Soviet-Asian Relations in the 1970s and Beyond

Bhabani Sen Gupta

The Praeger Special Studies program—
utilizing the most modern and efficient book
production techniques and a selective
worldwide distribution network—makes
available to the academic, government, and
business communities significant, timely
research in U.S. and international economic, social, and political development.

Soviet-Asian Relations in the 1970s and Beyond

An Interperceptional Study

PRAEGER SPECIAL STUDIES IN INTERNATIONAL POLITICS AND GOVERNMENT

Praeger Publishers   New York   Washington   London

Library of Congress Cataloging in Publication Data

Sen Gupta, Bhabani
    Soviet-Asian relations in the 1970s and beyond.

    (Praeger special studies in international politics
and government)
    Includes bibliographical references and index.
    1. Russia—Foreign relations—Asia.   2. Asia—
Foreign relations—Russia.   I. Title.
JX1555. Z7A77   327.47'05   76-24368
ISBN 0-275-23740-0

This study was funded by the Rockefeller
Foundation and by the Research Institute
on International Change, Columbia University. It was carried out with affiliation
granted by the Institute. The findings and
interpretations are exclusively the author's.

PRAEGER PUBLISHERS
111 Fourth Avenue, New York, N.Y. 10003, U.S.A.

Published in the United States of America in 1976
by Praeger Publishers, Inc.

Printed in the United States of America

to Elmore Jackson,
for his longtime concern about the
stability and progress of the South
Asian subcontinent

All that needs to be said to introduce this book is that it is probably the first attempt to study the relations with Asia of a world power on the basis of mutual perceptions. This approach should enable the reader to see how the Soviet Union and the Asian countries interact in complex ways and how their policies and actions are influenced by their self-images, their perceptions of the world and its major powers, and their mutual images of one another.

In the Third World, Asia has been and continues to be the combat ground of the Soviet Union with the United States and of the forces, ideologies, and objectives these two countries represent. In Asia both superpowers have had their disasters and success stories. The Soviet Union has had its disaster in China and the United States in Indochina. The U.S. success story has been Japan, and the Soviet success story has been India. What has limited, but has not been able to contain, the Soviet presence in Asia has been the might and power of the imperial United States. What has helped the Soviet Union spatially expand its presence in Asis has been the disarrayed retreat of the United States, exhaused from overspending its material and spiritual resources in the rice paddies of Asia. Now that the influence of the Soviet Union has advanced into the tropics and the screen of U.S. power is fading, how do the Asian ruling elites see the Soviet Union, and how does the Soviet Union regard Asia: That is what I shall attempt to determine in this book.

The Asian countries covered in this volume are Iran, India, and Bangladesh in South Asia; Indonesia, Singapore, Malaysia, Thailand, and the Philippines in Southeast Asia; and Japan.

I take this opportunity to thank the Rockefeller Foundation, which has made this study possible by granting me a fellowship for the study of international conflict extending from September 1974 through February 1976. I also wish to express my deep sense of gratitude to Dr. John Stremlau, head of the Study of International Conflict fellowship program, for the sympathy and kindness with which he responded to my requests, failings, and output.

The Research Institute on International Change at Columbia University first gave me a senior fellowship from February to August 1974 and then the affiliation necessary to carry on this study. I remain obliged to the distinguished director of the institute, Professor Zbigniew K. Brzezinski, and its administrative deputy director, Miss Sonia Sluzar, for numerous kindnesses over a period of eight years.

My Asian field study was made possible also by the willing and warm cooperation of a large number of individuals and academic institutions in the countries I was able to visit. It is far more difficult for an Asian scholar to visit Asian countries than to visit the United States and Europe. When I worked in Japan, in the five Southeast Asian countries, and in Iran, I realized much more vividly than before how diverse Asia is.

I have unforgettable memories of countless courtesies, big and small, and a readiness on the part of many people to help me find my way through a maze of half-known and unknown realities that, let me confess, we in India can hardly match. It would be impossible to mention all the persons who gave unsparingly of their kindness and time, but a few individuals and institutions must be named, since without their help and collaboration I could not have made much headway in my study.

I am particularly obliged to Professor Kenzo Kiga, of Keio University in Japan, a specialist on Soviet affairs; to Mr. Shigenobu Shima, director, and Mr. Yoji Hirota, executive director, of Oa Kyokai, the only institute in Japan that has engaged in systematic study of Communist societies over the last 15 years; and to the Director and faculty members of National Defense College, Tokyo, with whom I was able to have hours of immensely valuable discussion. Also particularly helpful were Mr. Hirokazu Hatano of the Asahi Shimbun, who was correspondent for his newspaper in Peking for a number of years and who has illuminating insight into Chinese politics and Chinese relations with Japan and the Soviet Union; Mr. Mikio Kato of the International House, Tokyo; Professor Tetsuji Yasuhira of the Tokyo Metropolitan University, a distinguished economist; Professor Ashoke Sirkar of Sophia University, who often acted as my interpreter and who found me a number of very useful contacts; and Mr. Kalyan Das Gupta, an Indian scholar of the Japanese language, who helped me understand the Japanese mind and the Japanese style of politics.

Of those who helped me in the Philippines, my most grateful thanks go to Mrs. Paz Puruganan of Manila, a Harvard-educated woman of great charm and inexhaustible hospitality, and to her husband, Mr. Greg Puruganan, a leading attorney; Mrs. Puruganan did everything for the somewhat lost professor from India, from fixing interviews to providing transport to help with shopping. I am grateful to President Salvador Lopez of the University of the Philippines for permitting my wife and me to live in the university guest house; to Professor Eva M. Duka Ventura, chairman of the University of the Philippines department of political science; and to the members of the political science and international relations faculty, especially Professor Amando E. Doronila of the Philippine Center for Advanced Studies.

In Hong Kong I had a most profitable interview with Fei Yiming, publisher of Ta Kung Pao, the leading Communist newspaper.

In Indonesia I was able to meet several scholars working at the Indonesian Center of Strategic and International Studies in Jakarta, through the good offices of its director, Dr. Yusuf Daud. I am particularly grateful to Dr. Adam Malik, the Indonesian Foreign Minister, who granted me a long interview at merely one day's notice and said, "I did this because one does not often meet an Asian scholar; one only meets Western reporters."

My work in Singapore was made enjoyable through the touchingly friendly cooperation of Dr. Karnial Singh Sandhu, the young and unusually active director of the Institute of Southeast Asian Studies, where not only Asian and Western, but also Soviet scholars engage in the study of Southeast Asian affairs. Similarly, in Kuala Lumpur I was fortunate to be the guest of my longtime friend Mr. Pran Chopra, former editor of The Statesman and now resident representative for Southeast Asia of the Press Foundation of Asia. No one has a deeper insight into Southeast Asian politics than this sensitive journalist and perceptive author. I should also mention Mr. Goh Cheng Teik, an academician turned political leader who is a junior minister attached to the Malaysian prime minister, who gave me two hours of his time talking wisely and knowledgeably in a downtown restaurant, not only about current Association of Southeast Asian States (ASEAN) politics but also about future trends and prospects.

In Thailand the ministry of foreign affairs appointed two senior officials to speak with me for two consecutive days; needless to say, the discussions were most instructive. Among others whose help I should like to record are Mr. Thanat Khoman, former foreign minister and a leading Thai statesman; Mr. Theh Chongkhadikij, chief editor of the Bangkok Post; Mr. Chaiyong Chavalit, resident representative of the Asia Press Foundation; Mr. Suluk Sivalak, an intellectual leader of the Left and Professor Kramol and Professor Kusuma of the Chalulongkorn University. I must also thank Mr. Satyendranath Ghosh of the Economic Commission for Asia and the Far East (ECAFE) and his wife, Mrs. Sandhya Ghosh, whose hospitality can never be forgotten.

In Bangladesh my work was made easier by the generous cooperation of Dr. Rounaq Jehan, then chairman of the department of political science at the University of Dacca. Among my meetings, discussions and interviews, I will never forget an evening spent with members of the Bangla Academy, two sessions with students of the Dacca University; conversations with Mr. Kamruddin Ahmad, former ambassador of Pakistan to a number of countries, who had lost a son in the freedom struggle and who had observed the whole film of events in 1971 as a close, penetrating student of human affairs. Conversations with my old friend, Kamal Hossain, then foreign minister of Bangladesh, and with Mr. Moni Singh, chairman of the Bangladesh Communist Party, were also extremely helpful. I also received most valuable help from my cousin, Mr. Dipta Sen, who was then the Dacca special correspondent of the Hindustan _Times_ of Delhi.

In speaking of Iran, the young Tehran woman who xeroxed for me free of cost a heap of newspaper reports bearing on Iranian-Soviet relations, and whose name I never asked, comes first to my mind. I had an illuminating interview with Mr. Amir Tahiri, the young and influential editor of Kayan International. Returning to Tehran for a second time in March 1975, I had the enviable opportunities of attending an international seminar on the Indian Ocean and the Persian Gulf and of long discussions with a number of Iranian scholars, including Dr. S. Chubin of the Institute of International Political and Economic Studies, an authority on Iranian-Soviet relations, and the director of the institute, Dr. Abbas Amiri.

An hour-long interview in Cairo with the Egyptian Foreign Minister, Ismail Fahmy, helped me gain a perspective of Soviet-Egyptian relations.

For the purpose of this book I have done no field work in the Soviet Union, but I have had useful interviews with Soviet correspondents located in Asia; Soviet scholars visiting India and the United States; Soviet scholars who attended the first international Slavic studies conference at Banff, Canada, which I also attended, as an invited delegate from India; and with Soviet officials at the United Nations.

With very few exceptions the persons I was able to interview, whether Asian or Russian, requested that they be not identified by name if they were to speak "frankly." For the same reason, while referring to the officials interviewed I have refrained in some cases from identifying their ministries.

In the United States I have had occasion to present the core of this study at a number of university seminars and to benefit from the comments and observations of a large number of scholars. For reading chapters of this volume with useful critical comments, my thanks go to Dr. William Barnds, Senior Research Associate, Council on Foreign Relations; Dr. George Tanham of the U.S. Committee for the Study of Conflict; Mr. Raymond Barghardt, a young officer of the U.S. Foreign Service with considerable experience of Southeast Asia; Professor Kenzo Kiga of Keio University, Tokyo; and Professor Mahammad Ayoob of the School of International Studies, Jawaharlal Nehru University, New Delhi.

Finally, a word of special thanks must go to my wife, who traveled with me in Asia, keeping a tight control of very limited funds, and took notes of my interviews and otherwise helped with research in the libraries.

CONTENTS

Soviet-Asian Relations in the 1970s and Beyond

THE SOVIET WORLD VIEW: SOVIET IMAGES OF ASIA

"Soviet foreign policy strategic plans have become part of the real life of the 1970s and have contributed to the transformation of international relations favorable to the achievement of its goals."[1] This claim, made by a Soviet scholar in May 1973, has been a recurrent refrain of Soviet writings on international affairs since the early 1970s. The focus of this study is on Soviet policies for Asia and on Asian responses to the general and specific tendencies of Soviet diplomacy. The strategic plans of Soviet foreign policy in Asia are, however, inseparably linked with the strategic thinking of Soviet foreign policy in general. They stem from the Soviet world view; from Soviet relations with, and perceptions of, the principal international actors; the Soviet self-image; the resource base of Soviet foreign policy--resource capability as well as the will to use that capability as an active instrument of diplomacy; and finally, the priority that Asian issues are given in the important question of allocation of foreign policy resources.

A distinguishing feature of Soviet foreign policy is its structural unity, a theoretical as well as operational global framework. The framework is contrived with Marxist-Leninist analytical tools, though in recent years a certain hospitality has been shown to some of the analytical paradigms of the Western social sciences. The Marxist-Leninist analytical framework may or may not inform Soviet foreign policy with an ideological content, but it certainly lends a thematic unity to foreign policy thinking.[2] Soviet scholars claim that the Marxist-Leninist analytical framework enables the decision makers to look for and identify the trends and processes of historical progression, the broad direction of historical change. At what pace the change will occur and what its particular manifestations will be, often remain unknown. The historical process often traverses a

zigzag course; at its major junctures, more than one outcome is objectively possible. This calls for alternative foreign policy choices
that are determined, not at random, but according to an analytical
system. Once the "natural laws" of history are comprehended accu-
rately within the context of a specific period of time, the objective
causes, trends, and prospects of development of each major event
have to be analyzed. It is essential to identify the "main link" in the
chain of complex and confused particles that constitutes each major
international event. Once the main link has been found, it is the task
of foreign policy "to set the entire chain in motion."[3] The Marxist-
Leninist analytical system, Soviet scholars affirm, leaves enough
room for the decision makers to select commitments, determine
priorities, allocate resources, keep alternatives in reserve, and
make adjustments in the light of success or failure. Moreover, it
allows for the strategic use of time in a combat the ultimate outcome
of which is never in doubt. It enables a patient pursuit of long-term
objectives along with concentration on short- to medium-term goals.
It forbids adventurism, counsels preservation of strength and consolidation of gains as part of the tactics of advance, and permits tactical retreat.[4]

To be sure, the Marxist-Leninist analysis is often influenced
by the historical experience of the Soviet decision makers; of their
Russian nationalism; and of their Russian prejudices, apprehensions,
and ambitions. In Asia this is evident in the conflict and cold war
with China, in the tortuous Soviet diplomacy in Japan, and in the per-
sisting quest for secure outlets to the warm waters of the Mediterranean and the Indian Ocean. The Soviet world view and the Soviet
perceptions of the major world actors and forces are, then, complex
products of the cognitive maps of the Soviet mind; which means they
are cognitive maps of the leading revolutionary power, of a superpower, of a global power, and of the resurgent Russian power. The
contradictions among these cognitive maps are, however, more apparent to the outside world than to the Soviets themselves. As far
as the Soviet decision makers are concerned, the contradictions are
resolved by a simple Leninist doctrine that obliterates all frontiers
between Marxism-Leninism and the interests of the Soviet state, that
is, Russian nationalism. What injures the Soviet state emasculates
the world socialist system and the world revolutionary movement.
Nationalist excesses are at times condemned as "adventurism," but
only when a particular prime actor has fallen. Nikita Khrushchev's
successors criticized his handling of the Cuban missile crisis and
his relations with China. As long as a particular leadership is in
control of the party and therefore of the state, however, it can pursue the national interests of the Soviet state in the firm conviction
that thereby it is also serving the interests of the socialist system
and the world revolutionary movement.[5]

The self-fulfilling merger of the Marxist-Leninist and Russian-nationalist cognitive maps of the Soviet mind is, however, meeting with some resistance, and even challenge, because of the growing pluralism in the Communist movement and the emergence of national-communist regimes in Asia. The Chinese Communists see the Soviet Union as a Russian superpower rather than as the leading socialist world power. This view, on the other hand, is rejected by the Communists who are in power in Vietnam and Laos as well as by those in North Korea. To the majority of the nonruling Communist parties in Asia, however, the Soviet Union is no longer the revolutionary power it once was. The national bourgeois elites in Asia tend to see the Soviet Union as the world's leading revisionist power, more interested in preserving the international status quo than in its revolutionary transformation. However, the nonrevolutionary perceptions of the Soviet Union by the non-Soviet world have not altered the self-image of the Soviet Union as the vanguard of the world revolution. Indeed, it is this Soviet self-image that still largely shapes the Soviet world view and the Soviet images of the principal international actors and forces.

THE SOVIET WORLD VIEW

Lenin, the founder of the Soviet state, saw the birth of the Soviet Union as the emergence of a new world system challenging the old. He exclaimed in 1920, "We have entered a new period in which we have won the right to our fundamental international existence in the framework of the capitalist states."[6] At the Geneva conference, George Chicherin offered "peaceful coexistence" of the "old system" and the "rising new social system" in a world in which "a united front of Soviet republics [was] confronted by the capitalist environment."[7] Some 50 years later in the 1970s, the Soviet Union still offers peaceful coexistence of the two world systems, but with one major difference: in the Soviet perception, the capitalist environment is no longer dominant and the world balance of forces has shifted definitely and decisively in favor of the challenger.

In an epoch of the "general crisis of capitalism," the 1970s, in the Soviet view, are marked by a deepening and intensifying capitalist crisis. Imperialism is still powerful; its resources have multiplied as a result of the dramatic revolution in science and technology; but in the 1970s imperialism has lost its initiative in international affairs, and the initiative has passed to the socialist system.

This fundamental change seen by Soviet leaders in the correlation of world forces has been brought about by a multiplicity of developments and events. First, there has been "enormous growth and

development" of the economic, military, and political power of the
Soviet Union and the socialist bloc.

Second, there are the multiple financial, economic, social,
and political crises that have stricken the capitalist powers in the
1970s. These crisis have led to a sharp decline in the capitalist
economies, creating the most prolonged and severe depression since
the 1930s and bringing in their wake serious challenges to the social,
political, and economic stability of the capitalist system.

Third, the economic crisis, more than anything else, has revealed the political ineffectiveness of the military doctrines of the
capitalist powers, particularly the doctrine of "strategic superiority."
The leading imperialist power, the United States, has been "forced"
to seek accord with the Soviet Union, limiting the strategic arms
race at the level of "parity."

Fourth, the "unprecedented successes" of the national liberation movement against imperialism, especially the Communist victories in Indochina, have mortally undermined the worldwide anti-
Communist security system erected by the United States since World
War II. The imperialist powers have lost their "control" of the
"local conflicts" in Asia, Africa, and Latin America. No longer
can they determine the outcome of these conflicts through military
intervention. The balance of forces in the national liberation zone
has shifted decisively in favor of the "anti-imperialist front," which
is the active rear of the world socialist revolutionary forces.

Fifth, the intensifying capitalist crisis has exacerbated the
"intercapitalist" contradictions, disrupted the cohesion and unity of
the capitalist powers, and created fierce intercapitalist competition
for world raw materials and markets.

Sixth, the energy crisis has exposed the Achilles' heel of the
capitalist economy by pitting the petroleum-owning states of the
Middle East and the Persian Gulf against the international oil monopolies, against, in fact, the most powerful single intercapitalist industrial enterprise. The cumulative impact of all these crises has generated an objective condition for a general restructuring of international relations on the basis of peaceful coexistence. [8]

In the Soviet view, the world remains essentially bipolar, that
is, divided between two opposing international systems, while the
capitalist system has become multipolar in the 1970s. The United
States no longer dominates the capitalist system. It has to reckon
with several rival centers of power within that system, notably the
EEC, Japan, and the multinational corporations. This polycentrism
in the capitalist bloc arises "first of all from the uneven economic
and political development of the capitalist countries, from a change
of relations among them with regard to power." The rise of new centers of power within the capitalist system enables the socialist

countries to develop cooperative relations bilaterally with individual
members of an internally split system. The imperialist states,
faced with "the crisis of the global strategy of their foreign policy,"
are "impelled" to make "a more sober and balanced evaluation of
their place and role in the present system of international relations,
a fresh evaluation of the possibilities of settling outstanding issues by
means of war, and, finally, to adopt a new attitude about negotiations
as a means of settling disputes in international life." This tendency
developed "rather obviously" in the Western European region. In the
1970s "it is beginning to influence in a certain way the policy of the
main country of modern capitalism, the USA as well."[9]

Polycentrism in the capitalist system has set off a "dialectical"
process of intercapitalist relationship. On the one hand, uneven development of capitalist economies "jeopardizes US imperialist hegemony in the capitalist world," and deepens interimperialist rivalries
in the strategic regions of the Third World. On the other hand, there
is the "tendency of the imperialist countries to join forces against the
rising strength of world socialism and the world revolutionary movement." This tendency is manifest in "imperialist integration." The
interimperialist contradictions are strong enough to prevent the rise
of a supranationalist capitalist power, but the cohesive tendencies in
the capitalist world are also strong enough to enable the capitalist
system to resolve many of its contradictions and pose numerous
sophisticated challenges to the socialist community. The principal
contradiction of the epoch, in the Soviet view, remains the contradiction between the two rival world systems. Intercapitalist contradictions, however, have assumed a secondary importance. In other
words, the capitalist strength and cohesion have weakened but not
withered, and imperialistm remains strong and highly resourceful.
The strategic task of Soviet foreign policy is to measure up to the
dialectics of the contradictions and cohesion of the capitalist system,
to separate the major centers of capitalist power from one another
by vigorous bilateral diplomacy, and to avoid doing anything that
might strengthen the unity of the leading capitalist powers.[10]

A policy of nonprovocation and sweet reasonableness, of manip-
ulation of the weaknesses of each capitalist economy, and of exploitation of the frictions among the major capitalist powers is all the more
advisable because, in the Soviet view, the current crisis of capitalism is not a passing ailment but a deepening malaise with little prospect of radical cure. Soviet analysts expect the crisis to get worse,
especially in Southern Europe, where capitalist development has been
uneven. In the Soviet analysis, modern capitalism is a "state-
monopolistic capitalism" in which the monopolies, with direct and indirect state patronage, dominate the political, social, and cultural
life of the people and tend to influence, and even control, foreign

policy. The "basic irreconcilable contradiction" in modern capitalism is the one between "the unparalleled process of product com-
munization" and "the domination of private ownership relations."
This contradiction, which is most manifest in the United States, is
now surfacing in the other leading capitalist countries also. From
this basic contradiction stem the political, economic, and social tensions, conflicts, and instabilities of the capitalist system and of the
individual developed capitalist countries. The process of intercapitalist integration has led to an "internationalizing of economic life"
in the capitalist system, but because this has been happening under
the domination of the international monopolies, it is triggering sharp
conflicts both within and among the individual nations. The relentless
competition to close the technology gap is "Americanizing" the economies of West Germany, France, Britain, and Italy. This is creating
a conflict situation between the international monopolies, which are
dominated by the United States, and their national partners on the one
hand and the independent big business houses, as well as medium-
sized and small enterprises, on the other. In Italy, in Japan, and to
some extent in France, this has created a "double economic structure," increasingly polarizing the regional imbalances and eliminat-
ing the weaker enterprises. In each major capitalist country, Soviet
analysts see struggles developing "between the forces of progress
and reaction."[11] In 1974 the leading ideologue of the Communist
Party of the Soviet Union (CPSU), Mikhail Suslov, declared as follows:

> The crisis of capitalism is becoming deeper and
> deeper, encompassing all aspects of life in the
> bourgeois countries. The false theory of the
> apologists of capitalism, who maintain that capi-
> talism has gotten its "second wind," that it is
> capable of providing answers to burning prob-
> lems of economic, social, and cultural develop-
> ment, has been refuted. In reality, capitalism
> is sinking deeper and deeper into a morass of
> contradictions.[12]

THE SOVIET VIEW OF THE UNITED STATES

In the 1970s the Soviets see the United States as the leading
country of modern capitalism rather than as the leader of the capitalist camp. Soviet foreign policy analysts claim that in the changed
correlation of forces within the capitalist system, relations with the
United States no longer occupy the pivotal place in Soviet foreign
policy, although the exclusive superpower relationship does demand
special consideration.

> It is true that signs of <u>a kind</u> of bipolarity are
> manifest in a <u>certain sense</u> in the concrete
> policy and in some or other role of states in the
> international arena, particularly in case of the
> biggest powers like the USSR and the USA which
> today bear a special responsibility for the pre-
> vention of a world war and the maintenance of
> peace. [13]

The new situation demands much more sophisticated studies by Soviet
foreign-policy makers of the United States as the number one actor in
the world. In the Kremlin foreign policy apparatus, reports one
Soviet analyst, the United States is now studied not merely in terms
of its internal balance of forces and the balance of forces between two
competing international systems, but also in terms of the contradictions and cohesion of the capitalist system, the strength and weakness of the socialist bloc, and major developments in the national
liberation zone. The primary task is to distinguish between the role
of leading capitalist power and that of leader of the capitalist system.
The opportunity exists to generate pressure on the United States for
detente and peaceful coexistence by establishing bilateral cooperative
relations with the other major capitalist countries and also to exert
pressure upon these countries by working out cooperative relations
with the United States. [14]

The single most important strategic goal of Soviet foreign policy
in the next decade is a stable, "irreversible" process of detente with
the United States. Soviet analysts identify five factors that are manifest in the 1970s that work in favor of a Soviet-American detente.
First, there is a growing realization in the United States that it is no
longer possible to translate military power into political power.

Second, the politically counterproductive strategic arms race
has also become economically unacceptable.

Third, the policy of containment of communism and of the
Soviet Union has "demonstrably" failed. Fourth, many Americans
realize that the United States cannot hope to resolve its socioeco-
nomic and political problems without a radical reshuffle of its foreign and domestic policy priorities and a turning from confrontation
to negotiation. Finally, the United States can no longer mobilize the
other major capitalist countries and a good portion of the Third
World in a policy of confrontation and containment. [15]

The best-known Soviet specialist on the United States, Georgi
Arbatov, argues that the two superpowers, "given all the fundamental
differences in their class nature and social systems, and given the
whole depth of political contradictions," [16] still have parallel or co-
inciding interests in many major problems. They alone can prevent

a thermonuclear war. It is as much in their own interest as in the
interest of mankind that they agree on limitation of strategic arms,
and, over time, on nuclear disarmament. It is also in their mutual
interest that no "local war" in which they may be involved escalates
to a nuclear confrontation. They can gain equally from large-scale
economic, scientific, and technological collaboration.

Arbatov believes that Soviet-American relations in the 1970s
will be shaped by the answers the two superpowers may find for
three principal questions. (1) What should be the basis of their bilateral relations in the changed international ambience? (2) What
position should be adopted "in the face of the unprecedented upsurge
in the national liberation movement?"--meaning, how should they
deal with tensions and conflicts in the Third World? (3) In what
direction should the tremendous new opportunities and forces released by the scientific and technological revolution be channeled and
how should its negative consequences be averted? A stable detente
is possible, Arbatov asserts, only if the United States recognizes
the right of the socialist system to exist on a basis of equality, if it
refrains from interfering in the internal affairs of the socialist countries, and if instead of intervening in the local wars, the United
States would discuss its differences with the Soviet Union over specific developments in the Third World. Implicit in the last "if" is
the claim that the Soviet Union is now entitled to at least an equal
position with the United States in resolving crises and conflicts in
the developing world. [17]

In the 1970s the Soviets see the United States as caught in the
coils of multiple crises involving domestic as well as foreign policy
priorities. The ruling class is divided and split. Arbatov wrote in
1974 that detente had proved to be "extremely difficult and complex"
for the United States because it demanded a "revision of certain basic
postulates which almost acquired the force of an immutable dogma."[18]
The pro-detente forces in the United States were able to take certain
welcome initiatives in the early 1970s, but the anti-detente forces
were "trying to consolidate and counterattack in the mid-seventies."
Detente, therefore, was "still not sufficiently stable"; the process
had not become irreversible. However, the forces that caused the
changes in U.S. policy toward the Soviet Union, Arbatov added, would
"most likely continue to operate in the forseeable future too, exerting
an influence on US policy. . . . It makes it possible to assess the
prospects for the development of Soviet-US relations in the seventies
with a certain degree of optimism."[19]

SOVIET GAINS FROM THE CAPITALIST SYSTEM

In the 1970s the Soviets have picked up quite a few marbles in
their dealings with the capitalist powers and in their manipulations

of the troubles within the capitalist system. The Soviets regard the
results of the Nixon visit to Moscow in 1972 as a kind of watershed
in the intersystem relationship. "The present balance of forces between the USSR and the United States was reflected in the agreement
concluded in May 1972 on the question of limiting strategic offensive
weapons and antimissiles," writes a Soviet analyst. "The agreements . . . show the collapse of the cold war policy conducted by
American imperialism for more than a quarter of a century."[20]
Bilateral diplomacy has enabled Moscow to secure formal Western
recognition of a postwar political map of Europe and the admission
of East Germany to the United Nations. A crowning success of the
Soviet European diplomacy was the conclusion, in the summer of
1975, of the agreement on "European security," the signatories of
which included the United States and Canada. Negotiations for the
SALT II accords were stalled in 1974-75 without losing the entire
momentum, but the deadlock seemed to have broken as a result of
Henry Kissinger's visit to Moscow in January 1976.[21]

     Through a series of bilateral agreements, the Soviet Union has
been able to secure a large-scale transfer of advanced capitalist
technology for further development of strategic sectors of the Russian
economy. West Germany, France, Britain, and Italy have each concluded agreements running to over $1 billion to build a variety of in-
dustrial plants in the Soviet Union, while Japan has committed over
$1 billion for the development of the forest and fuel resources of
Siberia. In 1972 and 1975 the Soviets bought over $2 billion worth
of food grains from the United States to overcome the shortages
caused by poor harvests. They have signed a five-year agreement
with the United States providing for the purchase of 6 to 8 million
tons of wheat each year. The collapse of the U.S.-Soviet trade
agreement in 1975, over the issue of emigration, does not appear to
have hurt the Soviet Union too much. According to a New York Times
report, despite the congressional limits placed on credits to Moscow
from the U.S. Import-Export Bank, the Soviet Union has concluded
a number of major deals with U.S. corporations through subsidiaries
in Japan and Western Europe. The contracts run across a broad
range of technology and include chemical and fertilizer plants, trac-
tor factories, paper mills, and the like, as well as purchases of
computers, construction machinery, and oil exploration equipment.
Beyond these immediate projects, U.S. concerns are said to be talking about long-range deals taking them into the 1980s. Some proposals, which the Soviets are considering, involve joint ventures in
which management would be shared by Russian and American execu-
tives. In the spring of 1975 the Bank of America offered to form a
banking syndicate to lend the USSR $.5 billion to finance imports from
the United States, thus enabling the Soviet Union to get over the limitations imposed by Congress on credits from the Export-Import Bank.[22]

These substantial gains, which will enable the Soviet Union to modernize its economy and to develop the still-vast untapped natural resources of Siberia without having to bring about painful structural changes in its economic bureaucracies,[23] have infused the Kremlin with a certain amount of self-confidence in seeking avenues of collaboration with the capitalist powers. Mikhael Suslov told a visiting delegation of U.S. Congressmen in June 1975 that the Soviet Union would "go on successfully developing our economy even without the benefit of the development of Soviet-American trade."[24] More realistically, Arbatov wrote in 1974 that "given the present situation in the world markets and the aggravation of the competitive struggles and the lack of many resources in short supply, the USSR could easily find other partners for many of the deals that are now being discussed with U.S. firms."[25] The Soviets claim that the real importance of their economic accords with the United States is political. However, they are in a position to say this only because they can obtain from the U.S. multinational corporations what they may be denied by the U.S. government as a result of congressional emphasis on the political aspects of these economic relations.

DETENTE AND PEACEFUL COEXISTENCE

If the Soviet concept of peaceful coexistence of the capitalist and socialist systems has been misunderstood and misinterpreted in the non-Soviet world, that is not because of any ambiguity on the part of the Soviet leaders. Detente itself, in French, may mean relaxation of tensions, or it may mean the triggering of new conflict. The Soviets have always, in fact with some stubborn consistency, explained that by detente or peaceful coexistence they do not offer a "class peace" to the capitalist system or accept a convergence of the basic interests of the two systems. The best definition of detente and peaceful coexistence, one that would satisfy the most orthodox Soviet idealogue, is the Nixonian definition, which is, movement from an era of confrontation to an era of negotiation. An authoritative 1963 Soviet publication defined peaceful coexistence as "an absence of cold and hot war, peaceful settlement of disputes and cultivation of economic relations between the socialist and capitalist countries."[26] Nine years later another authoritative publication declared that peaceful coexistence "rests on a system of principles that make it possible to avoid a major international conflict in the course of development of revolutionary processes within individual countries."[27] The system of principles is to govern the mutual relations of the two opposing class systems, capitalist and socialist. Strictly adhered to, these principles would eliminate war or threat of war to

settle international disputes and would entail mutual recognition of
each other's independence, sovereignty, and territorial integrity,
and noninterference in each other's internal affairs. Within this system of political relationship, peaceful coexistence provides for the
development of mutually advantageous economic, scientific-technological, and cultural relations.

Numerous pronouncements have left no doubt whatsoever that,
in the Soviet view, peaceful coexistence will neither bury the international class struggle nor end the ideological combat of the two opposing systems, but will only change their forms. For the first 50
years of the life of the Soviet state, Moscow offered the capitalist
system peaceful coexistence from a position of weakness. In the
1970s it offers peaceful coexistence from a position of strength.[28]
If the capitalist states have entered into cooperative relations with
the socialist countries, have recognized the Soviet Union's equality
in strategic power, and have offered negotiation in place of confrontation, they have not done so because of a sudden upsurge of peaceable-
ness in the capitalist bosom but because of the hard and cold reality
of the ascending military, political, and economic power of the socialist system and because the world balance of power no longer favors
the capitalist system. This self-reinforcing perception of the relative strength of the two world systems was reflected in 1975-76, when
Moscow strove for the SALT II agreements without yielding to U.S.
pressure to lower, if not abandon, its intervention in Angola. Current Soviet writings make it abundantly clear that under a system of
peaceful coexistence the Soviets expect conditions to be created for
further strengthening of the socialist system, further improvement
of conditions for the success of the national liberation struggles, and
an intensification of the class struggles within the capitalist countries.
The Soviet support for the national liberation struggles would increase
rather than diminish.[29] In essence, peaceful coexistence means a
long-lasting international balance of power dominated neither by imperialism nor by socialism. It is, however, a balance clearly in
favor of the socialist system, a transitional stage during which the
world revolutionary forces would become increasingly strong. The
capitalist countries will have to accept peaceful coexistence because
there is hardly any alternative.

By the mid-1970s, U.S. statesmen and scholars seem to have
realized that peaceful coexistence or detente can only be a "concert"
of cooperation and conflict. When the Soviet Union intervened in the
Angolan civil war, airlifting 12,000 Cuban troops and transporting
massive quantities of military aid by air and sea to the Popular Movement for the Liberation of Angola (MPLA), Henry Kissinger first
warned the Soviet Union that its action violated the process of detente, giving the impression that the United States would not proceed

with the strategic arms limitation negotiations unless the Soviet
Union backtracked from Angola.[30] Moscow did not take the warning
very seriously; it continued to back the MPLA with an impressive
demonstration of its new capability for intervening effectively in military conflicts far away from the Soviet Union.[31]

Where Moscow was apparently prepared to accommodate the
United States was in the exclusive sphere of superpower relationship.
Reportedly a concessional gesture on the arms limitation issue enabled Kissinger to visit the Soviet capital in January 1976, even while
the Soviet intervention in Angola continued. Zbiegniew K. Brzezinski,
the noted sovietologist, remarked, "Detente is going to be a mixed relationship with elements of both conflict and cooperation."[32] Marshall
Shulman, another well-known specialist in Soviet affairs, added that
detente did not mean that the Soviet Union had renounced its ultimate
ideological commitments, nor that Moscow would not take advantage
of opportunities to advance Soviet influence. "It does, however, sig-
nify a lower tension policy."[33]

THE SOCIALIST SYSTEM: THE SOVIET SELF-IMAGE

In the Soviet view, the most important factor that has changed
the world balance of forces is the continued growth of the military,
economic, and political might of the Soviet Union and of the socialist
bloc; the increasing unity of the socialist block; and its economic integration. "On the basis of the economic successes and the strengthening of defense might, on the basis of the consolidation of the fraternal
countries of socialism, there has been a dynamic growth in the role and
influence of the world socialist system on international relations and
the course of world affairs."[34] The socialist system has now "entered a new phase of its development, which is marked, on the one
hand, by growing complexity of the task before it and, on the other,
by the emergence of even greater opportunities for tackling these
tasks."[35]

In order to exploit these opportunities, in the Soviet view, the
Soviet state must develop its economy at a fast pace, with massive
importation of advanced technology and managerial skills and of techniques of higher productivity. This is an essential precondition for
further socialist integration. Only with a high level of integration
can the socialist bloc hope to make the best use of imported technology without yielding to capitalist political and ideological subversion.
Integration is admittedly "a new and complex process," and its political problems are no less difficult than its economic and technological
ones.[36] The Brezhnev doctrine protects the political frontiers of the
socialist world. The Soviet Union "sees it as its internationalist duty

to guarantee the reliable defense of the entire socialist bloc, not
merely from external attack, but also from internal defection." It
is within the doctrine of collective sovereignty of the bloc that its
"voluntary" economic integration proceeds at a faster pace, "on the
basis of a thorough consideration and coordination of the interests of
the countries involved."[37]

"Difficulties and some differences in the approach" to specific
issues of integration do arise. "The socialist community has had
and still has to face difficult problems in its development." The
problems stem mostly from the uneven economic development within
the bloc and from "nationalism," the dying embers of which are constantly fanned by capitalist subversive efforts. In spite of the difficulties and problems, the Soviet government believes that the productive capability of the socialist bloc has made impressive progress,
and the Kremlin leaders appear to look toward the future with stolid
confidence. In the 1970s the socialist bloc, it is claimed, has become the world's "most important industrial hub." In 1971 Soviet industrial output was placed at "over 75 percent" of the U.S. industrial
output. The rate of growth was "almost twice as high." In the level
of development of heavy industry, the Soviet Union was seen to be
"already catching up" with the United States. It was claimed in December 1974 that the "output volume of the means of production in
the USSR is no lower than 90 percent of this kind of production"[38] in
the United States. The agricultural setback in 1975 led to a substantial lowering of the robustly optimistic anticipations of the early
1970s, but in a period of a universal economic slump, the Soviet
Union saw its economy as performing much better than the crisis-
ridden economies of the capitalist countries.[39] In any case, the
need to import huge quantities of food grains from the United States,
Canada, and Australia did not prevent the Soviet Union from spending
over $.2 billion on military assistance to the MPLA in Angola.[40] It
also did not diminish the overriding priority given to "continued military preparedness," an "unavoidable" necessity "as long as imperialism remains aggressive in its designs and ambitions." The military
might of the Soviet Union guarantees the success of both the socialist
revolution and the national liberation movement; the military and economic power of the Soviet bloc has ushered the world from the barren
wastes of the cold war to the green vistas of peaceful coexistence.
In the 1970s, Soviet analysts point out, the capacity of the socialist
bloc to mobilize its economic resources for military construction is
immensely greater than it was at any time in the past. Its material
and technological base is also extremely strong. The Soviet Union
alone has over a million "workers in science," 650,000 of them
specializing in the areas of natural and technological sciences, as
opposed to 530,000 in the United States.[41]

In order to catch up with the United States in industrial production, to maintain a steady improvement in the living standards of its people, and to meet the increasing resource needs of foreign policy, the Soviet Union has been transferring considerable attention and investment in recent years to the development of the vast untapped resources of the Siberian Far East.

A progress report printed in the New York Times[42] toward the end of 1975 made quite impressive reading. The most dramatic venture is the 2,000-mile Baikal-Amur Mainline railway, which is being laid north of the Trans-Siberian. Once commissioned in 1983, it will lay open regions to economic exploitation that in the 1970s are inaccessible, with the raw materials dispatched to the growing network of Pacific ports. The Soviet Union is building hydroelectric dams; with Japanese collaboration it is developing its timber and paper industries; and it is prospecting and drilling for oil and natural gas. On the Zeya River the first hydroelectric station in Siberia, with a planned capacity of 1.2 million kilowatts, started operating early 1976. Two more hydroelectric stations are planned on the turbulent Bureya River and yet another on the Kolyma. On the Kamchatka peninsula, underground steam has been tapped to provide geothermal power. Dogged development efforts have given cities like Khabarovsk, 40 miles from the border between the Soviet Union and China, an industrial growth rate well above the national average.

With Japanese technology and credits, major timber processing plants have sprung up close to Vladivostok, the Pacific port. In September 1975 a new railroad bridge across the mile-wide Amur River at Komsomolsk was put into operation, opening up a through route from the Trans-Siberian to Vanio, on the Pacific. Also with Japanese collaboration, the Soviets are building a deep-water port near Nakhodka, extracting coal and natural gas in Yukutia and drilling for oil and natural gas in the Sakhalin waters.

The grimly inhospitable climate in most of Siberia, its great physical distance from European Russia, and its acute shortage of labor--in an area larger than Western Europe, its population is only about 6 million--and applicable resources make Siberian development a herculean task. Nevertheless, the Japanese have gotten involved in this enterprise, and the Siberian coastal trade alone involves about 100 Japanese companies. The Japanese seem to have no doubt that the Soviet leaders have committed themselves to the construction of an industrial infrastructure in Siberia within the 1980s. Once this is accomplished, the Soviet impact on Asia will be immensely greater. As container traffic grows across the Trans-Siberian, Japan will have a "land bridge" with Europe and the Japanese stake in good neighborly relations with the USSR will be higher than at present. With large-scale exploitation of Siberian oil and natural gas, the oil power of the Soviet Union will be stable over a long period.

The military implications of the development of Siberian resources will also be significant. The lag in Soviet power in the Pacific relative to the power of the United States will be substantially narrowed, while it will be overwhelming in terms of the military capability of Japan and China. In fact, the Soviets calculate that once they have been able to process the vast raw materials of Siberia, they may well become an indispensable source of supply of many scarce strategic raw materials for the industrial complexes in both Japan and the United States.[43]

THE NATIONAL LIBERATION ZONE

The Soviet expectations for the national liberation movement have risen in the 1970s as a result of the perceived shift in the world balance of forces in favor of socialism. The contradictions between the developing nations and the capitalist-imperialist system are believed to have become deeper and larger, providing new opportunities for striving for the strategic goals of Soviet foreign policy. At the same time, the developing countries themselves are seen as passing through a period of increasing social and political polarization that gives rise to more and more conflicts, both at domestic and international levels. Soviet international affairs analysts and decision makers appear to be greatly concerned about how the anticipated instabilities and conflicts in the national liberation zone are to be fitted into the operational instrumentalities of Soviet foreign policy in a way that will maximize the gains and minimize the risks and costs.

Ever since the Bolshevik revolution, the Soviet leaders have elevated to a "natural law" of history the Leninist assumption that Marxist socialism and the anti-imperialist struggles of the colonial and semicolonial peoples all over the world are parallel flows of a single revolutionary stream eroding the imperialist world order. Nevertheless, it has only been since the mid-1950s that Soviet leaders have been actively trying to lead the two flows to a confluence. Despite this "law" of history, the politically independent nations of the former empires of the imperialist powers have remained the "economic rear" of the world capitalist system, with strong political and military links with the metropolitan powers.[44] The strategic objective of Soviet foreign policy is to detach this capitalist rear, or help in its detachment, not by exporting revolutions, for which most of these countries are not prepared anyway, but by manipulating the contradictions between them and their capitalist patrons and, political opportunity and foreign policy resources permitting, to place at the disposal of the bourgeois ruling elites of these countries economic, military, and political instruments with which to defy the imperialist interests.

Soviet analysts argue that in the 1970s the socialist bloc has substantially greater foreign policy resources and also greater political opportunities for penetrating the national liberation zone. The single most significant new foreign policy resource is the Soviet capability for intervening directly in "anti-imperialist struggles" far from the frontiers of the Soviet Union. The political opportunities are seen in the changes that have, in the Soviet analysis, taken place in the internal conditions of many of the developing countries; in relations of the newly independent countries with the capitalist system; and in their relations with the socialist bloc.

As a result of all these changes, there has been a qualitative change in the national liberation movement. In each geopolitical region of the world, there is now an "anti-imperialist vanguard," described as follows: "The establishment and growth of a vanguard of new states with a socialist orientation is a new phenomenon in the national liberation movement, which has emerged in the course of the struggle between the two (international) social systems."[45] Soviet analysts now differentiate the developing countries and divide them into three groups according to their degree of militancy toward imperialism and their model of development. Those with a "consistently" anti-imperialist policy and a "socialist orientation" constitute the vanguard. Next come the countries that are developing along capitalist lines but are wedded to political and economic independence and therefore must "implement" an anti-imperialist political and economic policy. In the third group are those countries "with limited political and economic independence," which are tied to the imperialist economic and military system.[46]

In the 1970s the struggles both within the new nations and between them and the capitalist system are showing an ever-sharper "development edge." Internally, the focus of the struggle has shifted from political to social liberation, from growth to development.[47] Internationally, the struggle is now for independent development; one significant aspect of this struggle is what has come to be known as resource nationalism. "The struggle for economic independence is a form of development of the anti-imperialist national liberation movement, its new stage."[48] The struggles at both levels tend to internationalize the developmental conflicts in the Third World. The struggle between the two competing world systems determines world economic relations; it inevitably invades the struggle between the developing countries and the capitalist system. Contradictions within the developing countries also tend to outstrip the national framework and become international in character. The struggles at the two levels enmesh, obliterating the frontiers between the socialist struggle and the struggle for national economic and social liberation.[49]

   Soviet analysts argue that because of the growing impact of
the world socialist system on international economic relations, the
imperialist powers have been "forced" to adopt a more flexible,
more accommodating attitude toward some of the economic demands
and actions of the new nations. The nationalization of foreign-owned
companies, for example, no longer invites reprisals. On the resource question, too, the capitalist system now tries to respond
more positively than in the past to the collective pressures of the
developing nations.[50] However, the Soviet government assumes
that modern state-monopolistic capitalism is unable to meet the
developmental requirements of the new nations and that the capitalist
type of development cannot resolve the inflammable tensions and
conflicts that the Soviet analysts see as gripping most of the developing countries, particularly in Asia, where a majority of the countries have taken to the capitalist path.[51] What is growing in most
of these countries is "dependent and distorted capitalism." The
bourgeoisie in power are a "reformist, largely conciliationist
class." Through its political behavior and economic activities this
ruling bourgeois class "deepens the contradictions and weaknesses
of local capitalism, . . . narrowing its already limited opportunities." The bourgeoisie in the former colonies and semicolonies
are essentially a product of a straw revolution, because by itself,
without acting in cooperation with the forces of socialism, the national liberation revolution "cannot play the decisive role in the
world struggle against imperialism" nor, in the conditions of the
1970s, provide the wherewithal for radical social change.

> Deliverance from direct colonial yoke has changed
> but little the life of the majority of the peoples in
> the former colonies. The achievement of political
> liberation . . . has not yet been reinforced by eco-
> nomic independence. . . . Reactionary forces ham-
> per in every way the socioeconomic reforms pro-
> claimed in a number of countries under pressure of
> the working people. . . . The periods in which the
> promises proclaimed by the new governments were
> to be fulfilled have expired, but the living conditions
> of the working people continue to be woefully bad
> and the income level between different sections of
> the population grows wider. . . . The difference
> between the incomes of a handful of exploiters and
> those of the masses is becoming the basis of a
> mounting social struggle.[52]

In the Soviet view, then, the process of development is creating a dual polarization. At the world level it is increasing the gap between the developing countries, or at least those who have taken to the path of independent development, and the leading capitalist nations. At the domestic level it is increasing the gap between the ruling bourgeoisie and the mass of the population.

These two polarizations, which augment each other, are likely to generate conflict. In the Soviet perception, most of the developing countries in Asia have entered a period of social tension and even upheaval, as the impoverished peasant masses break their way into the political process. In almost all Asian countries, the peasants are not under proletarian (Communist Party) leadership; there is not even an effective alliance between the peasantry and the industrial proletariat. The peasant masses are therefore liable to be exploited by Maoist extremists and other leftist adventurers.[53]

The danger of social and political upheavals can be diminished, if not altogether averted, if the developing countries in Asia adopt noncapitalist models of development and if, at the international level, they join with the "vanguard" in the national liberation zone and the socialist countries in opposing imperialism and neocolonialism.

The Soviets expect the conflicts in Asia, at each of the two levels mentioned above, to multiply and intensify in the last quarter of the century. At the international level they expect many of the conflicts to center around two main questions. (1) Will the "anti-imperialist regimes" get stronger, or will they fall in the face of "counterrevolutionary coups"? (2) Will the developing countries continue to remain an "integral part of the capitalist system," or will they become "new areas that have slipped away from the capitalist system"? Both questions are expected to be resolved largely by the struggle between the two world systems.[54]

THE SOVIET VIEW OF WAR AND CONFLICT

The Soviet view of war and conflict has changed significantly since the exit of Khrushchev in 1964.[55] The current Soviet outlook corresponds to the prevailing Soviet strategic perception of the world balance of forces and is fed by the substantial increment in the military capability of the Soviet Union, particularly in its ability to intervene in overseas conflicts.

The Marxist-Leninist doctrine sees inherent conflict in the process of the historical development of human society. Each epoch is characterized by a central, basic contradiction and by several secondary ones. In the "deepening crisis" of capitalism in the 1970s and the worldwide "transition from capitalism to socialism," the central contradiction is between the two opposing international social systems. The transition to socialism, whether on the level of individual nations or at the international level, is generally attended by class conflict. The forms the class conflict will take and the chances that it will turn into violent civil war are determined by specific contextual forces. In the 1970s the Soviets see an unprecedented scale of conflicts raging at each level of international relations, and they regard many of these conflicts as contributing to the historical transition from capitalism to socialism.

War is a different thing. It is always started by imperialism and will exist as long as there is imperialism. Socialism does not start war. It only "defends the peace," because it needs peace for rapid development and for competition with the capitalist system. Wars can be "just" or "unjust," depending upon which forces are at war with which and on their objectives and purposes. All imperialist wars are "unjust" wars of aggression; so are all wars made by the "oppressor" against the "oppressed." Revolutionary wars, whether they are fought for social revolution or for political independence, are "just" wars. The Soviet state and the socialist system support all "just" wars and oppose all "unjust" wars.[56]

Within these postulates, significant changes have occurred in the Soviet view of war and conflict. In the Khrushchev period nuclear war was seen as a "supra-class war"; but it is now viewed as the "ultimate manifestation of the international class conflict."[57] The imperialists, in Soviet opinion, have not abandoned their designs for a nuclear confrontation with the socialist bloc in spite of the shift in the international balance of forces in favor of socialism. The Soviet Union must therefore maintain its strategic preparedness, although prevention of nuclear war remains "the supreme task of Soviet foreign policy."[58] However, if a nuclear war is unleashed by the imperialists, it will make a Soviet retaliation "inevitable." The next world war will be fought between two great coalitions of states; it could be a short nuclear war, or it could be a protracted nuclear-conventional war. The Soviet Union is battle-ready for both and must continue to be so; that, in the Soviet view, is the greatest guarantee that a nuclear war will not annihilate the world.[59] Implied in this strategic posture is an assertion of Soviet might, of the capability of the Soviet Union to fight a nuclear war and win, should such a war be imposed upon it by the imperialists. In short, the current Soviet stance on nuclear war basically mirrors that of the United States.

Of even greater significance is the current Soviet view of "local wars." When in the 1950s a debate on "local war" strategies was set off in the United States by the publication of Henry Kissinger's Nuclear Weapons and Foreign Policy,[60] the Soviets had no "limited

war" doctrine. Indeed, they did not even have a Russian word for
the American expression "local war," for which the phrase
"lokal'niye voiny" was introduced into the Russian vocabulary. V. D.
Sokolovskii's Soviet Military Strategy, a standard Soviet text, did
not recognize "local" or "limited" wars in its second edition, published in 1963, but still saw the future of war in terms of "enormous
geographic expanses" and as fought between two great coalitions.[61]
Soviet strategic analysts persistently took the view that "the era of
local wars is over" and that a local war could only be the "prelude
to a general universal nuclear war."[62]

This stance was given up after the fall of Khrushchev. The
third edition of Sokolovskii's work, printed in 1968, recognized the
existence of "local wars" and identified them with the wars of national liberation.[63] Since then, Soviet strategic thinking about
"local wars" has crystallized. These wars are now seen as characteristic of the 1970s. The central contradiction of the 1970s continues to be the one between the two opposing social systems; the
most important secondary contradiction is between imperialism and
the forces of national liberation. "Local wars" are "just" when they
are fought against aggressors and oppressors and "unjust" when they
are wars of aggression and oppression. Thus a "just" local war can
be fought within a single nation-state, such as the Bangladesh national
liberation war in 1971 and the ongoing "war" between the British and
the people of Northern Ireland.[64] The military might of the socialist
bloc does not exist to prevent local wars. A 1973 Soviet military
publication contains the following:

> the military might of the socialist countries is not
> viewed as a condition or a means for prevention of
> all wars generally, that is, civil, national-liberation,
> or in the defense of the sovereignty of peoples. The
> communists have always recognized that along with
> reactionary and unjust wars, there are also progres-
> sive and just wars. At present there are circum-
> stances when the suppressed classes and peoples are
> forced to fight for there is no other way out. Such
> wars cannot be "prevented," and they are legitimate
> and just. The socialist nations and the communist
> and workers' parties of the entire world actively
> support the liberation struggle among peoples.[65]

The imperialists see limited goals in "local wars," the analysts continue, because they too are afraid of the consequences of a
wider, nuclear war. However, the imperialists "constantly" consider the possibility of a "transition to nuclear war." The socialist

countries and their allies in the national liberation zone must remain
constantly vigilant if they are to defeat the imperialist designs.[66]

"Local wars" are also seen as politically useful. Wars of
national liberation release their own momentum of revolutionary
change, and they polarize classes and peoples within countries and
in geopolitical regions. "The events in Indochina and the Middle
East have shown that imperialist aggression hastens the maturity of
the people falling victim to it as well as of the people in other countries, shows them who is their friend and who is their foe, and
tempers them in the struggle against imperialism." These wars,
then, make it easier for the Soviet Union to pick up friends and allies.
Since the great majority of these friends and allies happen to be
leaders of the national bourgeoisie, the gains are limited and far
from stable. Although bourgeois "circles" are anxious to get rid of
imperialist dominance, they are not prepared to make a "clean
break" with imperialism; nor are they prepared to "democratize"
their countries beyond a certain limit, because they are afraid of
radical, revolutionary change. Worse, they often try to split the
revolutionary forces, and they sometimes collapse into the arms of
an imperialist or reactionary coup.[67]

The forces of national liberation cannot hope to win the "local
wars" against imperialism without the active support of the Soviet
bloc; nor can they gain their political and economic independence
without socialist assistance. This, however, is not the only "natural
link" between the twin streams of world revolution. In the 1970s
Soviet analysts have put forward a further argument for involvement
by the Soviet Union in local wars. These wars are waged by the
imperialists, not merely to regain their positions in the "peripheral
zone" of capitalism, but increasingly to gain "forward positions" in
their central combat with the socialist bloc. The Soviets therefore
intervene in these wars in defense of state interests. However,
this intervention must be selective, never undertaken in a spirit of
adventurism, but always after careful examination of the objective
forces involved in each conflict, of the risks, costs, and benefits.
The supreme consideration must always be that of safeguarding the
interests of the socialist revolution, that is, of the Soviet bloc. As
one military analyst puts it, "There may be a situation in which an
armed uprising is just and holds promise of success at a given time
within a certain country but may result in substantial negative results
for the world revolutionary process."[68]

THE SOVIET VIEW OF CHINA

Much of the Soviet diplomatic efforts in Asia, as we shall see
in this study, are consumed by the effort to limit the influence, and

tarnish the image, of China as ruled by Mao Tse-tung. When the
Brezhnev-Kosygin team came to power in 1964 it attacked Khrushchev
for, among other things, his China policy. They have not been able
to improve Soviet-Chinese relations, but they have been able to keep
the conflict limited to hot words and competitive diplomacy in the
midst of slowly rising trade relations. After the armed clash on the
Ussuri River in Manchuria in March 1969, the Soviets threatened a
preemptive nuclear attack on China.[69] This threat, together with
the rapid stationing of a million Soviet troops along the Sino-Soviet
border, sobered the Chinese, who responded by building a network
of underground shelters in their principal cities. Talks on the
border dispute began in September 1969 and have been going on in-
termittently since, without any sign of the deadlock being broken.

The Sino-U.S. diplomatic breakthrough in 1972 made China the
third major world power. The Soviets have since been haunted by
the specter of bilateral or trilateral alliances among their three
Pacific-Asian adversaries, China, the United States, and Japan. At
the same time the Soviet leaders have tried to wink at Mao: in 1973
Brezhnev secretly offered to conclude a no-war pact on the basis of
peaceful coexistence. Chairman Mao refused to wink back. However, neither Mao Tse-tung nor the Soviet leaders have formally
denounced the 1950 Sino-Soviet treaty, which does not expire until
1980.

The perceptions of China by the present Soviet leadership were
formulated after the 9th congress of the Chinese Communist Party
(CCP) in 1969, and these perceptions do not appear to have changed
significantly since. A lengthy thesis in Kommunist in March 1969
set forth the conviction of the Soviet leaders that Maoism would
flourish in China as long as Mao was alive and perhaps even after
his death. The thesis conceded that the return of the Communist
Party of China (CPC) "to the path of scientific socialism will be a
complicated and difficult process, attended by all sorts of unexpected
occurrences."[70] Moscow and its allies must therefore be ready for
a long and difficult struggle against "the theory and practice of
militant Maoism."[71] Since then, presumably at the bidding of the
Party, Soviet scholars have written a large number of monographs
on Chinese history, on the history of the Chinese Communist revolution, on Maoism, on the history of Sino-Soviet relations, and on
the Sino-Soviet border.[72] Numerous "scholarly" articles on China
have also been published in the Soviet journals. China is almost a
daily target in the Soviet media, much as is the Soviet Union in the
media in China.

From this wealth or welter of literature, six main Soviet
images of Mao's China emerge. First, there is the image of a great
revolution "grossly distorted" by Mao Tse-tung, who has been helped

by the objective conditions of Chinese society, that is, by backwardness, by the absence in China of a large and dominant working class,
and by its highly complex class mix.

Second, Mao had been anti-Soviet since the late 1930s, certainly during the second world war, and once in power he progressively succumbed to "blind anti-Sovietism."

Third, under Mao China has become a hegemonist, chauvinistic
power, keen on restoring the imperial glory of the ancient Chinese
empire. National chauvinism rather than scientific socialism is the
guiding force of Mao's foreign policy.

Fourth, Mao presides over an unstable regime. Behind and
under him a fierce struggle for power has been going on, and no one
can be certain what will happen in China after Mao's death.

Fifth, since 1972 Mao's China has become a collusive partner
of American imperialism. It is now an open defender of the U.S.
military presence in Asia.

Sixth, China has been promoting subversion in most of the
neighboring countries, which would be ill-advised to allow themselves to be seduced by its blandishments.

These six blown up images of China, along with others less
prominent, are constantly projected by the Soviet media to the
people of the Soviet Union as well as to the rest of the world.

At the same time, however, Soviet analysts claim that Maoism
is the product of the "specific conditions of China's reality," and that
it "cannot, and does not, have any chance of success in other countries." It has "suffered defeat on an international scale," which is
evident in the failure of Peking to put together a Maoist international
movement. Its capacity to infiltrate the socialist system is said to
be extremely limited, though not its ability to persuade the United
States, Japan, and the Western European countries to slow down the
process of detente. [73]

Nobody seems to know with any measure of certainty what kind
of factional and pressure-group support the Soviet leaders have in
the Chinese Communist Party. Are those Chinese Communists who
have been, and are still being, accused of being revisionists and
capitalist-roaders, the ones who favor a Sino-Soviet reconciliation?
In the Chinese military, are the "modernizers" actual or potential
supporters of a Peking-Moscow detente? The feeling is growing in
the United States that after the passing of Mao there will be some
significant effort in both capitals for at least a limited rapprochement
between the two Communist giants. In the mid-1970s both seem to
be using this option as leverage against the United States. The CCP
central committee sent an unusually warm message of greetings to
the CPSU on the occasion of the 57th anniversary of the Soviet revolution in 1974. [74] In late 1975 the Chinese suddenly released three

members of a Soviet helicopter crew, accepting the Soviet explanation that the aircraft had unwittingly strayed into Chinese airspace
over Sinkiang a year and a half earlier. This was a most unusual
gesture on the part of the Peking authorities. The New York Times
reported in August 1975 that according to some diplomats in Moscow
"it would be in [the Soviet] interest to try to patch up its quarrel with
Peking, which has put the Kremlin at a disadvantage in dealing with
the United States."[75] According to C. L. Sulzberger, Brezhnev advised the United States, Britain, and France in 1975 that the Soviet
Union was in no sense worried about China's hostility "now," but
that at the end of the century Peking would be a formidable power.
He asked for a stronger Soviet-Western cooperative relationship,
especially "fuller and speedier arms limitation" between the two
superpowers. "If not, he warned, Moscow had only one obvious alternative: restoring the old alliance with China-after-Mao."[76]

The old alliance will probably never be restored. It would be
most difficult for the Soviet Union to reorder Moscow-Peking friendship on the basis of true equality. A limited understanding, on the
other hand, is within the realm of possibility.[77] The China policy of
the Soviet Union now consists of three simultaneous activities: (1)
active diplomacy to reduce the influence of China, (2) a continuing
war of shrill words, and (3) a readiness to mend fences. In the
short to medium term, the China problem is compartmentalized and
under control. In the long term, the Soviets want to build up a permanent situation of strength in the Far East, which will be important
except in the unlikely event of an openly pro-Moscow regime being
installed in Peking as a result of the inevitable power struggle after
the demise of Mao.

A CRITIQUE OF SOVIET PERCEPTIONS

Do the Soviet perceptions of the realities of the relationships
between the rivals and adversaries of Moscow, as sketched in the
foregoing pages, conform with the realities themselves or only with
Soviet perceptions of the same realities? Are the Soviet perceptions
realistic, or is there a big red divide between Soviet visions and the
realities of international relations?

It would appear that on a broad spectrum of issues, the Western
perceptions of international realities in the 1970s mirror or nearly
mirror the Soviet perceptions, even though Soviet interpretations
vary substantially, often fundamentally, from those offered in the
West. Since the early 1950s, because of the continued growth of the
capitalist economy, despite occasional recessions; the rapid and
wide absorption by the capitalist economy of the advantages of the

scientific and technological revolution; the miracles of West German
and Japanese economic ascendancy; and the general stability of the
Western political system, no serious attention had been given in the
non-Soviet world to the Soviet concept of "the general crisis of
capitalism." In the 1970s, however, even hardened anti-Marxists
in the West concede that capitalism, which means not merely the
capitalist economy but also the entire liberal-democratic political
system in the advanced capitalist countries, is faced with a grave
"systemic" crisis from which recovery is going to be slow and
painful.[78] The emergence of the European Economic Community
(EEC) and Japan as economic giants has undoubtedly introduced
qualitative changes in intercapitalist relationships. The world
energy crisis has demonstrated that the unity of the capitalist camp
is fragile and that the United States is no longer the field commander
of the "free world" in its central combat with the Soviet bloc.

With economic affluence, the relationship of Western Europe
with the United States has changed from dependence to equality. Its
self-confidence restored, each major Western European power has
been seeking to affirm its own independent foreign policy. Gaullism
was a deviation in the 1960s, but it has become a trend in the 1970s.
The first major initiative to reorder East-West relations in Europe
came from Chancellor Willy Brandt's Ostpolitik; once the Federal
Republic of Germany accepted the postwar political map of Europe
and recognized the right of the German Democratic Republic to
exist as an independent nation, the cold war on the continent lost its
reason to exist. Ostpolitik led to the Helsinki accord in a remarkably short period of time, ushering Europe, in the Soviet view, from
the cold war to peaceful coexistence.

The Western Europeans still continue to value the protective
shield of the North Atlantic Treaty Organization (NATO), but they
are reluctant to share its costs at a time when the burden has begun
to hurt the United States. An extreme fringe of the Western European mood in the 1970s is reflected in the defense posture of the
Progress Party in Denmark, which captured 15 percent of the votes
in the 1975 national election. The Progress Party would reduce the
Danish army to one Russian-speaking person, who could awaken the
defense minister at the appropriate moment and proclaim the capitu-
lation of Denmark.[79] The Atlanticism of the postwar period is on the
wane.

The ideological cohesion of the capitalist system is threatened
by the increasing strength of the Communist parties of Italy and
France and even more by the newly acquired democratic face of
these parties. The "historical compromise" offered by the Italian
Communist Party, that is, its offer to serve in a coalition cabinet
with the Christian Democrats, and the "democratic platform" adopted

by the French Communist Party at its 1976 congress, together with
the increasing wish of the socialists of Southern Europe to work together with the Communists, bring Communist participation in one
or more major Western European governments during the 1970s
within the realm of political probability. Henry Kissinger has warned
that this might create serious problems within the Atlantic relationship.

Soviet perceptions of the economic and political problems
within the capitalist system are, then, not removed from the realities. The contemporary Soviet image of the United States is more
than confirmed by the U.S. self-image; in fact, the Soviets probably
have a much higher image of their adversary than many Americans
have of their own nation. No documentation is required to prove that
the United States is no longer the leader of the capitalist world, that
it is no longer the world's policeman, that it is obliged in the 1970s
to correct the overextension of its power in the three previous decades, and that this has generated a searing national debate over such
emotive questions as what the international obligations and commitments of the world's number one power really are. Gulliver knows,
more than anyone else, that he is in trouble.[80]

The self-perception of the Soviet Union, however, raises a
number of caveats. Marxism-Leninism is an optimistic philosophy;
its ultimate success is printed on the pages of history. In the period
since 1917 the Soviet state has become enormously powerful; it is
now a legitimate candidate for the summit of power. This great increase in might exposes the Soviet Union to the critical eyes of the
entire world. Its claim to leadership in human affairs generates
numerous demands, both within its own frontiers and in the rest of
the world, that it demonstrate the qualities of leadership.

Within the Soviet Union there is a mounting pressure for development rather than growth, for an improvement in the quality of
the lives of Soviet citizens, not in terms of the developing world but
in terms of the most developed world. This is not to suggest that
the Soviet system has neglected the material and cultural life of its
citizenry altogether, but that it will be required to devote much more
attention to it in the years to come. The Stalinist terror has disappeared to a large extent, but neither the Soviet state nor the Soviet
citizen has been released from the deep sense of insecurity that
made terror an entrenched relationship between the government and
the governed.

The blunt truth is that the Soviet government is respected and
feared in the developing countries for its economic and military
power, rather than revered for the higher civilization it claims to
have built for its own people. Soviet aid is welcomed. In times of
peril the Soviet Union is a valuable ally. In the painful task of nation

building, the Soviet Union is often a source of assistance not generally forthcoming from the capitalist countries.

Nevertheless, there is little enthusiasm in the developing
countries, particularly in Asia, for Soviet scholarship or for the
Soviet personality. This may be partly because of the "captive"
intellectual and moral values of the elites of the newly liberated nations, their deeply rooted orientation toward the Western world.
However, a certain disdain for the Soviet system is now clearly
visible, even among the majority of the Communists in Asia. In
Japan, for instance, many people who are Communists or supporters
of the Communist party record their dislike for the Soviet Union in
public opinion polls. In Europe the Communist parties of France
and Italy are now openly critical of those aspects of the Soviet system that continue to do violence to cherished human values such as
human dignity and the basic freedoms, which found a profound cham-
pionship in the writings of Marx.

A critical examination of the socialist system and of the Soviet
economy is outside the scope of this study. The impressive economic growth of the socialist system since the early 1960s is recognized even by its political opponents. It has certainly shown a great
deal of unity and cohesion, in a period when the Western alliance
has been in agonizing disarray. However, the world is not convinced that the socialist system consists of nations that are in effect
each others' equals. The Brezhnev doctrine has institutionalized
the supremacy of the Soviet Union, which is now admittedly the
arbiter of the limits of sovereignty of the individual members of the
commonwealth, including its own. Socialist integration proceeds
within the framework of the doctrine; it is "voluntary" because it
must be so. The ability of the Soviet Union to hold the bloc together,
evidently not by force alone, may be admirable, and may certify
the ability of the Soviet leaders to maintain their power, but the
Soviet Union has yet to demonstrate to the world that it can live in
fraternal equality with a coequal Communist power, that the socialist world system will not necessarily be a system that is dominated
by the Soviet Union. The conflicts between the Soviet Union and
China have seriously undermined the Marxist-Leninist claim that
the world will be free of war and conflict once socialism has taken
command. The Soviet explanation that Maoism is not Marxism-
Leninism, but only a Chinese chauvinistic distortion thereof, means
in effect that Soviet wisdom and Soviet interests must decide which
Communist system is true and which is not.

One should hasten to add, however, that the Soviet system is
not unaware of the challenge and has been trying to meet the demands of leadership, however slowly. The CPSU maintains webs of
"fraternal relations" with a number of Communist parties that have

declared their independence and that are at times critical of the
Soviet Union. The massive aid by the Soviet Union to Hanoi has not
made North Vietnam a subsidiary ally. However, this tolerance has
been shown only outside the Soviet bloc, and only to those Communist
parties that operate in the developed capitalist countries or which
have captured political power in Asia.

For all practical purposes a differentiation already exists
between the Soviet bloc and the "world socialist system." The
Brezhnev doctrine covers the Soviet Union and Eastern Europe, but
presumably not Cuba, North Korea, Vietnam, Laos, Cambodia, nor
indeed Yugoslavia. It is far from certain that Moscow would commit
its strategic military power to the defense of the socialist countries
outside the bloc. If the Communists come to power in any Western
European country in alliance with the socialists, that country might
be admitted to the socialist system, but it would certainly remain
outside the pale of the Brezhnev doctrine. In other words, the
pluralistic trends that already exist within the socialist system are
bound to get stronger with the passage of time. Intersocialist relations will have to rest on a theory more plausible than the theory of
proletarian internationalism, which is, as Jan Triska puts it, "an
assortment of hortatory speculations--unspecified, imprecise, and
unsystematic."[81]

In the 1970s the Soviet economy is moving out of the period of
rapid industrialization and into a period of maturity. The rate of
growth of the aggregate industrial output of the Soviet Union has been
impressive by world standards. Particularly impressive has been
the rate of investment. The share of output returned to the economy
as investment has been nearly twice that of the United States.[82] In
a command economy, investment has been concentrated on selective
sectors, industry, especially heavy industry, getting the lion's
share. Under Stalin, agriculture was generally neglected, while the
peasantry was exploited to serve the interest of industry. The imbalance between industry and agriculture that was thus created is
characteristic of all underdeveloped economies pressed to rapid
industrialization. Soviet economic growth has so far been generally extensive in character, achieved by increased inputs rather
than by efforts to get the maximum results from the inputs. Productivity has been neglected. This has created another imbalance,
between quantity and quality. The Soviet press is full of complaints
about the quality of the goods turned out, and not merely consumer
goods.

The Soviet economy has entered a period of increasing complexity and sophistication in which both imbalances need to be cor-
rected. The modern economy consists of innumerable interrelated,
interdependent, and interchangeable components. It is delicate and

sensitive to rough handling. Countless equations have to be resolved
at the same time. The essential inputs of a modern economy include
quality control and management. The Soviet economy now has to get
more from the same number or fewer inputs than in the past. Labor,
once abundant, is now in short supply, which makes labor productivity an overriding necessity. Modern managerial skill and a centralized bureaucracy go together poorly; plant managers not only
have to be given more responsibility, but also have to be made ac-
countable for the implementation of innovative skills. In short, a
wholesale process of decentralization of the Soviet economy is considered necessary by many experts. No less important is the generation of new technology and its rapid application in production on
a continuing basis. The Soviet Union is not lacking in technological
invention, but there is often a failure to adopt new technology without
a loss of valuable time. As two Soviet economists wrote in 1972,
"Although we do not lag behind foreign firms on the level of ideas and
technical solutions, we lose years and quality at every stage of the
introduction of the process, and our rate of technical progress is
declining."[83] In 1970 there were 388 inventions in the light industry
sector, reported Pravda, but only 35 of these were incorporated into
the plan for implementation.[84]

In its current phase the Soviet economy needs heavy inputs of
technology, whether generated within the country or imported from
abroad. Absorption of the new technology calls for across-the-board
improvements in organization and management. There must also be
a mechanism that can identify the need for changes and generate and
diffuse the changes throughout the economic system.

These are formidable tasks, especially for an overcentralized
system that is resistant to structural change. However, the Soviet
leadership is aware of the challenge, which is reflected in the economic debate that has become almost a daily feature in the Soviet
media. There is evidence of a growing self-confidence in the publication of more and more statistics, in regular scholarly discussions
with Western experts, and in the calmness with which the leadership
has accepted the severe shortfalls in grain output since 1970. The
emphasis in the five-year plans has now clearly shifted to intensive
development, to labor and capital productivity. The 1976-80 plan
says explicitly that most of the increase in output will have to come
not from capital and labor investment but from increased efficiency
and automation. The draft of the plan also reflects the concern on
the part of the Soviet leadership about the quality of Soviet goods.[85]

The failure to fulfill the growth targets of the 1971-75 plan was
probably because of the inability of the managers of the economy to
raise productivity to the level set in that plan. Heavy industry grew
by 38.9 percent instead of by the target of 41 to 45 percent. In

consumer goods the gap was even wider: 33.5 percent, against the
target of 44 to 48 percent. Overall industrial growth was 37.2 percent, compared to the set target of 42 to 46 percent. However, the
Soviet Union remained the world's leading producer of oil, extracting 491 million tons in 1975, a 32 percent growth from 1971, and
exceeding the plan target of 480 million tons. Electric power output
also passed the plan target, touching over one trillion kilowatt-hours
in 1975 and recording a 30 percent rise in five years. The goal of
steel production was nearly met: 141 million tons in 1975, compared
to the target of 142 to 150 million tons.

Individual consumer items showed a lower rate of growth and
in some cases a decline. The lowest growth rates were in fabrics,
radios, and butter. Television sets showed a 20.6 percent increase
in the five years, while the production of new housing units remained
more or less steady, hovering between 2.2 and 2.3 million units a
year. The steadily rising demand for consumer goods has not led to
a consumer revolt, indicating that the system maintains its grip on
consumer demand, which is reflected in the relatively low priority
given to consumer industries in the 1976-80 plan: 2.7 percent annual
growth, in comparison to 4.9 percent growth in heavy industry. In
1976 the Soviets expect to produce 520 million tons of oil and 147
million tons of steel. Evidently energy, heavy industry, machine
building, and basic foods are to receive the highest priorities in the
new five-year plan. [86]

Agriculture remains the Achilles' heel of the Soviet economy,
accounting for 20 percent of the aggregate output and locking up one-
third of the national work force. The poor harvest of 1975, a mere
140 million tons, dramatized the farm problem and led to conjectures
that the Soviet Union would remain a net importer of food grains for
years. [87] The poor 1975 crop was the result of weather calamities
unusual even in a country of notorious weather variations. Severe
droughts simultaneously hit both the Ukraine and Siberia-Kazakhstan,
that is, the entire crop-growing region. In fact, the structural reforms introduced since the death of Stalin and the transfer of more
and more state resources to agriculture have shown positive results.
The average annual output rose from 130 million tons during 1961-65
to about 190 million tons for the years 1971 and 1972; the latter year
actually brought in a record harvest of 222 million tons. Efforts to
improve the meat content of the citizens' diet and the resulting demand
for fodder have increased sharply in recent years. The Soviet Union
also has to devote about 5 million tons of wheat each year to the requirements of North Korea and North Vietnam.

In agriculture, as in industry, the emphasis has been steadily
shifting to productivity. In Khrushchev's time, certain fundamental
reforms were introduced both in agricultural organization and in

agricultural economic planning. The collective farms (kolkhoz) declined in importance, while the role of the state farms (sovkhoz)
increased. Under Brezhnev, intensive farming has been getting the
highest priority. Beginning in March 1965, the Soviet government
embarked on a vast program to upgrade agriculture, with greater
capital outlays for machinery, fertilizer, and storage facilities.
More than 131 billion rubles ($175 billion) were spent during the
1971-75 plan period. The new five-year plan has increased agricultural investment to one-third of the total funds available for investment (in the previous plan it was 20 percent). One ambitious program is the investment of 35 billion rubles in the next five years to
reclaim and enrich land in northern Russia, where the soil is poor.
Brezhnev has also sought to put agriculture on a more industrial
footing with interfarm factories, as has been done successfully in
Moldavia. Meanwhile, Soviet agronomists are discussing the prospects of growing sorghum, a fodder crop that is more resistant to
drought. The building of an agro-industrial infrastructure will take
time, but there is no sign of any unwillingness on the part of the
Soviet leadership. [88]

The Soviet leaders continue to hope to be able to bury capitalism, but for the present they entertain high praise for capitalist
technology. It is clearly the intention of the leadership to fill the
technology gap by large-scale imports from the capitalist world.
The importing of capitalist technology from Western Europe began
even in the mid-1950s. Detente has accelerated the process and has
made the United States and Japan among the major suppliers of advanced technological and managerial inputs to the Soviet Union.
Indeed, there has been a systematic rearrangement of Soviet foreign
trade since 1960, a diversion from the less-developed socialist and
nonsocialist countries to the developed capitalist countries. No
doubt the Soviets have gained substantially from the technological
fallout of detente. In the importation of technology, the crying needs
of agriculture seem to be receiving equal attention with the needs of
industry. It will not be surprising if by the mid-1980s the advanced
capitalist powers are seen to have given a most welcome helping
hand to making the Soviet Union reliably self-sufficient in farm
products. [89]

In light of this discussion, it is easy to see how important
detente is for the further economic development of the Soviet Union
and for its candidacy for the global summit of power. It is also easy
to see why so many people in the West oppose detente except on the
basis of an equal give-and-take. [90] The Soviets believe that detente
is being promoted by objective conditions in international relations
and that it is not entirely dependent on the wishes and whims of the
Western political actors. Many of these actors, on the other hand,

hold the view that the Soviet economy is hostage to detente and
therefore that Moscow can be made to pay a higher ransom than it
has so far, but only if the Western powers know how to exact it. In
the mid-1970s this tug of war has generated almost mirror perceptions of detente in the Soviet Union and the Western world. There
are hardliners and softliners in both camps, which makes the process
of detente extremely dynamic. A sharp contest of wills and capabil-
ities between the two competing systems marks the current period of
international relations; the contest will probably go on for years.
It seems probable that, in the superpower relationship, areas of
cooperation will become differentiated from areas of competition and
conflict. Kissinger, for example, attempted such a differentiation
in early 1976 when he separated the area of strategic arms negotiations from that of trade and economic relations, arguing that in view
of Soviet intervention in Angola the Administration would not renew
its effort to get Congressional approval for a nondiscriminating
trade agreement with the Soviet Union, but that it would pursue the
SALT II negotiations with Moscow because another strategic arms
race could cost the United States $20 billion in the next five years,
a burden it was scarcely in a position to bear.[91] If such a differentiation becomes somewhat institutionalized in Soviet–American relations, Moscow will have won a major point on both the theoretical
and the operational sides of international relations.

The Soviet perceptions of the Third World, the national liberation zone, are not generally reciprocated either in the Western world
or in most of Asia, as we shall see in this study. The enormous
conceptual and theoretical work done in the USSR on the national
liberation phenomenon has had little impact on the West and has been
generally ignored in the developing countries.[92] With the exception
of Communists, the non–Soviet world has refused to recognize
symbiotic linkages between the national liberation movement and the
world socialist revolution.[93] The claim that these linkages exist is
seen as nothing more than an extravagant Marxist-Leninist ideological flourish, with no empirical evidence to prove its validity. The
Soviet development models have gained little currency either in
Western scholarship or in the developing countries themselves, including those that have close relations with the Soviet Union.[94] Thus,
although the Soviets claim that over .1 billion people today live in
countries pursuing noncapitalist development, the non–Soviet world
neither seeks out, nor is willing to see, the national democrats or
the revolutionary democrats as constituting the vanguard of the anti-
imperialist movement.[95]

The Western powers do not recognize the main challenge to the
capitalist system as coming from the anti-imperialist struggle.
Contrary to the Soviet view, neither the Western powers nor the

Third-World nations see the balance of power in the "gray areas" as having shifted in favor of the militant anti-imperialists and the socialist countries. Moscow strives for access to, and influence in, the great capitalist rear, yes; but the threat to the capitalist world does not come from Cairo, Algiers, New Delhi, or Baghdad but from Moscow. It used to come from Peking, and may come from there once again. The Soviet strategic goal is to detach some of the key Third World countries from the world capitalist system. Even this has proved to be a difficult, long, and far from even process. To the Soviet leaders, each developing country is a potential ally in the anti-imperialist struggle, but the number of actual allies is small, and that of reliable allies is smaller still. During its first period the struggle was, or has been, anti-imperialist, its objective being national political independence. The strongest and most enviable Soviet ally has therefore been the national bourgeoisie rather than the ineffectual Communist parties or groups that exist in most of the new nations.

Soviet foreign policy is designed to influence the national bourgeois leaders of the new nations mainly in three directions. It endeavors to persuade them (1) to wage the struggle against imperialism both on the international and domestic fronts; (2) to develop ever wider and deeper economic, political, and military linkages with the socialist bloc; and (3) to introduce "democratic reforms" within the domestic sphere and pursue "socialist" policies even when these are not "scientific." The process of influencing, as Holsti points out, is an actor's ability to establish orientations; fulfill roles; or achieve, sustain, and defend objectives through the behavior and action of another independent actor. The process is fostered by mutual responsiveness in terms of values, felt needs, and the short- to long-term objectives of the national interest.[96] Durable influence building requires an evolving, dynamic relationship, an interdependence tested in the crucible of time. The Soviet Union enjoys certain environmental advantages in the new nations that are denied to the United States, since the latter is generally seen as the defender of the old order and of entrenched interests. In the initial stages of nation building, when the main tasks for the national bourgeois leadership are to enlarge and complete political sovereignty, to establish economic independence, and to assert sovereign rights over natural resources, it is relatively easier for the Soviet Union to merge its influence-building efforts with the nation-building enterprise of the national bourgeois leadership, particularly when the country concerned is engaged in a struggle with one or more of the imperialist powers. Where the Soviet leaders have proved to be more or less successful, the anti-imperialist struggle has provided mutual value responsiveness. Soviet aid has met felt needs. Soviet

political and military support has helped achieve, sustain, and defend shared objectives. Soviet global interests and the national
interests of the courted nation have converged. The entire process
has helped to establish a certain limited orientation.

This relationship of influencer with influenced, however, is
highly dynamic, especially where there is more than one bidder for
influence.[97] The competitive ambience leaves the local actor with
considerable autonomy of action. The imperialists themselves are
resourceful; they quickly learn to cut losses and to adjust their policies to the caprices of changing realities. Moreover, as Soviet
analysts often point out, the bourgeois leaders are uncertain bets.
Even the national democrats and revolutionary democrats often
vacillate between the two systems, being reluctant to break with the
capitalist world. At the first opportunity they strike out at their
external benefactors. Anwar Sadat of Egypt was able to expel Soviet
advisers in 1972 and return to the capitalist fold in 1975. India,
with all its extensive relations with the Soviet Union, still sells 45
percent of all its exports to the advanced capitalist countries.

Influence-building relations with such uncertain elements are
by nature transactional and involve bargaining and mutual attempts
at persuasion, arm twisting, and even threats. The Soviets see
friendships or alliances as resting on transactions that cover four
broad areas that may be described as areas of convergence, preference, tolerance, and resistance.[98]

1. Convergence of orientations and interests provides the
foundation of the relationship, as will be evident in the course of this
study. Orientation and interests may cover both external and internal
issues. Generally, however, there is a greater convergence of the
external policies, interests, and objectives of the Soviet Union and
its Third-World allies than there is of domestic policy stances.
Soviet analysts concede that the Soviet Union can exert very little
influence on the domestic policies of regimes with which it has close
relations.

2. The preference area of the relationship relates to the issues
on which the Soviet Union tries to persuade or pressure its allies to
adopt certain specific actions or stances, sometimes with success
and sometimes without. For instance, during 1967-71 the Soviets
tried to persuade India to call publicly for the withdrawal of American
troops from Vietnam, but failed; India called for the withdrawal of
all foreign troops, including, by implication, North Vietnamese
troops, from South Vietnam. However, in 1969, after the Sino-Soviet
border clash on the Ussuri River, the Soviet Union was able to get
from India a statement supporting the Soviet position on the Sino-
Soviet border dispute.

3. The tolerance zone of the relationship, which is often quite dynamic and which is larger than commonly believed, permits the ally to deviate from the Soviet-approved line so long as Russian interests are not hurt. When India exploded a nuclear device in May 1974 and annexed Sikkim in 1975, the Soviets accepted the actions even though they did not entirely approve of them. Similarly, they tolerated the quest by Iraq for Western arms in 1975, when the conclusion of the Baghdad-Tehran accords reduced the dependency of Iraq on the Soviet Union.

4. The resistance area covers issues on which the Soviets resist, with various forms of pressure and threat, the adoption of certain postures and actions by their allies. For instance, the Soviets would resist any Indian move to improve relations with China on the basis of major concessions, as they would resist any move on the part of India or Iraq to invite large-scale American private investment in their economies. If any ally or friend elects to act in despite of Soviet resistance, the relationship will be strained. Soviet friendship with the national liberation actors, then, is fraught with many problems in spite of the fact that, unlike the West, the Soviets have a philosophical appreciation of the impact of the anti-imperialist movement on the general progress of history and they link the anti-imperialist struggle symbiotically with the world socialist revolution. The local actor, like the Rebel in Baudelaire's poem, quite often turns around and shouts, "I will not" to the influencer, even when the latter claims to be armed with the wisdom of history.

What makes Soviet perceptions of developments in the national liberation zone truly interesting is the conviction of Soviet analysts that the general trends and processes in the Third World are turning in the 1970s against both the capitalist system and the national bourgeois political actors. This perception has been created partly by the Communist victories in Indochina. For the first time since the second world war, four Asian countries have been finally detached from the capitalist system. The only other country to be so detached during this period was Cuba. Also, the anti-imperialist struggle is now being waged in areas that are rich in energy resources and therefore vital to the capitalist economy. For instance, the establishment of the complete sovereignty of the Arab and Persian Gulf countries over their natural resources would hurt the international cartel of oil companies, the largest industrial enterprise of the capitalist world.

Several other perceived realities in the developing zone have also contributed to the current Soviet view. One is the withering of the quality of leadership of the national bourgeois leaders. A second is the belief that in a number of the new nations the liberation struggle

has entered its second stage and is now increasingly becoming a
struggle for the economic and social liberation of the broad mass of
people. A third is the emergence of what Soviet military analysts
call a "new type of war," which means wars and military conflicts
among the developing nations in which the imperialists have no dis-
cernible role. [99]

All of these perceived realities have led to a general downgrad-
ing of the national liberation movement as an autonomous revolutionary force in the analytical writings during the post-Khrushchev period.
Soviet analysts now stress that unless it is in firm alliance with the
socialist system the national liberation struggle can hope to achieve
but little. It can neither wrest meaningful economic independence
from the imperialist bloc nor advance its own domestic momentum
of progressive social change. [100] If these articulations have any
meaning for the conduct of Soviet foreign policy, the Soviets can be
expected to demand a higher price in the future for their friendship
and alliance than the Third World actors have been willing to pay so
far. In other words, the Soviet Union would very much like to avoid
the kind of setback it suffered in Egypt in 1972 and 1975. It now has
a greater capability to intervene in local wars and military conflicts,
but the price of intervention will probably be higher in the 1970s and
1980s than it used to be in the earlier periods. The Soviet Union
will probably also become increasingly involved in the domestic
polarizations in the developing nations. In 1975 it stood firmly by
Indira Gandhi when she declared an internal emergency, suspended
the civil liberties of the people, imposed a strict censorship on the
press, and seriously limited the independence of the judiciary--in
short, imposed an authoritarian system of government--in the name
of arresting a rightist offensive against her "progressive" social and
economic policies and against the close ties of India with the Soviet
Union. (See Chapter 5.)

There are similarities in the current Soviet and U.S. perceptions of Asia. Both governments perceive security vacuums created
by the retreat of U.S. power, widening gaps between the governing
elites and the governed masses, and the inevitability of conflicts and
tensions. The United States, however, is the withdrawing power.
The Soviet Union is for the first time in its history seeking a presence
throughout Asia. The United States became an Asian power by the
accidents of history. It does not belong to Asia, and it can always
pack up and go, in any case from a great deal of Asia. A latecomer
to the empire-building game, the United States is a Pacific power
with an Atlantic history, an Atlantic culture, and an Atlantic mind. [101]

Russia, however, is within and outside Asia, and Asia has
lived in the Russian mind for many centuries. It has stimulated each
Russian's historical imaginations; has given each one hallucinations

and moments of exaltation; and has caused each one fear and hope,
hatred and love. Prior to the Bolshevik revolution Russia went
through two different periods of Asian "ideology." For ancient Russia, Asia meant the alien hordes from the steppe, objects of hostility and often of fear. Under Peter the Great the educated classes of
Russia imbibed the imperial ideology of the Europeans and looked
upon Asia with a mixture of white, Christian supremacy and the zeal
of the crusading pioneer. It stimulated the Russians' desire to
dominate, to carry the flag of civilization to the uncivilized; it also
created in some Russians a romantic reverence for oriental cultures.[102]

Then, with the revolution, came the Eurasian concept, which
was formally inaugurated in 1921. Lenin discovered the Asian
character of the young Soviet state. He linked the Marxist-Leninist
revolution with the anti-imperialist struggles of the Asian colonies
and semicolonies. The road to world revolution now ran through
Peking, Shanghai, Calcutta, and Cairo rather than through Berlin,
Paris, and London. For the Soviets, Eurasia is both a geopolitical
and an ideological concept. It is part of the fluid of the Russian
historical experience. In a famous poem of Aleksandr Blok, composed in 1918, the young Soviet state found a new strength in its
Asiatic identity to challenge the Western interventionists.

> You are millions. We are hordes, and hordes
>   and hordes.
> Just try, fight us!
> Yes, we are Scythians! Yes, we are Asiatics,
> With slanting and greedy eyes!

The Bolsheviks inaugurated a new Asian policy for Russia by
denouncing the unequal and secret treaties and by offering friendship
to the nationalist revolutions in the East, from Turkey to China. At
home they believed that they were building a "system of states" on
the basis of a new relationship that included the right to secede,
which was never to be exercised. In the short time since the 1917
revolution the Soviet Union has achieved considerable development
in its central Asian republics, and the Soviet leaders have no doubt
in their minds that the experience they have gathered is relevant to
the young Asian countries outside the Soviet Union.[103] For many
centuries the warm waters of Asia and its tropical wealth had been
denied Russia by the imperial powers of Europe. For a quarter
century after the second world war, the United States denied the
Soviet Union a significant presence in Asia. Now, at long last, the
Asian frontiers are opening up for the Soviet Union, which calls
itself an Asian country. With a revolution over 60 years old, Russia

looks at Asia with a self-confidence it never had before and with
power it never wielded before. The steppe seeks its manifest destiny
in the tropics. [104]

The Asians, on the other hand, have never seen the Russians
as Asiatic, nor are they prepared to see the Soviet Union as an Asian
power. Eurasian by geography, yes, but European in civilization,
culture, traditions, language, color of skin, outlook, and behavior:
this is the most widely shared Asian image of the Soviet Union. With
the blurring of the Asians' ideological image of the Soviet Union, a
characteristic of the 1970s, as we shall find in this volume, the
Soviet Union is also seen in most of Asia as part of the affluent
North. This image gets clearer as Soviet advisers in Laos occupy
residential houses left by the Americans and as Soviet experts in
Kabul live a life that suits the average affluent European rather than
the average Asian.

NOTES

1. V. Gantman, "A Policy that is Transforming the World,"
Kommunist, no. 7, signed to press, May 8, 1973.

2. The advantages of the Marxist-Leninist analysis are recognized in Robert C. Tucker, The Soviet Political Mind: Studies in
Stalinism and Post Stalin Change (New York: Praeger), pp. 179-84,
and questioned in Vernon V. Asputurian, "Diplomacy in the Mirror
of Soviet Scholarship," in Contemporary History in the Soviet Mirror, ed. John Keep (New York: Praeger, 1964), pp. 250-55.
Soviet analytical tools, however, have become somewhat sharper
since this essay was written. For a description of the opposite,
"geometrical" U.S. image of the political universe, an approach
that is "too static and too frantic," see Stanley Hoffman, Gulliver's
Troubles, or the Setting of American Foreign Policy (New York:
McGraw-Hill, 1968), pp. 208-11. Hoffman says, "For a nation so
hopeful about the benefits of time, the United States is singularly
unwilling to let time operate, to trust the 'force of circumstance';
it is as though we knew we were whistling in the dark."

3. Gantman, op. cit. See also "The 24th Congress of the
CPSU and International Issues," report of a discussion organized by
the editorial board of International Affairs and the USSR Academy
of Sciences, scientific council on problems of the history of USSR
foreign policy and international relations, International Affairs,
August 1971; Alexander George, "The Operational Code: A Neglected
Approach to the Study of Political Leaders and Decision-Making,"
International Studies Quarterly (Beverly Hills, Calif., June 1969).

4. Nathan Leites, Kremlin Thoughts: Yielding, Rebuffing, Provoking, Retreating (Santa Monica, Calif.: Rand Corp., 1963); also Tucker, op. cit.; Asputurian, op. cit.; Hoffman, op. cit.

5. "The Supreme Internationalist Duty of a Socialist Country," Pravda, October 27, 1965.

6. V. I. Lenin, Collected Works, vol. 31 (Moscow, 1966), pp. 412-14.

7. Documents on USSR Foreign Policy, vol. 5 (Moscow), pp. 191-92.

8. Gantman, op. cit.; "The 24th Congress of the CPSU and International Relations," op. cit.; V. Gavrilov, "The Soviet Union and the System of International Relations," Mirovaya Ekonomika i Mezhdunarodnye Otnosheniia, no. 12 (1972).

9. Gavrilov, op. cit.

10. "The 24th Congress of the CPSU and International Issues," op. cit.

11. For a comprehensive and integrated Soviet view of modern capitalism see the seven studies brought out in 1972-73 under the overall title of The Economic and Politics of Modern Capitalist Countries, edited by V. Ya. Aboltin. The countries covered in the first six volumes are the United States, Britain, West Germany, France, Italy, and Japan; the seventh volume covers Sweden, Switzerland, the Netherlands, and Belgium. See also L. Leont'yev, "A Study of Modern Capitalism in the 1970s," Kommunist, no. 10 (July 1974); I. Gazminov, "Development of the Economic Crisis in the Capitalist Countries," International Affairs, October 1971; I. Trotsenko, "Agrarian Integration: Growing Inter-Imperialist Contradictions," International Affairs, March 1972.

12. Mikhail Suslov, Pravda, October 23, 1974.

13. Gavrilov, op. cit.

14. "24th Congress of the CPSU and International Issues," op. cit.

15. Georgi Arbatov, "On Soviet-US Relations," Kommunist, no. 3 (February 1973).

16. Ibid.

17. Ibid.; also Arbatov, "Soviet-American Relations in the 1970s," USA: Politics, Economics, Ideology, no. 5 (May 1975).

18. Ibid.

19. Ibid.

20. "The Path to Cooperation," Sovetskaia Rossiia, June 1, 1972; for similar comments, see Izvestia, editorial, May 31, 1972; "Fruitful Results," Krasnaya Zvezda, June 1, 1972; "Along the Leninist Course," Moskovskaia Pravda, June 15, 1972.

21. "SALT Breakthrough," New York Times, February 2, 1976.

22. David Shipler, "Soviet Buying Technology Despite US Trade Curb," New York Times, January 25, 1976. Shipler reported that several $1 billion deals were being negotiated, which would take project collaboration into the 1980s. Pullman, Inc. and its subsidiary, M. W. Kellogg, are building 13 ammonia plants in the USSR through licenses in Japan and France. Computer companies are selling through subsidiaries in Japan and France.

23. This has been one of the crucial points in the ongoing American debate on detente. The critics say that the Soviets are getting large-scale capitalist technology without paying any political price. See U.S., Congress, House of Representatives, Committee on Foreign Affairs, Subcommittee on Europe, Detente, 93rd Cong., 2d sess., May-July 1974 (Washington, D.C.: U.S. Government Printing Office, 1974); Zbigniew K. Brzezinski, "A U.S. Portfolio in the USSR?" The New Leader (New York), August 5, 1975.

24. New York Times, July 1, 1975.

25. Arbatov, "Soviet-American Relations in the 1970s," op. cit.

> There is cautious but growing optimism among
> Soviet and East European leaders that the long un-
> fulfilled Marxist prediction of a spontaneous col-
> lapse of capitalism may finally be at hand. . . .
> But leading economists and political theorists in
> the Soviet bloc leave no doubt that they believe the
> current economic crisis in the West is qualitatively
> different from earlier ones, and that it will be
> vastly more destructive to Western economic and
> political traditions than any of its predecessors.

Malcolm W. Browne, "Soviet Sees Gains in Woes of West," New York Times, July 10, 1975.

26. Preface, V. I. Lenin on Peaceful Coexistence (Moscow: Foreign Languages Press, 1963), pp. 9-10.

27. Problems of War and Peace: A Critical Analysis of Bourgeois Theories (Moscow: Progress Publishers, 1972), p. 247; see also pp. 267, 385. For the Soviet theory of peaceful coexistence as a "system" of international relations, see M. Avakov, "The Vital Force of Leninist Principle of Peaceful Coexistence," Kommunist Vooruzhennykh Sil, no. 23, October 1973; Georgi Zadorozhny, Peaceful Coexistence: Contemporary International Law (Moscow: Progress Publishers, 1968). For a sympathetic American interpretation, see Edward McWhinny, "Changing International Law: Method and Objectives in an Era of the Soviet-Western Detente," American Journal of International Law 59, no. 1 (January 1965).

28. The growing recognition of the principles of peaceful coexistence in no way means that the capitalist
states have abandoned their imperialist policy.
The essence of imperialism remains as it was; it
has not changed. But the time of undivided imperialist domination has receded irrevocably in
the past. The balance of forces in the world arena
has shifted radically in favor of the forces of peace,
social progress and socialism.

F. Ryzhenko, "Peaceful Coexistence and the Class Struggle," Pravda,
August 22, 1973.

29. "Such, then, are the facts. They show that with the introduction of peaceful coexistence into Soviet-US relations Soviet support
for the national liberation movements will increase rather than de-
crease, and opportunities for cooperation between the socialist nations and the developing countries will be greater." D. Volsky,
"Soviet-American Relations and the Third World," New Times, no.
36 (September 1973). "It is not by chance that it was in an atmosphere of relaxation of international tension that the Vietnamese
people won their signal victory over U.S. imperialist aggression or
that the people of Bangladesh gained their independence." Y. Kashlev,
"Detente and the Ideological Struggle," New Times, no. 37 (September 1973).

For one of the most forceful presentations of the Soviet
view of the impact of peaceful coexistence on the Third World, see
Boris Panomarev, "Actual Problems in the Theory of the World
Revolutionary Process," Kommunist, no. 10 (1973).

30. Kissinger said in December 1975 that "there is no question that our over-all relationship will suffer if we do not find an
adequate solution to the Angolan problem." The New York Times
commented, "The implication was: No Soviet move to settle Angola,
then less chance that the Russians will receive the grain they so
badly need and perhaps less chance of a new nuclear-arms pact."
New York Times, December 29, 1975.

31. "The Ford Administration's blunt warnings on the Soviet
Union's involvement in Angola appear to have had little effect on
Moscow's policy. . . . Even Soviet officials who study the United
States full time do not seem to take seriously the argument that Angola
could become a focus for powerful anti-detente and anti-Soviet feel-
ings among some segments of the American electorate." New York
Times, February 9, 1976.

32. Newsweek, January 19, 1976.

33. Ibid. In December 1975 Kissinger defined the detente as
acceleration of the process of moderating the potential conflict between

the Soviet Union and the United States by conscious acts of policy.
He said,

> In this respect, it requires conscious restraint by
> both sides. If one side doesn't practice restraint
> then the situation becomes inherently tense. . . .
> Unless the Soviet Union shows restraint in its for-
> eign policy actions, the situation in our relation-
> ship is bound to become more tense, and there is
> no question that the United States will not accept
> Soviet military expansion of any kind.

Statement at news conference in Washington, D.C., New York Times,
December 24, 1975.

34. "The 24th Congress of the CPSU and International Issues,"
op. cit.

35. Ibid.

36. The Soviet leaders acknowledge the importance of imported
technology for further development of the Soviet economy. Leonid
Brezhnev, in submitting the accountability report of the central committee to the 24th congress of the CPSU, said that "the improvement
of the system of foreign economic and technological ties will aid the
further rise of the economic effectiveness of the national economy."
Pravda, March 31, 1971. Soon after Nixon's 1972 visit to Moscow,
D. M. Gvishiani, deputy chairman of the State Committee for Science
and Technology of the Council of Ministers, indicated in an article
that cooperation with the advanced capitalist countries would enable
the Soviets to resolve "many unsolved problems in science and technology." "For the Good of Mankind," Izvestia, June 6, 1972. By
mid-1971 the USSR had concluded scientific and technological cooperation agreements with all of the major developed countries and with
46 developing countries. In early 1972 the USSR Academy of Sciences
reported that it had agreements for scientific cooperation with "practically all of the academies of science and most of the important
scientific organizations in the world." Vestnik Akademii Nauk SSSR,
no. 5 (May 1972).

37. The Brezhnev doctrine, that the sovereignty of the socialist bloc is collective and that the Soviet Union will not permit any
violation of the boundaries of the bloc, has become institutionalized
in Soviet writings on international politics in the 1970s.

38. "The 24th Congress of the CPSU and International Issues,"
op. cit.; see also Col. V. Rut'kov, "The Military-Economic Might
of the Socialist Countries as a Factor in the Security of Peoples,"
Kommunist Vooruzhennykh Sil, no. 23, December 1974.

39. The past year (1974) has demonstrated the immea-
surable superiority of socialism over capitalism.
The stability and consistently high rate of development of the economy and the steady rise in the well-
being of the peoples of the socialist countries stand
in sharp contrast to the picture of rampant inflation,
rising prices, energy crisis, decline in production,
and mass unemployment of the capitalist world. It
is characteristic that literally all the major capitalist states have been affected by the same severe
ailments.

"An Irreversible Process," Kommunist Vooruzhennykh Sil, no. 1
(January 1975).

40. William Griffith of MIT remarked, "To my mind what is
really remarkable is that the Soviets feel free to move into Angola in
a year when they are 70 million tons short of grain and cannot buy as
much as they need anywhere but here." Newsweek, January 9, 1975.

41. Rut'kov, op. cit.

42. Christopher S. Wren, "Soviet Far East Turning to Trade
with Pacific Basin," New York Times, November 25, 1975.

43. Ye. S. Shershnev, "Peaceful Coexistence and Economic
Cooperation," Kommunist, no. 1 (January 1975). Problems of
Japanese collaboration in Siberian development are discussed in
some detail in Chapter 7.

44. R. M. Avakov et al., Razvivayushchiyesya Strany:
Zakonomernosti, Tendentsii, Perspektivy (The Developing Countries:
Patterns, Trends, Prospects) (Moscow: Mysl, 1974), pp. 17-19;
K. N. Brutents, "The Easing of International Tensions and the De-
veloping Countries," Pravda, August 30, 1973.

To illustrate the theory that the developing countries begin
their career in the periphery of the capitalist system, I. M.
Kompantsev cites the case of Pakistan, the leaders of which, he says,
did not in the first years of independence see any "special usefulness"
in turning to the Soviet Union for economic aid. Pakistan i Sovotskii
Soiuz (Moscow: Nauka, 1970), pp. 193-97.

45. V. Lee, "The National Liberation Movement Today and the
Anti-Imperialist Struggle," Soviet Review (Moscow), February 8,
1972; R. Ul'ianovski, "The 'Third World'--Problems of Socialist
Orientation," International Affairs, September 1971.

46. Ibid. These categorizations have posed complex problems
for Soviet scholars, who concede that the Marxist "science" is still
not fully equipped to deal with all realities in the developing countries. For a perceptive analytical discussion of Soviet classification

problems, see Roger Kanet, "Soviet Attitudes toward Developing
Nations since Stalin," in The Soviet Union and the Developing Nations," ed. Roger Kanet (Baltimore: Johns Hopkins Press, 1974),
pp. 27-50. Kanet rightly points out, and he is confirmed by Soviet
scholars, that within a broad theoretical framework the Soviet leaders look at each developing nation contextually and formulate policy
in the light of particularist perceptions and analysis. See Kanet,
"Soviet Union and the Developing Countries: Policy or Policies?"
in Soviet Economic and Political Relations with the Developing World,
ed. Roger Kanet and Donna Bahry (New York: Praeger, 1975),
pp. 10-19. See also Elizabeth K. Valkenier, "The Soviet Union and
the Third World: From Khrushchev's 'Zone of Peace' to Brezhnev's
'Peace Program,'" same work, pp. 3-9. An incisive, if somewhat
cold-warish, study of the earlier Soviet formulations can be found in
Thomas P. Thornton, "Communist Attitudes toward Asia, Africa
and Latin America," in Communism and Revolution: The Strategic
Uses of Political Violence, ed. Cyril E. Black and Thomas P.
Thornton (Princeton: Princeton University Press, 1964), pp. 245-69.

47. In his report to the 24th CPSU Congress, Brezhnev saw a
process of polarization occurring in the national liberation zone. He
said, "The struggle for national liberation in many countries has in
practical terms begun to grow into a class struggle against the ex-
ploitive relations, both feudal and capitalist." Since then, Soviet
analysts have been focusing on the polarization process, which they
claim is differentiating the progressives from the reactionaries and
weaving closer links with the progressives and the socialist bloc.
V. L. Tyagunenko, "Paramount Task before Developing Countries,"
Mirovaya ekonomika i Mezhdunarodnye Otnosheniia, no. 11 (1971);
Tyagunenko, "World Socialism and National Liberation Revolutions,"
Kommunist, no. 8 (May 1973); K. N. Brutents, Sovremennye
Nasional'no Revolyntsii (Moscow: Izd. Politicheskoy Literatury,
1974), pp. 259-63. Brutents takes a cautious view of the "socialis-
tic" possibilities of the national liberation struggle, which he sees
to be still broadly "anti-imperialist." He also regards nationalism
as the strongest force in the developing countries; not only is it
"exploited" relatively easily by the imperialist powers, but it also
sometimes divides even the Communists. Ibid., pp. 479-80.

48. V. L. Tyagunenko, "World Socialism and National Liberation Revolution," Kommunist, no. 8 (May 1973).

49. Ibid. This point is also made by Brutents in Sovremennye
Nasional'no Revolyntsii, op. cit.

50. Ibid., pp. 295, 470-82; Tyagunenko, op. cit.; G. Mirsky,
"Important Problems of the National Liberation Movement,"
Kommunist, no. 9 (June 1974).

51. R. Ul'ianovski, "United Anti-Imperialist Front of Progressive Forces in the Newly-Independent Countries," Mirovaya Ekonomika i Mezhdunarodnye Otnosheniia, no. 9 (1972).

52. Tyagunenko, "Paramount Task before Developing Countries," op. cit.; Ul'ianovski, "United Anti-Imperialist Front of Progressive Forces in the Newly-Independent Countries," op. cit.

53. R. Ul'ianovski, "The Present Stage of the National Liberation Movement and the Peasantry," Mirovaya Ekonomika i Mezhdunarodyne Otnosheniia, no. 5 (1971).

54. Tyagunenko, "World Socialism and National Liberation Revolution," op. cit.

55. For in-depth discussion of contemporary Soviet strategic thinking, see Thomas W. Wolfe, Soviet Strategies at the Crossroads (Cambridge, Mass.: Harvard University Press, 1964); P. H. Vigor, The Soviet View of War, Peace and Neutrality; Michael MccGwire, ed., Soviet Naval Developments: Capability and Context (New York: Praeger, 1973), Part 1.

56. N. A. Lomov, ed., Scientific-Technical Progress and the Revolution in Military Affairs: A Soviet View (Moscow, 1973), translated and published under the auspices of the U.S. Air Force, p. 270.

57. Ye Rybkin, "The Leninist Concept of War and the Present," Kommunist Vooruzhennykh Sil, no. 20 (October 1973).

58. Ibid.

59. Lomov, op. cit., pp. 264-70.

60. Henry Kissinger, Nuclear Weapons and Foreign Policy, abridged ed., Philip Quigg, ed. (New York: Norton, 1969).

61. V. D. Sokolovskii, Soviet Military Strategy (Santa Monica, Calif.: Rand Corporation, 1963), pp. 308-09.

62. I. S. Buz, "Soviet Military Science on the Character of Contemporary War," Voennyi Vestnik (Military Herald), no. 6 (1958); N. Talenskii in Mezdhunarodnaia zhizn, no. 12 (December 1957).

63. V. D. Sokolovskii, Voennaya Strategiya (3rd ed., Moscow: Voenizdat, 1968), p. 222.

64. Lomov, op. cit., p. 270; V. Bokarev, "Ideological-Theoretical Principles of Military Science and Practice," Kommunist Vooruzhennykh Sil, no. 8 (April 1973).

65. Lomov, op. cit., p. 270.

66. Ibid.

67. Marxism-Leninism on War and the Army (Moscow, 1972), translated under the auspices of the U.S. Air Force, Washington, D.C., pp. 62-107.

68. Bokarev, op. cit.

69. The threat was contained in a long editorial in Pravda, May 16, 1969.

70. Ibid.

71. Ibid.

72. A. A. Gaber et al., Mezhdunarodnyye Otnosheniya na
Dal'nem Vostoke (International Relations in the Far East), vol. 1
(Moscow: Mysl, 1973); G. V. Yefimov and A. M. Dabinskiy, vol. 2
(Moscow: Mysl, 1973); P'in Ming, Istoriya Kitaysko-Sovetskoy
Druzhby (History of Sino-Soviet Relations) (Moscow, 1969); L.
Beskrovniy and others, "On the History of the Establishment of the
Russo-Chinese Border," Mezhdunarodnaia zhizn, no. 6 (1972);
V. M. Khostov, "The Chinese 'Bill' and Historical Truth,"
Mezhdunarodnaia zhizn, no. 10 (1964).

73. Lomov, op. cit., p. 264.

74. I was at that time traveling in Southeast Asia, doing field
work in connection with this study. I found much nervous curiosity
in the ASEAN capitals about the "true significance" of the CCP message. Did the Chinese send it because of their uncertainty about
U.S. policy during the transition from Nixon to Ford?

75. Christopher S. Wren, "Peking Display Worries Moscow,"
New York Times, June 3, 1975. The Soviet helicopter incident in
Sinkiang took place on March 14, 1974.

76. C. L. Sulzberger, "Brezhnev 'Cruise' to China," New
York Times, January 17, 1976.

77. "Barring a sharp worsening of Sino-Soviet relations, as
a result of a Soviet attack on China, for example, there is . . . an
obvious possibility that confrontation will be replaced sooner or later
by accommodation." Harold C. Hinton, Three and a Half Powers:
The New Balance in Asia (Bloomington: Indiana University Press,
1975), pp. 292-93.

78. One of the best studies of the crisis of the Western
democracies is Daniel Bell, The Cultural Contradictions of Capitalism (New York: Basic Books, 1975). Z. K. Brzezinski also has
written about the "cultural malaise" and has observed, "The international consequences of this crisis are not to be underestimated.
Today, democracy appears not only less vital, but less appealing.
It is hard to think of a period since the American Revolution when
the democratic system has had less appeal for the intellectual elite
of the world." "Manifest Destiny: Where Do We Go From Here,"
New York Magazine, March 3, 1975.

79. New York Times, February 12, 1976.

80. The Americans are in a self-deriding mood in the mid-
1970s, the cumulative result of Vietnam and Watergate. A typical
publication begins with these words,

> The United States of America enters the 1970's in
> a mood of retreat. The young giant of the West—

> the principal champion of its liberties and the
> guardian--is suddenly grown middle-aged,
> crotchety and fatigued. The optimism and the
> vigor so much admired and envied by older
> peoples has faded. . . . The central urge of
> American public opinion today is to pull back
> from the world.

Stephen Barber, America in Retreat (New York: Barnes and Noble, 1971).

81. Jan Triska, "The Socialist World System in Search of a Theory," in The New Communism, ed. Dave N. Jacobs (New York: Harper and Row, 1969), pp. 18-44.

82. Paul R. Gregory and Robert C. Stuart, Soviet Economic Structure and Performance (New York: Harper and Row, 1974), p. 404.

83. V. Nevelsky and M. Rostarchuk, in Izvestia, January 29, 1972.

84. Pravda, February 4, 1972.

85. New York Times, December 3, 1975. See Pravda, December 2 and 3 for official appraisals of the economic effort during 1971-75 as well as for a summary of the new five-year plan.
Kosygin in his report to the 25th CPSU Congress in February-March 1976 said that Soviet industrial output had grown at an average annual rate of 7.4 percent, compared with a 1.2 percent annual rate in the United States and the European Common Market countries. The 1.2 percent figure was called "roughly correct" for the United States by government and business sources. New York Times, March 2, 1976.

86. New York Times, December 3, 1975.

87. Christopher S. Wren, "Soviet Farm Failures," New York Times, December 9, 1975; Marshall I. Goldman, "The Soviet Economy: New Era or the Old Error?" Current History, October 1973.

88. Alec Nove, "Will Russia Ever Feed Herself?" New York Times Magazine, February 1, 1976; Wren, "Soviet Farm Failures," op. cit.

89. In 1965 Soviet imports were as follows: from Eastern Europe (CMEA), 58 percent; from the less developed countries (LDC), 23 percent; from the Western countries (West), 19 percent. The pattern changed in 1972 to CMEA, 60 percent, LDC, 17 percent, and West, 23 percent and in 1973 to CMEA, 54 percent, LDC, 19 percent, and West, 31 percent. The trade transactions with the West showed a distinct bias for industrial and agricultural technology. Steven Rosefielde, "The Changing Pattern of Soviet Trade," Current History, October 1973. For an in-depth study, see Rosefielde,

"Soviet Post-war Trade Policy," in From Cold War to Detente, ed.
Peter Potichniyj and Jane Shapiro (New York: Praeger, 1975). For
the problems and performance of the Soviet economy, see also
Raymond Hutchings, Soviet Economic Development (Oxford: Basil
Blackwell, 1972); Jan S. Prybyla, "The Soviet Economy: An Over-
view," Current History, October 1972, and Robert C. Stuart, "The
Soviet Economy: Prospects for the 1970's," Current History, Oc-
tober 1975.

90.   Leslie H. Gelb, "Detente's Supporters Under Fire in the
US," New York Times, December 29, 1975.

91.   Speech on Soviet-American relations in San Francisco on
February 3, 1976.

92.   Bhabani Sen Gupta, "An Approach to the Study of Soviet
Policies for the Third World," in Soviet Economic and Political Relations with the Developing World (New York: Praeger, 1975).

93.   Morton Schwartz, "The USSR and Leftist Regimes in Less
Developed Countries," Survey 19 (1973).

94.   Stephen Clarkson, "The Low Impact of Soviet Writings and
Aid on Indian Thinking and Policy," Survey 20, no. 1 (Winter 1974).

95.   Philip E. Mosley, "The Kremlin and the Third World,"
Foreign Affairs 46, no. 1 (October 1967).

96.   K. J. Holsti, International Politics: A Framework of
Analysis (Englewood Cliffs, N.J.: Prentice-Hall, 1972), pp. 164-70.

97.   For perhaps the most rigorous analysis of the influence-
building process, see Alvin Z. Rubinstein, "Assessing Influence as
a Problem in Foreign Policy Analysis," in Soviet and Chinese Influence in the Third World, ed. Alvin Z. Rubinstein (New York:
Praeger, 1975), pp. 1-18.

98.   This analytical framework was first developed in my "An
Approach to the Study of Soviet Policies for the Third World." Sen
Gupta, op. cit.

99.   Bokarev, op. cit.   The Soviets have intervened in some
of these conflicts, especially in the subcontinent; at the same time,
their theoretical position is that the differences leading to these conflicts should be settled through mutual negotiations.   In fact, Soviet
foreign policy has striven to resolve differences between India and
Pakistan and between Iran and Iraq, while taking advantage of actual
military conflicts to advance Soviet influence.

100.   Lee, op. cit.; Brutents, Sovremennye Nasional'no
Revolyntsii, op. cit., pp. 185-94, 253.

101.   Stanley Hoffman points out that the United States had no
postwar strategy for Asia.   A strategy designed essentially for
Europe, including massive retaliation, containment, and flexible
response, was applied to Asia during the Korean war and thereafter.
This strategy had "no relationship" with Asian politics.   Hoffman,
op. cit., pp. 152-53.

102. Nicholas V. Riasanovsky, "Asia Through Russian Eyes," in Essays on the Influence of Russia on the Asian Peoples, ed. Wayne S. Vucinich (Stanford: Hoover Institute Press, 1972), pp. 3-29.

103. This point has been forcefully made in Charles K. Wilber, The Soviet Model and Underdeveloped Countries (Chapel Hill: University of North Carolina Press, 1969). See also his "The Soviet Model of Economic Development: A Reexamination," in Soviet Economic and Political Relations with the Developing World (New York: Praeger, 1975), pp. 43-58.

104. The Great Soviet Encyclopedia, vol. 9 (translation of 3rd ed., New York: Macmillan, 1975), pp. 140-44, carries a five-page entry entitled "Eurasia," "the earth's largest continent." The editors say that "The need for a geographic designation for the entire continent is a result of the continuity of the landmass, the modern tectonic consolidation of the organic world and other manifestations of natural and historical unity as well as the necessity of taking into account the significance of territorial integrity in evaluating social and historical phenomena." There is no such entry in the Encyclopedia Britannica. The Australian scholar Jeoffrey Jukes recognizes the Soviet Union as an Asian power in his excellent book The Soviet Union in Asia (Berkeley: University of California Press, 1971).

The 1970s have brought major changes to the broad Asian strategic landscape.* These changes can be seen as much in the security systems of nations and regions as in the political architecture and economic pulsebeat of the Asian countries. The once-pervasive U.S. security system has collapsed in Southeast and South Asia and has become ambivalent in Northeast Asia. It is not that U.S. power has changed; what has changed is the Asian perceptions of U.S. power. The B-52s and F-111s have left Thailand; but the realities of U.S. power remain clearly visible in the presence of the Seventh Fleet and the Fifth and Seventh and Thirteenth Air Forces; in the 42,000 U.S. troops in South Korea, supported by tactical nuclear weapons; in the marine division and the air wing based on Okinawa, in the 100 or so military bases in Japan, and in the army division in Hawaii.

Nevertheless, the Southeast Asia Treaty Organization (SEATO) has died. No Asian nation believes that the United States will once again get involved in a war in the rice paddies of Southeast Asia. Asians are not even certain that the United States would fight another Korean war if the costs were too high. It is not merely that the U.S. physical presence has diminished on the Asian mainland, but also that the United States has reduced its commitments the most in Asia.[1]

The retreat of U.S. power from the Asian mainland has produced a wide spectrum of changes in the military security thinking and behavior of the nations in the three Asian regions. From Japan

_____

*The regional strategic environment in South and Southeast Asia and the strategic problems of the larger Asian countries are discussed further in Chapters 5 and 6.

to Iran, there has been a psychological shift from dependence on
U.S. power to security independence. In protecting their independence and territorial integrity, Asian elites have become more
inward looking. The inward stance has invested neighborly relations with an imporance that it had not been given before. For
Japan it is now as important to have good neighborly relations with
China and the Soviet Union as it is to preserve the substance of its
friendship with the United States. For the non-Communist countries
of Southeast Asia, living in peace and amity with China and Vietnam
has become a major task of foreign policy. The efforts of India
since 1972 have focused, without much success, on establishing good
neighborly relations with Pakistan. For Iran, living in peace and
good-neighborliness with the Soviet Union and Iraq is as important
as preserving its traditional friendly intercourse with the United
States and Western Europe.

The quest for good-neighborliness has given a new impetus to
regionalism. Helped by the process of dispersal of power on a
global scale,[2] the Asian countries are now seeking regional power
balances and regional security systems. In Northeast Asia a balance
involving the four powers that are preeminent in the military, political, or economic sense has for all practical purposes replaced
U.S. predominance. This quadrangular Pacific balance of power is
still uninstitutionalized, unstable, and therefore dynamic. The instability and dynamism stems not merely from the mobility that
informs the pair-relationships between Japan and China, Japan and
the Soviet Union, and Japan and the United States, as well as between China and the United States and between the Soviet Union and
the United States, but also from impending changes in the leaderships of Japan, China, and the United States.

However, the emerging four-power balance has already somewhat stabilized the situation in Korea by diminishing the option of
both Koreas to provoke a military conflict. Japan has become as
noncommittal about the defense of South Korea as China has about
the defense of the North, and the impacts of the two attitudes on the
two Koreas seem to have been identical. If the South Korean regime
collapses in the next five years or so, it will be because of a rebellion of the population against the repressive dictatorship or because
of a withdrawal of U.S. troops for domestic reasons, rather than
because of an invasion from the North.[3]

In Southeast Asia the U.S. withdrawal and the demise of SEATO
have strengthened the urge for neutralization and at the same time
have made progress in that difficult, uncertain, and time-consuming
effort. The five ASEAN countries, Indonesia, Malaysia, Singapore,
Thailand, and the Philippines, were expected to issue a neutralization blueprint in early 1975, but they did not or could not because the

Communist victories in Indochina changed the political and social
balance of forces in Southeast Asia. The declared "nonalignment"
of Vietnam, Cambodia, and Laos may have been somewhat reassuring to the non-Communist five, but no concrete progress toward
neutralization can now be expected until relations between this group
and the Communist states of Indochina have been normalized.

Several other factors have somewhat retarded the neutralization concept; these are the increasing Soviet presence in Vietnam
and Laos, the intensification of the Sino-Soviet competition in
Southeast Asia, uncertainties about the foreign policy of China, and
the death of Tun Razak, the prime minister of Malaysia, who was
the most persistent champion of the idea. However, in the wake of
the retreat of U.S. power, neutralization remains the regional
strategic stance of Southeast Asia, if only because it is considered
by the region to be the only plausible defense against becoming a
Chinese sphere of influence. [4]

In South Asia three different trends of regionalism have appeared in recent years. In the late 1960s the Soviets took the initiative, with the backing of Afghanistan and India, in regional economic collaboration among these three as well as with Iran and
Pakistan.

The initiative was frustrated by the determined opposition of
Pakistan. After the Bangladesh war of 1971 India and Pakistan,
meeting at the summit level in Simla in July 1972, agreed to settle
their outstanding differences and generate cooperative economic and
other relations through bilateral negotiations, keeping the external
powers out of the affairs of the subcontinent. Indo-Pakistani bilateralism, together with the then existing friendly relations between
India and Bangladesh, would, it was hoped in New Delhi, pave the
way for regional cooperation in South Asia and might even lead eventually to a regional security understanding. [5] However, bilateralism
between India and Pakistan failed to do more than limp; the two
countries did not resume diplomatic relations until the beginning of
1976. Meanwhile the friendship between India and Bangladesh died
with Sheikh Mujibur Rahman on August 14, 1975. [6]

However, the Shah of Iran, who had been projecting his country as a South Asian power since 1973, proposed during his visit to
Delhi in October 1974 that the countries of South Asia set up a regional security system. The concept was discussed between the
Shah and Prime Minister Indira Gandhi, and presumably also between the Shah and the prime ministers of Pakistan and Afghanistan.
However, no concrete direction has been given to the concept; nor
can any be expected as long as relations between India and Pakistan
remain unfriendly. Regionalism in South Asia may receive an impetus if Iran, Iraq, and the other Persian Gulf nations succeed in

putting together a regional security system that excludes the major
world powers. (This is discussed further in Chapter 5.)

MAJOR ASIAN ACTORS

Although regional security has not moved beyond the level of
fertilizing strategic concepts, changes in the global equations of
power have enhanced the stature of five Asian actors. Through the
good offices of the United States, China has acquired the form,
though not the substance, of a major world power. Friendship with
China is a primary input in the U.S.-Soviet detente, a complex relationship of cooperation and conflict.[7] Japan, with its great economic power and increasingly independent foreign policy, is a
strategic stalwart in Asia even though it lacks military might.
Indonesia is the leading power in Southeast Asia. India dominates
the subcontinent. Iran is determined to build itself up in the next
ten years as the dominant military and industrial power in the region of the Persian Gulf and the Middle East.

The four "local leviathans," however, have very little in common. Though located in Asia, Japan belongs spiritually to the rich
club of the industrialized capitalist countries. It enjoys a much
better political standing with the Soviet Union and China than with
the smaller and weaker Asian nations, who want Japanese capital
and technology but reject Japanese political and military power.
Indonesia, earning $5 billion in foreign exchange every year from
its oil exports, is still one of the poorest countries in Asia. Iran is
a leading member of the world's new rich, that is, of the 12 leading
petroleum-exporting countries. India, without oil and unable to
feed its over 560 million people, is the only Asian leviathan to have
derived its power from proven military capability.[8]

Japan

The competition among the three world powers for the friendship of Japan has altered the role of Tokyo in international politics.
Japan is no longer just a Pacific outpost of U.S. power but an autonomous security actor in the Pacific region and therefore in Southeast
Asia also. The Japanese ruling party has no intention of materially
changing the security ties of Japan with the United States. However,
the security treaty can be abrogated with one year's notice, and it
is no longer the stable relationship it used to be.

The economic power of Japan is hostage to international peace
and tranquillity. The mammoth industry of Japan would grind to a

halt if its sea lanes, which must constantly bring in supplies of raw materials, including petroleum, from Southeast Asia, the Middle East, and Latin America, as well as from Europe and North America, were closed. The Japanese have less military force than any of their smaller Asian neighbors. Just as a naval blockade could strangle Japan in a few months, in a few days a nuclear war would wipe out the industrial empire the Japanese have built with their own financial and managerial acumen. In the 1970s Japan is beset on all sides, as well as from within.

The Soviet Union wants Japan to adopt an independent foreign policy and to deny China the benefit of its steel and machinery and technology. It wants Japan to collaborate in the development of the fuel and other resources of Siberia, to loosen its security ties with the United States, and to cooperate with Moscow in setting up a collective Asian security system. Part of the leverage the Soviet Union has for diplomatic use in Japan is the Soviet Pacific fleet, with some 100 submarines, 40 of which are nuclear powered, and 55 major combat ships, many of which are larger and more powerfully armed than any in the Japanese and Chinese navies.

China, on the other hand, wants Japan to conclude a peace treaty that would, by implication, condemn the Soviet Union for seeking hegemony in Asia. China also has leverage in Japan, and its leverage is stronger than that of the Soviet Union because it is non-military and therefore politically more useful. Peking can influence Japanese politics, but Moscow can not. Japanese trade with China touched $4 billion in both directions in 1975, surpassing Japanese commerce with the Soviets by $1 billion. The Chinese can supply Japan with a considerable quantity of oil if the Japanese invest their capital and technology to develop Chinese petroleum resources.

The United States wants Japan to share its security burden in the Western Pacific, if not further south. South Korea wants Japan to provide security and to contribute to its economic development and its trade balance. North Korea wants from Tokyo everything the Japanese may extend to the South. The oil-producing countries, the countries of Western Europe, and Japan's client states in Southeast Asia have their own demands on the Japanese.

The rulers of Japan have taken advantage of the changes in world relations to increase the Japanese diplomatic autonomy, but as Richard Halloran, the perceptive New York _Times_ correspondent in Tokyo, points out, "The Japanese lack a guiding beacon, such as Secretary of State Kissinger's detente, or former West German Chancellor Willy Brandt's ostpolitik, or the late French President Charles de Gaulle's vision of 'grandeur.'"9

In the past the main importance of Japan to the United States lay in the military bases and in the logistic support Japan provided for U.S. military operations and force deployment in Asia. In the 1970s the primary importance of Japan to the United States is in its role as a supplier of imports, a market for exports, a partner in international finance, and the "swing nation in the balance of power in North Asia." In Halloran's view, "The United States doesn't want tension between Japan and the Soviet Union but neither would it approve of Japan leaning too close to the Russians. The gradual thickening of the ties between China and Japan may make China stronger and thus more effective for Mr. Kissinger's policy of playing the Chinese and the Russians off against one another."[10]

As the balancer in the four-power balance in Northeast Asia, Japan may incline toward one or the other of the major actors from time to time. It has, however, firmly indicated its unwillingness to join the United States as a security provider for South Korea or to contribute to its economic development, although it has offered to help in bringing about a dialogue between the two Koreas.[11]

Japan is also beset from within. The worst recession since the 1950s has hurt Japan more than it has hurt West Germany or France. Recovery is expected to be slow and painful. Inflation and unemployment have increased social tensions. The ruling coalition of conservatives and liberals has been steadily losing popular support over the years; its ability to govern Japan beyond the 1970s is seriously doubted by most Japanese people. If a new center-left coalition assumes power after the next election in 1977, the relations of Japan with the major powers may change, and these changes may affect its role in Asian affairs. (See Chapter 7.)

Indonesia

Indonesia is a nation of 13,000 islands and more than 130 million people. Its population is increasing at the rate of 2.5 percent a year. In per capita income ($110), it is one of the poorest countries in the world. Its per capita revenue from oil ($38.70) is the lowest of any of the member nations of the Organization of Petroleum Exporting Countries (OPEC). It has a military force of 344,000 men and a defense budget of about $300 million (2.5 percent of GNP). Its navy and air force are still largely equipped with Soviet weapons supplied between 1958 and 1965; much of this equipment needs to be replaced. Since 1966 Indonesia has been procuring military supplies entirely from the Western world. Between 1958 and 1965 Indonesia received $1.2 billion worth of Soviet military aid. Between 1950 and 1972 U.S. military aid amounted to $98.4 million; both military and economic aid from the United States has increased since then. In 1973 U.S. economic aid was over $230 million; it fell to $50 million

in 1974 but rose to $90 million in 1975. The United States has
agreed to double its military aid in 1976 and to increase its economic assistance to $180 million. In recent years U.S. military aid
has included three destroyers; three C-130 transport aircraft; and
patrol frigates, communication equipment, and surveillance systems. Under a three-year Australian aid program of $30 million in
military grants, Indonesia is to receive 14 F-86 sabre jets and also
surveillance aircraft and patrol boats.[12]

Despite its oil power, then, Indonesia, is still heavily dependent on external aid both for security and development. In fact, the
bulk of its oil income has been squandered by Pertamina, the state-
owned oil company. As a result, the foreign exchange reserves of
Indonesia have plummeted, from $2 billion in 1974 to $500 million in
1975.[13] The country has only just begun to exploit its other mineral
resources, which are coal, nickel, tin, copper, and bauxite. Its
industrial base, comprised mostly of extractive industries, is still
weak, and despite the abundance of its oil and its huge agricultural
manpower, it is not self-sufficient in food.

In the post-Vietnam period Indonesia is the focal point of the
U.S. and Japanese effort to promote Southeast Asian resistance to
Soviet and Chinese influence. This was made quite evident by
President Ford's visit to Jakarta in December 1975. The strategic
stance of Indonesia was explained by Indonesian Foreign Minister
Adam Malik on the eve of the Ford visit. "It is up to the United
States to keep a balance in this region," he said. "It is our duty in
Indonesia to keep outside powers from conducting their activities
here."[14] What he meant was that with the help of a U.S. balancing
presence in Southeast Asia, the countries of the region could themselves prevent both China and the Soviet Union from dominating the
region.

Indonesia is unable to play its leadership role in Southeast
Asia for a variety of reasons. The stance of its military leadership
is basically inward rather than outward. Relations with Malaysia
and Singapore are friendly without being cordial; the Southeast Asian
community is well aware of the fragility of the Indonesian political
system and economy. Relations with China have remained frozen
since 1965, and the firm anti-Communism of the Indonesian military
leaders inhibits the development of friendly relations with Vietnam.
The regime does not seem to be in immediate danger, but its popularity has been substantially eroded in the 1970s, especially among
the youth and the intellectual community. The economy has been
hard hit by the recession in the industrialized capitalist countries.
The Eurocurrency borrowings of Indonesia increased from $469
million in 1974 to $1,170 million in 1975.[15]

India

By defeating the Pakistani army in the December 1971 war,
India established its claim to be recognized as the dominant military
power in South Asia, although some saw the outcome of that war more
as a victory for the Soviet Union than as a triumph of Indian power. [16]
By exploding a nuclear device in May 1974, India, for all practical
purposes, promoted itself to the exclusive nuclear club. India has
the fourth-largest standing army in the world: 1,074,000 men, including the border security force. Its defense budget of some $2.5
billion consumes less than 4 percent of the GNP. Since 1966 the
largest supplier of military equipment to India has been the Soviet
Union; the Soviet component is most conspicuous in the Indian air
force and navy. Military assistance from the Soviet Union in the
form of credits totaled $700 million in 1973. With Soviet, British,
and French collaboration, India has built a strong indigenous defense
industry that makes or assembles MIG-21, HF-24, and Gnat inter-
ceptors; HS-748 transport planes for dropping paratroops; trainers
and helicopters; medium tanks; antitank weapons; some artillery; a
variety of small arms; naval escorts; and patrol boats. India exports a small quantity of arms and ammunition to a number of Asian
and African countries. India is the only Asian power with an aircraft carrier. Its four submarines are all of Soviet vintage.

Despite its military power, India is one of the world's poorest
countries. It is also the second most populous. The per capita income is a mere $93, and 43 percent of the population lives below
the poverty line. The country has neither oil power nor agripower.
Three military engagements in nine years have severely strained its
economic resources without narrowing its security gap. It is significant that the ten years since 1965, during which India fought two
wars with Pakistan, have been a period of overall zero-growth of the
economy, the per capita income rising by not more than 1 percent
annually. Much of the gains of the development of the earlier period,
as well as the once-buoyant promise of the so-called Green Revolution, have been largely wiped out in a decade of stagnant economic
growth. The military victory of 1971 brought the country much-
needed political stability, which had been shaken since the election
of 1967. In 1973-74, however, the fortress of centralized authority
was invaded by a multitude of problems, most of them offsprings of
war and of a no-growth economy, including runaway inflation, spiral-
ing prices, massive urban and rural unemployment, and widespread
corruption. To these were added two successive crop failures
caused by poor monsoons and a sudden quadrupling of petroleum
prices, wich created, in official admission, the "worst economic
crisis since independence." The green revolution withered as a

result of the scarcity of fertilizer and electric power. Petroleum
and food imports consumed nearly 75 percent of the export earnings
of India in 1974. Faced with mounting street violence spearheaded
by a disparate group of right-wing and populist leaders, the Indian
prime minister declared a national emergency in June 1975.

In early 1976 it seemed doubtful whether the parliamentary
democratic system would ever be fully restored. With plentiful
rains, however, the 1975 crop came to a record 114 million tons,
although India was still seeking to purchase several million tons of
grain in the United States with liberal credit. The authoritarian
regime quickly brought inflation down to 2 percent. The investment
rate was better than it had been for a number of years. Exports
were up significantly. The economy apparently grew wings after a
long period of time. [17]

The integrative role of India in the subcontinent suffered a setback, however. After the third coup in Bangladesh in four months
in 1975, a military regime seemed to have established itself in
Dacca in November behind a civilian presidential facade; this regime
was not overly friendly toward India. The turn of events pleased the
ruling elite in Pakistan, which now moved with alacrity to strengthen
relations with Bangladesh. [18] These events did not exactly enhance
the sense of security in Pakistan, since none of the major powers
was willing to underwrite the independence and territorial integrity
of Pakistan as they had in the 1950s. It has received a public security
commitment from the Shah of Iran, but no legally binding treaty
exists between these two close neighbors. [19]

Iran

Iran is probably the most spectacular oil power in the world.
With 136,292 square miles of territory and a fast-growing population
of 35 million, the Shah of Iran has embarked upon an ambitious program of military build-up and economic development that, if completed, would make his country not only the strongest military power
in the Persian Gulf region but also the largest manufacturing and exporting center in the area of the Middle Gulf and the Middle East.
The Shah's military budget for 1976 is over $8 billion, an 8 percent
increase from 1975 and more than three times the defense budget for
1973. His major military procurement program includes 6 Spruance-
class destroyers and 80 F-14 fighters from the United States and
700 Chieftain tanks from Britain. In 1975 Iran was reported to
possess 325 Chieftains and 880 M-60 and M-47 tanks made in the
United States. [20] The Shah has decided to build up the tank manufacturing capacity of Iran, probably with British collaboration. The

current build-up of armored might in Iran has been overshadowed by the even more dramatic plan for the expansion of its navy and for the addition of a vast number of sophisticated American-made aircraft to its air force. However, a sharp drop in oil income in 1975 compelled the Shah to shelve or delay some of the naval and air force expansion projects, particularly the $2 billion plan to build a large naval base at Charbahar on the Gulf of Oman in the southeast.

The spectacular industrialization program of Iran includes $15 billion dollars worth of deals with U.S. firms over a period of five years and a Japanese-aided petrochemical complex that may eventually cost $33 billion.[21] Iran is negotiating with the United States to buy six to eight giant nuclear power reactors worth $7 billion so it can have enough nuclear-generated electric power before the gushes of crude oil slow to a trickle.[22]

The Iranian army has not fought a real war. Since 1973, however, 3,500 Iranian troops have been fighting the pro-Soviet insurgents in Dhofar, Oman, who are aided by South Yemen. Organized insurgency ended in October 1975, but the Shah has been using Dhofar to train his troops in the use of sophisticated military hardware. The troops rotate in and out of Oman every few months, taking part in unannounced simulated missions. In October 1975 a squadron of Iranian destroyers appeared off the Dhofari coast and in two days fired 1,500 five-inch shells into a six-mile strip of inland territory.[23]

The Shah's arms build-up program is not so much a response to any felt threat to the security of Iran as it is a result of his wish to make Iran the most powerful nation in the Gulf region. Some Western military analysts say that Iran may face threats from any of three land fronts, "from the Soviet Union in the north, and perhaps from the Soviet Union from the east if Pakistan were to weaken further, and possibly from Iraq, although Iranian-Iraqi relations are currently cordial."[24] In an interview with John B. Oakes of the New York Times in September 1975, the Shah said that one reason for the arms build-up was to "establish a deterrent against any potential Soviet desire to penetrate southward." He also had the east in mind: "I don't think that you have envisaged out east. And if you had, you would be at one with me by letting nothing to chance-- everything that is east of this country including the Indian Ocean."[25] He told C. L. Sulzberger, also of the New York Times, that he was worried about the future of Pakistan as a result of the "independence movement" in the Pathan and Baluchistan areas. "I am less worried now," said the Shah in 1975, "provided that there are no dramatic changes in that part of the world. We encourage Pakistan to follow a policy of peace toward its neighbors. But we certainly could not sit back and tolerate an aggression against Pakistan--by anyone."[26] The

Shah's eastern concern mirrors U.S. strategic perceptions of the
South Asia and Persian Gulf region. Shortly after the debacle in
Indochina, James Schlesinger, the then U.S. defense secretary,
told a New York Times reporter that while the strategic outlook of
Iran was "satisfactory," it was far from stable. "Everything depends on the Shah." The report quoted Pentagon officials that the
Shah's death "would throw the entire Iran-Pakistan area into turmoil and might tempt the Soviet Union to undertake political or military adventure aimed at gaining a port on the Indian Ocean."[27]

The Shah's strategic posture has, then, an anti-Soviet orientation. However, as I shall argue later in this study, this orientation is more simulated than real. Iran has excellent economic and
commercial relations with the Soviet Union and has been engaged in
a strategic dialogue with Moscow since 1973. He told Oakes that
his arms buildup program had virtually no impact on the growing
friendly relations of Iran with the Soviet Union. "We have come to
understand that ideologies are separate from government-to-
government relations; at the government level, we are excellent
friends."[28]

What worries the Shah is not Soviet power but the built-in instabilities in the political architecture in the Persian Gulf. In
November 1971 the Shah's forces took possession of three strategic
Persian Gulf islands, Abu Musa, Greater Tumb, and Lesser Tumb,
in order to "protect" the access of Iran to the open sea. This
brought his relations with Iraq, which claimed the islands to be legally its own, to the breaking point. What was more, most of the
Arab countries sided with Iraq.[29] The Shah is afraid of a united
Arab front against Iran, but he is even more alarmed by the prospects of a radical political polarization in the Persian Gulf region.
When the Shah conceived his arms build-up program, his eyes were
riveted on the radical Baa'thist regime in Iraq, the close friendship
of which with the Soviet Union had enabled Baghdad to assemble, in
three short years, a formidable military machine.[30] The March
1975 accord reached between Iran and Iraq has replaced an age-old
antagonism with a burgeoning friendship. The two countries have
since concluded an agreement in principle to work together for a regional security system for the Persian Gulf.[31]

Between 1952 and 1972 Iran received military aid from the
United States worth $853 million. Since 1967 it has also received
Soviet military aid worth $110 million.[32] Iran has been purchasing
"considerable quantities" of Soviet military equipment, the Shah told
Sulzberger, "not tanks, but armored personnel carriers and artillery." He added, "I don't mind saying we are doing this to tell
some quarters in the United States--quarters with masochistic tendencies who always try and hurt their friends and allies, those who

wish to embargo the sale of all arms to the Middle East--to tell them
that we have other sources of weapons, including Russia."[33] The
Shah was obviously referring to his Central Treaty Organization
(CENTO) ally, Turkey, which also was trying to build friendly relations with Moscow and which in early 1976 was negotiating a treaty
of friendship and cooperation with the Soviet government.[34]

Iran's greatest insecurity stems from the closed authoritative
regime over which the Shah presides. Louis XIV's famous aphorism,
"L'etat c'est moi," applies more to Iran than to any other contemporary state in the world. The royal regime rests on no stable political and social institutions; the youth are alienated, and among the
middle class the traditional Iranian cynicism is still widespread.
Iran may well grow into a major military and industrial power if the
Shah's grand design is blessed with time. Should he fall before the
grand architecture of power has been built, Iran may plunge into the
deluge, pulling down much of the neighboring area with it.[35]

ZONES OF INSECURITY

None of the four local Asian leviathans is secure in its own
area; nor are they secure on the regional and global levels. Later in
this volume we have detailed the tensions and conflicts that have
plagued North, Southeast, and South Asia since the 1950s. It is in
North and Southeast Asia that the United States has fought two wars
to contain Communism. South Korea was "saved," but the whole of
Indochina has been "lost." Communism rules in six Asian states in
the mid-1970s; because of the Sino-Soviet conflict no socialist state-
system has emerged in Asia, but the balance of social and political
forces has changed, and the insecurities of the non-Communist
Asian regimes have increased. After Indochina there may be no
more of the classical wars of liberation in the three Asian regions
covered by our study; it is highly unlikely that the United States will
once again get involved in a war with Asian nationalism. However,
most significantly, the civil war in Pakistan in 1971 was also called
a war of national liberation by the Soviets and the North Vietnamese.

In the 1970s the focus of Asian tensions and conflicts has
shifted from outward to inward factors. Not a single non-Communist
country in Southeast Asia is free of Communist-led insurgencies.
In the subcontinent, 12 military actions have occurred in 24 years,
including two major wars between India and Pakistan and the only big
Asian war over a disputed frontier. An internal conflict, in which
others intervened, dismembered Pakistan in 1971. The "new"
Pakistan is also troubled with the independence struggles of the
Baluchis and the Pathans. It has a simmering war of attrition with

Afghanistan over the mutually contested Pathan tribal area. In Asia, then, internal forces are pitted against each other in multiple intermeshing confrontations involving disputed territory; ethnic groups; clashing nationalisms; and the many, many poor and the few privileged rich.

Among the smaller and weaker Asian countries, only Pakistan and Thailand have large armies, without feeling at all secure. Pakistan has 365,000 men in its military force, representing .62 percent of its population, the highest percentage in Asia. The defense budget consumes 8.31 percent of the GNP, which is too much for a country with a per capita income of $102.

Thailand, with its armed force of 217,400 men and with 7.3 percent of the GNP going into defense, resembles Pakistan, although the Thai per capita income is much higher, $210.

The least-armed nation in Asia is Sri Lanka, with a defense force of 8,600 and a defense budget of $17 million. The government of Sri Lanka might have fallen to the insurgents in 1971 if immediate military help had not been rushed from such diverse sources as China, India, and the Soviet Union.

Bangladesh has an armed force of 16,350 men, and probably many more civilians carry illicit weapons that may one day be politicized.

The bulk of the military forces of Indonesia, Burma, Malaysia, Thailand, and the Philippines is engaged in fighting internal insurgencies or in guarding the existing political regimes against onslaughts by potential insurgents. It is a shared characteristic of all Asian political regimes in the 1970s, including India, that the coercive arm of the state is being used with increasing intensity and brutality to suppress internal challenge even when the challenges are not violent.[36] A second shared characteristic is the decline of democratic political systems and the rise of authoritarianism. Democratic rights have disappeared from the whole of South Asia with the exception of Sri Lanka. In Southeast Asia these rights exist to some extent, but only in Malaysia and Thailand.

The political and strategic insecurities in Asia are reinforced by its economic realities. From north to south, the Asian economic landscape is marked by a single outpost of mature affluence, which is Japan, a zone of green that is threatening in the mid-1970s to pale into yellow, and a vast area of gray, turgid poverty. By per capita income, only Malaysia and Singapore are among the world's higher-income nations, while South Korea, Thailand, and the Philippines belong to the middle-income category.

Each of these five has been hit by the monetary, fiscal, and economic crises that have gripped the advanced capitalist countries in the 1970s. In South Korea, for instance, the average growth rate of the GNP was 10.5 percent in 1964-74 but fell to 8 percent in 1975 and is expected to tumble down to 4.5 percent in 1976. According to a recent study made by the Institute of International Policy in Washington, D.C., South Korea "is headed for default on her debts abroad and economic chaos at home."[37]

From Burma through the South Asian landmass, and taking the Indonesian archipelago and the island of Sri Lanka in its sweep, extends the great zone of Asian poverty, the home of a billion human beings. Nearly half of these people live below the Asian poverty line.[38]

These countries find themselves victims of both the weaknesses and strengths of the capitalist system with which their economies are strongly linked. The slump in the demand for their raw materials--tin, rubber, iron ore, manganese, bauxite, jute, tea, coffee, copra, coal, and forest products--has severely strained their export earnings.

The high cost of petroleum has either made development much more expensive than before or has led to a slowing down of development efforts; in most of these countries it has caused both. With depleted earnings from exports, the low- and middle-income countries of Asia, along with those in the rest of the world, have had to take over from the industrialized nations the task of financing the large payment surplus of the oil exporters, and they are rapidly growing broke in that process. Their ordeal was explained by a New York Times columnist in early 1976. In 1975, the columnist wrote, the collective surplus of the OPEC would be $50 billion on a current account basis. "But unlike 1973, when most of the surplus was reflected in deficits incurred by the industrial countries, the whole of this burden has now ended up on the back of the poor."[39]

The Asian non-Communist countries that were running deficit trade balances in 1975 were Japan, South Korea, Taiwan, Thailand, Philippines, Bangladesh, Sri Lanka, India, Pakistan, and Nepal. Only four of the nonoil countries were able to maintain a favorable balance of trade; these were Malaysia, Singapore, Burma, and Afghanistan.[40] According to the Times columnist, "most of these countries are no longer able to finance a deficit of this magnitude from reserves or commercial borrowings. The only resource therefore is to save money by continuing to reduce the imports from the industrial world."[41] The economic predicament in the early 1970s, more than political preferences, persuaded the Southeast Asian countries to seek alternative markets for raw materials and alternative sources of development assistance and fuel in the Soviet bloc and China.

The Asian countries, however, can hardly turn to the Soviet Union for the food grains in which most of them are deficient. They

must buy grains in North America, Canada, and Australia or in
Thailand, the only Southeast Asian nation with a large exportable
surplus of rice. According to the Food and Agriculture Organization
(FAO), Asia will need to import 47 million metric tons of food grains
in 1976, as against 37 million metric tons in 1970.[42] Food prices
have trebled between 1972 and 1974, and the high prices are expected
to continue. The FAO indicated that the developing countries would
spend more than $6 billion on imported foodgrains in 1975 and that
more than two-thirds of this amount would have to be absorbed by the
poorest 41 nations. According to Lester R. Brown of the Worldwatch
Institute, global food insecurities are greater in the 1970s than they
had been at any time since the second world war. Nowhere is the
impact of these insecurities greater than on South Asia, an area of
substantial food deficits. U.S. grain aid plummeted from about 18
million tons in the mid-1960s to 4.7 million tons in fiscal 1975. Developing nations will have to buy over 53 million tons of grain in
1975-76, of which only one-third is likely to be supplied by food aid.[43]

Oil power has generated resource nationalism, the political
overtone of which has pleased the Soviets and annoyed many in the
Western world and in Japan. There is a trend toward the formation
of cartels by nations owning important raw materials. The ASEAN
summit meeting in Indonesia, for instance, pledged cooperation in
sharing basic scarce commodities, particularly food and energy, and
in developing common negotiating positions on commodities and
tariffs in dealing with outside countries.[44] The Shah of Iran has
proposed a common market for the South Asian countries, and concepts of international groupings of countries producing such vulnerable
commodities as coffee, jute, iron ore, manganese, copper, rubber,
and tin are in the air. As the world community gropes for a new
international economic order, the rich and poor nations have begun
to strive for a stable new equilibrium in their basic economic relationship.[45]

The years immediately ahead will remain bleak, however. The
major industrialized nations will take several years to recover from
the depression of the 1970s. Whether they can recover with their
political and social institutions intact is one of the major questions
that loom across this decade.[46] It is far from certain that the drastic
deterioration in the terms of trade of the developing countries, that
is, in the amounts of goods they can buy abroad with the earnings of
their exports, will improve before the 1980s. The trade drift will
continue at least as long as the industrial nations have not recovered
from the slump, and for some years more, real resources will continue to flow from the poorer to the richer countries.[47] Meanwhile,
foreign aid, which has fallen from .52 percent of the GNP of the industrialized nations in 1960 to .32 percent in 1975, is expected to
drop still further.[48]

A continuing economic decline for even a few years may be
politically destabilizing for the Asian countries, particularly the
high- and middle-income ones, whose people, having tasted good
times, may not submit to serious deprivation without protest or even
defiance. The demands for structural social change may grow among
the urban youth, unionized workers, and deprived middle classes;
worse, the peasantry may well be drawn into confrontations with the
political regimes, which rest fundamentally on the support of privileged minorities and the coercive power of the state. Internal political and economic strains may urge political actors to ignite interstate conflicts. These conflicts will, of course, bring in newer
instabilities in their wake and pave the way for intervention in "local"
problems by the major world powers.

In the 1970s, then, the Asian strategic environment is characterized by a physical U.S. retreat from Southeast Asia; by the
emergence of four autonomous local actors, each determined to play,
and capable of playing, a major role in the regional balances of
power; by trends toward regional economic and defensive cooperation, which will take time to be institutionalized, assuming they do
not lose their momentum; by possibilities of intrastate and interstate
polarizations and conflicts; by political and economic instabilities in
most of the Asian countries; and by the decline of democratic freedoms and the rise of authoritarianism. The late 1970s will probably
bring no respite to any of the Asian countries.

How will the Asian strategic setup relate to the world strategic
environment in the next five to ten years? There is a lot of talk in
the air about a new international political and economic order. International orders are difficult to change in peacetime; the predominant tendency is almost always to make the adjustments necessary
to avoid major transformations. The crises of the 1970s have forced
the liberal, forward-looking advocates of change to take the defensive
in many of the industrialized countries, particularly in the United
States. In times of distress, nations, like individuals, shrink in
their outlook and tend to fall back to preserve what they have. They
become conservative, protectionist, inward-looking, even isolation-
ist. The Western world is caught in agonizing self-doubts. A group
of U.S. historians, assembling at a research institute in Washington
one day in the autumn of 1975, came to the conclusion that the United
States had entered the phase of its decline and fall, as the Roman
empire had done many centuries before.[49] Even the decline and fall
of the United States, if it must come, will be slow and protracted;
the United States will remain the world's number one power for the
rest of this century. Whether under U.S. initiative the world of
capitalism can break out of its current shackles and reemerge with
a renewal of vigor and promise, is a different matter.

Speculation may soar, but predictions must be cautious and plausible. The advanced industrial nations probably will no longer be suffering the effects of the slump at the end of the decade. By that time, however, the political color of Southern Europe will probably have changed. It is more than likely that the Communists will rule in Italy, together with other political forces, after the next election. If this happens, and if the Italian Communists play their cards well, the pattern may be repeated in France after the election of 1978.[50] In Japan, too, the next election may bring a center-left coalition to power.

The oil power of the OPEC will diminish sharply in the next five to ten years, but the agripower of the United States, Canada, and Australia will survive this decade. With 38 countries operating, building, or planning to build more than 260 major nuclear reactors, nuclear energy will make its mark on the fuel map of the world, all the risks of radiation, sabotage, and terrorism notwithstanding.

However, it is doubtful whether the growth rates of the developed countries will once again recapture the high percentage points of the 1960s. The United States will probably lose its technological superiority to Western Europe.[51] The world export-import market will probably find a balance in the next ten years between producers and consumers. A balanced market power may bring about agreements covering tin, copper, bauxite, lead, zinc, iron ore, rubber, coffee, and cocoa.[52] The world monetary relationship may stabilize around the reforms and adjustments that have followed the grave crises of the last few years.

As all this happens, several political upheavals will almost certainly occur in Asia, though it is difficult to see how in any Asian country except Thailand the Communists can expect to come to power. In any case, democracy will not be the wave of the coming decade.

Will there be a stable strategic balance between the United States and the Soviet Union? The current balance is tentative and unstable, and in both countries a strong wish exists to stabilize it. Probably both will move toward a stable strategic balance despite the opponents and critics, who have no alternative to offer. However, even a stable strategic balance can generate an arms race. Each superpower will succeed in maintaining and improving its position within the balance, probably at higher levels of maintained force than at present.[53]

Even if the strategic balance remains stable, the world will face the danger of local wars that would be much more devastating than the ones that have occurred so far. Both superpowers have been building up their conventional war machines. The invention of precision and "smart" weapons is changing the stances and doctrines of conventional warfare of the major powers.[54] The mobility of conventional forces has been greatly enhanced by the introduction of very large subsonic and supersonic transport aircraft. The Soviets have demonstrated their naval and air transport capability to intervene in distant conflicts.[55] The competitive and matching interventionist capability of the superpowers may lead to a mutual stand-off. At the same time, there is also the grim prospect of both of them getting involved in a local war, in which case the war would not remain local.

The reckless arms transfers by the leading industrial powers, especially the United States, to the oil-rich nations of the Persian Gulf and the Middle East amount to a thoughtless contribution to local tensions and conflicts. The next Arab-Israeli war, if it comes, will surpass all the previous wars in devastation of human life and resources, even if the superpowers stay out of it. Much of these arms and weapons may find their way to terrorist groups and to client states of the oil-rich countries in other parts of the world.[56]

The Western powers are also competing with one another in selling powerful nuclear reactors to Third-World nations without safeguards adequate to prevent the making of nuclear weapons. France has sold such a reactor to South Korea and is about to sell another to Pakistan. West Germany has concluded a deal with Brazil that promises technology for uranium enrichment and ultimately may provide a second way of making nuclear weapons. The Shah of Iran has made it clear that he will not accept "unreasonable restrictions" on the U.S. sale of the six nuclear reactors he has ordered.[57] The champions of nonproliferation of nuclear weapons, then, are themselves creating the objective conditions for proliferation. More than 20 countries can make nuclear weapons if they wish to, and it will not be surprising if several of them do elect to go nuclear. A major change in the strategic relationship between Japan and the United States would induce Japan to declare itself a nuclear power. Even the possession of a powerful nuclear reactor by Pakistan, without the strictest possible safeguards, would provide India with enough impetus to launch a nuclear weapons program. Iran is a candidate for nuclear might. Israel may already be in possession of nuclear bombs.[58]

These are symptoms, not of a symmetrical international order, but of one that is becoming dangerously unmanageable. Regarded optimistically, they are symptoms of a painful and groping transition of the world from one order to another. During the transition, the pillars on which the old order stood firmly for so many years are cracking. The alliances have lost their inner vitality and zeal. Nowhere in the world except in Europe is there a stable military balance. Even the European balance is becoming unstable because of political changes that run counter to the basic values behind the alliance system. Within and among nations, the emphasis has shifted from economic growth to equity. The primary concerns of nations

have extended from military security to energy, food, raw materials,
international trade, and their positions in the world monetary system.
There has been an unfathomable increase in the overkill power of the
two mightiest nations of the world, but it has become impossible to
translate this power into instruments of political advantage. [59]

In an insecure, unstable, and uncertain Asia in an insecure,
unstable, and uncertain world, the Soviets have embarked upon an
ambitious influence-building enterprise in the 1970s. It is not surprising that they have embraced their optimum strategic objective--
Asia--in their proposal for an Asian collective security system.

NOTES

1. Drew Middleton, "U.S. Studies Post-Vietnam Strategy,
Views Abroad of U.S. Power," New York Times, July 6, 1975.
Middleton said that the Pentagon review had led to the conclusion
that U.S. power in Asia had not changed significantly in the logistical
sense, but that Asian perceptions of that power had changed sharply.

2. Stanley Hoffman, "Groping Toward a New World Order,"
New York Times, January 11, 1976.

3. For the emerging four-power balance in North Asia, see
Robert A. Scalapino, Asia and the Major Powers, Implications for
the International Order, AEI-Hoover Policy Study No. 3 (Stanford:
Hoover Institute on War, Revolution and Peace, 1972); Ralph N.
Clough, East Asia and U.S. Security (Washington, D.C.: the Brookings Institution, 1975). President Ford's Pacific Doctrine, outlined
in Honolulu on December 7, 1975, recognized the interests of the four
major powers in the Pacific and added, "Equilibrium in the Pacific is
essential to the United States and to the other countries of the Pacific."
New York Times, December 8, 1975.

4. The heads of government of the five ASEAN countries held
their first meeting in eight years at Denpasar, Indonesia, in February
1976. They failed to agree on regional security. The communique
issued at the end of the meeting said nothing about neutralization.
Apparently the neutralization concept, which is discussed in some detail in Chapter 6 of this book, has received a setback. For reports
of the meeting, see the Washington Post and the New York Times reports for February 24-25, 1976.

5. K. P. Mishra, "Trilateralism in South Asia," Asian Survey 14, no. 7 (July 1974).

6. For background to the cooling off of relations between India
and Bangladesh even before the assassination of Rahman, see Bhabani
Sen Gupta, "Waiting for India: India's Role as a Regional Power,"
Journal of International Affairs (New York) 29, no. 2 (Fall 1975).

7. When Henry Kissinger was traveling to Peking in October 1975, the reporters accompanying him were briefed that "relations among Peking, Moscow and Washington were entering a new phase and that the key to the new phase was relations between Moscow and Washington." New York Times, October 19, 1975.

8. James W. Howe, "Power in the Third World," Journal of International Affairs 29, no. 2 (Fall 1975).

9. Richard Halloran, New York Times, January 18, 1976.

10. Ibid. Halloran reported earlier, "The Japanese Government has so far been unwilling to guarantee that the United States will be allowed to use the bases to support military action in Korea or elsewhere, thus making their usefulness questionable. They are also insecure since any anti-American mob of demonstrators can march in and close them down." New York Times, September 14, 1975.

11. New York Times, September 16, 1975.

12. David A. Andelman, "Indonesia: One of the Richest and Yet Poorest Countries of Asia," New York Times, December 5, 1975. The statistical figures are from the New York Times, December 5 and 28, 1975.

13. New York Times, January 25, 1976.

14. Quoted in Andelman, op. cit.

15. New York Times, December 19, 1975.

16. James Reston in the New York Times, December 17, 1971.

17. New York Times, December 25, 1975.

18. A. T. Choudhri, "Pressures on Bangladesh," Dawn (Karachi), November 30, 1975. This Pakistani analyst described the Bangladesh army as "generally anti-Indian," and suggested that the army was ruling the country with the help of "rightists." See also Colin Legum's report in Observer (London), November 18, 1975. Legum reported that after the August 14 coup the Indian army moved a short distance inside Bangladesh, but stopped because of a "Russian warning to Mrs. Gandhi that overt Indian action would have brought in the Chinese."

19. Prime Minister Zulfikar Ali Bhutto told a correspondent of the Japanese newspaper Yomuiri that Pakistan and Iran were so close to one another that "we regard them to be like one country." Dawn, November 29, 1975.

A significant change in Pakistan's security stance since 1972 is seen in its concern about internal stability. The Pakistani delegate to the 1975 session of the UN General Assembly made this clear during the debate on the proposal to turn the Indian Ocean into a peace zone. He said that the impact of external security factors impinged on internal variables; regional states must be assured against insecurity from both within and without. Ibid.

Dawn, November 22, 1975, suggested that the attempt by Dacca in April 1975 to lease out 5,000 square miles of its territorial

water in the Bay of Bengal to some U.S. oil companies for exploration had evoked strong Indian reaction.

20. New York Times, February 16 and 18, 1976. Iran may
also acquire a through-deck destroyer or mini-carrier with either
helicopter (ASN) missions or fixed-wing aircraft (VOSTOL) like the
Harrier "for projection of power at some limited distance from its
shores," and perhaps also submarines. Shahram Chubin and
Mohammad Fard-Saidi, Recent Trends in Middle East Politics and
Iran's Foreign Policy Options (Tehran: Institute for International
Political and Economic Studies, 1975), p. 76.

21. New York Times, February 18, 1976.

22. "Nuclear Iran?" New York Times editorial, March 12,
1975. This nuclear purchase program ran into some difficulty in
early 1976 as a result of U.S. insistence on safeguards. The Shah
said in January, "We gave them the guarantees that these reactors
will be used only for peaceful purposes and not for nuclear weapons.
But they asked unnecessarily for additional guarantees that we won't
give." New York Times, January 20, 1976. The $7 billion nuclear
reactor purchase proposals are covered by the $15 billion the Shah
intends to spend on U.S. goods in 1976-81.

23. Eric Pace, "Shah of Iran Uses Oman to Train Armed
Forces," New York Times, January 25, 1976.

24. New York Times, June 15, 1975; R. M. Burrell, "Iranian
Foreign Policy: Strategic Location, Economic Ambition and Dynastic
Determination," Journal of International Affairs 29, no. 2 (Fall 1975).

25. John B. Oakes, New York Times, September 24, 1975.

26. C. L. Sulzberger, New York Times, October 5, 1975.

27. New York Times, May 12, 1975.

28. Oakes, op. cit.

29. Roy P. Thoman, "Iran and the Persian Gulf Region,"
Current History, January 1973. Iranian strategic thinking, however,
takes into account an adversary Soviet naval presence in the Persian
Gulf region. See Chubin, op. cit., pp. 74-77.

30. Chubin, op. cit., pp. 60-73. In 1975, Iran possessed
1,125 tanks, including 900 Soviet-made T-54/55s, 90 T-34s, 45
PT-76 amphibians, 30 M-24s, and perhaps over 60 newer Soviet
T-62s. Iraq also had 1,300 armored personnel carriers, including
some British-made Saracens, in addition to various Soviet-made
models. New York Times, February 16, 1976.

31. New York Times, May 11, 1975.

32. Trevor N. Dupny et al., The Almanac of World Military
Power (3rd ed., New York: R. R. Bowker, 1974), pp. 176-78.

33. Sulzberger, op. cit.

34. New York Times, January 1976.

35. See New York Times, June 11, 1975 and February 22, 1976.

36. These statistical figures are taken from Trevor, op. cit., and from a chart printed in the New York Times, December 25, 1975.

37. As reported in the New York Times, December 25, 1975.

38. From this analysis, the Communist states of Asia have been excluded. By per capita income, North Korea and South Vietnam belong to the middle-income group, while Cambodia and Laos are among the poorest of Asian countries. North Korea is reported to be unable to pay interest on its $1.7 billion external debt, including $700 million to Moscow and $73.3 million to Tokyo. New York Times, February 26, 1976.

39. Paul Levis, "The World Economy: Searching for Strength," New York Times, September 14, 1975.

40. Time, February 25, 1976.

41. Levis, op. cit.

42. New York Times, December 7, 1975.

43. Politics and Responsibility of the North American Breadbasket (Washington, D.C.: Worldwatch Institute, 1975.

The world's poorest countries have been spending almost as much on imported food grains as on imported oil. It has been estimated that while oil imports have been responsible for an $11 billion increase in the balance of payment deficits of the non-oil-producing developing countries, another $8 billion increase in deficits was attributable to grain purchases. The United States earned $11.2 billion in fiscal 1975 from grain shipments, up from $2.6 billion in 1972. There is now a strong tendency in the United States to use its agri-power for economic and political objectives rather than for humanitarian purposes. Ann Crittenden, "Grain Prices--Punishing the Already Poor," New York Times, December 7, 1975.

The Soviets have to supply 5 million tons of food grains every year to North Korea and North Vietnam. In 1973 Moscow gave India, at a time of grave food shortage, a wheat loan of 2 million tons; earlier, in 1972, it rushed .2 million tons of wheat to Bangladesh when the newly born republic was threatened with famine. One reason why food grain prices are likely to remain at their current high levels is that the Soviets have contracted to buy 6 to 8 million tons of grain in the United States each year for five years beginning in October 1976.

44. New York Times, February 25, 1976.

45. The quest began at the special UN General Assembly session in 1975, at which the United States made a number of constructive proposals. These proposals, which were aimed at correcting some of the acute imbalances in North-South economic relations, have been under international scrutiny and negotiation since September 1975. For background to the world economic, monetary, and raw material crises, see William P. Bundy, ed., The World Economic Crisis (New York: Norton, 1975).

46. Michael Crozier, Samuel Huntington, and Joji Watanuki, The Crisis of Democracy (New York: New York University Press, 1975).

"Today Southern Europe appears much more similar to a Third World torn by divergent social and nationalist forces than to the image of a West European society united in its refusal of Communism and in its demand for American protection." Pierre Hassner, "The Dilemmas of Flexible Containment," New York Times, May 30, 1975. "A specter is haunting Europe--the specter of Finlandization." C. L. Sulzberger, "What Is Yours Is Negotiable," New York Times, July 30, 1975.

47. The Organization for Economic Cooperation and Development (OECD) has estimated that because of the shift in the terms of trade, the industrial countries will gain $7.5 billion from transactions with the poorest nations. New York Times, December 7, 1975.

48. Ann Crittenden, "Vital Dialogue Is Beginning Between the Rich and the Poor," New York Times, December 28, 1975.

49. New York Times, November 13, 1975.

50. For developments in Communist politics in Italy and France, see the New York Times, February 10, 1976; November 18, 1975. For background, see Neil McInnes, The Communist Parties of Western Europe (New York: Oxford University Press, 1975); Ronald Tiersky, "The French Communist Party and Detente," Journal of International Affairs 28, no. 2 (Fall 1974).

51. New York Times, January 25, 1976.

52. From 1953 to 1969 consumers dominated the world raw materials market; in 1972-74 there was a producers' market for petroleum but not for other raw materials.

53. Geoffrey Jukes, The Strategic Situation in the 1980's (Canberra: Strategic and Defense Studies Center, Australian National University Press, 1968).

54. New York Times, February 23, 1976.

55. Drew Middleton, "Soviet Improve Air Transport," New York Times, February 7, 1976.

56. The United States earned $11 billion from arms transfers to developing countries in fiscal 1975, up from $2 billion in 1967. Other major sources of large purchases of arms are the Soviet Union, France, Britain, and China.

57. See note 22.

58. New York Times, January 25, 1976.

59. Seymon Brown, The Changing Essence of Power (Washington, D.C.: the Brookings Institution, 1973); Zbigniew K. Brzezinski, "The Changing International System and America's Role," New York Times, October 5, 1975.

3

THE SOVIET SECURITY
MODEL FOR ASIA

It is somewhat startling to think that the Soviet Union, the leader of the world revolution, should ride through Asia in the 1970s upholding the banner of security. In 1969 Leonid Brezhnev, in no more than a single sentence, tersely put "a system of collective security in Asia" on the agenda of Soviet foreign policy.[1] He did not speak, and has not spoken since then, in a tone of apocalypse. Official Soviet pronouncements on Asian collective security have been miserly, mystical, and mellow. Brezhnev himself has not publicly spoken more than 1,500 words on the subject in six years. Andrei Gromyko has given it five small cryptic paragraphs in five out of his probably 100 speeches and statements; Aleksei Kosygin even less. On the other hand, Soviet analysts and propagandists have produced a profusion of journalistic appetizers but not the main course. Since the Soviet Union has not committed itself, the Soviet collective security system in Asia is not only still a club in search of members,[2] but it is also still in search of a comprehensive and comprehensible theory. Its architecture contains no more than some tentative drawings on political parchment. In contrast with this indifferent and clumsy external manifestation, the concept of collective security has figured forcefully in Soviet diplomatic intercourse with more than a dozen Asian governments. No Asian head of government or foreign minister has been in Moscow since 1972 whom the Soviet leaders have not pressed to subscribe, if not to the concept of an Asian collective security system, at least to the principles that, in the Soviet view, should govern inter-Asian relations.

In the 1970s the Soviets have markedly expanded their physical presence in Asia. They have treaties of peace and friendship with Iraq in the Persian Gulf and with India in South Asia. Anwar Sadat's anti-Soviet policy since 1972 has diminished the importance of the

Soviet-Egyptian treaty, but the Soviet Union has treaty relations with
Somalia, which has a strategic Indian Ocean location, and a 15-year
economic cooperation pact with Iran. Since May 1975 the Soviet
Union has built up a major presence in Vietnam and Laos.[3] It has
also established commercial and economic relations with all countries of Southeast and South Asia. The Soviet navy has established
its permanent presence in the Indian Ocean. From Japan to Iran, the
Soviet leaders have been conducting strategic dialogues with a host of
Asian leaders. They have looked approvingly at Asian initiatives to
form regional security systems excluding the major world powers.

Security-related issues, then, have become a major plank of
Soviet diplomacy with the Asian countries. Since diplomacy is contextual, Soviet policies must vary from country to country,[4] although
they may well have a broad thematic unity. In the 1970s collective
security appears to provide a thematic unity to the Soviet foreign
policies for the different Asian countries. In other words, with each
of the Asian countries that are strategically important for the Soviet
Union, Moscow is now seeking some strategic understanding. This
has necessarily lent a diversity to Soviet security diplomacy in Asia.
Whether the relationship is one of treaty-bound alliance, one of long-
term economic collaboration, or one of low-level commercial and
economic cooperation, security is invariably part of the ongoing
dialogue.

The experience of the last five years has shown that although
the formal launching of an Asian collective security system under
Soviet leadership or even with Soviet participation would still be extremely difficult, it would not be so difficult to construct bilateral
security-oriented relations with individual Asian nations nor to be
linked with indigenously sculpted regional security systems as an
external guarantor, at par with the United States and, in North and
Southeast Asia, with China.

In his report to the 25th Congress of the Communist Party of
the Soviet Union (CPSU), Brezhnev indicated that the Soviet security
diplomacy in Asia would proceed on the basis of bilateral and multilateral linkages. Brezhnev did not mention collective security.
"The Soviet Union," he declared, "intends to continue its active participation in the search for ways of consolidating peace and security
on the Asian continent . . . through bilateral contacts and also on a
multilateral basis." This does not mean that the Soviet leaders will
give up the goal of collective security; what it does mean is that the
emphasis will continue to be on seeking bilateral and multilateral
security relations with flexibility of response to the given balance of
forces. This kind of strategy would permit the Soviet Union to take
part formally in a four-power balance in the West Pacific region; to
be linked with an eventual Southeast Asian neutrality system as an

external guarantor of its viability; to seek suitable participation in a
Persian Gulf security system; and all the while to try to build bilateral
security relations with as many Asian countries as might be willing to
offer or accept such a relationship.

EXISTING SECURITY LINKS

Some Western analysts have argued that the Soviet Union has
already assembled the rudiments of a security subsystem in the
Middle Eastern and South Asian region, linked with the Warsaw Pact
"central security system."[5] Between the central security system
and the subsystem, they see the possibilities of three types of mutual
support functions: (1) logistic, including provision of military training, supply of military advisers and equipment, use of facilities or
bases; (2) defensive, meaning direct military intervention by countries within the subsystem, or by the subsystem itself if the central
security system is in jeopardy; and (3) offensive, meaning a situation
in which the entire security system could be utilized to mobilize large-
scale military operations against an enemy of the Soviet Union. The
weakness of this argument lies in the instability and ambivalence of
the security relations of the Soviet Union with the non-Communist
regimes in the Middle East and South Asia and the extreme reluctance of these nations to get involved in any "Russian war."

As long as the Soviet Union has security relations with a number of countries in regions that are logistically interlinked, it may,
in specific crisis situations, use the facilities in one to help another
of their allies. Thus there were reports, denied by India, that during the 1971 war between India and Pakistan the Soviets transferred
some military equipment from Egypt to India.[6]

It has been Soviet policy to encourage its Third-World allies
to cooperate with one another and even to conclude security-oriented
treaties.[7] The Soviets have persistently tried to enlarge economic
and political cooperation between Iraq and India, and they have succeeded to some extent. Iraq is now one of the major sources of
India's crude imports, and India is building a number of projects in
Iraq. In the military field, India trains Iraqi pilots in the use of
sophisticated Soviet-made planes.

However, the strategic links between the two countries are not
strong enough to induce the one to go to the support of the other in the
event of a military conflict. Not only has India not concluded a
security-oriented friendship treaty with Iraq, but Prime Minister
Indira Gandhi started building friendly relations with Iran in 1974,
even risking Soviet displeasure. (See Chapter 5.) In fact, the
strategic cooperation between India and Iraq has so far been of a

much lower level than the strategic cooperation between Iran and
Pakistan, which are both members of the CENTO alliance. Iraq itself is less dependent on the Soviet Union for its own security and for
safeguarding its interests in the Persian Gulf area after the conclusion of the Iran-Iraq accords than it was before.

Egypt, which had for all practical purposes put its friendship
treaty with Moscow into cold storage, unilaterally denounced its
treaty of friendship and cooperation with the Soviet Union in March
1976.

In South Asia the India-Bangladesh treaty has no longer the
friendly content it used to have as long as Sheikh Mujibur Rahman
was alive and in power. The Soviet-sponsored or backed treaty system in the Middle Eastern and South Asian region, then, is far from
stable. It can hardly be called a security system or subsystem.

The Soviet Union is not looking for friends and allies in Asia
from whom it can get military support; instead it is looking for allies
and friends that are in need of Soviet security support. To the extent
that Soviet strategic interests and the interests of an Asian ally converge, there is room for security collaboration. The common enmity
with China lends Indo-Soviet friendship a certain stability of shared
strategic interests. It is not improbable that India will extend a certain amount of strategic support to Moscow in the event of an armed
conflict between the Soviet Union and China; but even there, India will
be strongly inclined not to get too deeply involved, unless involvement
is compelled by Chinese conflict behavior. It can be taken for granted
that in the event of a Soviet-U.S. war the Asian allies of the Soviet
Union would do their best to stay nonaligned.

In Asia, as in the Middle East and Africa, the Soviet Union has
taken advantage of local conflicts to enhance its presence, build its
influence, and recruit friends and allies. In the classical conflict
between the Western powers and Asian nationalism, it has been relatively easy for Moscow to justify its intervention on ideological and
moral grounds. Thus, in the Middle East the Soviets have sided with
Arab nationalism against Israel, the image of which in the Arab world
is one of an advanced outpost of Western imperialism. In Indochina
also, the Soviet Union has had the opportunity to side with Asian
nationalism against French, and then U.S., imperialism. In the
subcontinent, India sought a security alliance with the Soviet Union
in 1971 not because it felt threatened by Pakistan but because it found
itself isolated from, and threatened by, the United States and China.[8]
Iraq concluded its friendship treaty with the Soviet Union in 1972 because it was afraid that its nationalization of the Iraq Petroleum Company would invite retaliation by the Western powers.[9] In his confrontation with Malaysia, Sukarno asked for and received Soviet support because behind Kuala Lumpur stood the superior might of Britain

and its ally, the United States. From all these cases emerges the
typology of Asian conflicts, which has enabled the Soviet Union to
build its presence and influence in individual Asian countries. Each
of these conflicts has involved, directly or indirectly, the major
world powers. The Soviets have supported those who have perceived
the United States or China or both as their actual or potential enemies.

Through carefully selected intervention in Asian conflicts involving the major Western powers and/or China, the Soviets have
succeeded in breaking through the wall of containment the United
States had erected, by a chain of interlocking military alliances,
during the cold war period. The multilateral Asian alliances have
collapsed. The United States is in the process of readjusting its
Asian presence. Firm U.S. security commitments remain only to
South Korea and Japan.[10] Meanwhile, the Soviet presence has en-
larged, both on Asian land and in Asian waters. After the experience
of Vietnam, the classical-type Asian conflict, that is, conflict between nationalism and imperialism, is not likely to occur again.
On the other hand, inter-Asian conflict potentialities have not
diminished. In a world of dispersed power, several power aspirants
have emerged on the Asian scene. The old balance of power has
broken down in more than one Asian region, and social polarizations
are forming in several Asian countries. The political system of almost every Asian country is fundamentally unstable. On the one
hand the retreat of U.S. power has generated quests for regional
security systems, while on the other hand these quests are being
undermined by rivalries, mutual hostilities, mistrusts, suspicions,
and fears, as well as by unresolved interstate disputes.

THE SOVIET POSITION IN 1969

It is in the broad context of the Asian realities of the 1970s
that we have to examine both the Soviet concept of collective Asian
security and Soviet diplomacy aimed at realizing that strategic goal.
When the concept was put forward by Brezhnev in June 1969, he certainly could not have anticipated the traumatic events that have shaken
Asia in the last six years, although a broad outline of the coming
security picture in Asia could have been drawn. The British government had announced its decision to withdraw strategically from all
Asia east of Suez by 1971, and the United States was seeking the ways
and means of an honorable withdrawal from Vietnam. The long postwar period of Western strategic dominance of Asia appeared to be
coming to an end. At the same time, the challenge from China looked
more menacing than ever before. Only six months before, Brezhnev
had faced the participants at the conference of world Communist and

workers' parties, and the Chinese and Soviet armies had engaged in
a major clash on the Ussuri river; the two communist giants had appeared to be poised on the brink of war.[11]

The Soviet leaders had determined the main course of Moscow
policy with regard to their two principal adversaries: accommodation with the United States was to proceed side-by-side with firm containment of China. China had to be contained both militarily and diplomatically. At the military level, the troop concentration along the
border with China and the open threat of a preemptive nuclear strike
produced the desired impact. Peking agreed to resume border "negotiations" as a result of the surprise meeting in September 1969* between Kosygin and Chou En-lai.[12] Border incidents stopped. The
4,150-mile Sino-Soviet border has been peaceful since then.

When Brezhnev put forward, in the most cryptic manner, his
idea of a collective security system in Asia, his Asian vision must
have been dominated by his perceptions of a United States about to
retreat from Southeast Asia and a China that had to be militarily subdued and diplomatically isolated. He put forward his proposal for
collective Asian security as a replacement of the U.S. security system. In this, the very concept was the projection of the Soviet Union
as the other power, which had a better, more durable, and more acceptable security system to offer the Asian nations.[13]

What exactly was the thrust of Asian diplomacy in Asia in 1969?
The Soviets had no treaty relationship with any nation either in the
Middle East or in Asia, but since 1968 Kosygin had been pursuing the
proposal to set up a system of regional economic collaboration covering the Persian Gulf and the South Asian region. Nikolai Podgorny
had visited North Korea and Mongolia; Aleksei Kosygin had gone to
India, Pakistan, and Afghanistan; and a senior official of the Soviet
external affairs ministry had toured Burma, Laos, Cambodia, and
Japan. This unusual transference of diplomatic attention to Asia was
caused not merely by the need to apprise the various Asian governments of the "dangers" posed by Maoist China, but also to demonstrate Soviet interest in the friendship and good will of the Asian
countries.

The Soviets had been somewhat stimulated by the Indian idea of
an "Eastern Locarno Pact," that is, an agreement among a group of
Asian countries to respect one another's sovereignty and territorial
integrity without any obligation to come to anyone's aid in any contingency.[14] The idea was discussed between Indira Gandhi and
Kosygin during the latter's visit to New Delhi in early 1969.

---

*The meeting was a surprise to the world though it had been
arranged before Kosygin left Hanoi.

Visiting Pakistan in May 1969 for the second time in 13 months, Kosygin had strongly pressed President Yahya Khan to join an economic grouping with Iran, Afghanistan, India, and the Soviet Union; in return, he had promised generous Soviet economic aid and a considerable amount of military assistance. The economic grouping proposal had already received Indian and Afghan approval; Afghanistan had even offered to host a proposed conference of the five countries.

Pressed by Kosygin, Yahya Khan had agreed to take part in a conference at the level of deputy ministers but had backed out immediately after the Soviet premier's departure from Rawalpindi because of strong opposition in his own government, as well as in Pakistani political circles and in the press. Yahya Khan had also given the Chinese ambassador a full account of the Kosygin mission, with a categorical assurance that Pakistan would join no grouping, economic, political, or strategic, that might invite the opposition and anger of China.[15] Because of Pakistani opposition, the economic cooperation conference could not meet; but the Soviets had not abandoned the idea.

This, then, was the thrust of Soviet diplomacy in Asia when Brezhnev proposed a collective security system to replace the U.S. security system in that continent. Soviet strategic thinking for Asia, at that formative stage, probably had three dimensions: the replacement of the U.S. security system by a system or systems with Soviet participation, if not under Soviet auspices; the isolation of China; and the launching of the security praxis on a limited, regional scale in the southern flank of the Soviet Union, where a network of roads linking the Soviet Union, Afghanistan, and Iran were being built or were in the planning stage.[16]

REITERATION OF THE SECURITY PROPOSAL IN 1972

From the time of the June 1969 pronouncement until late 1972, no Soviet leader spoke about collective security in Asia except Gromyko, who gave the subject two sentences in his address at the 25th (jubilee) session of the UN General Assembly. His main purpose, apart from planting the concept on the bank of the East River, was to counter the widespread anti-Chinese orientation the Soviet proposal had taken in Asian minds. Gromyko proclaimed that the Soviets envisaged the "participation of all Asian states in Asian regional cooperation."[17]

The Soviets, in fact, had reason to be disappointed with the responses the Brezhnev proposal had received in Asia and outside. Richard Nixon, in propounding the Guam (or Nixon) Doctrine only a month after the Brezhnev speech, gave the Soviet Union no partnership in a new security order for Asia. The Chinese had condemned the collective Asian security concept as a move to encircle China and had warned the Asian countries to have nothing to do with it.[18] Asian responses had been generally negative or lukewarm. Except for the Indian foreign minister, who supported the Soviet proposal in 1969 only to back out a little later, almost all Asian leaders saw it as primarily an anti-China move.[19] Brezhnev's report to the 24th Congress of the CPSU in early 1971 was sternly anti-imperialist. The peace program it offered called for anti-imperialist solutions of the conflicts in the Middle East and Southeast Asia and for detente with the Western powers, especially the United States.

When Brezhnev and Kosygin picked up the Asian collective security proposal once again in 1972 and gave it a skeletal framework, the situation in the Middle East and Asia had changed vastly in favor of the Soviet Union. The Paris peace talks had opened between the United States and North Vietnam, partly through Soviet good offices, thus conferring on Moscow, for the second time since 1954, the coveted role of a peacemaker in Southeast Asia. The Soviet Union had concluded treaties of friendship and cooperation with Egypt and Iraq in the Arab world and with India in South Asia. India, on its own part, had signed a friendship treaty with Bangladesh that was largely modeled on the Indo-Soviet treaty. The Bangladesh liberation struggle and the India-Pakistan war had established the Soviet Union as the most influential external power in the South Asian region. Nixon had conceded this in his "Emerging Structure of Peace" report to the Congress; it was "out of the question," he had declared, that the United States could "compete with the Soviet Union" to match the political ties that existed between Moscow and New Delhi.[20]

To be sure, Nixon had moved with an earthshaking initiative to open up relations with China so that the United States could make strategic use of the Sino-Soviet conflict to strengthen its bargaining position in relation to the Soviet Union. However, the Shanghai communique did not seem to hurt Soviet interests beyond the point of tolerance. The Nixon "shock," of equal force to Moscow and Tokyo, had opened a dialogue between the Soviets and Japan. Although Gromyko could not get what he wanted in his talks with the Japanese leaders in January 1972, the deadlock had broken in Soviet-Japanese relations and a new process of hard and sustained bargaining had begun. (See Chapter 7.)

Detente with the United States had not halted. The two superpowers had concluded an agreement in the autumn of 1971 on measures to reduce the danger of nuclear war, and in May 1972 the U.S. president was arriving in Moscow for crucial negotiations.

The Soviets had resumed their Asian collective security diplomacy with some vigor. Gromyko had argued for Japanese support.

During the visit of Zulfikar Ali Bhutto to Moscow in March 1972,
Kosygin had pleaded strongly with the Pakistani president for the
endorsement of Pakistan.[21] The reaction of the president of Bangladesh had been more than favorable, and India was presumably in a
mood to collaborate. The relations of the Soviet Union with Turkey
and Iran had improved markedly.

The time had come, then, not merely to revive the collective
security concept publicly, but also to reveal what it really meant.
Kosygin started the process while welcoming the prime minister of
Afghanistan on March 12, 1972. An Asian collective security system,
he declared, could be based on "such principles as renunciation of the
use of force in the settlement of issues in disputes between states,
peaceful coexistence of states with different social systems, and the
development of mutually advantageous cooperation; that is, principles
which comply fully with the UN Charter and are in no way directed
against any state."[22]

Six days later, addressing the Soviet Trade Union Congress,
Brezhnev was more explicit. He reminded his audience that questions involving relations with Asian countries had of late been receiving "an ever larger place" in Soviet policy. This was under-
standable, since "almost two-thirds of the Soviet Union's territory
is located on the Asian continent."[23] The role of Asia in world affairs was growing rapidly, according to Brezhnev, largely because
of the success of the national liberation movement and because of its
economic development. In both fields the Soviet Union had been playing a crucial role. It had "successfully developed" fraternal relations with Mongolia, North Korea, and North Vietnam, and it had
very good relations with Afghanistan, Ceylon, and Burma, while its
relations with Iran and Turkey were steadily improving. The
strength of Soviet relations with India was symbolized in the treaty
of peace and friendship concluded in 1971. The newly born republic
of Bangladesh was the latest addition to the Asian friends of the
Soviet Union. Between the Soviet Union and Pakistan there were "no
conflicts and no contradictions of interest." Recently there had been
"a noticeable turn for the better" in Soviet-Japanese relations.

Having submitted this impressive list of Soviet foreign policy
gains in Asia, Brezhnev made the following statement about Asian
security:

> The idea of guaranteeing security in Asia on a
> collective basis is arousing increasing interest
> in many Asian countries. It is becoming in-
> creasingly clearer that the real path to security
> in Asia is not the path of military blocs but the
> path of good-neighborly cooperation among all

the states interested in this. Collective security
in Asia must, in our view, be based on such
principles as renunciation of the use of force in
relations between states, respect for sovereignty
and the inviolability of borders, noninterference
in internal affairs and the broad development of
economic and other cooperation on the basis of
full equality and mutual advantage. We advocate
and will continue to advocate this kind of collective security in Asia, and we are ready to
cooperate with all states with a view to implementation of this idea.[24]

THE PROPOSAL AS ELABORATED BY
LEONID BREZHNEV IN 1973

In 1973 the conclusion of the Paris agreements for a ceasefire
in South Vietnam and withdrawal of U.S. troops raised Soviet confidence in the idea of an alternative security system in Asia. In three
major speeches that year, Brezhnev took up the theme, giving further
insights into the whys and hows of his proposal. Already in December
1972 Brezhnev had offered "full participation" to Peking, which only
provoked China even more strongly.[25] Because he was speaking on
Asian soil of the Soviet Union, the concept of this system dominated
his speech at Alma-Ata on August 15, 1973.[26] Brezhnev referred to
the decision by the Soviet bloc leaders, during their meeting in the
Crimea on July 30 and 31, that the "zone of detente" be "extended to
the whole world."[27] "We regard it as important that Asia be included
in this process on a broad front," he reiterated.

The Soviet Union, he claimed, had played a vital role in the liberation of the Asian peoples from the yoke of imperialism and colonialism. "The chronicles of the Asian peoples' liberation struggle do not
contain a single page that is not imprinted with effective support and
solidarity on the part of the Soviet Union, on the part of our people,
on the part of our Party."[28]

Asia was now in motion. "Its movement cannot help but be extremely difficult in view of the tenacity of the old order and the opposition of imperialism and reaction."[29]

Asia needed lasting peace, easing of tensions, and good neighborly relations for progressive development and radical social change.
There had been a remarkable improvement in the Asian situation.
The long and difficult war in Indochina had ended in the victory of
the Vietnamese people. Preconditions had been created for normalization of relations within the subcontinent. Tension in the Korean

peninsula had decreased as a result of the initiative of North Korea for peaceful democratic unification.

"Finally, and this is very important, the policy of the peace-loving states is having an increasing influence on the situation in Asia."[30] Among these states, "an outstanding place is held by such a great country as India."[31] There were negative forces too (Brezhnev did not name them); but the healthy forces, supported by the Soviet Union, were making headway. The Soviets were firmly convinced that Asia "can and must live according to the laws of peace, and the realistic path toward this end is collective security."[32] Of course, Asia would need time and considerable effort to attain this desirable goal.

Why did Asia need collective security? Because, Brezhnev said, this was the only way to rule out war, armed conflict, and imperialist aggression for the sake of free development and social and political renewal, for stronger political independence and success in building independent economies, and for mutually advantageous good neighborly relations.

The system that the Soviet Union was projecting called for equal participation by all countries, without exception. It would give no one any unilateral advantage. The concept was not one of Soviet genesis. Many of the principles upon which it could be built had been proclaimed at Bandung in 1955, while others had been reflected in a number of international documents relating to Asia. The Soviet Union could not build a collective security system in Asia. "Every Asian nation is called upon to make a contribution to its creation."[33] Brezhnev sought to "Asianize" the Asian collective security concept.

His other references to the idea in 1973 were at Tashkent in September and at the World Peace Congress in Moscow in October. At Tashkent he sounded somewhat pessimistic. "At first glance it may seem that positive tendencies are not making such clear headway [in Asia] as they are in Europe."[34] He likened Asia to an enormous flywheel, slowly gathering momentum and inexorably building up its force of acceleration. At the World Peace Congress he was soberly optimistic. He saw a "gradual development" among Asian nations of the kind of good neighborly relations that would correspond to the basic principles of peaceful coexistence; upon these foundations, over time, it should be possible to build a collective security system. He stressed the universality of the system and said that it would be "completely ridiculous" to think that such a vast country as China could be isolated in Asia. Then he immediately launched an attack on the Chinese leadership for their policy of tension and conflict with the Soviet Union and other socialist countries.[35]

The Peace Congress communique listed security and cooperation in Europe and peace and security in Asia as the two achievable
objectives of the world peace movement. In defining the content and
purpose of the system, the document supplemented Brezhnev's earlier
statements. Peace and security in Asia, it declared, is threatened
"primarily by the imperialist policies of aggression, subversive activities and the pitting of Asians against Asians."[36]

The Asian peoples had scored numerous successes in their
struggle against imperialism and reaction. As a result, "a decisive
change in favor of peace and freedom has taken place in the balance
of forces" in Asia.[37] The highly dangerous conflicts and crises that
still remained in Asia could be overcome only by united efforts to defeat imperialism. The collective security system, then, would be
essentially anti-imperialist; the ambience in which it could take shape
would come only after the defeat of imperialism and native reaction.

What would the system give the Asian countries? It would remove the hotbeds of war. It would enable the Asian nations to overcome the consequences of foreign aggression and interference and
would pave the way for social progress in individual Asian societies.

How could Asia move toward collective security? By intensifying the struggle to rid the continent of foreign military bases and military blocs; by the admission of Bangladesh to the United Nations; by
complete normalization of relations within the subcontinent; and by
transformation of the Indian Ocean into a zone of peace. These were
among the essential elements of Asian security. The governments
and the public forces of the Asian countries had to coordinate their
efforts to gain peace and security. They must proceed from the
fundamental principles of peaceful coexistence to take into account
the constructive ideas and principles that are advanced.[38]

A year later, when Brezhnev spoke on Asian collective security
at Ulan Bator, the capital of Mongolia, he tried to Asianize the concept still further. The Soviet leaders had not advanced a new concept; it had emerged from the historical endeavors of the Asian nations. The five principles of peaceful coexistence that had been incorporated for the first time in the Sino-Indian agreement of 1954,
known as the Bandung declaration, were ideas and concepts of security and regional cooperation that had been advanced from time to
time by different Asian leaders. They were included in the principles
of international relations endorsed at the Algiers conference of nonaligned nations. Many other constructive proposals had emanated
from the Asian countries themselves. The construction of a collective Asian security system would require

> persistent and consistent practical steps by many
> states and careful consideration of many opinions
> and positions. . . .

> Just as great rivers are formed from dozens
> of small rivers, from hundreds of tributaries
> and brooks, so in international politics a truly
> major undertaking is frequently the result of
> many attempts, of many initiatives--large and
> small--that merge into a single mighty stream.[39]

SOVIET POLICY GUIDELINES AS REVEALED
IN THE PROPOSAL

A scrutiny of Brezhnev's formulations leads to a number of
the guidelines of Soviet foreign policy operations in Asia during the
1970s and beyond. First, the Soviet Union wants the Asian nations
to believe that it has entered the Asian scene not to create conflicts
and confrontations, but to bury them; not to divide Asia into zones
of varying political colors, but to erect a canopy of peaceful coexistence in countries with different political and social systems.

Second, the Soviet Union has neither the capability nor (therefore) the intention of imposing a security system on Asia; the "collective" must emerge as a result of Asian quests for security.

Third, the forces that may favor the Soviet model of security
are not yet consolidated even in any Asian region; hence the need for
"struggle."

Fourth, the Soviet leaders are uncertain and flexible about the
spatial aspects of Asian security. While striving for a pan-Asian
security system as a distant goal, they would concentrate on bilateral
and regional security relationships as foundations of an eventual pan-
Asian security edifice.

Neither Brezhnev nor the numerous Soviet analysts who have
persevered in attempting to "sell" the collective security concept to
Asia have been able to offer a credible theoretical framework for
collective security. The only theoretical framework provided by
Soviet analysts is that of peaceful coexistence, which as we have
noted is at best a set of vague and lofty principles governing the
practice of international relations among states with opposing social
and political systems. Peaceful coexistence, Soviet analysts concede, presupposes a balance of international forces that is decisively in favor of the forces of socialism and of militant, anti-imperialist
national liberation. Peaceful coexistence formalizes not only the
legitimacy of the socialist system but also its right to be recognized
by the opposing world system as a coequal partner in the mosaic of
interstate relations. The capitalist-imperialist system, which was
nourished on wars of aggrandizement and which is congenitally inclined to intervene in the affairs of the socialist and national liberation countries, will seek security in peaceful coexistence only when

its claws have been cut and it has realized that aggression will not
pay. A Soviet analyst gave the following explanation:

> For the governments of the capitalist states to
> accept the principle of peaceful coexistence, it
> was obviously essential that they should be con-
> vinced of the absolute hopelessness of their wishes
> for external suppression or internal decay of the
> socialist society. In other words, the growth of
> the power of the socialist countries and of their
> international cohesion and internal stability has
> been and remains the decisive factor insuring
> the effectiveness of the policy of peaceful co-
> existence and, consequently, the transformation
> of the idea of collective security from a possi-
> bility into a reality. [40]

Collective security in Asia, then, is predicated on the growing
might and cohesion of the socialist countries, in the face of which the
imperialist powers will be obliged to abandon the path of aggression
and intervention and adopt the path of peaceful coexistence. However,
there is no socialist community in Asia. The Soviet Union, with all
its claim to be an Asian power, is still regarded by most Asians as
belonging to Europe. The socialist countries in Asia with which the
Soviets have fraternal relations are weak and developing. China, the
one powerful socialist country in Asia, is the principal adversary of
the Soviet Union. Asia clearly lacks the stable polarized balance of
military and economic power that prevails in Europe and makes
peaceful coexistence objectively possible.

The Soviet analysts themselves are aware of the diversities
and disharmonies of Asia. They stress the "dissociation" rather
than the cohesion of the Asian states. As one of them puts it, "In a
word, Asia still lacks what it takes to carry on a successful struggle
for security and cooperation. . . . In Asia . . . there is still no
common platform for rebuffing imperialist aggression and for guaran-
teeing security and cooperation."[41] Asia is far from ready for the
Soviet-type collective security.

The Soviets must nevertheless project the concept of collective
security in Asia for several strategic reasons. First, it legitimizes
Soviet partnership in Asian security systems. Second, it fortifies
the Leninist theory that socialism and national liberation are the two
streams of a single anti-imperialist force. Third, it puts a facade
of stability and security on Soviet foreign policy operations and, hopefully, weakens the ideological rejection of the Soviet Union by the
Asian nations. Fourth, it responds, albeit rhetorically, to the most

widely shared felt need in Asia. Since World War II Asia has seen more conflict and tension, more bloodshed and devastation, than any other world region.

ASIAN ATTITUDES TOWARD THE PROPOSAL

The Soviet argument that peaceful coexistence is an insurance against interstate conflict and warfare is at best a utopian hortative wish without empirical evidence. The Soviets themselves make it clear that in the international ambience of peaceful coexistence, the contradictions between imperialism and the forces of national liberation, on the one hand, and between the forces of reaction and those of radical change, on the other, will be sharper. What is the guarantee that these contradictions will not lead to conflict and war? The conclusion of the 1954 Sino-Indian treaty incorporating the principles of peaceful coexistence did not prevent the two largest nations of Asia from fighting a border war eight years later. The claim that socialism eliminates war has been disproved by the history of the intersocialist relations of the postwar period. By propagating Asian collective security and by conducting anti-China polemics in the same breath, the Soviets have made it all the more difficult for the various Asian leaders to see their collective security drive as something that is not primarily designed to isolate China from the mainstream of Asian affairs.

The Asian ruling elites have therefore not been seduced by the inflated promises of the Soviet security model. For them China is the predominant Asian power, and many of them need China in order to keep their own distance from the Soviet Union. However, although the Asians have politely turned down Soviet initiatives for assembling a collective security system, in the 1970s they have not turned down the Soviet claim to be involved in whatever security arrangements may emerge in the Asian geopolitical regions. Even where they are unwilling to extend formal membership in a proposed regional security system to the Soviet Union, they realize that any such system will need to be guaranteed by Moscow as much as by Washington and Peking in order to be viable.

The Soviets themselves have given the impression that what they are aiming at during the coming years is not a pan-Asian balance of power dominated by Moscow, nor even regional Asian balances under Russian domination, but balances in which the Soviet Union is an equal partner with the United States and is able to tilt the balance somewhat in its favor with the support of the national liberation forces. In other words, having achieved a strategic balance with the United States in the bipolar international system, the

Soviets are seeking what an Australian scholar has perceptively termed the balances within the various subsystems. [42] (I should prefer to call it "inner" balances.) The Soviet claim to inner balances in Asia and in other world regions is based on the proven capability of the Soviet Union to intervene in distant conflicts, on the scale of its relationship with some of the local powers, on its naval presence in the Indian Ocean, on the Communist victories in Indochina, and on the humbling of U.S. power in Asia. The cochairmanship of the Geneva conference formalizes the Soviet claim to an "inner balance" in the Middle East. Similarly, the Soviet Union demands equal access to the blue waters of Asia. It also demands relations with Japan that would match those Japan has with the United States and a status in Southeast Asia that would equal the position of China. Perhaps only in the South Asian and Persian Gulf region is the Soviet Union striving for a leadership position in an economic and security grouping.

The need for "inner balances" prompts the Soviets to insist upon the withdrawal of the United States from its bases in Asia, especially because, in the post-Vietnam era, the Chinese have become supporters of a continued U.S. military presence in North and Southeast Asia, as well as in the area of the Persian Gulf and Indian Ocean. The urge for inner balances can also be seen in the Soviet endorsement of the proposal to set up an indigenous security system in the Gulf region and the move for the neutralization of Southeast Asia. [43] The Soviets, then, are not actively seeking the erection of a pan-Asian security system, although this concept surfaces in Soviet formulations on Asian security. [44] In fact, the quest for security systems in a diverse and disharmonious continent such as Asia cannot but be varied. The way in which the Soviet Union has been pursuing a variety of security objectives in the different regions of Asia can be seen in an analytical study of its diplomacy of collective security during the 1970s.

The Soviet leaders have had numerous and sustained dialogues on security with a dozen Asian heads of government or foreign ministers. Among these are the Shah of Iran; the prime ministers of India, Pakistan, Afghanistan, and Bangladesh; the leaders of the government of Iraq; the prime ministers of Sri Lanka and Malaysia; the president of Burma and the prime minister of Singapore; the foreign minister of Indonesia; the prime ministers and foreign ministers of Japan; and the leaders of the Communist regimes in North Vietnam, North Korea, and Mongolia. Since in the Soviet view the road to security relations is paved by economic cooperation, the concept of collective security has figured in the conversations of Moscow with the leaders of even those Asian countries with which economic and commercial relations have been opened or resumed during the last few years, such as Thailand, the Philippines, and Indonesia. Security, however, has been discussed in depth and with intensity only with the Persian Gulf and South Asian group of countries and with Japan. So far the negotiations have been bilateral, but with the Persian Gulf and South Asian group they have assumed the aspect of multilateral exchanges, since the same kinds of Soviet proposals have been taken up with each of these countries and the reaction of one has weighed heavily with that of another within the group. Consultations have taken place between India and Afghanistan and between Iran and Pakistan. Finally, it is only in this region that the Soviets have persevered, and are still persevering, in setting up a system of economic cooperation that includes the full-fledged participation of Moscow.

In asking for Japanese support for collective Asian security, the Soviet leaders have specifically demanded that Japan withdraw from its security treaty with the United States; dismantle the U.S. bases on its territory; develop an independent foreign policy that would serve its own, rather than U.S., interests in Asia; and build up a "balanced" relationship with the Soviet Union, the United States, and China. The Soviets have actively sought to prevent Japan from inclining toward Peking; a Sino-Japanese alliance, blessed by the United States, is something that the Soviets dread more than any other power combination. The Soviet Union has offered Japan, in return for good-neighborliness and equal friendship, opportunities to develop, and share on a long-term basis, the plentiful fuel and forest resources of Siberia. It has also agreed to return to Japan two of the four islands in the Kurile group, which Moscow had taken over after the defeat of Japan in World War II. The Soviet Union has offered Japan a treaty of friendship and nonaggression and a peace treaty, if the Japanese are willing to conclude one on the basis of the return of two of the four islands.

The Japanese, as we shall find in this book, have doggedly and systematically spurned the Soviet offers; however, the Japanese leaders have not rejected the concept of collective security as such. They have refused to discuss security relations with the Soviet Union until all of the four disputed northern islands have been returned to Japan; they have refused to break off their security ties with the United States; and they have pleaded their absolute inability and unwillingness to be a party to any anti-China initiative by the Soviet Union. Some Japanese scholars of international relations have said that the Soviet security concept should be discussed "in theory" in developing a new security system for Asia.[45]

SOVIET PRESSURE FOR ACCEPTANCE

The utmost Soviet diplomatic exertions for collective security have been with Iran, Pakistan, Afghanistan, India, and Iraq. We have already noted the Kosygin proposal for an economic grouping of the five South Asian countries.

Pakistan

Yahya Khan's backing out from his initial support for an inaugural economic cooperation meeting of the five countries caused Moscow great disappointment and anger. G. W. Choudhuri, a former member of the Yahya Khan cabinet and a former foreign policy adviser to President Ayub Khan, has detailed the strong carrot-and-stick pressures the Soviet leaders brought to bear upon the two Pakistani presidents between 1968 and 1970 in hopes of securing their participation in the proposed economic grouping.[46] Yahya Khan's "betrayal" might have argued in 1971 for Soviet support for the Bangladesh liberation struggle.

When Bhutto, the first president of the "new" Pakistan, visited Moscow in early 1972, the Soviet leaders candidly told him that not only did they not regret their intervention on behalf of the Bangladesh liberation movement, but they would act in the same manner in events were to repeat themselves.[47] This was interpreted by the Pakistanis as a veiled threat of possible Soviet intervention in the Baluchi and Pathan unrest in Pakistan. There is no evidence that the Soviet Union has so far directly intervened in these Pakistani domestic conflicts; the Baluchi and Pathan rebels, however, have been getting moral support from Moscow. In 1973 the Pakistani security forces raided the embassy of Iraq in Rawalpindi and seized a quantity of arms meant for the Baluchi insurgents. Baghdad Radio has openly supported the "struggle for Baluchi independence." The Soviets, then, have not refrained from playing power politics to bend Pakistan to their initiative in setting up a South Asia and Persian Gulf economic grouping. However, Pakistan has not bowed. On the contrary, it has kept China fully informed of each and every thrust of the collective security diplomacy of Moscow.[48]

Iran

The collective security concept was discussed between the Soviets and Iran during the Shah's visit to Moscow in November 1972; during Kosygin's visit to Tehran in June 1973; during Prime

Minister Amir Abbas Hoveida's return visit to the Soviet capital in
the following August; and during the Shah's visit to the Soviet Union
in November 1974. The joint communique issued after Hoveida's
conversations with the Soviet leaders incorporated endorsement of
the concept of Asian collective security by Iran and an Iranian readiness to strive in that direction. The communique read as follows:

> Taking into account the need for joint effort and
> cooperation by all Asian countries in the work of
> ensuring peace and security on the Asian continent
> on the basis of nonuse of force or threat of its use,
> respect for sovereignty, the inviolability of borders,
> noninterference in one another's internal affairs and
> the development of all-round cooperation based on
> mutual respect and equality of peoples, the two
> sides expressed the intention to promote the reali-
> zation of the idea of creating a collective security
> system in Asia embracing all the countries of
> this continent.[49]

This has been the most support the Soviets have obtained so
far in Asia for their security proposal. The Iranian support was
subsequently beamed by Moscow radio to Pakistan and other countries. Why did the Shah of Iran back the Soviet proposal? The
author was told by responsible persons in Tehran in March 1975 that
the Shah was in favor of economic cooperation among the South Asian
nations and even more between Iran and the Soviet Union. What he
sought in 1973 was some formal basis for stable relations with the
Soviet Union, and nothing suited him better than the principles of
peaceful coexistence. If Iran and the Soviet Union could build good
neighborly relations on the basis of nonuse of force, noninterference
in each other's internal affairs, and mutual respect for sovereignty
and territorial integrity, not only would the Shah feel secure from
the north, but it would also be possible for him to strengthen economic relations with the Soviet Union. The Shah had no idea of promoting any Asian collective security system with Soviet participation,
the author further learned; what he was interested in was a security
system for the Persian Gulf region that would exclude the major
powers but be guaranteed by each one of them. A South Asian regional security system, if and when it was founded, could well be
linked to such a regional security system.

India

The Indian attitude has been somewhat mystical. As noted,
India had broached the idea of a loose "Eastern Locarno pact" among

an unspecified group of Asian countries. Presumably in 1971, at
the time of the conclusion of the Indo-Soviet treaty, the Soviets did
not press India for formal support for their Asian collective security
proposal. In fact, the Soviets tried to play down the security aspect
of the treaty in 1971, apparently because they did not wish to notify
China and the United States that they were launching a security system in South Asia.[50] After the India-Pakistan war, India moved,
with Soviet support, to promote bilateralism with Pakistan, while
the Soviet emphasis was on normalization of relations within the subcontinent. Individual Indian ministers sometimes spoke in favor of
Asian collective security, but Indira Gandhi's public posture was that
India was not interested in any military pact. It was probably understood between the Soviet and Indian leaders that India should be one
of the last, and not one of the first, countries to formally endorse
the Soviet security model or to take any unilateral or joint step in
that direction. The support of India would be the kiss of death for
the concept as far as Pakistan and several other smaller Asian countries are concerned.[51]

The Soviet leaders probably changed their minds in 1973. The
main purpose of Brezhnev's nearly week-long visit to New Delhi in
November 1973 was probably to obtain the support of India for collective security in Asia. The subject was not formally on the agenda,
but it undoubtedly figured prominently in the four meetings Brezhnev
had with the Indian Premier. Speaking of his first round of talks with
Indira Gandhi, Brezhnev reported as follows to the members of the
Indian parliament: "We agreed to consider together the new things
that life is confronting our countries with, to outline further steps
that would help deepen and expand Soviet-Indian cooperation, and to
determine fields of future joint work for the good of our peoples, for
the sake of peace."[52]

In his address, he spoke at some length and with a great deal
of emphasis about the need in Asia for a collective security system
and about Soviet efforts in that direction. The final communique on
the Brezhnev talks with Indira Gandhi, however, revealed that India
was not ready to go even as far as Iran on the question of Asian collective security. In fact, the phrase "Asian collective security" was
not even mentioned. All that the communique said was as follows:

> The Soviet Union and India reaffirmed that they
> attach special importance to the broad develop-
> ment of mutually advantageous cooperation and
> the strengthening of peace and stability in Asia,
> based on the joint efforts of all states in this
> largest and most populous part of the world.
> The Soviet Union and India have agreed on the

need to promote the creation of conditions in
which peoples can live in an atmosphere of
peace and goodneighborliness, so that resources, including human resources, can be
channeled into solution of social and economic
problems; an upswing in the peoples' living
standards and in their economy and culture depend on this above all.

The two sides believe that relations between all states should be based on such principles as the renunciation of the use of force
in relations between states, respect for sovereignty and the inviolability of borders, noninterference in internal affairs, and the broad
development of economic and other cooperation
based on full equality and mutual advantage.

In both sides' opinion, the transformation
of the continent of Asia into a continent of lasting peace, stability and good cooperation will
undoubtedly facilitate the further normalization
of relations among countries and the strengthening of world peace. [53]

Other Asian Countries

Between 1973 and 1975 the Soviet leaders sought support for
their security model with the prime ministers of Afghanistan, Sri
Lanka, and Malaysia and the foreign ministers of Singapore and
Indonesia. [54] All that they could obtain was vague endorsement of
some of the general principles of peaceful coexistence that had been
enunciated by Brezhnev as the foundation of an Asian collective
security system.

The Malaysian case is rather interesting. When Tun Razak
visited Moscow in October 1972 he and Kosygin tried to sell each
other their own security models. Kosygin had some words of praise
for the Southeast Asian neutralization proposal but claimed that the
Soviet model was better. Razak, in reply, made no mention of the
Soviet model and argued that neutralization of Southeast Asia was a
more practicable proposition and assured the Soviet Union that the
legitimate interests of all the great powers would be protected in the
event of neutralization. The joint communique recorded that the two
sides had explained their proposals and agreed that "the interests of
the security of Asian peoples, call, above all, for urgent elimination
of the conflicts and seats of tension existing in that area. "[55]

This nearly exhaustive account of Soviet diplomatic efforts to promote the proposal for collective security in Asia shows that while Moscow has notified almost all Asian governments of the seriousness of its intention to persist with its model, so far it has not succeeded in shoring up any "hardware" support. It has not been able to soften up the major actors in any Asian region even to the extent of obtaining complete rhetorical support for the Soviet model. The Soviet Union is still the loner in the field of Asian collective security. Its promotional efforts are being shared by no Asian country, not even among those with socialist regimes, with the sole and not very helpful exception of Mongolia.

CONCLUSION

The Asian response to the Soviet collective security proposal would have been more positive if the Soviet leaders had begun by offering an equal position to China and the United States in the system. Brezhnev has, in effect, opened the system to China only if the Chinese leaders agree to behave, if they abandon their anti-Sovietism and if they are willing to cooperate with Moscow and its allies. The Soviet proposal will gather strength if relations between Moscow and Peking are normalized in the years to come. With China pulling in the extreme opposite direction, it is not possible for the Soviet Union to mobilize enough Asian support for its security initiative.

Brezhnev has never said in so many words that the United States cannot be included in the collective Asian security system, but he had excluded "American imperialism." Some Soviet scholars have implicitly suggested a U.S. role in a new Asian security system or balance of power.[56] Several aspects of the existing situation indicate possibilities, however nebulous at present, of Soviet-U.S. cooperation in a future security system, if not for the whole of Asia, at least for its more important regions. As noted, a four-power balance is already in existence in North Asia. The Pacific Doctrine of Gerald Ford offers a possibility of friendly relations between the United States and Hanoi. If the Geneva conference mechanism succeeds in bringing a stable peace to the Middle East, with the United States and the Soviet Union as underwriters of an Arab-Israeli peace agreement, its impact is bound to be felt on all Asia.

The proposal for collective Asian security reflects the strength as well as the weakness of the Soviet Union in Asia, its hopes and also its fears. The Soviet self-image of a Eurasian nation impels Moscow to seek its manifest destiny in the tropics and blue waters of Asia. The dream that has soared in Russian breasts for many centuries now appears to be descending to the level of reality. This is the time when Soviet ideologues would like to confirm the Leninist theory of the symbiotic unity of Marxist socialism and the forces of national liberation. Whatever the urges and impulses of the ideologues, however, the statesmen in Moscow are sobered by the limitation of expendable resources and the frailty of rewards. Asian realities are unusually stubborn and recalcitrant. Asian revolutions have a habit of going off track, of being delivered before the Soviet Union is ready to receive them. Even when an Asian Communist nation does not become arrogantly hostile, it is almost always less than completely friendly; in any case it is a drag on Soviet resources. Few Asian nonruling Communist parties are pro-Soviet; almost all of the Communist parties in Southeast Asia have a Maoist orientation. The prospect of these Communist elements riding to power on the crest of peasant upheavals cannot be very inspiring to the CPSU leaders.[57]

Inherent in the Soviet leaders' collective Asian security diplomacy is the tactical Soviet line of working with the national bourgeois regimes to make them stable and secure in their own national, as well as in the Asian, environment. The ideological objective is to encourage independent capitalist development and in specific cases to inject "socialism" into the arteries of weak capitalist systems, rather than to promote revolutionary explosions.

The main problem for the Soviet Union in Asia is that the majority of the Asian actors are not convinced that Moscow is more interested in promoting security and stability than it is in replacing the United States as the dominant Asian power and in reducing China. To persuade the Asian countries that they are offering a security system or systems that would not in effect polarize Asia still further and usher in a new generation of conflicts, the Soviet architects of collective security will have to build the edifice from above as well as from below. That is, they will have to secure the cooperation of the United States, China, and Japan and with the European powers with Asian interests that are still substantial, which in recent years have demonstrated some wisdom with regard to their Asian policies, and it will also have to deal successfully with the leaders of the various Asian countries, who as we have seen are not inclined to rely for security solely on Soviet promises.

Meanwhile, in order to establish their claim to emerging Asian security orders, the Soviets have been building up their power presence in the blue waters of Asia.

NOTES

1. For analyses and commentaries on the Soviet proposal for Asian collective security, see Arnold L. Holerick, The Soviet Union's "Asian Collective Security Proposal": A Club in Search of Members (Santa Monica, Calif.: Rand Corporation, 1974); Alexander O. Ghebhardt, "The Soviet Collective Security System," Asian Survey 13, no. 12 (December 1973); Geoffrey Jukes and Ian Clark, "The Soviets and Asian Collective Security 1969-74," in Soviet Economic and Political Relations with the Developing World, ed. Roger Kanet and Donna Bahry (New York: Praeger, 1975); Ian Clark, "Collective Security in Asia: Towards a Framework of Soviet Policy," Roundtable, no. 252 (October 1973); Harold C. Hinton, "The Soviet Campaign for Collective Security in Asia," Pacific Community 7, no. 2 (January 1976); Ian Clark, "The Indian Subcontinent and Collective Security--Soviet Style," Australian Outlook 26, no. 3 (December 1972); Victor Zorza, "Collective Security," Survival, August 1969; and Bhabani Sen Gupta, "Soviet Thinking on Asian Collective Security," Institute of Defense Studies and Analyses Journal (New Delhi), April 1973.

2. Holerick, op. cit.

3. Fox Butterfield, "Hanoi-Soviet Tie Worries Peking," New York Times, November 3, 1975.

4. Roger Kanet argues that Soviet policies vary from country to country in the developing world. See his "Soviet Union and the Developing Countries: Policy or Policies?" in Soviet Economic and Political Relations with the Developing World, op. cit.

5. Avigdor Haselkorn, "The Soviet Collective Security System," Orbis 19, no. 1 (Spring 1975).

6. Time, December 20, 1971; New York Times, March 31, 1972; Anthony McDermott, "Sadat and the Soviet Union," The World Today, September 1972.

7. Pravda wrote on March 31, 1971 that "for its part the Soviet Union invites those countries which accept [its] approach to conclude appropriate bilateral or multilateral treaties" among themselves.

8. Bhabani Sen Gupta, "South Asia and the Great Powers," in The World and the Great-Power Triangles, ed. William E. Griffith (Cambridge, Mass.: MIT Press, 1975), pp. 223-28.

9. "A sense of isolation and fear of Western intervention if the Iraq Petroleum Company were to be nationalized were the major factors that prompted Baghdad to seek an alliance with the Soviet Union in the early months of 1972. Moscow took advantage of such an agreement." R. M. Burrell and Alvin J. Cottrell, Iran, Afghanistan, Pakistan: Tensions and Dilemmas (Washington, D.C.: Center for Strategic and International Studies, Georgetown University, 1974), p. 4.

10. The Korean commitment is controversial, while the U.S. security treaty with Japan is now terminable by either party at one year's notice.

11. For an account of the clash and a detailed critique of the Sino-Soviet border dispute, see Tai Sung An, The Sino-Soviet Territorial Disputes (Philadelphia: Westminster Press, 1973), pp. 156-63.

12. Pravda, in an editorial on August 28, 1969, brandished Soviet nuclear might and threatened a preemptive nuclear attack. The Soviet deputy defense minister, Matvey V. Zakharov, reportedly said soon after the Pravda editorial that the Soviet action against China might take the form of a surprise blitzkrieg. Washington Post, October 9, 1969. The possibility of a Sino-Soviet nuclear war was also discussed by the controversial Soviet journalist, Victor Louis, in a dispatch in the Evening News (London), cited in the New York Times, September 18, 1969.

The dialectics of the Sino-Soviet conflict make it truly unique in the annals of interstate conflicts. For some 15 years it has been fought mostly with piercing invective, and although it has destroyed an alliance and a friendship, it has not quite harried the connection to death. The leaders of both countries have been anxious to keep the conflict under control; saber-rattling has almost always been followed by unilateral or mutual climb-down. The Chinese have been careful not to provoke Moscow to the point of no return. China has sometimes spoken in two voices: the official voice pleading moderation and the revolutionary voice denouncing the USSR. See the two very different statements on the question of border negotiations issued in Peking within 24 hours in October 1969, one suggesting that the "status quo should be maintained and there should definitely be no resort to the use of force," and the other belligerent in tone and sternly anti-Soviet in content. Both statements can be found in Peking Review, October 10, 1969. See also Peter J. Kumpa's interpretation in the Baltimore Sun, October 12, 1969.

In January 1971 the Soviet government handed Peking the draft of a "special treaty" on the nonuse of force, with a provision that neither side "shall use against the other armed forces employing any types of weapons including (a) conventional, (b) missile, and (c) nuclear." The Chinese rejected the proposal. In his report to the 10th congress of the Chinese Communist Party, Chou En-lai said that disputes between Peking and Moscow should not impede normalization of relations on the basis of the five principles of peaceful coexistence and that the border question should be settled "peacefully, through negotiations, in conditions ruling out any threats." Brezhnev, in a public response to Chou En-lai's statement, remarked in September 1973, "We have already declared that we are ready at this time to develop relations with the CPR [Chinese People's Republic] on the basis of the principles of peaceful coexistence, if Peking

does not deem it possible to go further in relations with a socialist
state."

13. This is how Brezhnev put forward his embryonic concept:

> The burning problems of the current relations do
> not conceal from our view long-term tasks, name-
> ly, the creation of a system of collective security
> in those parts of the globe where the dangers of
> another world war, of armed conflicts, are con-
> centrated. Such a system is the best replacement
> for the existing military-political groupings. . . .
> We are of the opinion that the course of events is
> also putting on the agenda the task of creating a
> system of collective security in Asia. (Pravda,
> June 8, 1969.)

14. This hitherto little-known fact was disclosed to the author
by a highly competent source in New Delhi in February 1975. The
source cannot be identified.

15. G. W. Choudhury, "Reflections on Sino-Pakistan Relations," Pacific Community 7, no. 2 (January 1976). Kosygin argued
with Yahya Khan that China could not be a true friend of Pakistan and
that the Chinese were trying to destabilize East Pakistan. Pakistan
Times, July 11, 1969; Hindustan Times, May 23, 1969. See also
Choudhury, India, Pakistan, Bangladesh and Major Powers: Politics
of a Divided Subcontinent (New York: Free Press for the Foreign
Policy Research Institute, 1975).

The strongest opposition to the economic grouping proposal
came from the Pakistani military, with strong backing by the foreign
office. The leader of the Pakistan People's Party, Zulfikar Ali
Bhutto, was also hostile to the idea, as was the press in general.
Bhutto observed in an article, "An overland link through Pakistan
would give India access to the frontiers of the Soviet Union and under-
mine the strategic importance of this country. . . . If Pakistan opens
its frontiers to India to promote regional commerce, would India allow
Chinese convoys to use the Tibet-Nepal Highway to reach East Pakistan,
Burma and Ceylon through the length and breadth of Indian territory?"
Cited in A. P. Jain, ed., India and the World (Delhi: D. K. Publishing House, 1972), p. 195. See also Dawn, June 3 and 11, 1968. For
the Indian reaction, see The Times of India, September 12 and 16,
1969.

16. Under the Indo-Soviet agreement of March 1970, New
Delhi was to finance the construction of a road from Kandahar, in
Afghanistan, to the Iranian border to link up with another road built
by Iran to Sandar Abbas, on the Persian Gulf.

17. Gromyko said, "The Soviet Union has advanced the idea of setting up a collective security system in Asia. We can now state that the fundamental approach on which our proposal is based--the peace-loving orientation of a security system in Asia and its collective nature-- envisaging the participation of all Asian states in Asian regional co-operation--is meeting with general support." Pravda, October 23, 1970.

18. Within weeks of Brezhnev's June 1969 statement, Peking denounced his Asian collective security proposal as "something . . . picked up from the garbage heap" of the policy of John Foster Dulles with the primary purpose of "encircling" China. Hsinhua, June 28, 1969.

Another sample of Chinese attacks on the Soviet proposal follows:

> The Soviet social imperialists have tried to coerce and cajole Japan into taking part in an "Asian collective security system." The calculations of these men in the Kremlin are that once Japan comes into the "system," it will submit to the Soviet Union and give up its northern territories. And once Japan bites the hook of this so-called "Asian security system," the Soviet Union will get the upper hand in its rivalry with the United States in Asia. Former Japanese Vice-Foreign Minister, Shinsaku Hogen, pointed out on July 26 that the Soviet Union would intensify its offensive against Japan and pro-pose again the setting up of an "Asian security system" following the "European security conference" with the aim of maintaining the status quo of northern territories. (Peking Review, August 29, 1975.)

19. Indira Gandhi, during her visit to Afghanistan in 1968, welcomed South Asian economic cooperation as a contribution to Asian security. The Indian foreign minister, Dinesh Singh, visited Moscow in September 1969. The Indian press speculated that he would discuss Asian collective security with Kosygin. On the eve of the foreign minister's journey, Indira Gandhi observed that India was opposed to a security pact but favored regional economic cooperation. Dinesh Singh, however, declared while he was in Moscow that "India welcomes the proposal of the Soviet Union on the notion of a system of collective security system in Asia," and particularly stressed the system's economic aspects. Pravda, September 21, 1969. In De-cember, however, Dinesh Singh remarked that the Indian government

did not believe in the notion that the big powers act as the "guardian of security for India or its neighbors." The Statesman, December 19, 1969; The Times of India, September 12 and 16, 1969. In February 1972, however, the Indian foreign minister, Swaran Singh, interviewed by Tass, described the Soviet collective security concept as an "initiative aimed at promoting peace and security and reducing international tension." In May he told the Indian parliament that "the idea of collective security for Asia, put forward by the Soviet Union, was good and that the security and stability of the region was essential for the countries concerned." Cited in Basant Chatterjee, Indo-Soviet Friendship (Delhi: S. Chand & Co., 1974), pp. 234-35.

20. U.S. Foreign Policy for the 1970's: The Emerging Pattern of Peace, report by Richard Nixon to Congress (Washington, D.C.: U.S. Government Printing Office, 1972), p. 150.

21. The author learned from authentic Pakistani sources that Kosygin tried hard to win Bhutto away from China and offered substantial economic assistance if he would reduce the relations of Pakistan with Peking. In an interview reported by Karachi radio on March 2, 1973, Bhutto said that "the question was: Asian security against whom? Pakistan wanted to maintain good relations with China as well as the Soviet Union." In 1975, when asked for his views on the Soviet collective Asian security proposal, Bhutto told a Japanese correspondent, "We are not ready for it. But that is Japan's position also. Japan's position and ours are similar on this matter." Dawn, September 12, 1975.

22. Pravda, March 15, 1972. Jukes and Clark, op. cit., stress the "apparent abruptness" of the decision to revive the Asian collective security proposal and ask why it was not mentioned in the articles carried in Soviet journals in December 1971 and January 1972 to mark the first anniversary of the UN General Assembly's Declaration on the Strengthening of International Security. They also wonder why Kosygin made no mention of Asian collective security during the visit of the Bangladesh president, Sheikh Mujibur Rahman, less than two weeks before the visit of the Afghan premier.

23. Dawn, September 12, 1975.

24. Pravda, March 21, 1969.

25. Pravda, December 22, 1972.

26. Pravda, August 16, 1973.

27. The meeting had reached the general "conclusion" that

significant positive changes have taken place in the international situation as a whole. The principles of peaceful coexistence of states with different social systems are finding ever wider international recognition; mutually advantageous

economic ties between the socialist and capitalist countries are expanding and more and more
favorable prospects are opening up for constructive new steps to promote the consolidation of
peace and international security. (Pravda,
August 1, 1973.)

28. Pravda, August 16, 1973.
29. Ibid.
30. Ibid.
31. Ibid.
32. Ibid.
33. Ibid.
34. Pravda, September 23, 1973.
35. Pravda, October 27, 1973.
36. Pravda, November 3, 1973.
37. Ibid.
38. Ibid.
39. Pravda, November 27, 1974.
40. In Soviet international politics, collective security is, in
effect, a "system of relations" among states with different social
systems. It is not a mechanism contrived to punish with collective
superior force a deviant power bent upon committing aggression.
Within the collective security system, the opposing social systems
will continue to compete with one another on a broad, nonmilitary
front. In such an ambience, the steady ascendancy of the socialist
system and corresponding decline of the capitalist system is considered to be historically inevitable. The "change in the correlation of
forces" between socialism and imperialism renders the use of force
in international relations increasingly futile. The "social guarantees"
against war grow "gigantically." See V. Sobakin, "Collective Security: Historical Experience and Modern Times," Kommunist, no. 4
(March 1974), from which the quotation in the text is taken. This
theory is predicated on the assumption that the socialist system will
never use force. How are the nonsocialist states to be convinced
that this has been, is, and will be so?
41. Vladimir Kudryavtsev, "The Road to Peace and Security
in Asia," Moscow News, no. 33 (1972); also, Victor Mayevsky,
"Collective Security in Asia: A Ripe Problem," Pravda, July 1,
1972.

In their security environment, Europe and Asia are so
vastly different that the conclusion of the summit conference on
"security and cooperation" in Europe in August 1975 was not likely
to have much of an impact on Asian affairs. The Soviets, however,
have tried to persuade the Asian countries, as well as themselves,

that the political fallout of the Helsinki Declaration is bound to be
profound in Asia. See Kudryavtsev, "Asia: Problems of Security,"
Pravda, August 28, 1975. He wrote, "Everything that happens in
Europe is echoed, directly or indirectly, in the rest of the world.
. . . The Asian countries have an acute need for peace and security
for their economic and cultural development and for overcoming the
colonial legacy. . . . All this makes the problem of creating a security system in Asia extremely urgent." Kudryavtsev suggested that
the ten principles of international relations incorporated in the Helsinki document could provide a security praxis in Asia. This is a
slight improvement on the skeletal framework that was offered by
Brezhnev in 1972. Some U.S. analysts also believed that the Helsinki document would help Moscow push its security model in Asia.
See Ronald Hilton, "Games Nations Play," New York Times, July 17,
1975. In fact, the impact of the Helsinki Declaration on Asia has
been marginal.

42. Ian Clark, "Soviet Concept of Asian Security--from Balance 'Between' to Balance 'Within'," Pacific Community 7, no. 2
(1976). Clark has probably been the most persistent student of the
Soviet security model for Asia and has come out with some interesting insights into Soviet strategic thinking.

43. For Soviet views of the Southeast Asian neutralization proposal, see Kudryavtsev, "Southeast Asia at a Fork in the Road,"
Izvestia, January 7, 1972. He wrote, "Possibly neutralization would
be conducive to the creation of a system of collective security in
Asia; the proposal for this system is cherished by all those who seek
the normalization of the situation in Asia and the ensuring of peace
and security in that region." See also V. Matveyev, "For Collective
Security in Asia," Izvestia, January 6, 1972; V. Pavlovsky, "Problems of Regionalism in Asia," International Affairs, no. 4 (April
1969); and Pavlovsky, "Collective Security: The Way to Peace in
Asia," International Affairs, no. 7 (July 1972).

Concerning Soviet support for a Persian Gulf security system, see Moscow Radio in Persian 1630 GMT, January 23, 1975.

In pursuance of Soviet collective security diplomacy, the
proposal was formally put forward by a Soviet delegate at the March
1972 session of the UN Economic Commission for Asia and the Far
East (ECAFE) in Bangkok, while a roving Soviet ambassador sounded
several Southeast Asian governments on the proposal at the same
time. Bangkok Post, March 21, 1972. At the Paris peace talks,
Soviet and Polish delegates pushed the Asian collective security concept, apparently without support of Hanoi. The Indian Express, February 28, 1972.

44. Matveyev, one of the leading analysts of Asian security affairs, observed in Izvestia on January 6, 1972, that "it is practically

inconceivable to build a system of collective security on a compara-
tively small and restricted area." However, no Soviet analyst has
said categorically that there should be a pan-Asian security system.
Although Brezhnev and his colleagues have used the singular in their
speeches and statements, Soviet analysts have been giving the impression that what is practicable is a series of regional security
systems.

45. Kei Wakaizumi, "Japan's Role in International Society:
Implications for Southeast Asia," in Japan as an Economic Power
and its Implications for Southeast Asia, ed. Kernial Singh Sandhu
and Eileen P. T. Tang (Singapore: Singapore University Press,
1974), pp. 75-87; Yoshikazu Sakamoto, "Changing Japanese Attitude
Toward World Affairs," Peace Research in Japan (Tokyo: University
of Tokyo, 1971); Shinkichi Eto, "Japan and America in Asia During
the Seventies," Japan Interpreter 7, nos. 3 and 4 (Summer-Autumn
1972).

In December 1970 the chairman of the Japanese Socialist
Party (JSP), Tomoni Narita, after his return from a visit to Moscow,
announced at a press conference that the JSP supported collective
security in Asia. He wanted Japan to convene a conference of Asian
countries to devise a collective security system. Mainichi, December 21, 1970. The JSP is the only Japanese political party to have
taken a positive stand on the Soviet model.

46. Choudhury, India, Pakistan, Bangladesh and Major
Powers: Politics of a Divided Subcontinent, op. cit.

47. Pravda, March 18, 1972.

48. When a coup in July 1973 overthrew the Afghan monarchy
and a republican regime was proclaimed with Daud Khan as president, some people saw the Soviet Union behind this event. Daud had
the backing of the Afghan military, which is equipped almost entirely
with Soviet-made weapons and whose officers are trained in the USSR.
However, even Daud has not formally committed himself to the Soviet
security model.

The former Bangladesh foreign minister, M. A. Samad,
who presided over the fifth commission of the World Peace Congress
in Moscow in October 1973, was given by some Soviet officials a
draft of an Asian collective security treaty for his own private reading. An Indian participant at the Congress, who gave the author this
information, added that the same draft had been shown by Soviet officials to a number of Asian governments, including the governments
of Pakistan, India, and Afghanistan. However, the author could not
get confirmation of this report from any other source. Asked about
it in Dacca in early 1975, Samad, who had since lost his cabinet
post, said, "No comment."

An international conference was held in Dacca in May
1973 to discuss the concept of Asian collective security. It was

organized by the "peace" front and attended by delegates from more
than 20 countries. The final document, however, made no reference
to the Soviet collective security proposal, and Pravda, in a commentary on May 29, said that the conference noted "considerable difficulties" in the way of a collective security system in Asia. Smaller
and much less publicized "international" seminars on collective Asian
security have taken place at Aden, New Delhi, and Katmandu.

The Moscow visit of the prime minister of Sri Lanka in
November 1974 led to joint support for the principles of peaceful coexistence without any mention of collective security. Pravda, November 17, 1974.

49. Pravda, August 3, 1973.

50. See the interpretation of the treaty in an "advertisement"
run by the Soviet embassy in New Delhi in Indian Express, September
4, 1971. It said that the Indo-Soviet treaty had nothing to do with the
Brezhnev proposal for a collective security system in Asia; its significance was entirely bilateral and mostly developmental. See also
the Pravda editorial of August 11, 1971. It was only in 1972 that the
Soviets openly played up the security aspects of the Indo-Soviet treaty.
See Chapter 4 for further discussion.

51. The author owes this insight to an Indian foreign service
official who asked that he not be identified.

52. Pravda, November 28, 1973.

53. Pravda, December 1, 1973. During Brezhnev's visit the
Soviet Union signed with India a 15-year economic cooperation agreement and an agreement for cooperation between the national planning
organizations of the two countries. Brezhnev's India visit was probably designed to make up the loss of influence the Soviets had suffered in Egypt since 1973, but the absence of Indian support for the
Asian collective security concept seemed to have robbed the visit of
some of its intended success.

54. Podgorny visited Kabul after the coup mentioned in Note
48. The joint communique on his talks with Daud said nothing about
collective security. The Times of India, May 26, 1973.

55. Pravda, October 1972.

56. L. Kutakov, for instance, has recalled in a review article
the Soviet efforts in the 1930s to "involve the United States in the
creation of a collective security system in the Far East and the
Pacific." See his "A Major Contribution to the Study of the History
of International Relations," Kommunist, no. 14 (September 1974).

V. P. Lukin and G. A. Orionova, reviewing Robert A.
Scalapino's Asia and the Major Powers: Implications for the International Order, AEI-Hoover Policy Study No. 3 (Stanford: Hoover
Institute on War, Revolution and Peace, 1972), have suggested "useful" scholarly exchanges on the question of a four-power balance in

the Western Pacific region. See USA: Economics, Politics, Ideology, no. 12 (1973).

57. The Communist Party of Malaysia calls itself "a revolutionary party armed with Marxism-Leninism-Mao Tse-tung thought; it echoes the CCP line about Soviet "social-imperialism." There are two Communist parties in the Philippines; the Moscow-oriented PKP and the Peking-oriented CPP-ML. The PKP projects itself as a nationalist, progressive party following a responsible, parliamentary policy; its leaders offered their cooperation to President Ferdinand Marcos in November 1974. The CPP-ML pursues the line of armed struggle. The most important Communist "front" group in Singapore, the Barisan Sosialis Malaya, has practically no contact with the Soviet Union, though its cadres go to China via Hong Kong. The Communist Party of Thailand (CPT) turned to Peking and Hanoi in the early 1960s for ideological training and logistical support. It remains pro-CCP and is highly critical of the CPSU. Richard F. Staar, ed., Yearbook on International Communist Affairs 1975 (Stanford: Hoover Institute Press, 1975), pp. 376-82, 401-07, 414-21, 425-27. Also Gene Z. Hanrahan, The Communist Struggle in Malaya (Kuala Lumpur: University of Malaya Press, 1971); Justus M. van der Kroef, "Communist Fronts in the Philippines," Problems of Communism, March-April 1967; and U.S., Department of State, Bureau of Intelligence and Research, World Strength of the Communist Party Organizations (Washington, D.C.: U.S. Government Printing Office, 1973).

Strategic parity and a "blue water" navy are the two inputs of Soviet military power that have altered the Washington-Moscow balance of power in favor of the USSR in the 1970s. With a powerful oceangoing navy, the Soviet Union now both looks and acts like a global power. In overall naval strength the Soviets still lag behind the United States; if the naval power of the Atlantic allies of the United States is taken into account, the Western position stands as distinctly superior to that of the Soviet bloc. In spite of this weakness, however, the Soviets have gained or are about to gain in the high seas what they have already gained in strategic arms: the status of a coequal power with the United States. In certain waters, in the eastern Mediterranean and the Indian Ocean for instance, the Soviets have already neutralized U.S. naval power, if they have not established naval superiority.[1] Also, in the northwestern sector of the Indian Ocean, "the Soviets have organized themselves into the position of being the dominant external power, able to display both naval and air forces, and with an amphibian capacity which can be strengthened as required."[2] From this dominant position, the Soviets have adopted an assertive diplomatic role in the strategic Persian Gulf region. In the 1970s Soviet naval power has been actually deployed as an instrument of coercive, preventive, and friendly diplomacy in the Asian-African basin of the Indian Ocean. The political climate in this basin is no longer favorable for U.S. naval intervention; nor is the U.S. political will to intervene as strong in the 1970s as it used to be in the earlier decades. The Soviet Union has been trying to take advantage of both factors to project its naval power in the Indian Ocean basin.

Soviet naval power has generated a global debate because it brings the might of the Soviet state in full view of all international actors, big and small, close to the USSR or far away. In the Western world the debate centers on the quantitative and qualitative reaches of Soviet naval power and on the doctrine that lies behind it as well as the objectives for which it is being used. In Asia each country is required to take into account this newest differential in the global power calculus and to examine whether, why, and to what extent its own strategic interests clash or converge with Soviet naval power. The debate in the Western countries, particularly the United States, has generated two main views, which one strategic analyst has categorized as "alarmist" and "realist." While the alarmists see in the Soviet naval penetration of the oceans and seas a menacing threat to Western political and economic interests and urge decisive countermeasures even at the risk of an expensive naval arms race, the realists consider the latest development in Soviet military power as inevitable and urge mutual restraint leading, hopefully, to accords on naval arms control, at least in the Indian Ocean.[3] At the beginning of 1976 the U.S. defense department was reported to have come to the conclusion that "in most of the scenarios, an acceptable maritime balance of power currently exists" between the two power blocs, even if not between the two superpowers. The Pentagon also concluded that "the United States and its allies deploy naval forces in peacetime which are, and are seen to be, at least equal in striking power and superior in sea-control capability to the naval forces deployed by the Soviet Union and its allies."[4]

In the Asian-African basin of the Indian Ocean, the debate is not so much on the Soviet naval buildup as on the beginning of a superpower naval arm race. This debate centers on the concept of turning the Indian Ocean region into a zone of peace. The peace-zone concept, however, is pitted against not only the competing naval power of the major nations but also the rising naval aspirations of the principal regional powers, India, Iran, and Indonesia.

The Soviet navy is certainly far from having the capability that is needed to "control" the seas, but it has reached a capability that can "deny" that control to the United States. The current Soviet objective is to gain a parity of effective strength with its adversary on the waters of the planet. In 1971 Brezhnev said that Moscow would be willing to "solve" the problem of a great-power naval arms race, but only if it got an equal bargain.[5] As a price for naval arms control accords in such politically sensitive waterways as the Indian Ocean, the Soviets demand the elimination of the "military bases of the imperialist powers." In the annual UN debates on the proposal for a peace zone in the Indian Ocean area, the Soviets have made it clear that a peace zone with the preservation of Western military bases "would not put the USSR on an equal footing" and would be injurious to the interests of the socialist bloc.[6]

SOVIET NAVAL CAPABILITY

In January 1976 the Pentagon "quietly abandoned," largely for financial reasons, the long-standing goal of expanding the U.S. fleet to 600 ships by 1985. To justify this decision, the Pentagon publicized its revised view of Moscow's naval expansion program, which was markedly less alarmist than the views aired before a congressional committee by the chief of naval operations, Admiral James L. Holloway, III. The revised Pentagon view was that the Soviets had decided to stabilize their naval force levels in order to concentrate on two areas of the greatest importance to Moscow, which were antiship capability and antisubmarine warfare. The Pentagon believed that in spite of a large shipbuilding capability the current Soviet fleet of 550 surface ships and submarines would remain fairly stable in the next few years.[7]

Financial limitations must inhibit the Soviet naval expansion program also, especially because of the recent shift of emphasis to the building of a strike force with larger, more combatworthy, and therefore costlier ships. The "forward" naval strategy advocated in 1972 by the chief of the Soviet navy, Admiral Sergei G. Gorshkov, is now symbolized by the aircraft carrier.[8] The Soviets have already launched two aircraft carriers, the Kiev and the Minsk, each displacing 45,000 tons; a third is under construction. Western analysts believe that eventually six Kiev-class carriers will be built. These ships are not attack carriers comparable to the U.S. carriers of the Nimitz, Forrestal, or Midway class; nor will they be nuclear powered or fly long-range attack aircraft. They are seen by most Western analysts as primarily defensive, flying vertical take-off and landing (VTOL) aircraft in defense of surface ships and on antisubmarine missions. They will be able to carry about 70 aircraft, in comparison with the nearly 100 larger planes flown from a U.S. attack carrier. Nevertheless, these aircraft carriers give the Soviet fleet the ability to project surface sea power beyond the cover of shore-based aircraft. With these carriers flying strike and fighter aircraft, the operational area of the Soviet fleet can be markedly expanded. The deployment of three aircraft carriers would also have an important political impact.[9]

The Soviet navy held its second global exercise in five years in April 1975, with about 220 ships and a higher level of air activity than in previous exercises. All four fleets, Northern, Baltic, Black Sea, and Pacific, took part. The purpose was evidently to demonstrate its strike capability, about which many Western military observers were still somewhat skeptical.[10]

In building naval power, the Soviet decision makers have attached the greatest importance to the overriding task of defending the

socialist bloc, particularly the USSR, from the devastating danger
posed by the introduction of the U.S. Polaris-Triton-Poseidon fleet.
In the first years of the 1960s the emphasis was on nuclear submarines backed by missile-armed aircraft and on an antisubmarine
defense system to counter the Polaris missile. In the mid-1960s
the decision to substantially augment the number of surface ships
was taken. However, once a major surface capability was acquired,
the assertive use of the naval forces in distant areas could no longer
be refused. The decision to this effect was probably taken in 1967.
The decision to build aircraft carriers was probably influenced by
the great political gains of forward deployment since the Arab-
Israeli war of June 1967. [11]

The Soviet leaders now recognize that a naval force capable of
quick and effective deployment in areas far away from Soviet shores
is essential for the exercise of Soviet global power. Admiral Sergei
G. Gorshkov, who is also a deputy defense minister, observed in
his famous articles on the growth of Soviet naval power and policy
that "all of the modern powers are maritime states. . . . Navies
have always played a great role in strengthening the independence of
littoral states, and those without navies have not been able to hold
the status of great powers for long." [12] In a foreword to a Soviet
naval publication, Gorshkov asserted in December 1974 that as a
result of the policy decisions made in the 1960s the Soviet Union had
acquired within the short period of a decade, "a long-range fleet and
a major strategic weapon" capable of opposing a strong naval enemy,
and of exercising substantial influence on "the course and outcome
of an armed struggle on the great oceans and continental theaters of
military operations." [13] The initial concentration on a nuclear missile fleet was designed to create a strategic naval offensive force
that could destroy "major enemy groupings of the enemy, and above
all [crush] his military-economic potential." [14] Having achieved
that objective, the Soviet navy has embarked upon the second stage
of its expansion with the goal of achieving naval combat capability of
a global character. The emphasis, during this phase, is on the
building up of a strike force. "In the future, clearly the strike force
will become the main method of utilizing naval forces," Gorshkov
declared. [15]

Elaborating on this theme a Soviet naval analyst observed,
"The moment will come in combat operations when it is necessary
to consolidate the success achieved, to occupy and hold a certain
space, which will require a landing on the enemy's territory by
large troop groups." [16] He specifically mentioned the U.S. landings
in Korea and Vietnam.

The acquisition of a powerful blue water navy enables the
Soviet leaders to speak about the global reach of Soviet power much

in the same manner, albeit with different rhetoric, as U.S. statesmen used to speak of the worldwide frontiers of U.S. power in the
1950s and 1960s. Brezhnev, in his report to the 24th congress of
the CPSU, claimed that "the founding of a contemporary fleet of the
Soviet country has forever marked the end of the high-seas dominance
of the fleets of Western governments. The interests of Communist
construction demand this."[17] A year later Gorshkov, in a startling
sweep of Soviet strategic thinking, linked the local wars in the national liberation zone to the security and state interests of the entire
socialist community and, by implication, brought the local conflicts
within the operational jurisdiction of the Soviet navy.

> Today these wars can be regarded as a special form
> of the manifestation of the "flexible response" strat-
> egy. In seizing individual areas of the globe and in
> interfering in the internal affairs of countries, the
> imperialists are striving to gain new advantageous
> strategic positions in the world arena, which they
> need for the struggle with socialism and in order to
> facilitate carrying out missions in the struggle with
> the developing national liberation movement. There-
> fore local wars can be regarded as a display of the
> more decisive operating methods of imperialism
> against the movement of national independence and
> progress.[18]

Gorshkov has outlined the principal objectives of the use of
Soviet naval power as follows. First, the naval power is intended to
defend the socialist community from external aggression, to protect
the interests of this community beyond its borders, and to demonstrate the economic and military might of the Soviet Union in all
parts of the globe.

Second, a powerful navy would enable the USSR, as it has other
powers throughout history, to "solve problems of ties between peoples," that is, to reward allies, create new friends, and punish
enemies.

Third, the navy would provide an effective support to negotiations with Soviet adversaries.

> Many examples from history attest to the fact that
> problems of foreign policy have always been solved
> on the basis of taking into account the military might
> of the "negotiating" sides, and that the potential
> military power of one state or another, built up in
> accordance with its economic capabilities and

political orientation, have permitted it to conduct a
policy advantageous to itself and to the detriment of
other states not possessing a corresponding military power. [19]

THE INDIAN OCEAN

In terms of each of these objectives of Soviet naval power, the
Indian Ocean is seen by the Soviets as an area of vital interest and
concern. Through this ocean flows a considerable part of the Soviet
east-west internal trade, and its importance for Soviet domestic
trade will increase in the 1980s, when larger quantities of Siberian
oil will have to be transported across the seas to European Russia.
The Asian-African basin of the Indian Ocean is politically important
to the USSR. The Soviet Union is bound to three countries in the
basin by treaty relations, and it has trade and economic linkages
with almost every country. The strategic wealth of the countries of
this basin is becoming increasingly attractive, if not essential, for
the development of the Soviet economy. The ocean littoral falls
within the national liberation zone and contains much of the "vanguard" of the national liberation struggle. The imperialist powers
are involved in the local conflicts and wars, creating actual and potential clients for the Soviet Union. The U.S. Polaris-Poseidon
fleet in the Indian Ocean poses a direct nuclear threat to the deep
reaches of the USSR. A demonstration of Soviet naval power in the
Indian Ocean, where the U.S. navy is not in a sea-control position,
could help Moscow in its strategic arms control negotiations with
Washington.

Soviet military and political analysts frequently refer to the
economic, political, and strategic importance of the Indian Ocean
basin. They make no secret of the Soviet readiness to help the
littoral countries dislodge the Western powers from their "stranglehold" of the basin's wealth. The Indian Ocean basin, writes a Soviet
military analyst, is "one of the strongest resources of raw materials
(oil, rubber, tin, gold, diamonds, and so forth), from whose rapa-
cious exploitation American and other Western monopolies derive
fabulous profits."[20]

In the Persian Gulf region itself, notes another Soviet military
analyst more specifically, the U.S. monopolies reap an annual profit
of $1.5 billion for an investment of $2 billion in the petroleum industry. Of the 40 or so types of strategic raw materials imported
by the United States, this analyst goes on, "around 20 are imported
from the Indian Ocean area."[21]

In the 1980s the industrialized capitalist countries, including
the United States, notes a third Soviet military analyst, will need
about 4 billion tons of oil per year, 70 percent of which will have to
be imported from the Gulf region. The sea lanes of the Indian Ocean
are of crucial importance for the capitalist countries' foreign trade.
"The shipment of cargo along the routes--Persian Gulf (191 million
tons per year), Europe and South and Southeast Asia, and Europe and
Australia and New Zealand--have attained particularly great significance. To this might be added cargo shipments from the Persian
Gulf and West Africa to Japan (about 145 million tons a year), South
Africa, and the Pacific Ocean. "[22]

Purporting to quote the Military Review, one Soviet analyst
declares that "the country which can influence this region in the future . . . and control the new center of the world will be the dominant force throught the world. "[23]

Soviet analysts see, or want the leaders of the littoral countries to see, the Indian Ocean basin as still dominated by the imperialist powers. Noting that the Indian Ocean basin has 37 naval
bases and refueling stations, "many more than the littoral countries
can use for their own naval forces";[24] 100 seaports, most of them
exporting strategic raw materials; and 900 airfields, with a total
capacity of up to 25,000 aircraft, one Soviet naval expert says that
across "the entire coastal part" of the Indian Ocean is a "large semi-
circle of Anglo-American military bases"[25] extending from South
Africa to Australia. When the naval base on Diego Garcia is completed, all these strong points, he adds, will form a single

> strategic triangle. . . . Apart from the large semi-
> circle of bases, there is also a group of important
> [imperialist] bases in the northwestern part of the
> Indian Ocean. These include, in particular, the
> U.S. base at Bahrain and the British base at Masira.
> . . . . The network of bases . . . cannot be re-
> garded as an isolated case. It is an integral part
> of the imperialist powers' unified base system, and
> its aim is to unify their military presence in two
> other regions of the world--the Atlantic and the
> Pacific. [26]

The imperialist powers use, or would like to use, their Indian
Ocean bases for "broad maneuver" by their armed forces, for
"rapid transport of their forces from one ocean to another," and
"for the building and concentration of forces in any particular region
in order to exert pressure on the independent states of Africa and
South and Southeast Asia. "[27]

The Soviets therefore take a dim view of the upcoming U.S.
naval base on the island of Diego Garcia and have sought to make the
greatest possible use of the objections registered by many of the
littoral countries to the building of this base. In attacking the U.S.
decision to build the base, Soviet propaganda has been projecting to
the littoral countries the danger of U.S. intervention in their internal
affairs and to the United States the misgivings and apprehensions of
the littoral nations with regard to the base. The latter projection
is obviously designed to strengthen opposition within the United
States itself to the building of a large naval and air base on the
Indian Ocean island. [28]

This opposition has come from several important sources,
since it goes to the heart of the U.S. foreign policy dilemma of the
post-Vietnam period, which is whether the United States should extend or contract its global commitments and military burdens. The
strongest advocate of the base continues to be the U.S. navy. Admiral R. Zumwalt, Jr., then chief of naval operations, told a congressional committee in March 1974 that without the Diego Garcia
base the United States would not be able to project military power
into the Indian Ocean region. He saw in this region the potential to
produce major shifts in the global power balance in the next decade.
He added, "It follows that we must have the ability to influence
events in that area, and the capability to deploy our military power
in the region is an essential element of such influence."[29] Responding to one of the main objections raised in Congress, Zumwalt
argued that expansion of the Diego Garcia facility would not set off
a naval arms race in the Indian Ocean, since the Soviet Union was
already "on the move" in the region and was expanding its naval
presence. The Soviet Union, he said, possessed a support system
in the region "substantially more extensive than that of the United
States,"[30] with access to harbors or airfields in Somalia, Iraq, and
Southern Yemen.

Zumwalt's view was contested in a report by a panel of UN experts released on May 11, 1975. Appointed by the secretary-general
at the request of the General Assembly, the panel said that the construction of a full-fledged naval and air base on Diego Garcia would
almost certainly prompt the Soviet Union to seek a similar installation in the area. "The instabilities inherent in the Indian Ocean area
will not easily permit a mutual balance to be maintained successfully by the two great powers over a period of time. And the chances
of great power rivalry interacting with local conflicts, and then escalating, are high."[31]

In Congress the request by the Administration for funds for
building the Diego Garcia base met with strong opposition, and in
late 1975 only a relatively small amount was approved by Congress

to keep the construction work going. The Administration took the view that the base was needed to ease the logistic burden of supporting naval operations in the Indian Ocean. It argued that the United States must offset a growing Soviet naval presence in that ocean and that a projection of U.S. military power into those waters would promote stability in the region and protect the sea lanes leading to the Middle Eastern oil supplies. The opponents of the base saw in it "an extension of a policy of the United States trying to be policeman of the world,"[32] and feared that the base could be the "stepping stone to a three-ocean navy."[33] They noted that in November 1974 the nations bordering on the Indian Ocean had issued a statement opposing the construction of a U.S. naval base on Diego Garcia.

Congressional support for funding the construction of the Diego Garcia base over a number of years gained somewhat after then U.S. Defense Secretary Schlesinger displayed before the Senate Armed Services Committee in the summer of 1975, pictures taken by a U-2 plane in April of the Soviet naval "facility" at the Somalian port of Berbera, which commands the strategic approaches to the Red Sea. Schlesinger claimed that the Soviet Union was "in the process of establishing a significant new facility capable of supporting their naval and air activities in the northwestern Indian Ocean."[34]

The U-2 pictures enabled the Administration to win a point in its debate with Congress, but it did not answer the doubts and questions that still remained in American minds.

> Why have the Soviets in the past six years gradually expanded their naval presence in the Indian Ocean and why do they now seem intent on establishing a support facility in Somalia? Is their purpose merely to extend their geopolitical influence into the Indian Ocean by showing the flag in much the same manner that Western navies here have been doing for decades or do they have a more sinister motive of interdicting the crucial sea lanes leading out of the Persian Gulf? . . .
> But are the Soviets really likely to take the risk of attacking Western shipping when the price may be an all-out nuclear war? Cannot the United States already project naval power in the Indian Ocean if it wants? By constructing a base at Diego Garcia, is not the United States contributing to a superpower naval race in the Indian Ocean, which may or may not have been started by the Russians?[35]

Neither in the Western countries nor in Asia are there uniform, generally acceptable answers to these questions. The analysts are as divided as are the political leaders, and therein lies the biggest advantage of the Soviet Union. In the Cold-War days, any signal of assertive Soviet power united the Western allies and the majority of their Asian clients to a rigid and firm response of resistance. In the 1970s the non-Soviet world is split and splintered; even in the United States the reaction to the rapid buildup of Soviet naval power is mixed. On the whole the "alarmists" may claim more headlines, but the "realists" seem to determine policy decisions.

On their own part, the Soviet Union has not tried to conceal its naval doctrine or naval policy. The doctrine, as Robert W. Herrick has noted, is sea denial rather than sea control. In the Third World the policy is to build a strong Soviet naval interventionist capability in order to neutralize Western naval power rather than to interdict the highways of Western maritime trade and commerce. The policy, in short, is not to provoke a nuclear war with the West but to persuade the West not to provoke a nuclear war with the USSR by hurting Soviet interests in those areas in which Soviet diplomacy has developed a stake. The Soviet policy, wherever possible, is to establish forward positions of Soviet influence through timely, decisive intervention, in the knowledge that the Western response would not lead to a head-on clash.

The Soviet leaders believe that objective changes in the international situation, rather than a sudden reasonableness on the part of Western statesmen, have made it possible for them to penetrate the high seas. The first and foremost objective condition is the enhanced strength of the socialist system, the progressive buildup of the military and economic power of the Soviet bloc. The second factor, parallel to this, is the deepening crisis of the capitalist system, the decline in the economic and military power of the Western powers and the divisions in their ranks. The third factor is the political and military successes of the national liberation struggle in its numerous conflicts with imperialism. These successes, according to Soviet analysts, have strengthened the "democratic, national-patriotic and progressive" forces in the national liberation zone and brought about a general polarization between the developing nations and the imperialist powers. The developing nations find in the USSR a source of economic and political help, and as Soviet relations with these countries grow and deepen, their ties with the imperialist system tend to loosen. Countries belonging to the national liberation zone, Soviet analysts claim, find in the Soviet naval presence on the high seas an assurance against imperialist intervention in their internal or interstate conflicts. The Soviets, then, concede that in peacetime the role of the Soviet navy in the blue

waters of the world is manifestly political. One Soviet military analyst wrote as follows in July 1973: "The presence of our ships . . .
constantly inhibits the violation of the peaceful atmosphere of this
area [the Middle East] and plays a restraining role. If our foes examine our navy ever more frequently and see in it an interference
with their adventurist schemes, this means that it justifies the mission assigned."[36]

The political mission of the Soviet navy has been demonstrated
several times in the Indian Ocean region in the 1970s. During the
India-Pakistan war of December 1971 the Soviet Union clearly used
its Indian Ocean fleet for coercive diplomacy.[37] The next year
naval power was employed for similar diplomatic objectives in
Iraq.[38] In 1973 the Soviet fleet in the Indian Ocean supplemented
the much larger fleet in the Mediterranean, to neutralize the U.S.
fleet in the Arab-Israeli war. In January 1976 a Soviet flotilla
cruised close to the Angolan coastline as the OAU debated its role
in the Angolan civil war. These diplomatic uses of naval power
made a considerable impact on the littoral countries as well as on
Western observers of Soviet foreign policy operations. Wrote the
French sovietologist, Michel Tatu, "Landings of the type carried out
by the United States in Lebanon in 1958 and in the Dominican Republic in 1965 would be more hazardous, if not entirely out of the question, today. On the other hand, a landing of Soviet 'marines' to support some 'progressive' regime or to help some minority faction in a
power struggle is no longer inconceivable."[39]

The use of the Soviet navy for friendship diplomacy was seen
in Bangladesh when a 20-unit fleet stayed for two years (1972-74) in
the Bay of Bengal to clear mines and salvage ships at the ports of
Chittagong and Cox's Bazar, free of cost.[40] After completing the
Bangladesh mine-clearing operations, the Soviet vessels entered the
Red Sea in June 1974 to assist with the clearing of mines from the
Straits of Jubal at the southern end of the Gulf of Suez. A U.S.
strategic expert has described this kind of operation as follows:
"By entering quietly, by building up a presence gradually, and by
performing tasks for which it will be appreciated, the Soviet Union
has already begun to establish a favorable basis from which its
presence [in the Indian Ocean] could easily--and without serious political risks--be expanded."[41]

In terms of naval and air bases, port visits, and ship days,
the Soviet presence in the Indian Ocean is still much smaller than
the naval presence of the three major Western powers, the United
States, Britain, and France. The competition, however, is between
the two superpowers. The British naval role has been progressively
diminishing, and it is not certain whether the French would place
their facilities at the disposal of the United States in the event of a

Soviet-American naval confrontation in the Indian Ocean area.
Neither of the superpowers can control the Indian Ocean; each, however, can deny the ocean to the other. The question is, what kind
of a naval arms race can be generated by the competitive sea-denial
policies of the two superpowers.[42] The report released in 1974 by
the UN panel of experts shows clearly that while the naval presence
of the Western powers in the Indian Ocean area was still far greater
than that of the USSR, the Soviet presence had been steadily increasing during the 1970s.

     Since 1970 a typical deployment of Soviet ships has consisted
of one or two destroyers, possibly with surface-to-air missiles, or
sometimes one cruiser of the Kresta or Kynda class; two fleet mine-
sweepers; two oilers; two to four supply ships; and two hydrographic
or oceanographic ships. The submarines are normally F-class deisel
powered attack ships or sometimes E-II-class nuclear powered
cruise-missile firing units. The Soviets also operate up to 40 fishing trawlers in the Indian Ocean, some of which are presumably
fitted with electronic surveillance equipment. Ships are relieved at
about six-monthly intervals; normally, therefore, the force is larger
only for a brief period between the arrival of fresh ships and the
departure of the others.

     On two occasions during the early 1970s the Soviets deployed
a sizable combat presence in the Indian Ocean. The first was during
the 1971 India-Pakistan war, when there were 20 warships, 13 surface ships, and 7 submarines. Four of these ships, some with
surface-to-surface missiles, were sent after the United States had
dispatched a task force headed by the aircraft carrier Enterprise.
"As soon as the American ships had left the Indian Ocean, the extra
Soviet warships also left. The India-Pakistan war led therefore to
record force levels for both the United States and the USSR--14 warships and auxiliaries for the United States and 26 for the Soviet
Union."[43]

     The second occasion was when an exceptional number of Soviet
ships were sent into the Indian Ocean in October 1973 during the
Arab-Israeli war. The Soviet navy then dispatched additional warships to make up its squadron in the Indian Ocean from the usual
number of less than six to a maximum number of ten surface ships
and four submarines. In March 1974 the Soviet deployment in the
Indian Ocean consisted of six surface ships and five submarines.[44]
In 1975 the Soviet naval presence generally consisted of close to
30 ships, including eight or nine warships. The Soviet helicopter
carrier Leningrad was deployed in the northwestern sector of the
ocean in March 1975.

     Western analysts believe that the reopening of the Suez Canal
in June 1975 has enabled the Soviet Union to double its Indian Ocean

fleet, if it so decides, with far greater ease and at much less cost
than it could during the closure of the canal. The UN experts, however, saw no special benefit accruing to the USSR as a result of the
reopening of the canal. The Suez Canal cuts 7,000 miles off the
South African route of the Soviet navy and enables Moscow to base
its Indian Ocean fleet on the Black Sea instead of at Valdivostok; but
the canal also enables the U.S. Sixth Fleet, with its home port at
Piraeus in Greece, to send its ships into the Indian Ocean with
greater ease and convenience. [45]

According to a Soviet military analyst, long cruises in the
southern latitudes have become a daily matter for the Soviet navy. [46]
However, the United States has a big lead over the USSR in the number of naval visits, though the number of ship-days spent in the
Indian Ocean indicates a stronger Soviet presence. According to the
UN report, Soviet ships paid 162 calls to Indian Ocean ports between
1968 and 1971, while in 1971 alone ships of the U.S. navy visited
157 ports in 20 countries in the Indian Ocean region, excluding
Thailand and Bahrain. In 1973 the USSR had about 9,000 ship-days
in the Indian Ocean, counting all types of ships; this was about double
the totals for 1970 and 1971. The number of ship-days for the U.S.
navy in the Indian Ocean in 1973 was over 2,000. "The statistics
can be chosen to support various arguments. Numbers of ship-days
can be used to indicate a greater presence of Soviet ships than
American ones. But frequency of port visits can be used to indicate
a greater American presence." [47]

INFRASTRUCTURE

The United States has a much stronger and larger logistical
naval infrastructure in the Indian Ocean region than has the Soviet
Union, but the Soviet infrastructure appears to be politically stronger.
The U.S. base facilities relate both to conventional naval war and to
strategic nuclear war. The U.S. nuclear war base facilities are
located at the North West Cape in South Africa, at the Kagnew Station
base near Asmara in Ethiopia, at the island of Diego Garcia, and at
two bases in Australia. [48] Conventional base facilities exist at
Bahrain in the Persian Gulf, at Asmara, in Mauritius, at Mahe, in
Australia, and on Diego Garcia. [49]

However, a study conducted by the Pentagon in 1975 expressed
concern over the reduced ability of the United States "to project
military force" into the Western Pacific and Indian Oceans in the
post-Vietnam era. In the changed strategic situation, said the study,
many installations on which U.S. naval and air forces had been
based in the past "will be unavailable and the ability of the area

powers to challenge United States forces will be enhanced. "[50] The scope of military missions in the area is therefore "likely to be seriously limited unless steps are taken to develop alternative, forward, politically invulnerable support bases for American operations. "[51]

The logistical infrastructure of the Soviet fleet consists of a chain of supply points, deep-sea mooring buoys, and fleet anchorages established around the entire western and eastern coastline of the Indian Ocean. The Soviet navy has floating buoys off the Seychelles and Mauritius and in the Chagos archipelago, as well as north and south of Socotra. The Soviet Union claims that it has no naval and air bases in the Indian Ocean littoral, but this is dismissed in the Western countries as mere propaganda. In the northwestern sector of the ocean the Soviet Union has established its naval presence most clearly and has treaty-bound friendships with India, Iraq, and Somalia. It has also built and developed port facilities at Aden, Mukulla, and Hodeida in Southern Yemen and at Umm Qasr in Iraq, with facilities in excess of what these two countries can utilize. The USSR has built a military airfield near Mogadishu and has acquired bunkering facilities, although these are by no means exclusive, at Mauritius and Singapore. In a daring diplomatic initiative, the Soviet government asked the labor government in Australia for facilities to build a satellite tracking station in that country. This was refused by Melbourne, but half-way between Australia and South Africa, Soviet and French scientists have been carrying out atmospheric and metereological research on the Kerguelen Islands. The Soviets are also conducting oceanographic and other intelligence activity in the Indian Ocean. A dramatic example of this came in January 1971 at the time of the British Commonwealth prime ministers' conference in Singapore. Four Soviet ships sailed through the Malacca Straits in full view of the prime ministers, perhaps monitoring some of the port's communication.

The most controversial Soviet "base" or "facility" is located at Berbera, Somalia. As already noted, the U-2 pictures taken in April 1975 disclosed an extensive Soviet-controlled "facility"; this was, however, denied by both the Soviet Union and Somalia. The Somali government invited U.S. reporters and congressmen to visit the area, but when they did arrive at Berbera they were refused access to the facility. This facility probably includes a capability to communicate with submerged hunter-killer submarines, both nuclear and conventional. This would give the Soviet Union at least facility in the Indian Ocean region that is related to nuclear strategic war.

Drew Middleton quoted Pentagon officials in April 1975 for the report that the Soviet Union was stockpiling long-range guided missiles at Berbera. These so-called cruise missiles were said to be

intended for the surface ships and the submarines of the Soviet
squadron deployed in the Indian Ocean. "Now that the Soviet squadron
is assured of rapid resupply of its cruise missiles . . . the Russians and their Arab friends from Iraq to Southern Yemen could in
an international crisis control the exits from the Persian Gulf and
from the Suez Canal and Red Sea supply lines."[52] Pentagon officials
felt, according to Middleton, that "the accumulation of Soviet and
Arab military strength in the area offers the Soviet Union strategic
options that would be serious challenges to both Israel and the United
States in another [Arab-Israeli] war."[53]

THE PERSIAN GULF

For all strategic purposes the Middle East and the Persian
Gulf regions are strongly interlinked. The center of oil power is the
Persian Gulf region, but the Arab countries of this region are, with-
out exception, deadly hostile to Israel, which is the political outpost
of the United States in the Middle East. Since the 1973 Arab-Israeli
war, the Shah of Iran has also adopted a pro-Arab, if not an anti-
Israeli, posture, further weakening the U.S. political base in the
Gulf region. Iran and Saudi Arabia are friendly with the United
States, the latter more than the former, but both expect Washington
to bring about a Middle Eastern peace that would satisfy the major
Arab demands, which are Israeli withdrawal from all, or most, of
the territory occupied in the June 1967 war and a national home for
the Palestinians. Most of the Persian Gulf countries have been
arming feverishly in the 1970s, primarily with U.S. cooperation,
but paradoxically this makes the U.S. position in the Gulf less rather
than more stable in the absence of a settlement of the Arab-Israeli
conflict. Furthermore, the radical regimes in Iraq and South Yemen
exert a certain polarizing impact on the Gulf region, while the ambition of Iran to become the undisputed dominant security provider in
the region tends to make the Shah independent of both the United
States and the USSR, rather than a strategic ally of Washington.

The only U.S. naval base in the Persian Gulf is in Bahrain,
for which, in 1975, the United States agreed to pay the ruler, Sheikh
Mohammed, six times the amount it had been paying before, without
any assurance of the stability of the base. The Bahrain base is used
for the Middle Eastern force of the U.S. navy. The installation
covers a 10-acre space with piers and limited airport facilities.
The naval force stationed at the base consists of two destroyers,
two aircraft, and a 500-foot command vessel armed with three-inch
guns. There are 475 U.S. military personnel. The naval force
has important electronic equipment that monitors military traffic

throughout the region. The navy ships cruise the Persian Gulf and also visit ports from the Gulf of Aqaba and the Red Sea to the Indian subcontinent.

In 1973, during the Arab-Israeli war, the ruler of Bahrain announced that he would abrogate the agreement under which the United States used the base, requiring the U.S. navy to pull out within a year. The ruler, however, reconsidered his decision in 1974 at U.S. request and permitted the agreement to continue at a much higher financial cost to Washington. The base, however, continued to remain politically unpopular not only in the Gulf region but also in Bahrain itself. Bahrain, with little oil, is the one Gulf country that has not embarked on an arms buildup program. Its parliament, with limited power, has a radical political temper. In March 1975 the ruler's foreign minister told the New York Times that the continued use of the naval facilities by the United States would depend on the U.S. attitude toward the Arab cause in the Middle East.[54] The British foreign secretary, James Callaghan, told reporters at Doha in November 1975 that the United States would "soon" close down the Bahrain naval base.[55]

The importance to Iran of the U.S. base in Bahrain diminished after border and other accords were reached in the spring of 1975 between Tehran and Baghdad. As long as Iraq remained an enemy, with its strong military, political, and economic ties with the Soviet Union, the Shah probably wanted the U.S. base at Bahrain to remain. In August 1975, however, the Iranian prime minister, Amir Abbas Hoveida, told the New York Times, "We can keep the seas free and we don't need the presence of the superpowers." The Shah himself had told the same newspaper a year before that "in order to ask the Americans and the Soviets not to be present in the Indian Ocean militarily, we must show that there is no need for them there."[56]

The Soviet leaders have been calling for the withdrawal of the U.S. naval base in Bahrain for a long time. This demand is backed by the argument that there is no Soviet naval base in the Gulf. Soviet economic relations with Bahrain and Kuwait are steadily expanding. In a recent visit to the USSR, the ruler of Kuwait reportedly showed an interest in the purchase of Soviet arms. The accords between Iran and Iraq, as noted, have diffused local tensions in the Persian Gulf. Once the U.S. naval base at Bahrain is withdrawn, the Soviet leaders will be in a better position to bargain with the littoral powers for a coequal status with the United States in a regional security system.

As long as the U.S. naval base on Bahrain exists, the Soviet leaders will continue to take a dim view of the expanding naval power of Iran. As noted, Iran has been building a vast naval base, at an estimated cost of $1 billion, at Charbahar, on its southeastern coast adjoining Pakistan. To the west of Charbahar lie the Persian Gulf and the Strait of Hormuz, where Iran has been building up its military presence to assure the safe passage of oil tankers. The main contract for the Charbahar base has been given to a British concern, but several U.S. firms are also involved. Though financial stringencies have slowed down the progress of naval base construction, Iran continues to expand its navy with U.S. help. The U.S. government advised Congress in 1975 of its decision to sell Iran three diesel-powered submarines of the postwar Tang class, 287-foot craft designed for high speed while submerged. The Iranian government has not disclosed precisely what functions the Charbahar naval base will have, relative to those of the big bases further west at Bushire and Bandar Abbas. Western military analysts predict that Charbahar will serve as a base for certain landing ships, fast patrol boats, and submarines.[57]

The Persian Gulf region is one of the most conflict-prone areas in the world, although no serious interstate conflict has broken out so far. The Shah would like to bring the small sheikhdoms under his influence, if not under his domain. At the invitation of the Sultan of Oman he dispatched several thousand troops to fight the insurgents in Dhofar; these troops are to remain in Dhofar for an indefinite period, even though the insurgency was flushed out in October 1975.[58] Iraq has its claim on Kuwait. Saudi Arabian relations with Iraq are far from friendly. The Saudis would like to extend their domain to the Gulf sheikhdoms. The Union of Arab Emirates continues its precarious existence; its disintegration would please all of the Gulf states except Iran, as well as the Soviet Union.

By extending moral and material support to the insurgents in Dhofar the Soviet Union has maintained its radical image in the volatile Gulf region, but it is more interested in working with "independent" actors, like the Shah if he chooses to lean equally on both the capitalist and socialist blocs and does not permit the imperialist powers to gain military footholds in Iran and in the Gulf region.

In the absence of a regional security system, the dismantling of the U.S. naval presence in the Persian Gulf will be again for the Soviet Union. The Soviet naval presence in the northwestern Indian Ocean and the close Soviet ties with Iraq and good economic and political relations with Iran will make the Soviet presence felt in any interstate or intrastate conflict. It would not be difficult for the Soviet Union to demonstrate support for the forces it favors. In the event of the construction of a regional security system, the overall balance of political forces in the Gulf will not be distinctly in favor of either power bloc, but the Soviet Union would be one of the external powers that would guarantee the security of the region. Soviet analysts expect the social and political forces in the Gulf region to polarize further in the coming years.

In 1969 the Soviets were willing to help Pakistan construct a naval base primarily for submarines at Kwadar, a small peninsula 50 miles east of the Pakistani-Iranian border. This move was seen in India as a reply to the refusal of India to give the Soviet Union base facilities.[59] Vice-Admiral N. X. Smirnow, deputy chief of staff of the Soviet navy, was quoted as saying that a powerful Pakistani navy was a precondition for peace in the Indian Ocean.[60] The project was dropped for reasons unknown; it created very unfavorable reactions in Washington, Peking, and also New Delhi.

In January 1973 Prime Minister Bhutto of Pakistan was reported to have offered the United States an air and naval base on the shores of the Arabian Sea close to the Iran border.[61] Nothing, however, has since been heard about it. Bhutto could hardly invite the United States to build a naval facility on the Arabian Sea after the Arab-Israeli war of 1973 and in view of the Shah's distaste for foreign military bases in the Persian Gulf region. Besides, Bhutto cannot afford to provoke the Soviet Union too much. In any case, he probably feels protected by the naval power of Iran. The two allies have been cooperating to develop sea transit between their countries, with Turkey as a third partner.[62]

One indicator of an increased Soviet presence in the Indian Ocean region relative to that of the United States is the number of littoral countries that have received superpower aid to build their navies. The United States has transferred naval equipment to nine littoral countries: Australia, Burma, Indonesia, Iran, Malaysia, Pakistan, Saudi Arabia, Singapore, and Thailand. The Soviet Union has transferred naval equipment to seven: Bangladesh, Egypt, India, Indonesia, Iraq, Somalia, and South Yemen.[63]

THE INDIAN VIEW OF SOVIET NAVAL POWER

Of the countries belonging to the Asian basin of the Indian Ocean, India has the largest, most populated, and strongest naval power. The close relations of India with the Soviet Union make the Indian view of Soviet naval power in the Indian Ocean particularly significant. The Soviet Union has been playing the leading role in enabling India to expand its own navy; the entire submarine fleet of

India has been acquired from the USSR.[64] There have been reports in the Western press of Soviet naval bases in India, and although these reports have been vigorously denied in New Delhi, the denials are not universally believed. In fact, the Soviet Union has not asked India for base facilities but has sought only limited facilities for berthing and recreation. Soviet engineers helped to expand the shipyard at Vizag.[65] As long as the British security system continued in the area "east of Suez," the 3,000-mile coastline of India was more or less secure. India could therefore concentrate on the defense of its land frontiers in the northeast, north, and northwest. Since the Indian security scenario was dominated by Pakistan and China, neither of which was a sea power, the Indian Ocean did not substantially enter the thinking of Indian strategic planners for more than two decades of independence. However, a perceptive Indian historian, K. M. Pannikar, predicted even in the 1940s that the "future of India will undoubtedly be decided on the sea."

The threat from the sea became visible after some two centuries when the U.S. task force, led by the nuclear carrier Enterprise, threatened India from the Bay of Bengal in 1971. The Indian navy had done well in several engagements with the Pakistani navy in the Arabian Sea but was no equal to the U.S. task force. India therefore welcomed the Soviet offer to neutralize the U.S. naval force. This demonstration of Soviet alliance—the risking of a naval encounter with the United States to honor a Soviet commitment to India—established with Indian military planners and political leaders the value of Soviet friendship beyond any reasonable doubt. The events of 1971 established a certain harmony between Indian and Soviet interests in the Indian Ocean. This harmony has persisted through the mid-1970s in view of the poor state of Indian relations with the United States and China and of the continued Indian perception of a Sino-U.S. collusion against the Soviet Union. In other words, India cannot rule out the need for Soviet naval support in a future military conflict with Pakistan or China.

In fact, the defeat of Pakistan in 1971 and the upsurge in Indian military power and prestige has, paradoxically, brought into bolder relief than before the vulnerability of the Indian coastline and thus of its major industrial and cultural centers. India can now be effectively threatened from the sea, and even if it were threatened from the landward side, it is only from the sea that effective assistance could be forthcoming.[66]

India is opposed to a superpower naval arms competition in the Indian Ocean and has been a supporter of the Asian-African efforts at the United Nations to turn the Indian Ocean area into a "peace zone." Like Iran, the second strongest naval power in the Asian basin of the Indian Ocean, India is strongly opposed to domination of

the ocean by a single world power. However, while Iran wants a
U.S. naval presence to balance the Soviet naval presence in the
Indian Ocean, India wants a Soviet naval presence to balance a U.S.
naval presence. The brunt of Indian attack in the 1970s has been
the U.S. base-building on Diego Garcia, because India fears that if
it were equipped with a major base in the Indian Ocean the United
States could more easily intervene in a future conflict in the subcontinent. India cannot be sure of Soviet counterintervention if the
U.S. navy in the Indian Ocean is too strong and if the price of counterintervention becomes too high. Indian spokesmen have criticized
neither the Soviet presence in the Indian Ocean nor specific instances
of the use of the Soviet navy as an instrument of coercive diplomacy.
On the other hand, these spokesmen have consistently held that the
Soviet Union has no bases in the Indian Ocean region.

The outcome of the 1971 war with Pakistan has reduced the
dependence of India on the USSR, but this reality has not been recognized by the Chinese, who continue to perceive India as more or
less a Soviet satellite. India would be less dependent on Moscow if
it could build a more powerful navy, but this cannot be done without
Soviet assistance. A report in the Far Eastern Economic Review in
1974 said that Indian strategists were contemplating the development
of a nuclear-powered submarine and a fleet of "at least 20 to 25
oceangoing submarines. There is a proposal to spend 10,000 million rupees ($1.2 billion) for a ten-year plan of naval development,
including missile ships, and half that sum on the Air Force."[67]
India argues that it needs a much stronger navy, not only to defend
the coastline, but also to protect its growing foreign trade, of which
15 percent is carried in Indian ships.

India would support superpower naval arms control in the
Indian Ocean, leading to a stable limited naval presence of the Soviet
Union and the United States, each neutralizing the political impact of
the other.[68]

SOUTHEAST ASIA

The sea lanes of Southeast Asia connect the Pacific and the
Indian Oceans; the shortest and most-used link between the two is
the Malacca Straits. The ports of Burma, Singapore, Malaysia,
Thailand, and Vietnam are windows on the Indian Ocean, while the
ports of the Philippines open in the direction of the Pacific. A
Soviet naval presence in Southeast Asian waters impinges directly
on the southern flank of China.

It frightens Japan, too, because the shipping lanes connecting
Japan with the major sources of its fuel and raw material supplies

traverse the Southeast Asian waters. The Japanese take a serious view of the prospect of Soviet control of these sea lanes. Indeed, several of the strategic plans the Japanese have conceived to safeguard their interests stem from this prospect. These include the projected Kra canal in southern Thailand; Japan's expanded naval and sea power; and a loose defensive arrangement with Indonesia and Australia.69 The Soviets can, and probably do, use their naval buildup in the Indian and Pacific Oceans as an input of their vigorous diplomacy with Japan. Of all Soviet shipping movement, 13 percent takes place in the Sea of Japan and the Sea of Okhotsk.

The Japanese are alarmed by every indication of a Soviet "forward" naval capability. A powerful Pacific fleet would enable the Soviet Union to strongly influence the balance of power in the area, especially since neither Japan nor China is a naval power. If the Soviet naval presence in the strategic sectors of the Indian Ocean becomes stronger than that of the United States, the Japanese will be under strong pressure to come to a strategic understanding with the USSR. (See Chapter 7.)

China takes the dimmest view of Soviet naval activity in the Indian Ocean, particularly in the post-Vietnam period. The Chinese have no naval presence in the Indian Ocean area. However, China would like to dominate the South China Sea, the East China Sea, and the Yellow Sea, which wash its shores from Hainan to Luta. Unnoticed by the outside world, China has built up what is now regarded as the third-largest navy in the world. With 230,000 officers and over 100 vessels, including 60 submarines, one of which is probably nuclear powered, the Chinese navy is larger than the French and British navies put together.70 The capability of this navy was demonstrated in January 1974 when the Chinese, in a swift combined air and sea operation, seized control of the tiny Parcel Islands from the pro-U.S. regime in South Vietnam. According to Japanese sources the Chinese have been observing Soviet naval maneuvers in the Yellow Sea. The Soviet Union accuses China of harboring the intention to convert the South China Sea, with its promise of vast deposits of oil, into a Chinese lake. So far the Chinese navy has not ventured outside its coastal waters; its declared mission is to turn "China's coastline into a great wall of steel." The three Chinese fleets are deployed to guard the northern, eastern, and southern shores of China.

With most of its combat ships of Soviet vintage of the 1950s, China does not have the ability to contain Soviet naval power; hence its hope that the United States will continue to operate its naval bases in Thailand and the Philippines. The relations of China with the Southeast Asian governments are not of such a nature as might enable it to mobilize littoral opposition to Soviet naval penetration of the regional waters and sea lanes. Since Vietnam the Chinese have become even more concerned about Soviet naval activity in these waters and in the Indian Ocean. In the view of Peking this is nothing short of a Soviet encirclement of China.[71]

Apart from bunkering facilities in Singapore, the Soviets do not have port facilities in Southeast Asia. They may gain access to the facilities built by the United States in some of the South Vietnamese ports if their relations with Communist Vietnam continues to improve and if Vietnam feels threatened by China. Moscow suspects that the United States will continue to enjoy the naval facilities it has built in Thailand; together with Vietnam, the Soviet Union can be expected to keep pressure on Thailand to deny these facilities to the U.S. navy.

The Soviet merchant marine has, however, established its presence in Southeast Asian waters.[72] Soviet ships call regularly at all ASEAN ports. Moscow runs a joint shipping service with Singapore and has just started another with the Philippines. These shipping lines are fairly active on the Pacific sea routes off the west coast of the United States. The Soviet trade with Singapore and South Korea is among its largest with Third-World countries, while its trade with Malaysia and the Philippines is also steadily increasing.

When I visited the five ASEAN countries in November-December 1974 to study elite perceptions of the Soviet Union, I found that nothing had brought home the reality of Soviet power more clearly to the elite groups in Manila, Bangkok, Singapore, Jakarta, and Kuala Lumpur than the Soviet naval presence in the Indian Ocean and the actual use of Soviet naval capability as an instrument of diplomacy. As long as the Soviet Union lacked an interventionist capability, its power was distant. The interventionist naval power of the USSR became disturbingly visible to the Southeast Asian elites during the India-Pakistan war of 1971, and it raised the question of the free passage of Soviet ships through the Malacca Straits. Indonesia and Singapore even suggested that the littoral nations had the right to deny passage through this narrow but vital waterway to any power they considered hostile. However, by the end of 1974 Southeast Asian opposition to the passage of Soviet ships through the sea lanes of the region was not so rigid. I asked each of the 250 persons I interviewed in the five ASEAN capitals whether he or she would like to see the Soviet Union given an equal right of passage with the United States: 67 said yes; 110 said no; and the rest were not certain. However, when asked if they expected their governments to deny the Soviet Union the right of free passage in peacetime, 195 said no and the others were not sure. Elite resistance to Soviet naval use of the Southeast Asian sea lanes was stronger in Singapore and Indonesia than in Malaysia and the Philippines. This resistance has probably further mellowed since the traumatic events of 1975.

The overwhelming wish of the Asian countries is for an agreement among the world naval powers, which would limit the presence of the navies in the waterway. This wish finds its expression in the resolutions adopted by the UN General Assembly declaring the Indian Ocean to be a "peace" and a "nuclear-free" zone. The littoral nations, however, are not in a position to persuade the superpowers to come to a naval arms control agreement; nor is there a great deal of harmony among naval interests and aspirations of the major littoral nations themselves. The larger littoral countries look with suspicion at each other's growing naval power, while the smaller countries are as much afraid of the naval strength of their more powerful neighbors as they are of the navies of the world powers. In this circumstance, the initiative for naval arms control must come from the two superpowers themselves. It is the Asian hope that the major powers will work out a balance eventually. [73]

In the early 1970s, both the United States and the Soviet Union were reported to be willing to engage in talks aimed at limiting their naval activities in the Indian Ocean. Australian newspapers noted that both Brezhnev and unnamed high U.S. officials had expressed their wish to talk. These papers reported that an actual discussion had been initiated. [74] The outbreak of the Arab-Israeli war of 1973 probably halted the probings. Moscow and Washington were both under pressure to increase their naval presences in the Mediterranean and the Indian Ocean. In March 1974 the Indian Ocean was discussed between Indonesian Foreign Minister Adam Malik and the visiting Soviet deputy foreign minister, Nikolai Firyubin. The Soviet official said that the Indian Ocean should be seen as the "open sea," open to all nations without discrimination. Asked by Malik whether the Soviets would withdraw their naval force if the United States did so, Firyubin replied that "this matter should be reached later in the process of detente. "[75]

NOTES

1. New York Times, January 30, 1976. The U.S. defense secretary, Donald H. Rumsfeld, was reported to have conceded that in view of the Soviet naval buildup, the ability of the U.S. navy to operate in the eastern Mediterranean in wartime "would be, at best, uncertain. "

2. T. B. Millar, "The Military-Strategic Balance, " paper read at the conference on the Persian Gulf and the Indian Ocean in International Politics, Tehran, March 25-27, 1975.

3. The debate is nowhere better reflected than in the annual hearings of the various committees of the U.S. Congress, especially

the appropriations and armed services committees of the House and
the Senate and the joint committee on atomic energy. The "alarmist-
realist" categorization has been made by Norman Polmar in Soviet
Naval Power: Challenge for the Seventies, Strategy Paper No. 13
(New York: National Strategy Information Center, 1972). For the
"realistic" view, see, among others, Robert W. Herrick, Soviet
Naval Strategy (Annapolis: U.S. Naval Institute, 1968); David
Fairhill, Russian Sea Power (Boston: Gambit, 1971); Michael
MccGwire, ed., Soviet Naval Developments: Capability and Context
(New York: Praeger, 1973); and Geoffrey Jukes, "The Indian Ocean
in Soviet Naval Policy," Adelphi Paper No. 87 (London: International Institute of Strategic Studies, 1972). For the "alarmist" view,
see R. M. Burrell and Alvin J. Cottrell, The Indian Ocean: A Conference Report (Washington, D.C.: Center for Strategic and International Studies, Georgetown University, 1971); and articles in successive issues of Proceedings, the monthly journal of the U.S. Naval
War College. For a useful bibliography of articles and papers, see
K. P. Mishra, "Survey of Recent Research: International Politics
and the Security of the Indian Ocean Area," International Studies
(New Delhi) 12, no. 1 (January-March 1973).

For an objective and perceptive discussion of superpower
naval arms control possibilities, see Barry N. Blechman, The Control of Naval Armaments: Prospects and Possibilities (Washington,
D.C.: The Brookings Institution, 1964). It includes the proposed
draft of a naval arms control treaty for the Indian Ocean. In March
1975 the then labor Prime Minister of Australia, Gough Whitlam, in
identical messages to the United States and the USSR, urged them to
exercise mutual restraint in the Indian Ocean. New York Times,
March 26, 1975.

4. New York Times, January 30, 1976.

5. Pravda, June 12, 1971.

6. Speech by Soviet delegate, Roschin, in the General Assembly's December 1973 debate, cited in T. T. Poulose, ed., Indian
Ocean Rivalry (New Delhi: Young Asia Publishers, 1974), pp. 136-38.

7. New York Times, January 27 and 30, 1976. Admiral
Holloway told a congressional committee in 1974 that "if the United
States is to maintain the margin of superiority that we enjoy today--
although it is a slim one--over the Soviet Union, we must have a
minimum of 600 active ships by the mid-1980's."

To build up to a 600-ship fleet, the U.S. navy would have
to build about 85 ships a year at the cost of $9 billion a year in 1976
dollars, requiring a doubling of its budget, which has grown from
$2.4 billion in 1969 to a proposed $6.3 billion for fiscal 1976. For
an appraisal of U.S. shipbuilding progress and problems, see New
York Times, May 4, 1975.

8. In 1967 Gorshkov had declared that "the process of the sun setting on aircraft carriers . . . has begun." The carrier, he added, had "no future." In 1972 he changed his view and implicitly conceded that the aircraft carrier still had a significant role to play in a forward naval strategy. See Sergei G. Gorshkov, "Navies in War and Peace," Morskoy Sbornik, February 1972 through February 1973; E. T. Woolbridge, "The Gorshkov Papers: Soviet Naval Doctrine in the Nuclear Age," Orbis 13, no. 4 (Winter 1975).

For the financial implications of the Soviet naval expansion program, see Raymond Hutchings, "The Economic Burden of the Soviet Navy," and Michael MccGwire, "The Economic Costs of Forward Deployment," in McGwire, op. cit., pp. 176-238; also New York Times, May 20, 1975.

9. Drew Middleton, "Russians Reported Building A Third Aircraft Carrier," New York Times, Obctober 28, 1975. Also Norman Polmar, "The Soviet Aircraft Carrier," Proceedings (Naval Review), 1974.

10. New York Times, April 19, 1975. The Soviets have a growing naval infantry. For the importance of the Soviet marines in naval operations, see Arty P. Yakimov, "The Combat Employment of the Naval Infantry in Landing Operations," Voyenno-istoricheskiy zhurnal, no. 11 (November 1974). The Soviet Union also has 12 or 23 airborne divisions, with a mobilized strength of 7,500 each. Military Review, March 1975; New York Times, October 26, 1973; Graham H. Turbiville, "Soviet Airborne Troops," Military Review, April 1973.

11. MccGwire, "The Turning Point in Soviet Naval Policy," in MccGwire, Soviet Naval Developments: Capability and Context, op. cit., pp. 203-04.

12. Gorshkov, op. cit., February 1973 issue.

13. Gorshkov, foreword to Combat Path of the Soviet Navy (Moscow, 1974).

14. Gorshkov, "Navies in War and Peace," op. cit.

15. Gorshkov, "Certain Questions Concerning the Development of the Naval Art," Morskoy Sbornik, no. 12 (December 1974).

16. N. Pavlovick, "Basic Factors in the Development of the Art of Naval Warfare," V.-I.-Z., no. 12 (December 1974).

17. Quoted in "Na Strazhe morskikh rabezhei," Kommunist Vooruzhennykh Sil, no. 12 (June 1971).

18. Gorshkov, "Navies in War and Peace," op. cit.

19. Ibid.

20. G. Melkov, "The Sources of Tension," Kransaya Zvezda, June 9, 1974.

21. V. F. Davydov and V. A. Kremenyuk, "United States Strategy in the Indian Ocean," USA: Economic, Politics, Ideology, no. 5 (May 1973).

22. K. Tikov, "The Indian Ocean on the Charts of the Pentagon," Morskoy Sbornik, no. 7 (July 1973).

23. Davydov and Kremenyuk, op. cit.; the quotation, slightly
distorted in translation, can be seen in Military Review, December
1970.

24. Tikov, op. cit.; this is an informative paper on the political and military geography of the Indian Ocean basin.

25. Ibid.

26. Ibid.

27. Melkov, op. cit.

28. Soviet commentaries on the United States naval policy in
the Indian Ocean region recognize the existence of a "sober school of
thinking." See the articles listed above, notes 20-27.

29. New York Times, March 21, 1974.

30. Ibid. Zumwalt told the Times, on the eve of his retirement, that the Soviet Union's "capability to deny us the sea lines,
which is their job, is greater than our capacity to keep the sea lines
open, which is our job." New York Times, May 14, 1974.

31. "Report of the Ad Hoc Committee on the Indian Ocean,"
May 3, 1974, included in Poulose, op. cit., p. 283.

32. New York Times, May 23, 1975.

33. Ibid.

34. Ibid.

35. John W. Finny, "The Soviets in Somalia: A 'Facility,'
Not a Base," New York Times, July 6, 1975.

36. I. Borzov, "The Mighty Fleet of the Soviet Union," Vestnik
Protivovozdushnoy Oborony, no. 7 (July 1973). Gorshkov himself
wrote that the Soviet navy demonstrated "to the peoples of friendly
and hostile countries not only the power of military equipment and
the perfection of the naval ships, embodying the technical and economic might of the state, but also its readiness to use this force in
defense of state interests." Gorshkov, op. cit., February 1973 issue.

37. James McConnell and Anne M. Kelly, "Superior Naval
Diplomacy in the India-Pakistan Crisis," in MccGwire, Soviet Naval
Developments: Capability and Context, op. cit., p. 451.

38. Alvin J. Cottrell, "The Soviet Navy and the Indian Ocean,"
paper read at the conference on the Persian Gulf and the Indian
Ocean in International Politics, Tehran, March 25-27, 1975.

39. Michel Tatu, "Soviet Navy in Indian Ocean--'Progressive'
Gunboat Diplomacy," Le Monde, April 26, 1970.

40. For details of the Bangladesh operations, see Bhabani
Sen Gupta, "Moscow and Bangladesh," Problems of Communism,
March-April, 1975.

41. Cottrell, op. cit.

42. Alvin J. Cottrell and R. M. Burrel, "No Power Can Hope to Dominate the Indian Ocean," New Middle East (London), September 1971.

43. New York Times, May 23, 1975.

44. "Report of the Ad Hoc Committee on the Indian Ocean," op. cit., p. 267.

45. Miller, op. cit.; Cottrell, op. cit.; "Report of the Ad Hoc Committee on the Indian Ocean," op. cit.

46. V. Kruglyakov, "Tropical Maximum," Krasnaya Zvezda, January 18, 1975.

47. "Report of the Ad Hoc Committee on the Indian Ocean," op. cit.; Poulose, op. cit., p. 268.

48. Ibid., p. 269.

49. Ibid., p. 272.

50. Drew Middleton, "Pacific Regions Worry Pentagon," New York Times, January 25, 1976.

51. Ibid. The study recommended "large submersible platforms--in essence super submarines" and stable semisubmersible floating concrete platforms "which could be towed slowly to any conflict area in the world," rather than aircraft carriers, which had become vulnerable.

52. Drew Middleton, "Soviet Reported Stockpiling Missiles at African Base for Indian Ocean Ships," New York Times, April 7, 1975.

53. Ibid.

54. Eric Pace, "Bahrain Says Continued US use of Naval Station Depends on Support to Arab Cause in Mideast," New York Times, March 9, 1975.

55. Dawn (Karachi), November 29, 1975.

56. Eric Pace, "Iran Pushing Construction of Naval Base in South," New York Times, August 26, 1975. For Iran's anxiety to keep the Persian Gulf region free of polarization and conflict, see also Amir Tahiri, "The Persian Gulf and the Indian Ocean: Attitude of the Non-Arab Littoral," paper read at the conference on the Persian Gulf and the Indian Ocean in International Politics, Tehran, March 25-27, 1975; Alvin J. Cottrell, "The Political Balance in the Persian Gulf," Strategic Review 2, no. 1 (Winter 1974).

57. Pace, "Iran Pushing Construction of Naval Base in South," op. cit.

58. New York Times, January 11, 1976. Aid to the insurgents from South Yemen and Iraq probably diminished after the conclusion of the accords between Iran and Iraq.

59. The Statesman, June 29, 1969.

60. George G. Thomson, Problems of Strategy in the Pacific and Indian Oceans (New York: National Strategy Information Center, 1970), p. 37.

61. The Times of India, quoting New York Times, January 23, 1973.

62. Thomson, op. cit., p. 40.

63. "Report of the Ad Hoc Committee on the Indian Ocean," op. cit.

64. For the Soviet content of the Indian Navy, see Arms Trade Register: The Arms Trade with the Third World (Cambridge, Mass.: MIT Press, 1975), pp. 33-36.

65. The Statesman, May 10, 1973; see also W. A. C. Adie, Oil, Politics and Seapower: The Indian Ocean Vortex (New York: National Strategy Information Center, 1975), p. 46.

66. Thomson, op. cit., p. 40.

67. The Far Eastern Economic Review, June 2, 1974.

68. For a more detailed analysis of Indian perceptions of the superpower naval arms race in the Indian Ocean, see Sen Gupta, "The Indian Ocean and the Persian Gulf: The View from India," paper read at the conference on the Persian Gulf and the Indian Ocean in International Politics, Tehran, March 25-27, 1975. For an Indian naval officer's view that the USSR can not dominate the Indian Ocean, see Proceedings (Annapolis), October 1970. See also Poulose, op. cit. for several papers articulating the Indian viewpoint.

69. Frank Mount, "Southeast Asia's Global Strategic Context," Southeast Asian Spectrum (SEATO, Bangkok) 2, no. 4 (July 1974).

70. Fox Butterfield, "China Has Built Big Power Navy," New York Times, August 10, 1975.

71. According to Jane's Fighting Ships, 1975, the Chinese have about 60 diesel-powered attack submarines, mostly of Soviet design, but they have built two of their own design, including a Han-class with a tear-drop shaped hull that was launched in 1972 and is thought to be a nuclear vessel. Cited in ibid.

72. The Soviet merchant fleet consists of 6,575 ships and has been growing at the rate of something like a million tons a year, an impressive performance, and to some people a disturbing one. In 1974 the Russians built 90 transport ships, including the first 105,000-ton petroleum and ore carrier and 150,000-ton Krym tanker. Vodnyy, July 18, 1974. "Starting almost from the scratch twenty years ago, [the Soviet Union] has come to challenge traditional sea powers like the United States and Britain on their own terms. In short, there has been a massive shift in the strategic balance--and it is still continuing." David Fairhill, "Soviet Merchant Marine," Brassey's Annual: Defense and Armed Forces (London), 1973.

73. The Singapore foreign minister, S. Rajaratnam, has observed, "So what is more likely to happen in the Indian Ocean, given the present mood of the two superpowers, is the establishment of a sane balance of great power interests. In the course of this, there

will be moments of tensions and crises. Small and weak nations fringing the ocean will be subjected to new strains and stresses which may not cripple those who do know the game." "Singapore and the Indian Ocean," in Poulose, op. cit., p. 160.

74. Melbourne Age, April 27, 1971; Canberra Times, June 14, 1971.

75. Adie, op. cit., p. 57.

The Soviet Union is generally perceived as the dominant external power in South Asia.[1] The Soviet intervention and presence-
building in this Asian region has proved to be more effective and
durable than those of its two rivals, the United States and China.

Over the last 20 years, the USSR has built its presence in
three Asian regions, the west, the south, and the southeast, using
primarily two foreign policy tools, development assistance and
politico-military intervention in local "anti-imperialist" conflicts.
Armed conflict between the forces of national liberation and those of
imperialism has paved the way for Soviet penetration of the Arab
world and of Vietnam.

It has not been so in South Asia. When Khrushchev descended
on India in 1955, his briefcase carried no offer of military aid. India
was not involved in any conflict with the imperialist powers. India,
however, did have a conflict with Pakistan over Kashmir, and Pakistan was a military ally of the United States. Khrushchev's surprise
offer of Soviet political support for India in its dispute with Pakistan
over Kashmir and his similar offer to Afghanistan a little later in its
Pakhtoonistan dispute with Pakistan did amount to intervention in
local conflicts. Nevertheless, the main image of the USSR projected
by Khrushchev to the subcontinent and to all of Asia was the image
of socialist development; that is, of the spectacular growth of the
military and economic power of Russia under the Soviet system and
the ability and willingness of the socialist bloc to give meaningful
help to "peace-loving, anti-imperialist" newly liberated nations such
as India in their political and economic development.

This was a clever and skillful role projection on the part of the
Soviet Union. Its success was assured not only by the needs of India,
but also by the Indian historical psychology. Unlike Japan and China,

the subcontinent had no historical devil image of imperial Russia; the British had kept their empire insulated from Russian penetration. Also, the leaders of the Indian nationalist and intellectual movements had been profoundly influenced by the anti-imperialist overtones of the Bolshevik revolution. Since the early 1930s certain emotional and intellectual linkages had been established between Indian nationalism and Soviet communism. Even in the Muslim League, which is less secular and more conservative than the Indian National Congress, there were many Western-educated Muslims who admired the Soviet Union both for its anti-imperialism and for its rapid economic development.[2] During World War II the Indian Communist Party (CPI) had lost whatever strategic position it used to have in the nationalist struggle for independence. The political "arrangement" of 1947, which led to the transfer of power to the two sovereign states of India and Pakistan, found both countries firmly in the control of the national bourgeoisie. By the mid-1950s the CPI, despite its pro-Soviet orientation, was not offensive to Indian nationalism, since it had already decided to operate within the system of parliamentary democracy and was supporting the "progressive" foreign policy of the government in New Delhi. This government, led by Nehru, who was a long-time admirer of the Soviet experiment, had been waiting for eight years for the friendship of Moscow and had refused to be provoked by the Soviet invectives against his regime and himself during the Stalin period.[3]

Subjective as well as objective conditions, then, have helped the Soviet Union build its steadily expanding presence in South Asia since the mid-1950s. This effort has not met with any major reverse or setback, although, to be sure, events have defied Soviet anticipations, and the rewards have not been equal to Soviet expectations. Even Soviet-Indian relations, the most steadfast Soviet friendship in the non-Communist world, have not been entirely free of stresses and strains. On the whole, however, Soviet diplomacy in South Asia has not been thrown out of gear, nor has it been effectively challenged by the two other major powers. In the Soviet Union both the scholarly community, which has done considerable work on India, and the political leaders, who now describe Indo-Soviet friendship as "traditional," that is, above the ups and downs of daily events, look upon the Soviet success in the subcontinent with some pride. One Soviet scholar ascribes this success to the "soundness" of the Soviet model relative to the U.S. and Chinese models in South Asia. The Soviet model, he claims, is based on a correct geopolitical appraisal of the realities in South Asia and of the relations of the region with the outside world. Its persistent thrust has been to build friendly, cooperative relations with the "progressive" forces of democracy and nationalism and therefore with India, which is by far the largest,

strongest, and most stable power in the region. It has been a "positive model" aimed at "positive goals" through "positive cooperation"
between world socialism and the forces of national liberation. In
contrast, according to this scholar, the U.S. model has been based
on "barren anti-communism," and is therefore reliant on conservative, reactionary forces and regimes that cannot survive the "con-
vulsions of development." The Chinese model since the early 1960s
has been based on even more empty anti-Sovietism: it has "sown
storms and reaped whirlwinds" in one Asian country after another.
The net result has been a growing hiatus between these two powers
and the "progressive and dynamic nation-builders" in South Asia.[4]
     Whatever the merit of this self-fulfilling, somewhat simplistic
"model" building, in the 1970s the Soviet Union is more involved in
the affairs of South Asia than the United States or China. One result
of this deepening involvement is that the Soviet role in the region has
become diversified. The Soviet Union is now as much involved in the
security of South Asia as it is in its economic and political development. This diversified role has been acquired by successful, inex-
pensive intervention in three wars in South Asia, the Sino-Indian
border war of 1962 and the India-Pakistan wars of 1965 and 1971.
Its intervention on behalf of India in all of these wars has imparted a
large strategic content to the treaty-bound Indo-Soviet friendship.
At the same time the Soviet Union has claimed the subcontinent, because of its geographical closeness to the USSR, virtually as its
sphere of influence, a claim that is contested by China, although
China is not in a position to hurt Soviet interests too much. In the
1970s the Soviets have a spatially large strategic design for the inter-
linking regions of South Asia and the Persian Gulf, which none of
the regional actors has so far accepted. The design is for the security of the two regions, to be brought about by multilateral economic
cooperation; by bilateral settlement of interstate differences and disputes; and, over time, by political and strategic collaboration, all
of these with Soviet participation and involvement, though not formally under Soviet leadership. The Soviet policy makers, then, have
given themselves the long-term task of establishing a broad strategic
symmetry in the two intermeshing regions. Soviet analysts believe
that only by the establishment of multifaceted regional and inter-
regional cooperation, under the benign protection of the socialist
system, can the two regions be insulated from imperialist and Chinese intervention. This strategic design has introduced a new dynamism into Soviet relations with the two major regional powers, India
and Iran, neither of which is willing to subscribe to the Soviet strategic design nor ready to reject it altogether. Each has its own
power interests and ambitions in South Asia. The Soviet strategic
design for the regions has also begun to be reflected on its conflict

with China and its competitive coexistence with the United States in
the Third World.

THE STRATEGIC DISHARMONY OF SOUTH ASIA

The Soviet leaders have been striving to bestow a broad strategic harmony on a region that has been stricken with sharp strategic
disunity since the collapse of the British imperial system in 1947.
India and Pakistan view each other both as independent threats and
as symptoms of their internal disunity.

With independence, India had a new set of frontiers to defend
and develop. By the early 1950s its security scenario came to be
dominated by Pakistan in Kashmir and by China in the Himalayan
reaches of the subcontinent; the security of Sikkim, Bhutan, and
Nepal loaded India with an "imperial" defense responsibility too
large for its resources, as Nehru confessed to his biographer,
Michael Brecher.[5] The security gap began to widen with penetration of the subcontinent by external powers in the 1950s. The process of intervention was initiated by the United States and was
promptly picked up by the Soviet Union, China following in a matter
of years. While the Soviet Union remained by and large a consistent
supporter of India and China an even more consistent backer of Pakistan, the United States frequently shifted its position, depending on
which of the two Communist giants it sought to contain at particular
junctures of its containment policy. These shifts appeared to indicate that the United States had no "autonomous" policy for South Asia,
nor any permanent interests, and that the importance of the region
to U.S. policy makers increased and declined in response to the
vicissitudes of its central engagement with the Soviet Union and/or
China.

The military pact of the United States with Pakistan in 1953
not only formalized the strategic cleavage between India and Pakistan
but also linked this cleavage with the global conflict between the two
Cold-War blocs. However, this did not intolerably increase the defense burden of India, since it was effectively counterbalanced by the
strategic political support for India by the Soviet Union and by the
development assistance India received from the United States and
the USSR. Indeed, the period of 1953-59, when U.S. and Soviet intervention balanced each other at a relatively low level of involvement, was an unbroken period of peace in the subcontinent.[6] The
balance, however, was overthrown by Chinese intervention in the
1960s. The border crisis with China spiraled the defense expenditure of India upwards, and after the border war of 1962, defense became its first priority. The need for U.S. military aid to the anti-

China defense effort of India betrayed, in Pakistani eyes, the tenuous-
ness of Washington's military commitment to Pakistan. In Pakistani
perceptions, the two superpowers were now working together to
strengthen India, the mortal enemy of Pakistan. Pakistan could now
turn with assurance of support only to China. In 1963 Zulfikar Ali
Bhutto, then foreign minister of Pakistan, asserted that "the largest
power in Asia" would come to his country's rescue if it were "attacked
by India."[7]

In the early 1960s, however, a promise of strategic symmetry
in the subcontinent came from parallel Soviet and American aid to
build up India as a countervailing power in Asia in relation to the
Chinese People's Republic and from a U.S. initiative, in conjunction
with Britain, to resolve the deadlock on Kashmir. According to
Chester Bowles, then U.S. ambassador in New Delhi, Nehru agreed
to "support a genuine effort by [the U.S.] government to negotiate a
political settlement that could end the fighting in Southeast Asia,"
that is, in Vietnam, as well as to "negotiate a ceiling of military expenditure with Pakistan."[8]

The promise proved to be fleeting. The Indian government resented the arm-twisting by the United States and Britain to force it
to make concessions to Pakistan on the Kashmir issue, and India
abandoned its halfhearted conciliatory moves when China, in a tour
de force, concluded a border agreement with Pakistan, conferring
tentative sanction on Pakistani control of two-thirds of the state of
Jammu and Kashmir.[9]

The main reason for the withering of the promise probably lay
in a shift in U.S. priorities after the death of John F. Kennedy. The
United States lost interest in India on the political and developmental
planes. Increasing involvement in the Vietnam war led to a general
U.S. disengagement from the uncommitted nations of the Third World
in terms of economic aid. By the mid-1960s, anxiety to avoid direct
military conflict with the Chinese evidently persuaded Lyndon Johnson
to lower the U.S. anti-China profile in South Asia also. Washington
found it wiser to concede to Moscow the primary diplomatic and
strategic role in South Asia because of the greater Soviet stake in
containing China and because of the relative political unimportance
of India to the United States. India turned to the Soviet Union and
got everything it had asked from the United States and more. The
Indians were pleased, because the United States, having conceded to
the Soviet Union the major role in controlling conflict in the subcontinent, could not possibly come to the help of Pakistan in an Indo-
Pakistani military conflict.

This expectation was confirmed in the war between India and
Pakistan in September 1965. For the first time the United States
remained officially neutral in a war involving one of its allies. The

USSR and China faced each other as direct contenders in the subcontinent. In a major strategic initiative, Moscow intervened in the India-Pakistan war, armed with the theory of geographical propinquity. The conflict, as Kosygin told the prime minister of India and the president of Pakistan, was taking place in an area close to the borders of the Soviet state, compelling Moscow to offer its diplomatic services to bring the two warring parties together. At the same time, the Soviet government warned other countries to keep out of the conflict. Inherent in the Soviet diplomatic initiative was the claim that South Asia, being geographically close to the USSR, was a natural sphere of Russian interest.[10]

After the Tashkent agreement, Moscow gradually unfolded its own strategic design for South Asia. The visit by the Shah of Iran to the Soviet capital in 1965 had led to an improvement in Soviet-Iranian relations, and in 1966 a program of Soviet economic and military assistance to Iran was initiated.

After the Tashkent accord the Soviets ceased to support the Indian position on Kashmir and adopted a posture of "neutrality," which paved the way for a diplomatic initiative to improve relations with Pakistan. The transfer of Soviet military aid to Pakistan, however small in quantity, involved the risk of alienating India. The Soviets, however, took that risk.

There was resentment and anger in India, but the times had changed, and it did not cost Moscow too much. Kosygin personally assured the Indian leaders that the Soviet Union continued to regard India as the kingpin of its South Asian policy and explained that a Soviet presence in Pakistan was the only way to diminish Chinese influence and block "imperialist intervention" against Indian interests.[11]

The Indians were reassured in 1968 when Kosygin proposed, almost immediately after the first transfer of military equipment to Pakistan, an economic cooperation conference of Iran, Afghanistan, Pakistan, and India, with Soviet participation. It was suggested in the Soviet press that the four countries could have profitable trade with the USSR through the roadways and rail links already existing and likely to be constructed between the Soviet Union and Afghanistan on the one hand and the Soviet Union and Iran on the other. An authoritative Moscow newspaper foresaw a regional security system that would eventually emerge from economic cooperation among the South Asian countries.[12] The Afghan government, prompted by the Soviet Union, offered to host the proposed conference, which never took place because of the Pakistani refusal to attend. Thus the first attempt to unfold the Soviet strategic design came to nothing, although as a price for economic and military aid, Pakistan agreed to close down the extensive U.S. intelligence facilities in Peshawar.

SOVIET ANXIETY

During the latter half of the 1960s there was considerable anxiety in the Soviet Union about the drift of internal politics in India and about a possible pro-American shift in Indian foreign policy. During the brief prime ministry of Lal Bahadur Shastri, the primary Soviet concern, as judged from writings on India in the Soviet press, was to prevent the right wing from dominating the Congress party and the Indian government. The Soviet media welcomed the election of Indira Gandhi as prime minister after Shastri's sudden death in Tashkent. Within a short time, however, Soviet analysts began to note "the growing strength of the [Indian] capitalist monopolies with their close foreign ties."[13] After the 1967 general election, in which the Congress party lost power in as many as nine states, a Soviet analyst identified the cabinet of Indira Gandhi as "a coalition of the ruling party's centrist and rightist elements."[14] At a high-level academic symposium on India, the following question was posed: "Given the present balance of forces in the Indian National Congress, is not the election victory (of 1967) a triumph for big monopoly capital?"[15]

The Soviet concern stemmed not only from the analysts' perception of the rightward drift in the Congress party leadership but more particularly from the confrontation between the central government in New Delhi and the leftist-democratic coalitions that ruled West Bengal and Kerala. Both coalitions were dominated by the Communist Party of India (Marxist), or CPI-M, the parallel Communist party, which had been formed in 1964 after a split in the CPI. The Marxists were independent of Moscow and Peking but were nevertheless generally seen to be pro-Chinese. What placed the CPSU in an embarrassing situation was that the pro-Soviet CPI was also a partner of the two coalitions, and the confrontation between these two state governments and the Center was creating a polarization between the Congress party and the CPI and undermining the CPSU line of a broad united front of "democratic and left forces," meaning the "progressives" in the Congress party and the CPI.[16]

When Kosygin made a suddenly announced visit to New Delhi in February 1968, one leading Indian commentator likened its significance to that of the Khrushchev-Bulganin tour of India in 1955.[17] His talks with Indira Gandhi covered the whole gamut of subjects from economic affairs to political developments in India to foreign policy. The communique issued at the end of the talks indicated that the Soviet government remained fully committed to help India restore its economic health and remain steadfast to its foreign policy. Much of the conversations centered on China, which had built a sizable presence in Pakistan since Tashkent and was supporting several "revolutionary Communist" groups in India in 1968 and projecting to these groups a Maoist line of protracted armed struggle from rural bases.[18] Kosygin reportedly pointed out to Indira Gandhi that Pakistan was almost the only country with which Chinese relations had not been affected by the Cultural Revolution, and he impressed upon her the urgency of a parallel Indian and Soviet effort to loosen the Chinese hold on Pakistan. The Soviet premier also told her that Moscow would like India to fill the vacuum to be created in the Indian Ocean region by the British withdrawal from the Persian Gulf by 1971. India could not do this without internal stability and without some form of coexistence with Pakistan.[19]

The political crisis in India was resolved to Soviet satisfaction when Indira Gandhi broke away from the Congress party in late 1969 to form her own Congress party and, in order to prove her leftist legitimacy, nationalized 14 major Indian banks. In 1970 the CPI parted with the CPI-M and returned to the line of the "national-democratic" front of all democratic and left forces, including the "progressive elements" in Indira Gandhi's Congress party. In state-level elections in West Bengal, the Marxists emerged as the single largest party, with only a few seats short of an absolute majority in the state assembly. Nevertheless, the CPI joined in a coalition with the Congress party and other groups to keep the Marxists out of power. Likewise in Kerala, the old left coalition cabinet was replaced by a coalition of the Congress party and the CPI, headed by a CPI leader. In several other state elections, too, Indira Gandhi's party had electoral arrangements with the CPI.

In Pakistan a serious threat to political stability followed President Ayub Khan's heart attack in the spring of 1968. In November a full-scale agitation was launched in the urban areas of West Pakistan for the restoration of parliamentary democracy. In Punjab, the seat of the Pakistani power establishment, the leader of the agitation was Z. A. Bhutto.

Ayub Khan returned to the helm of affairs in the latter months of 1968, but he realized that military rule could not survive his death or retirement. In March 1969 he convened a roundtable conference of political leaders to decide on the restoration of parliamentary rule. The conference decided that a new national assembly, to be elected by universal adult franchise, but with equal representation for the two wings of Pakistan, would determine such controversial issues as provincial autonomy.

These decisions were immediately rejected by most political groups of East Pakistan, especially the Awami League led by Sheikh Mujibur Rahman, which since 1966 had been demanding "the largest possible autonomy" for East Pakistan, which the Awami Leaguers had begun to rename as Bangladesh, land of the Bengalis. The Awami League was particularly offended by the roundtable conference's offer of equal representation to the two wings. East Pakistan, or Bangladesh, with 55 percent of the total population of Pakistan, was entitled to a majority of seats in the national assembly; if it accepted an equal number of seats with the Western wing, the Awami Leaguers argued, it would never get the sanction of parliament for "maximum autonomy." The rejection of the conference proposals by East Pakistan led to large-scale riots in most parts of the eastern wing of Pakistan, in which thousands of East Pakistani Muslims killed hundreds of West Pakistanis and injured many thousands of them. On March 25 Ayub Khan bowed out of the Pakistani political scene, handing over power to the commander in chief of the army, General A. M. Yahya Khan. [20]

In November 1969, after an extensive tour of the two wings, Yahya Khan announced that elections to a constituent assembly would be held in the following October on the basis of one-man-one-vote. This concession to the East Pakistani elite was made because most members of Yahya Khan's cabinet were certain that a plurality of political parties in East Pakistan would deprive the Awami League of a dominant position in the constituent assembly. [21]

However, when the elections were finally held in December 1970, the Awami League captured not only all but two seats in the East Pakistan legislature but also an absolute majority in the national assembly. This created a confrontation between the Awami League and the West Pakistani power establishment, a united front of Bhutto's Pakistan People's party, which had emerged as the strongest West Pakistani group in the national assembly, and the military regime. Bhutto's refusal to let the Awami League rule Pakistan made it impossible for Mujibur Rahman to compromise in his demand for an autonomous Bangladesh with loose federal links with Pakistan.

After three months of highly complicated and often deceptive negotiations, Yahya Khan determined in the last days of March 1971 to crush the Bangladesh struggle with military force. Rahman was arrested and whisked away to West Pakistan. The Pakistani army, composed entirely of West Pakistan personnel, was ordered to restore law and order. The bulk of the Awami League leaders and 7 to 10 million refugees took shelter in India, where the Awami Leaguers proclaimed a "sovereign people's republic of Bangladesh" with Mujibur Rahman as president.

Thus began the Bangladesh civil war. India was immediately sucked into the war by the huge influx of refugees, which threatened to impose an intolerable burden on its already severely strapped economy; by the presence of the Awami League leaders and the

Bangladesh "government" on its territory; and by the deep sympathy
of the Indian people for the autonomy movement. [22]

By coincidence or by design, Indian and Soviet policy concerning the grave crisis in Pakistan ran parallel through the summer of
1971 until they converged in the autumn. Indira Gandhi was under
heavy public opinion pressure to intervene in the Bangladesh struggle,
to recognize the government-in-exile, and to help it raise a "liberation army." Although India did train the Bangladesh liberation army
from April or May onward, and although there was some coordination
between the Bangladesh partisans and the Indian border security force,
a paramilitary organization, Indira Gandhi refused to recognize the
Bangladesh government, operating from close to the East Pakistan
border. What she demanded was a political settlement between the
Pakistani government and the Awami League leader, Mujibur Rahman,
that would enable the refugees to return to their homes "in peace and
with honor." In other words, she supported the establishment of
Bangladesh within or outside Pakistan. [23]

The Soviet Union was the first major power to intervene openly
in the Pakistani crisis. Since 1968 Soviet relations with Pakistan had
produced more frustration than friendship. The Soviet leaders had
risked Indian displeasure by transferring military aid to Pakistan,
but they had not been able to loosen the ties of Pakistan with China
nor win the support of Pakistan for the regional economic grouping
that Moscow had been wanting to create. [24]

The Soviet leaders had hoped that Yahya Khan would yield where
Ayub Khan had been stubborn. Yahya Khan had visited Moscow in
1968 as chief of the Pakistani army; that visit had led to the protocols
for the supply of Soviet military equipment to Pakistan. Yahya Khan
paid his second visit to Moscow in June 1970, this time as president;
he agreed to expand Soviet-Pakistani collaboration. The Soviet Union
was to build the first steel plant in Pakistan and to help Pakistan develop nuclear energy for peaceful use. The foreign ministers of the
two countries were to meet from time to time to exchange views. The
first manifestation of the improved relationship was the five-year
trade agreement concluded between the two, covering the period
1970-75.

Why, then, did the Soviet leaders decide to intervene on behalf
of the Bangladesh movement? The considerations that weighed with
Moscow are not difficult to find. What the Soviets wanted was a
friendly regime in Pakistan, a prime minister who would be willing
to deepen the country's relations with the USSR; loosen its ties with
China; and under Soviet protection, proceed to build nonpolitical cooperative relations with India. The election of December 1970 created
opportunities that the Soviet leaders regarded with hope and enthusiasm. The Pakistani military constituted the hard-core pro-China,

anti-India, and therefore anti-Soviet, element. If the Awami League, led by Mujibur Rahman, could form a government in Pakistan, the prospects of Soviet-Pakistani relations would improve significantly and a new leaf could be turned on relations between India and Pakistan.

Another factor also weighed with the Soviet leaders. If the Bangladesh struggle were allowed to turn into a protracted nationalist guerrilla war, it would radicalize the eastern flank of the subcontinent and pose a dangerous challenge to the Indian political system. From this point of view it was also essential that the struggle be won relatively quickly by the Awami League and its leader, Mujibur Rahman.[25]

On April 3, 1971, Nikolai Podgorny sent a message to Yahya Khan in his capacity as head of the Soviet state, expressing concern at the sufferings and privations of the people of Bangladesh and urging an immediate stoppage of the bloodshed and a "peaceful political settlement" with the elected leaders of the people.[26] In itself, the message was an assertion of the role the Soviet Union had acquired in 1966 as the conflict manager in the subcontinent. Podgorny's message drew forth no immediate U.S. reaction, but there was a countermessage from Chou En-lai.[27] Yahya Khan not only ignored the Kremlin warning, which was followed up with diplomatic pressure, but also appeared in July to be succeeding, with U.S. help, in setting up a civilian regime in East Pakistan with the participation of a section of the Awami League leadership. The Indian foreign minister returned almost empty-handed from a worldwide diplomatic mission. During his brief visit to New Delhi in July, Henry Kissinger volunteered the chilling warning that in the event of Chinese action across the northern border, India could not expect U.S. help. The Indians saw Pakistan as successfully coordinating its policies with Peking and Washington. India stood isolated even in the Third World.[28]

THE WAR OF 1971

In the midst of this Indian predicament came the biggest diplomatic explosion of our time, which was the secret journey of Kissinger to Peking that was arranged through the good offices of Pakistan and the announcement of an upcoming Nixon visit to China. The Sino-American diplomatic breakthrough created identical perceptions in India and the USSR of an emerging "alliance" between the United States and China that would be directed against the Soviet Union. Since Pakistan was a firm ally of China, the new Sino-U.S. linkage could work in South Asia only to the detriment of India. Perceptions of a looming threat to the vital interests and even the survival of India cemented the Indo-Soviet relationship on August 9, 1971, with a 20-year treaty of peace, friendship, and cooperation.

The treaty committed the Soviet Union to meet the security needs of India in the event of aggression or threat of aggression.[29]

In signing the treaty, the Indians did not believe that they gave the USSR more than they expected to get from their ally. The Indian government claimed that the treaty ended the isolation of India, safeguarded its independence and territorial integrity, and was a deterrent to aggression from any quarter. The treaty generated the most stimulating debate on foreign policy in the history of India, a debate that was conducted not in terms of the idealism of the non-alignment of yesteryear but in terms of power politics, spheres of influence, and mutual gain. The test of the treaty, according to the elite consensus, lay in how India could use it to gain its own strategic objectives in the subcontinent, namely by securing Bangladesh by risking war with Pakistan, if necessary, but without getting involved in a war with China.[30]

War was very much in the air even in October and November, as Indira Gandhi returned from Moscow with the assurance of Soviet help if she were compelled to intervene militarily in Bangladesh.[31] The extent and implications of Soviet support were meticulously discussed in New Delhi during the extended visit in November by Nikolai Firyubin, a Soviet deputy foreign minister. At about the same time, a visiting Soviet expert on Asian affairs, Vladimir Kudryavtsev, who is also a member of the CPSU central committee, described the Bangladesh struggle as a war of national liberation and declared that in the event of an Indian war with Pakistan or any other country, the Soviet Union would play the part it had been playing in Vietnam.[32]

The war that was fought between India and Pakistan for two weeks in December could not be compared with the Vietnam war. Pakistan received no support from either of its major allies, China or the United States. The Soviet Union, on the other hand, stood firmly by India. Two days after the outbreak of the war, the Soviet Union warned all nations to keep out of it: the message was obviously addressed to Peking. The Soviet Union blamed the war on the refusal by Pakistan to come to a political settlement with the elected leaders of the Bangladesh people. It called for the speediest ending of bloodshed, and in the UN Security Council it vetoed three resolutions backed by the United States and China calling for an immediate cease-fire. When the U.S. government dispatched a naval task force into the Bay of Bengal, presumably to intervene in the Bangladesh war, the Soviets moved naval units into the same waters. The Soviet ambassador assured the Indian government that the Soviet Union "will not allow the Seventh Fleet to intervene" in the Bangladesh war.[33]

It could well be that Moscow risked a collision with the two other major powers because it was convinced that neither the United

States nor China would physically intervene on behalf of Pakistan. As soon as the war broke out, the White House reconciled itself to the emergence of Bangladesh; the United States and China were more worried about the Indian intentions for West Pakistan, more specifically the parts of Jammu and Kashmir under Pakistani control. An Indian attempt to recover these portions of Kashmir could have led to a wider war.[34] This neither the Soviets nor the Indians wanted. Indira Gandhi declared a unilateral cease-fire immediately after the Pakistani surrender in Bangladesh. Whether she did this on her own or under Soviet pressure, it was the crowning success for Soviet diplomacy during the war. It earned the USSR credit from Nixon himself for restraining India from a "conquest of West Pakistan."[35] This tribute enabled the Pakistani elite to see the Soviet Union as a savior of Pakistan.[36]

After the December war and the birth of Bangladesh, Moscow proceeded confidently toward the achievement of its long-cherished goal, the restoration of strategic harmony in the subcontinent. The overall balance of forces in the subcontinent looked deceptively favorable. The preeminence of India in the subcontinent was now universally recognized. The state-level elections in India in March 1971 and the national election a year later restored the predominance of Indira Gandhi's Congress party, with which the Moscow-oriented CPI was linked in an unofficial political alliance.[37]

The government of the newly created People's Republic of Bangladesh was beholden to India and the USSR, and the three countries were bound together by interlocking security-oriented treaties of peace, friendship, and cooperation. India was holding 93,000 Pakistani prisoners of war and was in physical occupation of several thousand square miles of Pakistani territory, including a new "line of actual control" in Jammu and Kashmir. Pakistan, caught in the trauma of a major military defeat, was faced with a rising tide of ethnic rebellion in Sind, Baluchistan, and the Northwest Frontier province.[38] It appeared that India had enough leverage to bend Pakistan to formal acceptance of its predominance in the subcontinent and to submission to its friendly embrace. It was toward this end that the Soviets now employed their diplomatic resources with renewed vigor.

AFTER THE WAR

During 1972-75, however, Indian and Soviet efforts for "complete normalization" of relations in the subcontinent were effectively blocked by Pakistan. With a remarkable combination of tenacity, virtuosity, and flexibility, President (or Prime Minister) Bhutto turned the position of weakness of Pakistan to a position of strength.

The essence of Bhutto's strategy was flexibility and intransigence.
His main objective was to prevent a united front of India and Bangladesh, backed by Moscow, that would wrest from him the diplomatic
recognition of Dacca and his agreement to enter into cooperative relations with India. For two years Bhutto withheld recognition from
Bangladesh, appearing all this time to be trying to win Pakistani public opinion for recognition "at the proper time." As long as he refused to recognize Bangladesh, the Chinese were ready to keep the
new nation out of the United Nations. In the meantime Bhutto convinced India and the Soviet Union that he was their best political bet
in Pakistan; the alternative was restoration of military rule with
even more dependence on China. Bhutto thus got his summit meeting
with Indira Gandhi at Simla in July 1972, where in return for a major
concession on Kashmir, that is, for recognition of the new Indian line
of control and an agreement not to change the status quo by force, he
obtained Indian withdrawal from the Pakistani territory occupied in
the war. [39]

The mellowing impact on India of his concession on Kashmir
transported Bhutto in 1973 to the achievement of his next objective,
which was to effect the repatriation of the war prisoners, still without recognizing Bangladesh. This was worked out in April, when
India and Bangladesh offered to repatriate the war prisoners and
civilian internees, except some 150 whom the Bangladesh government was still determined to try for war crimes. This would be
done if Pakistan would simultaneously send back to Bangladesh the
Bengalis forcibly detained in Pakistan and take back the Pakistanis,
mostly original residents of the Indian state of Bihar, who were still
living in Bangladesh. [40] An agreement on tripartite repatriation was
finally reached in August 1973 between India and Pakistan, with the
concurrence of Bangladesh. [41]

Bhutto's final triumph came in February 1974. On the eve of
a pan-Islamic conference in Lahore, a delegation of foreign ministers of seven Islamic countries flew to Dacca and worked out an
agreement under which Bhutto traded his recognition of the Bangladesh government for dropping of the proposal to try the 150 Pakistanis for war crimes. Bhutto killed three birds with a single stone:
he got the war crimes trial dropped; he recognized Bangladesh without submitting to pressure from India; and he got Mujibur Rahman,
despite his adherence to secularism, to share the Lahore platform
with other leaders of the Islamic world. [42]

By the time the first meeting of the foreign ministers of Pakistan, India, and Bangladesh took place in New Delhi in April 1974,
Bhutto had paid an astonishingly popular visit to Dacca, though its
political results fell far short of his expectations, and the Bangladesh
elite had lost much of its earlier enthusiasm for Indian friendship. [43]

Step by step Bhutto restored "normal" relations with India, but it was the traditional normalcy of mutually hostile neighbors, not the cooperative relationship that the Indians and the Soviets had hoped and labored for after the 1971 war.[44]

Ironically, the political systems of the three countries looked similar in the latter half of 1975, but they were very different from the way the Indians had expected them to be as a result of the 1971 war. In 1972 the Indian elite had seen, in the establishment of a secular, democratic, and "socialist" regime in Bangladesh and the installation of a parliamentary regime in Pakistan, a long coveted vindication of the Indian experiment with representative government.

Events, however, took an entirely reverse turn in mid-1975. Despite its secure majority in parliament, the government of Indira Gandhi faced a populist rebellion of unprecedented dimension. It proclaimed a state of national emergency on June 26, 1975; this was accompanied by the arrest of thousands of opposition leaders, the imposition of strict press censorship, and a severe curtailment of individual freedoms. By the end of the year it became clear that the national emergency would continue indefinitely and that India would not return to the pre-emergency political system of a full-fledged parliamentary democracy.[45]

In Bangladesh, Sheikh Mujibur Rahman dissolved the national assembly, abrogated the constitution, abolished the political parties, and brought the press under government control in February-March 1975. At the same time he installed a presidential system of one-party government. On August 15 he and members of his family were brutally murdered by a military junta. Between August and December control of the government changed hands as many as four times, but it still remained in the grip of the military, who ruled the nation under martial law.[46]

In Pakistan an armed rebellion in Baluchistan, widespread unrest in the Frontier province, and an unabated power struggle between the military and civilian political leaders and also among the civilian political leaders themselves led to the suppression of several opposition parties, to mass arrests of dissident political leaders, and to the abolition of popular government in two of the four provinces.[47]

The Soviet leaders welcomed and fully supported Indira Gandhi's assumption of authoritarian power, which they, as the CPI, saw as a response to an offensive from the right-wing and reactionary forces in collusion with external powers.[48] In contrast, the Soviet media took a dim view of Bhutto's suppression of the "democratic" opposition. The killing of Mujibur Rahman and many of his close political colleagues created apprehension in the Soviet Union that the foreign policy of Bangladesh might change, thus enabling China to build a presence in the eastern flank of the subcontinent.[49]

In the light of this broad outline of developments in the subcontinent during the 1970s, we shall now examine more closely the Soviet relations with India, Pakistan, and Bangladesh. As we shall see, Soviet policy for the subcontinent has for years tended to be coordinated with its policy for the Persian Gulf region, as the politics of the two regions themselves have intermeshed.

THE SOVIET UNION AND INDIA

Soviet relations with India expanded and deepened after the Bangladesh war. Between 1972 and 1974 the two countries concluded as many as 40 agreements or protocols for economic, technological, scientific, and cultural cooperation. No department of the Indian government is without some cooperative linkage with the Kremlin. The Soviet Union is now the largest trade partner of India in years when India does not have to import large quantities of food grains from the United States. For the last few years the trade balance has been in favor of India, enabling it to use part of the surplus to pay for military supplies. The Soviet Union is also not only the largest single supplier of its defense needs, but also the most important single source of assistance to its rapidly growing defense industry.[50]
Intergovernmental commissions of economic, technological, and scientific cooperation have been meeting regularly every year since February 1973. Each year the agreement has provided for greater collaboration than did the agreement of the year before. Although India has resisted the Soviet proposal for "integration" of the two economies, there exists between the two countries what the Soviet leaders call an "international division of labor," and a certain degree of coordination has come to be established between the planning bodies of the two countries, especially since the conclusion of a 15-year trade agreement. The Indian minister for foreign trade announced in 1973 that "structural changes" would be made in the foreign trade of the country to place increasing reliance on trade with the Soviet bloc, while the minister of commerce remarked a year later that the two economies had become "complementary."[51]
At the political level the high-water mark of the relationship was Brezhnev's five-day official visit to New Delhi in November 1973, his first visit to any Asian land as chief of the CPSU. In Brezhnev's own words, the visit brought about a "qualitative improvement in Indo-Soviet friendship and enabled the two governments jointly to plan long-term economic collaboration through the principle of 'international division of labor'."[52] During the visit the two countries signed a 15-year economic cooperation agreement. Since 1973

the Soviet Union has been the largest single supplier of such strategic Indian needs as kerosene, fertilizers, newsprint, heavy industrial equipment, and oil drilling and exploration machinery. In 1974 the Soviet government came to help India avert a large-scale famine by "lending" 2 million tons of wheat out of its own U.S. imports. The two countries are collaborating in a space program; the first Indian satellite was successfully launched in 1974 from a Soviet pad. Also in 1974 the Soviet Union resumed substantial collaboration with India in onshore oil exploration.

In the political field, the Soviet Union and India have worked together on all major international issues. After the announcement of the Nixon Doctrine, and more particularly after the 1971 war with Pakistan, India moved closer to Hanoi and to the provisional revolutionary government in South Vietnam, and in 1975 it welcomed the Communist victories in Indochina. [53] On the Middle East issue, India has been persistently pro-Arab. In the Arab world India has moved closer to Iraq and Syria since the death of Nasser. Although India no longer plays a leadership role in Afro-Asian and nonaligned forums, it has supported the admission of Communist regimes to the annual conferences of nonaligned countries, and at the United Nations it has voted with the Arabs on such polarizing issues as the listing of Zionism as a racist ideology. More importantly, Sino-Indian relations continue to remain deadlocked: the Chinese perceive India as no better than a Soviet satellite. Relations with the United States showed some improvement in 1974 but were still deadlocked in early 1976. [54]

A broad convergence of the regional strategic interests of India and the global strategic interests of the Soviet Union has continued through the mid-1970s. As long as the United States leans on China in order to improve its bargaining position with the Soviet Union, India will regard the Sino-U.S. friendship as working against its strategic interests simply because the two adversaries of the USSR are friendly toward Pakistan, while India is the friend of the Soviet Union. [55]

Among the three world powers, the Indians see only the Soviet Union as genuinely interested in the emergence of India as a major regional power. Indians argue that the main reason why India cannot have a balanced relationship with the United States and the Soviet Union is that the United States treats India at par with Pakistan, while the USSR regards India as an equal of China. That is why Indians see the status of their country as the leading South Asian power as impinging on Chinese and U.S. interests in the region but agreeing with Soviet interests. Therefore the Indian nuclear blast of May 18, 1974, was condemned in China and the United States but not in the Soviet Union. For the same reason, Indians argue, the

annexation of Sikkim in 1975 as an "associate state of the Indian
Union" provoked the anger of the Chinese government and was strongly criticized in the U.S. media, while the Soviet Union welcomed the
measure as a contribution to peace and stability in South Asia.[56]

In the absence of a strong U.S. profile in South Asia, China
cements the strategic linkage between the USSR and India. China
makes India as important to the Soviet Union as it makes the USSR
important to India. In 1970-72 India made several probings to improve its relations with China; a certain amount of improvement
would not have been contrary to the Soviet-Indian treaty of friendship.[57] The requirements of normalization of Sino-Indian relations
were discussed between aides of the two countries in Rangoon,
Cairo, Katmandu, and Moscow. After the events of 1971 the Chinese
leaders apparently concluded that India had become an even more
helpless tool than before for Soviet expansionism and an instrument
in the Soviet-led "encirclement" of China. Besides, the Indian intervention in the Bangladesh war and the "annexation" of Sikkim have
reinforced the Chinese perception of India as an "expansionist power."
In the mid-1970s the Indian elite do not see any real possibility of an
improvement in Sino-Indian relations as long as the Moscow-Peking
cold war continues. The Chinese support for a U.S. security role in
Asia; the transfer of Chinese weapons to Pakistan; the Chinese support for the simmering tribal insurgencies on the eastern border of
India; the Chinese effort to build up Maoist groups in India; renewed
tension on the Sino-Indian border; the Chinese plan for rapid industrialization, including modernization of the air force with large-
scale imports of sophisticated Western technology--all of these are
seen by the Indians, with the encouragement of the Soviet Union, as
irrefutable evidence of an immutable Chinese hostility to the status
of India as the dominant South Asian power.[58] This Indian perception of China increases the importance of the Soviet Union for India's
security planners on the one hand and reinforces the arguments for
an independent Indian nuclear capability on the other hand.

Paradoxically, the dismemberment of Pakistan has not narrowed the security gap of India but has probably widened it. The
India-Bangladesh border has not turned out to be the expected border
of peace and friendship. India maintains the same strength of troops
on this border as it used to when Bangladesh was East Pakistan.
Political instability in Bangladesh can easily endanger the social and
economic stability of West Bengal, and an unfriendly regime in Dacca
can cause much security concern in India.[59]

Though geographically smaller, Pakistan is not militarily
weaker, but perhaps stronger. In order to give itself a "protective
cover," truncated Pakistan spent 40 percent more on defense in
1973-74 than the united Pakistan had spent in 1970-71.[60] In 1973 the

geographically much smaller, but more defensible, Pakistan had an
army that was not weaker, either in number or in weaponry, than the
Pakistani army of 1971. Compared to India, Pakistan in the mid-
1970s has more diversified sources of defense support, including
China, the United States, and some of the oil-rich Middle East. The
security gap of India in relation to Pakistan becomes wider still if
the United States takes a greater interest in the security of Pakistan
than it has taken since the early 1960s, which is not improbable.
The Washington Post reported in March 1975, when the United States
resumed selling arms to the subcontinent, that the "intensifying geopolitical swirls" in South and Southeast Asia appeared to have enhanced the importance of Pakistan in the eyes of U.S. foreign policy
makers, who now believed that it was "no longer in American interest
to keep Pakistan defenseless."[61] The security planners of India have
to take into account a "hostile" U.S. naval presence in the Indian
Ocean as well as India's unwilling but inevitable involvement in the
intensifying Sino-Soviet cold war.

In the context of the prevailing international alignment of
forces, the connection of Pakistan with the United States immediately
reinforces the connection of India with the Soviet Union. After the
1971 war the Soviet Union replenished most, if not all, of the weapons
losses of India; as soon as the war had broken out, it had cut off transfer of arms to Pakistan. The Soviet Union, however, was resisting
Indian requests for long-range, deep-penetration Soviet aircraft to
replace the aging Canberras, and this created a certain strain on
Soviet-Indian relations.[62] The Soviet leaders apparently changed
their minds when Washington notified New Delhi and Rawalpindi that
it would be lifting the decade-old embargo on the sale of arms to
Pakistan and India. As India, and Afghanistan, reacted sharply to
the U.S. decision, the Soviet defense minister, Marshal Grechko,
paid a much-publicized visit to New Delhi in the company of his two
junior colleagues, Admiral Sergei G. Gorshkov, chief of the Soviet
navy, and Marshal Pavel Kutakhov, chief of the Soviet air force.
The three Soviet military leaders met their Indian counterparts for
intensive discussion. Grechko also delivered to Indira Gandhi a
personal letter from Brezhnev.[63] The talks apparently resolved
whatever differences had come to exist between the two governments
over defense supplies. Krasnaya Zvezda, the Soviet army newspaper,
reported on February 26, 1975, that the two sides had agreed to
further intensify and expand their relationship.

The timber of the relationship reflects the images the two
countries have of their friendship and of one another. Neither sees
the relationship as between two unequal powers. Indians see it as a
coalition in which collaboration for the attainment of shared objectives does not preclude effort by each to use its influence on the other

for the pursuit of its own strategic interests. Indians argue that the relationship so far has been entirely to India's advantage; India, they claim, has done nothing it would not have done even if it had been less friendly with Moscow. As a senior official of the Indian foreign office told me in January 1975, "If you make a list of what India and the Soviet Union have each got out of the friendship, you will find that we have got everything we wanted without surrendering on any issue of real concern to our national interest." In support of this widely shared view, the Indians point to the nuclear blast of 1974 and stress the fact that India has so far given no formal support to the Soviet concept of an Asian collective security system. "In fact," as a cabinet minister told me, "Iran has gone far ahead of India in endorsing the Soviet concept."

Prime Minister Indira Gandhi has repeatedly denied that the Soviet Union has any influence on India. During Brezhnev's visit she declared at a public reception that at no time had the Soviet Union tried to influence Indian decisions. [64] However, she knows that in most countries of the world her government is considered to be under Soviet influence. At a press conference at Kingston in April 1975 she conceded that "almost any time that I am met by various foreign dignitaries or the foreign press, the question is put to me about our being influenced by the Soviet Union." She called this "absolutely ridiculous," and made a rather revealing observation: "The USSR has come to our support at the right time at no cost to them, and perhaps the United States policy has given them the opportunity to do so."[65]

The Indians realize that the Indo-Soviet friendship has cost the USSR next to nothing. It has intensified the Soviet cold war with China, but it has so far not led to a Sino-Soviet confrontation except in rhetoric. The United States has not accused the Soviets of "expansionism" in India and has not made the Soviet support for New Delhi an issue in negotiating the detente between the two superpowers. [66] The costlessness or low cost of the Soviet connection, Indians argue, puts India in a strong bargaining position. The friendship, they believe, rests on a foundation of objective conditions, that is, upon the need for India by the Soviet Union in its confrontation with China and the need for the Soviet Union by India in its development and defense.

The structure of Indo-Soviet friendship is also not devoid of a subjective content. The most vocal constituency of the friendship is, of course, the Indian Communists. Even the Marxists who are critical of Soviet "revisionism" and of Soviet support for the "reactionary" government of Indira Gandhi want Indo-Soviet relations to be stronger. [6]

The real subjective strength, however, comes from the perception of the USSR by the national elite. With the exception of the elite belonging to the rightist and conservative groups, most Indians see the

Soviet Union not in terms of ideology but in the more convincing terms of military, economic, and political power. The USSR is not seen by the Indian elite as a revolutionary power out to extend the frontiers of Communism by subversion or force, but rather as the Other Power, which is broadly in sympathy with the national aspirations of the newly liberated countries and more at home with the "progressive" national bourgeoisie than with the Communists. The Indians are more impressed with the political stability of the Soviet system and its economic achievements and military power than with the Soviet personality and the quality of Soviet society. In the 1970s the USSR is seen by most Indian opinion makers as steadily overtaking the United States in strategic power and as capable of playing, and willing to play, the role of a global power. They are also impressed with the growing economic power of the Soviet bloc and with its increasing capability to compete with the capitalist system. [68]

Public opinion polls in the metropolitan areas of Delhi, Bombay, Calcutta, and Madras have shown that a large plurality of Indians belonging to all age groups and income and educational categories have greater confidence in the ability of the Soviet Union to "manage international crises" than in that of the United States. In successive polls in these areas, the USSR has also topped the countries Indians say they like most. [69]

Nevertheless, the Soviet connection produces resentment, misgivings, even serious concern in India and raises questions for which few can find the answers. Are the major powers, despite their noisy differences, moving toward a balance of power in which the subcontinent will be reduced to a Soviet sphere of influence? Will the Soviet connection get India involved in conflicts that it would be in its better interests to keep out of? How long can India do without U.S. friendship and Chinese good neighborliness? Will the Soviet friendship for Pakistan end up in a tilt? If there is a Sino-Soviet detente after the passing of Mao, can it happen without great cost to India? Can it happen without a Moscow-Peking "arrangement" for influence in the subcontinent? [70]

In the economic field the Indians are conscious of the advantages of paying for Soviet goods with Indian goods or in Indian currency. The Soviet bloc also provides a market for the products of Indian industry, which the advanced capitalist countries do not wish to buy. However, Indians often resent the Soviet pricing system and complain that they suffer at both ends, as buyers as well as sellers. In the economic ministries there is some concern about the quality of Soviet technology and not much respect for Soviet industrial efficiency. Planners and industrial bureaucrats are heard to complain that the composition and quality of Soviet aid do not always match the requirements of the present, increasingly sophisticated, stage of

Indian development. Indians also resent the fact that the Soviet Union still insists on delivering turnkey projects, refusing to transfer to competent Indian firms the roles of prime consultants and the task of preparation of feasibility reports. They resent the Soviet practice of maintaining large numbers of Russian personnel at plants when the jobs done by them could be done as well by Indians. In the ministries of the Indian government one can hear complaints about the hard bargaining that goes into most trade transactions with the Russians; about delays in the delivery of Soviet goods; and about Soviet resale of Indian goods and materials to third parties at a profit.

The weakest link in the Indo-Soviet connection is probably the communication gap between the two elites. Although the Indian elite, as noted, has high regard for Soviet military and economic power, its members seem to care little for the Soviet view of world affairs, for Soviet scholarship in the social sciences, and for Soviet models and theories of development. The Indian press carries current affairs analyses by several U.S. and British columnists and reporters but almost never by anyone from the USSR. Even books written on Indian agrarian problems by CPI experts carry few references, if any, to the impressive Soviet literature on the Indian agrarian situation. The Indian and Soviet elites speak two different political languages; the Indian political language is still very much the language of Western liberal democracy and Fabian socialism.

In sum, Soviet-Indian friendship remains strong in the mid-1970s and continues to be reinforced by the mirror perceptions in the two countries of the alliance between the United States and China. The close relations of Pakistan with the Chinese and U.S. governments and the hostility of China toward India make the Soviet connection supremely important for Indian strategic planners. The Indians believe that the USSR alone, among the major powers, supports the primacy of India in South Asia and treats it as a major regional power. They have no perception of India as being under Soviet influence. India would like to improve its relations with the United States and China but does not expect any significant development in that direction as long as these two major powers coordinate their policies for containing Soviet power and influence. The prevailing correlation of international forces impinging on the subcontinent imposes a strategic harmony on the Indo-Soviet friendship. India, however, has not supported the Soviet proposal for a collective security system for Asia and in fact has tended in recent years to downgrade the importance of the Indo-Soviet treaty. Although in 1972-73 hardly a month passed without an Indian cabinet minister visiting the USSR, the number of ministerial visits has declined sharply since 1974. The prime minister herself has not gone to Moscow since 1972 at the time of this writing (March 1976). She has not even returned the Brezhnev visit.

It was announced in May 1976 that she would be visiting Moscow in
June 1976, her first visit to the Soviet Russian capital since August-
September 1971. Far from signaling any "trouble" with the relationship, this may well indicate its stability and "normalcy." This
was indicated by Indira Gandhi on the last day of 1975 in her address
to the annual session of her Congress party. The United States, she
told her followers, was playing the same "destabilizing game" in
India that it had used to topple the Allende government in Chile, and
India was facing "the greatest danger of outside interference" in the
history of its independence. [71]

THE SOVIET UNION AND BANGLADESH

The importance of Bangladesh to the USSR lies mainly in its
impact on the balance of political and military power in the subcontinent. Since the 1971 war, the objectives of Soviet diplomacy in the
subcontinent have been (1) to restore stability in the context of a balance of power based on Indian primacy; (2) to promote normalization
of relations toward this end, with India and Bangladesh coordinating
their negotiating positions with regard to Pakistan; and (3) to deny
China and the United States any role, negative or positive, in the
process of normalization. These objectives imposed on Moscow the
quite formidable task of helping the new republic of Bangladesh to its
feet, while simultaneously promoting the primacy of India and en-
deavoring to mend fences with Pakistan.

The supportive role of Moscow in the early months of Bangladesh independence was expressed through a number of initiatives.
Moscow recognized Bangladesh on January 24, 1972, the first major
power, and one of the first nations, to do so. Within two weeks
Pravda announced that Sheikh Mujibur Rahman had been invited to
pay an official visit to the Soviet Union. [72] On February 7, Aeroflot
inaugurated a weekly service between Moscow and Dacca, the first
international route of the infant republic. By March, the Soviet embassy in Dacca had a staff of 90, many of the members of which were
fluent in the Bengali language.

Also in March a .2 billion taka ($12 million) trade deal was
concluded, involving the exchange of Soviet equipment and material
for the traditional exports of the area. Subsequent trade-and-aid
negotiations resulted in a three-year pact for a yearly trade worth
$435 million and a modest Soviet commitment to provide the equiva-
lent of $39 million to finance projects in the public sector. Almost
overnight some 400 industrial units were created by nationalization,
including jute and textile mills owned by Pakistani capitalists.

In the next few months the Soviet Union gave Bangladesh some aircraft for domestic use and a squadron of MIG fighter planes. The Soviet Union agreed to train pilots for the Bangladesh air force and also offered limited help in the field of irrigation, flood control, oil exploration, and communication. It showed particular interest in completing a power project near Dacca that it had begun to build four years before.

The most expensive and important service the Soviets gave Bangladesh was the clearing of the heavily mined shipping channels of Chittagong and Cox's Bazar, free of cost. Operating with a 20-unit Soviet fleet, the Russians completed the operation in two years, salvaging 17 ships ranging from a 15,000-ton freighter to small coastal ships and barges.[73]

Almost from the beginning, however, it was clear that the Soviet Union had no wish to assume a major role in the security and economic reconstruction of Bangladesh. In the closing days of the 1971 war, Moscow had turned down an Indian suggestion that it conclude a security-oriented treaty of cooperation and friendship with Bangladesh. After the war the Soviets welcomed Rahman's initiative to conclude a 15-year treaty with India. The terms of the treaty were arranged between Rahman and Indira Gandhi during their four-day meeting in New Delhi in February 1972. However, the treaty was not announced until Rahman's return from his state visit to Moscow.[74]

A joint communique issued after Rahman's conversations with Brezhnev and Kosygin lauded the "active and consistent support" by the Soviet Union for the Bangladesh liberation struggle, which, it said, "revealed the true friends and foes" of the new nation, an oblique reference to China and the United States. The communique spoke of the resolve by the two governments to "expand and deepen" areas of economic, cultural, and political cooperation. It identified avenues in which Soviet development aid would be forthcoming, and it provided for contacts between the political parties, trade unions, and youth organizations of the two sides. The communique stressed the importance of normalizing relations within the subcontinent through negotiations among the parties directly concerned and appealed to "peace-loving countries" to "administer a determined rebuff to all attempts at outside interference" in the affairs of the region.[75]

The Soviet Union was prevented by local and regional as well as global factors from assuming a larger role than it did in the life of the new Bengali nation. The problems faced by Bangladesh were so enormous, and its immediate and long-term needs for relief and assistance so pervasive, that in order to play a significant role in "building" Bangladesh, the Soviet Union would have had to transfer a massive quantity of material, equipment, and technical personnel to the new state, a course it was apparently not willing to pursue; nor was it asked to by Bangladesh and India.[76]

A strong Soviet physical presence would have been seen by the world as a direct bid to bring Bangladesh under Soviet influence, if not control; it would not have been liked even by India, which regarded the new nation as within its natural orbit of influence. Moreover, such a Soviet presence in Bangladesh would have alienated Pakistan and made normalization of relations in the subcontinent even more difficult. In any case it would have imposed a heavy draft on the limited transferable resources of the USSR, which were heavily strained in 1972 by the more important demands of Soviet allies and clients such as North Vietnam, India, Egypt, Syria, and Iraq. Therefore, since the initial gifts and credits of 1972, the Soviet Union has made no significant fresh commitments to Bangladesh. It did join other nations in sending emergency aid, especially .2 million tons of wheat, in August 1973 when large areas of Bangladesh faced a famine.

Trade, as opposed to aid, has continued at a fairly brisk rate, but not up to mutual expectations. A protocol signed in December 1973 provided for a 54 percent increase in the exchange of goods in 1974 over the level of 1973, but actual trade fell far short of that goal. Bangladesh could not deliver goods in which the Soviets were interested. Deliveries of Soviet equipment were often delayed, partly because the output of Russian factories lagged behind schedule, but more often because Bangladesh was not ready to construct planned projects.[77]

The Soviet Union might have assumed a bigger role in the development of Bangladesh if the new nation had adopted the Soviet model of "noncapitalist development" under a mobilization system of government. Soviet analysts came to the conclusion in 1972-73 that Bangladesh, with its extremely small and highly fragmented bourgeoisie, its lack of an entrepreneurial and managerial elite, and its preponderance of peasants with small holdings, was unsuitable for capitalist development and parliamentary democracy.[78]

The Awami League represented the landowning class and the small urban bourgeoisie.[79] The left itself was weak and fragmented. The Bangladesh Communist Party (BCP), which had been banned for 20 years, could boast in 1971 of only a skeletal underground organization. Its legally functioning front, the faction of the National Awami party led by Muzaffar Ahmad (NAP-M), had little influence outside the cities and towns. On the other hand the youth elements, radicalized during the liberation struggle, were inclined toward violent extremism and were potential recruits for a Maoist Communist party. Even in 1971, therefore, the Soviet Union, through the Communist party of India, had tried to bring about a united front of the India-based

Awami League leaders and the BCP and its front organization, the
NAP-M.[80] The efforts of the CPI failed, since neither the Awami
League leaders nor the Indian government had any enthusiasm for it.
However, a coordinating committee was formed with Awami League
and BCP and NAP-M leaders, though it had little impact either on
the liberation war or on the political course taken by Bangladesh.
Mujibur Rahman paid no heed to the BCP demand for a government
of "democratic and left unity." In the national election of March 1973
the BCP and the NAP-M could not shore up a single seat, although
the latter polled 1.5 million votes as against the 14 million polled by
the Awami League.[81]

In August 1973 a delegation of the BCP went to Moscow to meet
with the CPSU. It was agreed that the BCP and the NAP-M would
now concentrate their efforts on achieving the unity of "democratic
and national-patriotic forces," which in the context of Bangladesh
meant the Awami League, the Communist party and allied organizations, and the broad strata of "progressive" nationalist elements.[82]
In subsequent weeks the two groups again approached Rahman for the
formation of a "popular united front" among party organizations outside the government. This time Rahman, beset by a constant down-
turn in the economy and a rapid loss of public confidence in the ability of his government to set things right, as well as by the vitriolic
invectives from groups of Maoist and pro-Pakistani elements, accepted the proposal and himself inaugurated the front in October.[83]

The front had little impact on the politics of the new nation,
but it did help the BCP to expand its party organization to most of
the district and subdivisional towns in a short time and to set up a
skeletal peasant organization. At the same time the BCP lost a good
deal of its revolutionary image, particularly in the universities and
urban middle classes. In 1974 the popularity of the Rahman government touched rock bottom. The economy ground to a halt. The
treasury was practically empty. In December 1974 I found a deep
pall of gloom and an anguished sense of doom in the intellectual communities in Dacca and other cities. The Dacca city authorities were
burning 200 "unclaimed" bodies each week. Law and order had
broken down in much of the interior. The youth, who had spearheaded the Bangladesh struggle, felt that their revolution had been
betrayed. A relatively small number of political operators and
traders, most of them either belonging to, or with close connections
with, the Awami League, had fattened in three years at the expense
of the vast majority of the populace. Rahman himself was accused
of patronizing corruption, bureaucratic lethargy and inefficiency,
and nepotism. The most charitable in the intellectual community
saw him as a prisoner in the hands of a small clique of power-hungry,
newly rich people.[84]

Sensing that in order to retain his leadership Rahman would have to radically modify the political system, the BCP, reportedly with Soviet approval came out with a new political model for Bangladesh in late 1974. This model, as Moni Singh, the leader of the party, explained to me in a long interview, was designed to generate a political momentum of radical social change, vigorous mobilization of resources, increased production, and equitable distribution of the national output. The model prescribed a presidential system of government with a cabinet of "progressive, efficient and honest" persons drawn from the democratic and national-patriotic parties. Although there would still be a national assembly, it would have only limited power, and the cabinet would not be made responsible to it. Speaking about the model, Moni Singh asserted,

> Bangladesh has neither a strong capitalist class nor a class of big landlords. This makes it a very different society from India. We therefore need not live in a parliamentary system, which can only lead to stratification of the classes and which, in effect, legitimizes exploitation of the poor by the rich. The parliamentary system cannot but be a roadblock to significant social change. What we need is an efficient, honest, and ideologically progressive government, a government of progressive and democratic forces under the leadership of Sheikh Mujibur Rahman.

The capitalist powers, Moni Singh continued, were neither willing nor able to lift Bangladesh out of its economic travail. However, he said, "there are the socialist countries, which will give us all the help we need if we were to follow the correct political line and are able to mobilize our own resources to the maximum extent possible." The BCP, then, had little doubt that the Soviet bloc would underwrite the development needs of Bangladesh if Rahman adopted the political model it advocated.

Moni Singh said, "We strongly believe that the force of circumstances will compel the Sheikh to adopt our political line." He was wrong. In January and February 1975, as noted, Rahman dismantled the parliamentary system and set up a one-party presidential dictatorship with little or no change in his presidential cabinet.[85] Even then the situation was not entirely uncongenial for the Communists, who could now function from within the national party, the Workers' and Peasants' Awami League, that Rahman had launched. The authoritarian measures taken by Rahman were therefore welcomed in the Soviet Union.

The coup of August 15, however, created an entirely different
situation. Developments in Bangladesh now caused grave concern in
Moscow. Soviet analysts were worried that the new elements in
power in Bangladesh might change the course of the foreign policy of
the country. The gains of the war of national liberation might then
be lost, and Bangladesh might turn out to be a negative factor for the
stability and security of the subcontinent. Soviet commentators took
note of the predominance of "pro-Pakistani" elements in the Bangladesh army, of the arrest and detention of "progressive" people, of
the banning of the Workers' and Peasants' Awami League, and of the
gladness the developments since the coup had produced in Pakistan
and China. They were afraid that the "forces of imperialism, Maoism and internal reaction" might now ."carry out vigorous actions"
and that Bangladesh might be torn away from its "proven allies."
They warned that such a turn of developments in Bangladesh might
affect the situation in the subcontinent and that the situation in the
subcontinent might influence "people far away from that important
part of the world."[86]

Bangladesh vividly illustrates how impossible it is for a big,
strong power to influence, far less control, the events in a small,
weak nation. India could defeat Pakistan in East Pakistan and usher
in the republic of Bangladesh, but it could not shape the course of
events in the new nation. Although Indira Gandhi refrained from intervening in the affairs of Bangladesh, she made it quite clear, especially after the attack on the life of the Indian high commissioner
in October, that India could not be indifferent to what happened in the
neighboring country if its events had a spillover effect on the security and well-being of India itself.[87]

No Bangladesh government can survive in enmity with India,
and the new rulers in Dacca quickly started mending fences with their
big and powerful neighbor. However, foreign policy options are not
entirely closed to Bangladesh. In the current context of the balance
of power in the subcontinent, even a limited opening to China in Bangladesh may cause consternation in India. Political instability may
create a radical situation in Bangladesh that would pose a threat to
the eastern flank of India. In short, within four years of the birth of
Bangladesh, much of what India and the USSR had gained from the war
of December 1971 appeared to have been lost, at least for some time.
The future of India and the USSR in Bangladesh remains uncertain.

THE SOVIET UNION AND PAKISTAN

The change of political weather in Bangladesh has enhanced the
importance of Pakistan for the overall Soviet strategy in South Asia.[88]

The intractable problem here is the predominance of India as the regional power. Among the few things on which Pakistani and Indian intellectuals seem to agree is that the self-image of Pakistan will not permit it to accept a regional order in which India is the leading power. "Pakistan's sense of national prestige and honor makes it impossible for her to be a party to [any] scheme of Indian hegemony in [South] Asia," asserts G. W. Choudhuri in what is widely regarded as the best-written study of relations between Pakistan and India by a Pakistani scholar. If peace in South Asia means peace under Indian influence, he adds, Pakistan will be no party to it.[89] "Pakistan's perception of its own independence in the region," echoes an Indian expert on Pakistani affairs, "will not allow it to establish a relationship vis-a-vis India which is ordained by [India's] size and resources."[90] The Soviets are as much aware of this as are the other external powers. Nevertheless, they have been trying to wear down the resistance of Pakistan to neighborly cooperation with India. The uncertainty of Soviet-Pakistani friendship stems from the exactly opposite results sought from it by the two countries. The Soviet Union wishes to use its friendship to bend Pakistan to the acceptance of a regional order in the subcontinent in which India predominates; before this can happen, the friendship of the Soviets must be able to wean Pakistan away from China. The objective of the friendship of Pakistan for the Soviet Union is to enhance its own importance for China, which is the power it needs to counter India, and to sow seeds of discord in the wide pasture of Soviet-Indian friendship.

The Pakistani ruling elite have had a monolithic vision of the size, manpower, resources, and strength of India, all of which is a threat to the independence and integrity of Pakistan. Therefore, as an authority on the foreign policy of Pakistan has stated with some candor, "there is not the same degree of community of interests between the Soviet Union and Pakistan as there is between China and Pakistan."[91] The Soviet Union, he adds, wants to bring Pakistan and India together in order to erect a formidable barrier to China in South Asia. Pakistan, on the other hand, perceives China as the only major power that can help it maintain its independence from encroachment by India.[92]

Zulfikar Ali Bhutto came to power in Pakistan in the wake of the 1971 war, not to bow to the primacy of India but to resist it to the best of the ability and resources of Pakistan. In his first message to the people of Pakistan as their president, Bhutto spoke of revenge, and of undoing the "temporary humiliation" of the defeat in Bangladesh.[93] A year later he declared that Pakistan could not pursue its confrontation with India and must of necessity adopt a policy of "consultation and negotiation."[94]

However, this mellowness was a clever simulation to gain the objectives we have already noted. The Soviets played an important part as intermediaries between India and Pakistan. They succeeded in persuading India to soften its negotiating position. The Soviets have also hailed each and every accord reached between India, Pakistan, and Bangladesh since 1972. However, the cumulative return from all of the India-Pakistan agreements concluded by Bhutto has been to restore the relationship to the prewar level of ill-neighborliness. Pakistan's self-image in 1973 was that of a nation better equipped to stand up to Indian hegemony. "Today we have a far more compact frontier to defend without any danger of internal sabotage and with many friendly countries physically standing behind us as a second line of defense," declared Pakistan Radio on the occasion of the country's independence day in 1973.

What Pakistan wants is to enjoy the fruits of Soviet friendship without bending to the Soviet strategic design for South Asia. Soviet friendship is also important, because Pakistan wants to keep as many options as possible open in a fast-changing world.

For 25 years and more, the foreign policy of Pakistan has been searching in vain for an ally that could do as much for Pakistan as, for instance, the Soviet Union has done for India, that is, that would commit its political and military power to the defense of Pakistan in the event of a war with India. As long as the world was bipolar, the military alliance with the United States enabled Pakistan to hold its own against the much larger resource-base of India, but as soon as the cold war began to yield to a Soviet-American detente and the two superpowers could be seen working together to contain China, the foundation of the U.S.-oriented foreign policy of Pakistan collapsed.

It found itself surrounded by three large hostile powers. As Ayub Khan admitted, it was its "geographical location and the political compulsions inherent therein [that] have determined the course of Pakistan's foreign policy in recent years." Since Pakistan had to "accept the situation of implacable Indian hostility," the new policy was to "set up bilateral equations" with the Soviet Union and China "with the clear understanding that the nature and complexion of the equation should be such as to promote our mutual interests without adversely affecting the legitimate interest of third parties."[95] In other words, Pakistan sought to cultivate Soviet friendship without hurting China and vice versa. This policy received its underpinning from the perception by Pakistan of a long-term competition among the three major powers for areas of influence. "None of them," concluded Ayub Khan, "can afford to isolate and antagonize any of the developing countries completely."[96]

For over a decade the foreign policy of Pakistan has rested basically on the premises constructed by Ayub Khan. Although this

foreign policy has paid off handsomely in peaceful times, enabling
Pakistan to bask in the assistance derived from each of the three
major powers, it has failed to produce the ally Pakistan has been
looking for. In its two wars with India in six years, all it could get
from the United States, its treaty-bound ally, was either neutrality
or clumsy, ineffectual political support and no military assistance.
The lesson the Pakistanis have drawn is that the United States does
not regard its own stakes in the subcontinent to be so high that it
would engage in a military confrontation with India and the USSR by
intervening in behalf of Pakistan in an India-Pakistan war.

During the war of September 1965 the Chinese did issue an
"ultimatum" to India that threatened military action along the eastern
sector of the Sino-Indian border; the "ultimatum" did propel the UN
Security Council to demand a cease-fire before the war could hurt
Pakistan too much.[97] However, China's "activist" role in that war
was possible because the Soviet Union was neutral. The Chinese did
not even make the appearance of an intervention in Pakistan's behalf
during the 1971 war, while the Soviet Union stood firmly by India,
promising to take on the Chinese on the border and the United States
in the Bay of Bengal.[98] After the war Bhutto told the BBC that Pakistan had not "lost confidence in China's friendship or China's words."

Two years later he asked the United States either to give Pakistan the arms it needed or denounce the military treaty.[99] At the
same time he looked up to Iran for a protective wing. Nevertheless,
Pakistan continued to remain unprotected by any power that could
challenge the Soviet-Indian alliance.

The predicament of Pakistan stems from the extremely unequal
Sino-Soviet power equation; the unequal Soviet and Chinese stakes in
South Asia; and what has almost become a rule in relations among
the major powers, which is mutual recognition of "legitimate" spheres
of interest or influence. There is reason to believe that the United
States has more or less recognized the subcontinent as the legitimate
sphere of interest of the USSR.[100]

The Chinese have not; but the subcontinent is by no stretch of
imagination the legitimate sphere of interest of China, and in any
case Peking is incapable of taking on the Soviet Union in a military
conflict. A Chinese attack on India may provoke a Soviet attack on
Sinkiang, the home of Chinese nuclear power. If ever the United
States and China join together in a war with the Soviet Union--a
bizarre scenario--it would be most unlikely to happen in South Asia.
It is not without significance that the Chinese leaders politely turned
down Bhutto's offer of a Sino-Pakistani friendship treaty in February
1972; nor can the Pakistanis expect Iran to rush in where the Chinese
fear to tread.

Not only has Pakistan failed to discover an ally that can match the Soviet friend of its enemy, India, but the objective foundation of the enmity between Pakistan and India has been considerably eroded by the 1971 war and is likely to weaken further as a result of the changing pattern of the involvement of Pakistan with its neighbors, as well as the competition and conflict among the linguistic and ethnic elements of the Pakistani elite. The birth of Bangladesh has diminished the threat posed by India and Pakistan to each other's internal stability. It may or may not have destroyed the two-nation (Hindu-Muslim) theory on the basis of which the subcontinent was, according to the Pakistanis, divided in 1947.

It has certainly undermined the claim of Pakistan to be the guardian of the human rights and liberties of the Muslim community in India. This community no longer looks up to Pakistan with the respect and expectations of the pre-Bangladesh period. The almost total absence of Hindus in Pakistan puts India in a relatively advantageous position, since it can no longer be accused by Pakistan of using a Hindu minority to destabilize its internal politics. It is interesting to note that since 1972 there has been no Hindu-Muslim riot anywhere in the subcontinent. The Hindu-Muslim hostility that used to constantly feed the enmity between India and Pakistan has, then, been diffused by the creation of Bangladesh.

There is no dispute between Pakistan and India except over Kashmir. The land frontier has been defined and demarcated. The dispute over the sharing of the waters of the Punjab rivers was settled in the late 1950s through the good offices of the World Bank. The Kashmir dispute also seems to have been contained, by a mutual agreement not to change the status quo by force.[101]

Since 1972 the ethnic tensions and conflicts in Pakistan have tended to shift away from areas adjacent to India to those adjacent to Afghanistan and Iran. These tensions and conflicts stem at least partly from competition among the different provinces for development funds and political power. The political opposition to Bhutto's Punjab-based Pakistan People's Party (PPP) comes from the Baluchis and the Pathans of the two relatively deprived provinces. These provinces are adjacent to the Baluchi-speaking areas in Iran and to the Pushtu-speaking areas of Afghanistan. It is these two neighbors rather than India who are now involved in the domestic tensions and conflicts of Pakistan.

The Afghan involvement is of course not new; the Pakhtoonistan demand has had a certain sympathy in India. The Iranian involvement, however, is of very recent vintage. The Baluchi rebellion of 1973 compelled the Shah's intervention. He told a reporter of the New York Times that he would "seize Pakistani Baluchistan before anyone [else] did so."[102]

The Shah's intervention was welcomed by Bhutto and his supporters in Punjab, but it created considerable resentment in Baluchistan and the Northwest Frontier province. Bhutto has brought these
provinces under direct rule of the central government, thus depriving
the local political leaders of their legitimate claim to power. All
Pakistanis, then, do not perceive the Shah of Iran as a protector of
the integrity and independence of Pakistan against encroachment by
India. This predominantly Punjabi power establishment perception
is rejected by the elites of Baluchistan and the Northwest Frontier
province.

The Shah's intervention stemmed primarily from his concern
about the stability of the Baluchi-speaking portions of Iran. In recent
years the Shah has taken a hand in trying to resolve the tension between Pakistan and Afghanistan. In 1973 the Shah sent a special envoy
to Kabul in a bid to defuse Prime Minister Mahammed Daud's territorial dispute with Pakistan.[103] The next year Bhutto, on a visit to
Moscow, asked the Soviet leaders to intervene with Kabul. In March
1975 Daud himself journeyed to both New Delhi and Tehran to seek
support for the Afghan case against Pakistan. In October 1975 the
Indian foreign minister made a five-day visit to Kabul, immediately
followed by a two-day visit to Tehran.[104] If the Pakhtoonistan issue
has thus been "regionalized," Iran and the Soviet Union mean much
more to the disputants than does India, the involvement of which is
no more than marginal.

Whatever may be the long-term consequences of Iranian involvement in the internal politics of Pakistan, the Indian disengagement is beginning to have an impact on the Pakistani elite. In the
Pakistani press one comes across far fewer complaints about Indian
interference in the internal affairs of Pakistan than one used to before the 1971 war. If Pakistan and India each cease to see the other
as a threat to its internal security, and if each is no longer the
other's domestic problem, the two may be able, over time, to take
a rational view of their state relations and embark upon mutually
beneficial cooperation. This hasn't happened yet and probably will
not happen in the immediate future. Until it does, Pakistani-Soviet
relations must necessarily remain at a level considerably lower than
Moscow would like.

This, however, does not mean that the Soviets have no leverage
in Pakistan at all. Apart from what Moscow can do in terms of Pakistani development, Bhutto probably needs his Soviet connection to
keep the generals at bay. The political ambition of the military has
not died with the defeat in Bangladesh.[105] Although Bhutto needs
Soviet friendship and the promise of better relations with India in
order to stabilize his power, his competitive plus cooperative relationship with the generals does not permit him to move closer either
to Moscow or to New Delhi, even if he should wish to.

It is not clear whether he does, and relations between his government and the USSR have therefore remained less than warm. Bhutto has visited Moscow twice since 1972. Although economic relations have been resumed, he has not been able to persuade the Soviet leaders to resume military aid. Pakistan is no longer criticized in the Soviet media. On such issues as the friendship of Pakistan with China and the resumption of U.S. arms sales, Soviet attacks fly in the direction of Peking and Washington. However, the Soviet Union looked with grave displeasure at Pakistan's participation in CENTO naval exercises, while expressing its pleasure at Pakistan's withdrawal from SEATO and the British Commonwealth.[106] The Soviets, then, see a combination of both "positive" and "negative" trends in the foreign policy of Pakistan. The "negatives" are precisely those that enable Pakistan to defy the primacy of India in the subcontinent and resist the strategic design of Moscow.[107]

Brezhnev therefore is not entirely correct when he claims, as he did in his address to the Soviet Trade Unions Congress in 1973, that "no conflicts and no contradictions in interest divide" the Soviet Union and Pakistan. There are no bilateral conflicts between the two, but their strategic interests contradict because of the continuing strategic disharmony between Pakistan and India. The objective conditions for this disharmony have, in our view, mellowed since 1972, but the subjective conditions remain largely unchanged. However, there have been other developments in South Asia in the 1970s that have added a new dynamism to relations between Pakistan and India and created new problems as well as opportunities for Soviet foreign policy.

IRAN: A SOUTH ASIAN POWER

The most important of these developments are the rise of Iran as a South Asian power and the intermeshing of the politics of the Persian Gulf region with the politics of the subcontinent. We have just seen the role Iran has been playing in recent years in the internal problems of Pakistan as well as in its relations with Afghanistan. This role-playing began during the 1971 war, when Iran gave significant logistical support to its CENTO ally. After the war the Shah committed Iran to the maintenance of the independence and territorial integrity of Pakistan, a commitment Pakistan has not been able to secure from China.[108] The Shah justified his arms buildup program with the lessons of the 1971 India-Pakistan war.[109]

The alliance of Iran with Pakistan and the Shah's claim that Iran is a South Asian power created serious problems for India. Two-thirds of the oil imports of India come from Iran. A series of

economic collaboration agreements between India and Iraq had reinforced the Iranians' negative perception of India, which was seen in
Tehran not only as the enemy of a friend (Pakistan), but also as the
friend of an enemy (Iraq). The Indians similarly saw Iran not only
as a friend to Pakistan, willing to transfer arms and "military loans"
to its ally, but also as a rising power with interests and aspirations
in the Persian Gulf and South Asian region that were tied up with the
interests and involvements of the United States. The military correspondent of a leading Indian newspaper wrote the following in April
1973:

> As far as India is concerned, the most disturbing
> development in recent months has been the sudden
> emergence of Iran as a regional power based on
> large-scale acquisition of sophisticated arms from
> America and Europe, its oil policy, and politico-
> military alignments. Whether these developments
> will in the near future constitute a threat to India's
> security or not it is not yet easy to assess; what
> is more pertinent is whether Iran's regional am-
> bitions will aim at countering India's potential in
> the subcontinent and in the Indian Ocean.[110]

The Indian prime minister moved to improve relations with
Iran and found the monarch unexpectedly responsive. In early July
1973 an Indian journalist, invited by the Iranian government, was received by the Shah. The monarch told him that, far from encouraging the intransigence of Pakistan, "he was imploring [Bhutto] to pursue a policy not only of peaceful coexistence but of active cooperation
with India because it is evident to him that there could be no stability
in Asia without it. Iran's own interests require peace in the subcontinent."[111] A few days later the Indian foreign minister, Swaran
Singh, visited Tehran, where he met with the Shah and had extended
talks with his Iranian counterpart, Abbas Khalatbari. The Indian
visitor assured his hosts that New Delhi not only had no wish to intervene in the internal problems of Pakistan but was actually interested in a stable, united, strong, and friendly Pakistan. The Iranian
leaders, in turn, assured him that Tehran would "exercise its influence on Pakistan" for a peaceful settlement of the outstanding problems in the subcontinent.[112] The Simla agreement between Pakistan
and India was well received in Iran. Khalatbari's visit to New Delhi
in December 1973, by which time the sudden quadrupling of oil prices
had imposed a crippling burden on the Indian economy, paved the way
to Indo-Iranian economic cooperation. In February 1974 Iran agreed
to send India an additional million tons of oil a year for five years,

most of it on deferred payment; to finance part of the cost of expanding the capacity of the Madras refinery from 3.5 to 6.5 million tons; and to supply the additional crude for refinement.[113] Not only did Iran grant India welcome relief with this agreement in the matter of paying for imported crude, but the very pattern of the oil transactions between the two countries went through a fundamental change. Hitherto Iranian crude had been refined mostly at refineries in India that were owned and operated by foreign companies, but now Iranian oil was to be refined by state-owned refineries in India.[114]

Indira Gandhi's visit to Tehran in May 1974 and the Shah's return visit to India in October 1974 further expanded bilateral economic collaboration. Since 1974 India has been exporting to Iran steel, cement, sugar, textiles, and iron ore (developed with Iranian credit) and has contracted to build several projects in Iran, including a cold rolling mill at Isfahan and a pipe plant at Ahwaz. The Shah has suggested cooperation in the petrochemical field, in which Iran can advantageously produce intermediaries and India the final products for its own use.

Of greater potential importance is the strategic understanding that seems to have been growing between the Shah and Indira Gandhi since 1974. This understanding enables the two countries to see each other as autonomous actors. The Shah seems to have been able to convince Indira Gandhi that he is no conveyor of U.S. power in the Persian Gulf and the Indian Ocean. His primary interest lies in preventing polarizations and in promoting regional cooperation. What Iran needs is stability in the Gulf area as well as in Pakistan so that it can grow into an industrial power in the late 1970s and early 1980s.

On her part the Indian premier has tried to persuade the Shah, not without success, that India is not under Soviet control but retains its foreign policy autonomy; that India is genuinely interested in friendly cooperation with a stable and strong Pakistan and would welcome the Shah's efforts in that direction; and at the same time that India hopes the Shah will not increase the intransigence of Pakistan by transferring sophisticated military hardware to his ally.

The Shah, in return, is said to have assured the Indian prime minister that he has no intention of propping up the military power of Pakistan and that he will do whatever he can to push Pakistan toward cooperation with Afghanistan and India. It would certainly take time for Pakistan to reverse its state policy so dramatically. He would welcome any help India might be able to render in his efforts to improve the relations of Iran with Iraq.

The two leaders listened with interest to each other's views on how important it was at the present stage of international relations to insulate the various Asian regions from external intervention and how the regional powers could protect their independence of decision making and action from encroachment by the major powers.[115]

The Shah's policy of nonpolarization and cooperation in the
intermeshing regions of the Persian Gulf and South Asia was stated
with some forcefulness in a paper read by Amir Tahiri, editor of
Tehran's leading English-language newspaper and an occasional
trouble-shooter for the Iranian foreign affairs ministry, at a three-
day international seminar on the Persian Gulf and the Indian Ocean
held in Tehran in March 1975. Part of Tahiri's paper read as follows:

> Iran is anxious to prevent the polarization of the
> political situation in the region. During the past
> ten years Iran has reaped great benefits from
> correct and mutually profitable relations with
> both the United States and the USSR. It would
> thus wish to see the present balanced situation
> continue for at least another decade during which,
> as Iranian policy-makers assert, Iran would be-
> come strong enough to hold its own against all
> eventualities. Iran is unhappy about the reac-
> tionary stance of several Arab regimes in the
> peninsula and wary of hotbed radicalism in both
> Iraq and South Yemen. But it believes that any
> open attempt at challenging the status quo would
> immediately lead to polarization. In a polarized
> political setup Iran itself would be forced to
> stand and be counted on this or that side. And
> that, according to Iranian policy-makers, would
> not be "advantageous," to say the least.
>   Iranians, with some justice, claim a share
> in having weaned India away from Russia while
> enabling Pakistan to maintain some distance
> from both America and China. Iran was perhaps
> partly to blame for Iraq's rash decision to con-
> clude a 15-year pact with Russia. But Iraqi lead-
> ers are now conscious of the fact that the treaty
> in question has limited their freedom of maneuver
> in the Persian Gulf and the Arab world at large.
> With good relations between Tehran and Baghdad
> now a distinct possibility, Iraq is almost certain
> to adopt a more even-handed foreign policy that
> would lead to a reduction of its dependence on
> Russia. Iran also has been unhappy of Saudi
> Arabia's almost fanatical friendship with America.
> Riyadh's "exclusive relationship" with Washington
> is seen by Iran as an open invitation to polariza-
> tion. Iran also suspects the Saudis of trying to

sabotage the OPEC to please the United States
which has been fighting to lower oil prices.

The same dislike for polarization has been
manifest in Iran's policy towards Afghanistan.
The Daud coup was described by Tehran press
as a triumph for Russia. But Iranian policy-
makers did not take the same view and Iran
was one of the first countries to recognize the
new republican regime in Kabul. Later, Iran
began patiently cultivating the new regime's
friendship and succeeded in helping Daud take
his distance from the USSR. By the end of 1974
Irano-Afghan relations were better than they
had ever been since the emergence of Afghanistan
as an independent state.[116]

According to Tahiri, Iran, with its massive economic aid to
the South Asian countries--it gave India credits worth $1 billion;
Pakistan, $750 million; Afghanistan, $50 million; and Bangladesh,
$10 million between 1973 and 1975--has been able to reduce the de-
pendence of India and Afghanistan on the Soviet Union and the dependence of Pakistan on China and the United States. This may be short
of the truth. However, the basic foreign policy stance of Iran, which
is that the major powers in the Gulf region and in South Asia should
reduce their dependence on the three world powers and try to work
out regional cooperative relations, finds responsive ground in India
and in Iraq. For instance, Iraq joined Iran in calling for a regional
security system for the Persian Gulf, to be managed exclusively by
the littoral powers within two months of its dramatic accords with
Tehran providing for the withdrawal of Iranian support for the Kurdish
rebels and for a border agreement across the strategic Shatt al-Arab
river.[117]

However, neither India nor Pakistan has so far supported the
Shah's 1974 proposal for a regional security system for South Asia,
presumably because the power equations within such a system are
still highly controversial. During his New Delhi visit the Shah ridi-
culed CENTO, which pleased the Indians, but he showed no readiness
to dismantle it, which made the Indians suspicious. Similarly, he
gave a categorical assurance that in the event of a Pakistani attack
on India, Pakistan would get no help from Iran. This was pleasing
to the Indian ears, but his ambivalent statement about the transfer
of arms to Pakistan and the fact that a certain process of transfer
continued through 1975 was far from reassuring to India.[118]

Bhutto, on the other hand, was quite alarmed in 1974 by the
ascending scale of friendship between Tehran and New Delhi and

turned to the Arab monarchs of the Gulf region, with whom the relations of Iran are not exactly cordial, for military support.[119] The cooperation between India and Iran sharpens the religious animosity between the Pakistanis, who are <u>shiias</u>, and the Iranians, who happen to be <u>sunnis</u>; it also lends an edge to the sense of cultural and intellectual superiority of the Pakistani elite over the elite in Iran. I asked a Pakistani scholar who was doing research at a leading U.S. university how Pakistan would react to a South Asian security system dominated by India and Iran. His immediate comment was, "<u>Sic transit gloria mundi</u>."

The Indians, on the other hand, would probably welcome a strategic trade-off recognizing Iran as the dominant power in the Gulf region and India as the dominant power in the subcontinent. At the beginning of 1976 such a trade-off is not in sight. Although the Indians value economic cooperation with Iran for its healthy contribution to the Indian economy, they tend to look at Pakistan to measure the political importance of their friendship with Tehran. For instance, six weeks after the declaration of emergency in India on June 26, 1975, a leading Indian columnist wrote the following:

> Friendship with the Shah has been paying dividends
> and not just in terms of credits for the purchase of
> oil, the development of the Kudremukh iron ore
> mines and so on but also in terms of relations with
> Pakistan. For, it is difficult to believe that Mr.
> Bhutto and the Pakistani media would have been as
> reticent in the wake of the declaration of national
> emergency in this country if the Shah had not been
> as well disposed towards it as he is. Thus, Mrs.
> Gandhi is in a position to concentrate on domestic
> issues and not be distracted too much by the prob-
> lems of external security.[120]

THE SOVIET UNION, THE GULF, AND
THE SUBCONTINENT

In the 1970s Soviet foreign policy makers are aware of the intermeshing of the politics of the Persian Gulf and South Asian regions. The diplomacy and foreign policy resources of the Soviet Union have been deployed in part to promote helpful linkages between the two regions, especially between Iraq and India. Since 1972 Soviet dialogues with Iran have also linked the two areas. During his visit to the Soviet capital in October 1972, the Shah raised the subject of the crisis in Pakistan and the "ambitions" of India in his talks with

the Soviet leaders.[121] When Amir Abbas Hoveida, the prime minister of Iran, was in Moscow in August 1973, Kosygin named Iraq and
India as countries that had expressed to the USSR their apprehension
about the gigantic arms build-up program of Iran. He also compared
the efforts by the Soviet Union for friendly cooperation with Iran with
similar efforts to cooperate with Turkey, Iraq, India, Pakistan, and
Afghanistan, thus lending a spatial unity to Soviet policies for the
vast area covering the Northern Tier (the Near East), the Persian
Gulf, and the subcontinent.[122] Moscow Radio systematically projects
Soviet-Iranian cooperation to Pakistan as worthy of emulation. The
Iranian endorsement of Asian collective security is likewise projected to the entire Asian continent.

THE SOVIET UNION AND IRAN

Historically, pressure from Russia on Southern Asia has been
transmitted through Iran in the direction of the Persian Gulf. Soon
after the proclamation of the USSR, the Bolsheviks, with the help of
a group of Iranian revolutionaries, set up a "socialist republic" in
the province of Gilan in the mountainous area near the Caspian Sea.
The revolutionaries tried to "liberate" Tehran but failed. The Gilan
"republic" collapsed when it was attacked by the army of Reza Khan
in October 1921. The Soviet Union had lost in its first bid to beat a
friendly outlet to the Persian Gulf.[123]
After World War II the Soviets tried, once again without success, to set up a separatist satellite regime in Azerbaijan. The
dramatic leftward turn in Iranian politics in 1951 when Mosadeq
came to power and immediately nationalized the oil industry, raised
Soviet hopes of having a friendly government in Tehran.
The royalist restoration and the downfall of Mosadeq dashed
these hopes, and for nearly a decade and a half Soviet relations with
Iran remained poor. Although the Soviet leaders perceived Iran during this period as a client of the United States, the Shah did not conclude a military pact with Washington, nor did he permit U.S. military bases on his territory.[124] The security of the Persian Gulf remained more or less a British responsibility.
When Iranian-Soviet relations began to improve after the Shah's
visit to Moscow in 1965, the Persian Gulf region, like the subcontinent, was differentiated from the Middle East and Vietnam by the low
level of its military involvement with both superpowers.
Since then, the strategic situation in the Persian Gulf has vastly changed. The withdrawal of British power has created a "vacuum,"
and the upsurge of oil power presents a temptation as well as a deterrent to external intervention. Soviet perceptions both of the region

and of its political actors have changed. In the 1970s Soviet analysts see three political colors making up the Gulf landscape. At one end stand Iraq and Southern Yemen, the "progressive" regimes, with their numerous linkages with the Soviet bloc, while at the other end are Saudi Arabia and the other "reactionary, feudal" regimes, which are closely linked with the United States and other Western powers. In between stands Iran, a "modernizing" nation seeking to play an independent role in regional and world affairs. In spite of many mutual differences, the "progressive" and the "modernizing" Gulf countries share common interests and perspectives. Iraq and Iran, for instance, both stand for high oil prices and both advocate cooperative relations with the Soviet Union.

Soviet analysts see both "positive" and "negative" forces at work in Iran. The Shah is no longer seen as a feudal despot presiding over a U.S.-protected enclave of power. He is an enlightened monarch, a modernizing agent of great dynamism, a national patriot who has brought the oil resources of Iran under its own sovereignty and is competing with the international oil cartels rather than remaining one of their subsidiary allies. The Shah's "white revolution" has destroyed much of the old Iranian society and has given birth to a new middle class with a modern outlook. Industrialization is creating a new working class, while capitalist farming is creating a new rural proletariat. The middle class is asking for active participation in the process of government. Beneath the facade of charismatic respect for the Shah's leadership, there is also an undercurrent of alienation, cynicism, and even resistance to the authoritarian regime. The alienation is strongest among the university youth and the intellectuals. The Shah's popularity stems from his independence from the Western powers, especially the United States; the Iranian public would not permit the monarch to reverse the process and return to the imperialist fold. The Shah is aware of this; hence his anxiety to build cooperative relations with the Soviet bloc and to diversify the economic and political relations of Iran with the outside world.

Along with these "positive" images of the Iranian situation, Soviet analysts also have some "negative" images; the most negative is of the Shah's military buildup program, of the continued membership of Iran in CENTO, and the participation of the Iranian navy in CENTO naval exercises. The Soviet leaders also take a dim view of the Shah's continued close ties with the United States; of the presence of several thousand U.S. military advisers in Iran; and of the friendship of Iran with the Chinese People's Republic. The monarch's readiness to intervene against "progressive elements" in the Gulf region, his territorial ambitions, his commitment to the integrity of Pakistan, his "intervention" in the dispute between Pakistan and Afghanistan over the Pathan tribal areas, and his repression of the leftist elements in Iran are among the elements in the Shah's state-craft that cause anxieties in the Soviet mind.[125]

The broad Soviet foreign policy tactic in the Persian Gulf is twofold: to develop in-depth relations with Iraq and South Yemen and to bring about a "united front" of the "progressive and positive" forces. In other words, the Soviet Union wants to block the chances of a coalition of Iran, Saudi Arabia, and the Gulf sheikhdoms against Iraq and South Yemen. The operational thrusts of the tactical line can be seen in Soviet efforts since 1972 to bridge the gulf between Iraq and Iran and in the Soviet eagerness to expand and deepen economic collaboration with Iran.

Since the mid-1960s Soviet-Iranian relations have grown steadily, but few among the ruling elite in Tehran perceive the Soviet Union as a friend; nor does the Soviet Union see Iran as a friend or an ally. In both countries the relationship is described as good-neighborly, based on the principles of peaceful coexistence. The 2,500-kilometer frontier, the second-longest border of the Soviet Union after that with China, has been free of tension for many years. A network of hydroelectric dams and industries is now springing up in the border area. The road linkages between the two countries have improved. There is a weekly train service from Moscow to Tehran. Ships ply between the ports of the Soviet Union and Iran on the Caspian Sea. The Soviet Union claims to have ushered Iran to the threshold of industrialization by helping it build 70 "national economic enterprises," including the prize project of the 2-million-ton steel plant at Isfahan and a large hydroelectric plant on the Aras river on the border.[126] Iran, as noted, procures a limited amount of military equipment from the Soviet Union. Its defense minister, General Reza Azimi, visited Moscow in January 1973 for talks with Marshal Andrei Grechko. He also toured the Academy of Armored Troops, which trains commanders and engineers for the Soviet armed forces.

In addition to an existing natural gas deal between the two countries, a new 20-year agreement was concluded in November 1975 under which a 1,000-mile pipeline is to be constructed to supply 13.4 billion cubic meters of Iranian natural gas every year for consumption in West Germany and Austria. Iran is to pipe the gas to the Soviet Union for domestic consumption; the Soviet Union, in turn, will pipe an equal quantity of its own gas to West Germany and Austria. Work on the pipeline is to be completed in 1981, and the entire project is to cost $2 to $3 billion.[127]

A similar project involving Iran, the Soviet Union, and Japan has been under discussion since 1973. If it materializes, Iran will export large quantities of natural gas to the USSR, which will export most of the Siberian natural gas to Japan.[128]

We have already noted that a strategic dialogue has been going on between Tehran and Moscow since 1972. Between 1972 and 1974 the Shah and his prime minister each went to Moscow twice; in 1974 more Iranian ministers went to the USSR than members of the Indian cabinet. The Shah has been trying to convince the Soviet leaders that although for historical and other reasons he is determined to maintain his close friendly ties with the United States, he is equally willing to build up friendly and good-neighborly relations with the USSR. His objective is to build up Iran as an independent industrial power, and for this what he needs most is stability in the Persian Gulf region and on the subcontinent. Neither the Soviet Union nor the United States must polarize the political forces in the region. Neither should try to exploit the regional disputes, differences, and instabilities to its own advantage.

Iran wants the security of the Persian Gulf region to be managed by the littoral countries without the intervention of external powers. However, the legitimate interests of all nations in the Persian Gulf, including those of the USSR, would be respected. The Shah reportedly told the Soviet leaders that he might be able to offer a multi-billion-dollar portfolio of economic relations if he were assured that the Soviet Union would not intervene in local affairs in the Gulf and would contribute toward the stability and economic progress of the region. More specifically, the Soviet Union must not try to acquire naval bases in the Persian Gulf nor extend support, moral or material, to the radical elements; nor should Moscow in any manner promote the destabilization of Pakistan.

The Soviet leaders, in turn, are said to have assured the Shah that they share his desire to stabilize the Persian Gulf region; but they are also said to have argued that instability comes primarily from the machinations of imperialism, particularly the "imperialist stranglehold" of the oil resources of the region. What the Soviet Union had done in Iraq was to enable the regime in Baghdad to acquire control of its national resource.

The Soviet leaders are reported to have urged the Shah to progressively reduce his dependence on the imperialist powers. While responding to the Shah's sentiments about good-neighborly relations with the USSR, they pointed to the continued membership of Iran in CENTO and its participation in naval exercises with the U.S. and British navies. The Soviet leaders expressed anxiety over the differences between Iran and Iraq and offered to help, though not to mediate, in resolving the problems. They acknowledged and even welcomed the Shah's influence in Pakistan, but they hoped that the monarch would use it to persuade Pakistan to normalize its relations with India and Afghanistan and join in economic cooperation among the countries of the Persian Gulf and South Asia.[129]

Perceptional divergences still exist between Iran and the USSR, but they are not as wide as they used to be and there has been an effort on both sides to narrow the gaps. There is still no strategic harmony between the two neighbors, but the disharmony is not as strong as in the case of the USSR and Japan, as we shall see later in this study. The steady expansion of economic relations, particularly the commitment to long-term projects involving billions of dollars, also tends to generate a certain momentum for strategic cooperation.

Most members of the Iranian ruling elite have strong memories of Soviet intervention in Iran during the first decade after World War II; but some people in the Iranian government also recall that the two countries had an effective neutrality agreement from 1927 to 1939. Those who remember this period suggest that the relationship is now tending to return to some form of institutionalized neutrality.[130]

Elsewhere in the region, Soviet images of India and Indian images of the USSR are largely compatible; so are the mutual images of the Soviet Union and Afghanistan. Incompatibility is still marked in the Soviet-Pakistani mutual images, but neither regards the other as an enemy. On the whole, then, the Soviet images of Asia and the Asian images of the Soviet Union are most compatible, or least incompatible, in this region.

NOTES

1. During my six-month study tour of Japan, the Southeast Asian countries, and Iran, I saw for myself how in elite perceptions in this vast area, the Soviet Union is the dominant external power in the South Asian region. President Nixon conceded the dominant Soviet role in this area in his foreign policy report to Congress. See U.S. Foreign Policy for the 1970's: The Emerging Structure of Peace (Washington, D.C.: U.S. Government Printing Office, 1972), pp. 150-52. After the 1971 India-Pakistan war James Reston wrote that the "main thing" was not India's victory. "For the Soviet Union has emerged from this avoidable and tragic conflict as the military arsenal and political defender of India, with access for Moscow's rising naval power to the Indian Ocean, and a base for political and military operation on China's southern flank." "Who Won in India?" New York Times, December 17, 1971. (For the Japanese perception of the outcome of the war, see Chapter 7.)

2. For linkages between Indian nationalism and Soviet communism, see Jayantuja Bondyopadhyaya, Indian Nationalism versus International Communism (Chicago: University of Chicago Press, 1966), Chapters 5 and 6. For Nehru's reaction to Soviet Communism

before he became India's prime minister, see Arthur Stein, India and the Soviet Union (Chicago: University of Chicago Press, 1969), Chapter 1.

3. Nehru was once shown by a senior civil servant a sheaf of Moscow radio attacks on him and his government. He glanced at the extracts and remarked, "The heat is not against us though it looks like it. The heat is against the British. The British have always tried to keep the Russians out of this subcontinent and the Russians cannot believe that the policy has changed. . . . If we can show the world that we are, in fact, an independent country, the world will change its attitude towards us." Cited in Stein, op. cit., p. 26.

4. Nikolai Sirota, of the Institute of World Economy and International Relations, Moscow, at a seminar at the School of International Studies, Jawaharlal Nehru University, New Delhi, January 8, 1972.

5. Nehru told Brecher that India's military weakness precluded a more activist line of action in response to the Chinese advance into Tibet. Michael Brecher, Nehru: A Political Biography (London: Oxford University Press, 1959), pp. 90-91.

The Labour government of Britain that engineered the 1947 transfer of power to a partitioned subcontinent hoped that India and Pakistan would continue to belong to the British security system for the Persian Gulf, the Indian Ocean, and Southeast Asia. For Clement Atlee's instructions to Lord Louis Mountbatten, see Alan Campbell-Johnson, Mission with Mountbatten (London: Hale, 1953), p. 31.

6. U.S. military transfers to Pakistan were rather limited, and strict rationing of spare parts restricted the fighting ability of Pakistan to not more than 30 days. The United States obtained from Pakistan a promise not to use U.S. arms against India; this promise had a restraining effect on the Pakistani political leaders. The defense budget of India remained relatively low throughout this period, consuming less than 2 percent of the GNP. In 1959, when the Sino-Indian border crisis exploded in bloody encounters, Ayub Khan proposed to Nehru a "joint defense" of the subcontinent against any Chinese aggression. Nehru, however, paid no serious attention to the proposal. It is interesting that the Ayub Khan initiative was attacked both in the Soviet Union and in China; in fact, it was one of the rare occasions in the late 1950s when the Chinese media attacked Pakistan.

7. New York Times, July 18, 1963.

8. Chester Bowles, "America and Russia in India," Foreign Affairs 49, no. 4 (July 1971).

9. For details, see Bhabani Sen Gupta, The Fulcrum of Asia: Relations Among China, India, Pakistan and the USSR (New York: Pegasus, 1970), pp. 131-33.

10. For a detailed treatment of the Soviet and Chinese roles in the 1965 India-Pakistan war, see ibid., Chapter 4.

11. There is no reliable information about the exact value of Soviet arms transfers to Pakistan. Ayub Khan told a press conference in Tehran on July 21, 1968, "In fact, what we may get from the USSR will fill up gaps here and there." Dawn reported on July 12 that there were indications in Rawalpindi that "Russian arms supplies to Pakistan would be defensive in nature, that they would be far less than what India has been receiving," and that they were being given on the express condition that Pakistan would not use them against India.

It is interesting that after the Soviet decision to supply arms to Pakistan, a U.S. newspaper saw the United States and the USSR still sharing the same objective in South Asia, that is, containment of China. "Both are distressed that Rawalpindi relies on China for arms and both would like to wean Pakistan away from this dependence. At the same time, both regard India as their principal client on the subcontinent and dislike creating an unfriendly climate here." Washington Post, dispatch from its India correspondent, quoted in Dawn, July 12, 1968.

12. The Soviet initiative was inspired in part by the British decision to withdraw from the Persian Gulf region by 1971.

13. For samples of pessimistic Soviet analyses of political trends in India between 1965 and 1967, see New Times, January 19, 1965, for an ideological assessment of Morarji Desai, who contested both Shastri and Indira Gandhi for the prime ministership; New Times, March 2, 1966, for an ideological analysis of the Congress party; New Times, February 2, 1966, for an assessment of Indira Gandhi; New Times, October 9, for a gloomy review of the Indian economy; New Times, March 29, 1967, for an assessment of the major political parties; New Times, March 29, 1967, for a report on Mrs. Gandhi's cabinet; and New Times, November 29, 1967, for an analysis of the post-election political alignment.

14. A. Usanov, "The New Indian Cabinet," New Times, March 29, 1967.

15. The journalistic articles in mass circulation periodicals stemmed from in-depth studies of developments in India both at the party and scholarly levels. In International Affairs, April 1967, M. Savelyev saw the Indian monopolies extending their controls over "vital sectors" of the national economy; he also noted "largescale alignments" between the Indian national bourgeoisie and Western monopoly capital. The May 1967 issue of International Affairs carried a 20-page report of a seminar held in early 1967 with academic and party experts. The seminar came to the conclusion that "in India the national bourgeoisie and the landowners are in power" and

that "capitalist relations are developing apace." This was, of course, a much mellower Marxist-Leninist perception of the Indian political universe than the perception of the Chinese Communist Party. The CCP saw political power in India in control of the big bourgeoisie and the big landlords. However, the Soviet analysis of 1967 recognized India as a capitalist country and differed in one important respect from the CPI analysis: the landowning class, according to the CPI, was in control of political power in coalition with the national bourgeoisie, not at the central, but at the local level of the political system. See Bhabani Sen Gupta, Communism in Indian Politics (New York: Columbia University Press, 1972), Chapter 6.

16. Ibid., Chapters 6 and 7. For Soviet concern over the fate of the West Bengal and Kerala coalitions, see Moscow Radio Peace and Progress, in English 1130 hrs GMT, November 20, 1967; Moscow Radio in Hindi, 1130 GMT December 4, 1967, and Moscow Radio Tass International Service in English, 1910 hrs GMT January 26, 1968. In none of these or any other formulations was the Indira Gandhi government directly attacked. The target of attack was "feudal elements and monopolists."

17. Dilip Mukherji, "New Turn in Indo-Soviet Relationship," The Statesman, February 2, 1968.

18. Bhabani Sen Gupta, "A Maoist Line for India," China Quarterly, no. 33 (1968); Sen Gupta, Communism in Indian Politics, op. cit., Chapters 8 and 9.

19. Mukherji, op. cit.

20. There are several accounts of the 1971 political crisis in East Pakistan and the December war leading to the birth of Bangladesh. For a documentary study, see Bangladesh Documents (New Delhi: Ministry of External Affairs, 1971). For a study sympathetic to the Bangladesh liberation struggle, see Anthony Mascarenhas, The Rape of Bangladesh (New Delhi: Vikas, 1971). For an able presentation of the Indian viewpoint see Mohammed Ayoob and K. Subrahmaniyan, Liberation War (New Delhi: S. Chand, 1972). For the best Pakistani account, see G. W. Choudhury, The Major Powers and the Subcontinent (New York: Free Press, 1975). See also Choudhury, "The Emergence of Bangladesh and the South Asian Triangle," The Year Book of World Affairs (London: Institute of World Affairs, 1973); Sen Gupta, "South Asia and the Great Powers," in The World and the Great-Power Triangles, ed. William E. Griffith (Cambridge, Mass.: MIT Press, 1975).

21. That this was the firm anticipation of the Pakistan government was confirmed at a discussion at Columbia University in the autumn of 1970 by G. W. Choudhuri, then minister of constitutional affairs in the Yahya Khan cabinet. He was replying to a question put by the author.

22. On March 31, 1971, the Indian parliament unanimously adopted a resolution condemning the Pakistani action and extending the sympathy of India to the people of Bangladesh for "their struggle for a democratic way of life." When the flow of refugees passed the 3 million mark, Indira Gandhi developed her strategic perception of the crisis. "What was claimed to be an internal problem of Pakistan had also become an internal problem of India," she asserted on May 24. "Pakistan cannot be allowed to seek a solution of its political and other problems at the expense of India." Two days later she was more explicit, "It is a problem that threatens the peace and security of India, and indeed of Southeast Asia. . . . We are not concerned merely with the legal aspects of this situation. We are concerned with one thing and one thing only--our national interest and security, and naturally that of the heroic people of Bangladesh."

23. This was the position of Indira Gandhi up until the end of October. For India, a Bangladesh within Pakistan might have been a more welcome event. The author learned from several reliable persons in Bangladesh in December 1974 that Bhutto had, even in January 1971, decided to "get rid of the cancer" of East Pakistan. These sources were involved in the negotiations between Mujibur Rahman and the West Pakistan leaders during January and March 1971.

24. Yahya Khan had good reason for rejecting the Soviet initiative for a regional economic conference. Besides his predictable resistance to economic cooperation with India, the Soviet proposal was denounced by the Chinese, and Yahya Khan was neither willing nor in a position to offend China. Apart from the close relations of Pakistan with China, Yahya Khan had been acting since 1969 as a secret channel of messages between Washington and Peking.

According to William Barnds the Soviets were "offended" by Yahya Khan's unwillingness to displease China and halted arms shipments to Pakistan in 1969. "China's Relations with Pakistan: Durability Amidst Discontinuity," China Quarterly 63 (September 1975). If this is true, Yahya Khan's talks with the Soviet leaders apparently led to a resumption of arms supply. The Indian foreign minister told the Lok Sabha (lower house of parliament) on November 9, 1970, that his government had received an assurance from Moscow that it would not supply any more arms to Pakistan. The Statesman Weekly, November 14, 1970.

25. For the text of the message, see Soviet Review (Moscow), Supplement, January 18, 1972. The Soviet government tried to put pressure on Yahya Khan. Toward the end of November the Soviet ambassador to Pakistan, Alexei Rodionov, met Yahya Khan to convey his government's "demand" that Yahya Khan come to a political settlement with Mujibur Rahman and desist from escalating the crisis in the subcontinent. The Soviet government also warned Pakistan against

the "disastrous consequences" of its "warlike course." Patriot
(Delhi), quoting an Associated Press report from Rawalpindi and a
Press Trust of India report from Moscow. November 26, 1971.

26. We now know more reliably than before that the Chinese
government did not approve of the Pakistani military suppression of
the Bangladesh struggle and counseled a political settlement. Chou
En-lai's message, made public in Pakistan rather than in China, attacked the USSR for intervening in Pakistan's internal affairs.
Throughout the crisis the Chinese leaders and the Chinese media
supported Pakistan's sovereignty and independence, but pledged no
support to Pakistan's efforts to maintain its territorial integrity.
Peking Review, no. 15 (April 9, 1971).

27. In the spring and summer of 1971, peasant bases of the
so-called Naxalites and the CPI-M were being flushed out by 200,000
Indian armed security personnel in the districts of West Bengal. A
noted Indian journalist wrote in June, "Perhaps there is more substance in the argument that, if the Awami League leadership in Bangladesh is allowed to wither, then the new leadership will be of extreme
elements, many of whom already profess allegiance to Chairman Mao
Tse-tung and that the radicalization of Bangladesh could be very un-
settling for the rest of Southeast Asia." Chanchal Sarkar, "Explaining India's Stance," Hindustan Standard (Calcutta), June 24, 1971.

28. Kuldip Nayar, Distant Neighbors: A Tale of the Subcontinent (New Delhi: Vikas, 1972), p. 163. According to Harold C.
Hinton, "Kissinger told the Indian Government that his Chinese hosts
had expressed to him an intent to intervene in the event of an Indo-
Pakistani conflict, such as then loomed clearly on the horizon." This
message was reportedly conveyed to New Delhi by Secretary Kissinger
after his first visit to Peking. "The Soviet Campaign for Collective
Security in Asia," Pacific Community (Tokyo) 7, no. 2 (January 1976).

29. Of the 12 articles of the treaty, Articles 9 and 10 are related to security. "In the event of either Party subjected to an attack
or a threat thereof, the High Contracting Parties shall immediately
enter into mutual consultations in order to remove such threat and to
take appropriate effective steps to ensure peace and the security of
their countries." Article 9. "Each High Contracting Party solemnly
declared that it shall not enter into any obligation, secret or public,
with one or more States, which is incompatible with this Treaty. Each
High Contracting Party further declares that no obligation be entered
into between itself and any other State or States, which might cause
military damage to the other Party." Article 10.

Indira Gandhi proposed a friendship treaty to the Soviet
government about two years before it was actually concluded. This
means that she made the suggestion in 1968-69, when the principal
international events were the Soviet armed intervention in Czechoslovakia and the Sino-Soviet armed clash in the Ussuri river. What

precise considerations prompted her to make the proposal remain
unknown. My guess is that, in preparation for her confrontation with
the rightist leaders of her party, she thought a treaty with the USSR
would refurbish her progressive image at home.

    30. For a summary of the debate, see Bhabani Sen Gupta,
"The Soviet Union in South Asia," in The Soviet Union and the Developing Nations, ed. Roger Kanet (Baltimore: Johns Hopkins Press,
1975), pp. 123-26.

    Interestingly, the Soviet leaders themselves have been
highly flexible, if one could use that word, in interpreting the treaty.
When it was signed the Soviets undervalued its security content,
which was stressed by the Indians; later the reverse became the norm.
In an advertisement in The Indian Express of September 4, 1971, the
Soviet embassy in Delhi claimed that the treaty had nothing to do with
the Brezhnev concept of a collective security system for Asia; the
treaty had a "much more modest objective"; it gave "juridical con-
cretization to a manifold relationship" between the USSR and India
and contributed to "peace and stability and progressive social change
in Asia."

    31. For the understanding reached between Indira Gandhi and
the Soviet leaders, see Dev Murarka, "Twofold Gain for India,"
Western Times (Ahmedabad), October 16, 1971.

    32. The Times of India, November 16, 1971. Kudryavtsev
was also the first Soviet political leader to describe the Bangladesh
struggle as a war of national liberation.

    33. Jack Anderson in the Washington Post, January 10, 1972.
According to Anderson, the Soviet ambassador, Nikolai Pegov, told
the Indian government that "a Soviet fleet is now in the Indian Ocean
and the Soviet Union will not allow the Seventh Fleet to intervene."
Anderson also reported that, after Richard Nixon ordered the Seventh
Fleet to send a task force into Indian waters, plans were made to
"arrange provocative leaks in such places as Jakarta, Manila and
Singapore of the task force's approach. By the time the ships had
assembled in the Malacca Strait, both the Indians and the Soviet Union
were well aware that they were on the way." Washington Post, December 21, 1971.

    The Nixon Administration claimed that the task force had
been sent to rescue U.S. personnel stranded in East Pakistan. However, there is little doubt that the task force was meant to be a show
of force. The naval deployment was intended to (1) compel India to
divert both ships and planes to shadow the task force; (2) weaken
India's blockade against East Pakistan; (3) divert the Indian aircraft
carrier Vikrant from its military mission; and (4) force India to keep
planes on defense alert, thus reducing their operations against Pakistani ground troops. "The evacuation of American citizens was

strictly a secondary mission, adopted more as the justification than
the reason for the naval force." Anderson, Washington Post, December 31, 1971.

      34. This remains a controversial point. According to Ander-
son, the White House had genuine apprehension that after reducing
East Pakistan, the Indian army would turn against West Pakistan.
Ambassador Pegov reportedly told the Indian government that the
Soviet Union would not mind if it decided to take the whole of Kashmir,
but then the job must be finished quickly. Pegov also assured India
that the Soviet Union would neutralize any Chinese "adventurism"
across the border. At the UN Security Council, the Chinese delegate
asked his Soviet counterpart, in vain, for a categorical assurance
that there would be no Soviet action in Sinkiang. Washington Post,
December 16, 1971; New York Times, December 16, 1971; Peking
Review, no. 49 (December 10, 1971); Washington Post, January 10,
1972.

      According to C. L. Sulzberger, the United States and
China would have intervened if India carried the war into West Paki-
stan. "The Soviet Union understood the signal and then pressed India
for a cease-fire. I know this is true. I have just been in Peking and
Chou En-lai confirmed this to me." International Herald Tribune.
For a less firm Chinese position, see S. M. Burke, Pakistan's For-
eign Policy: An Historical Appraisal (London: Oxford University
Press, 1973), p. 404.

      It should be noted that some of the reports by Jack Ander-
son proved to be at variance with the original CIA reports that they
quoted. However, the Anderson reports were denied neither by the
Indian nor the Soviet governments. In fact, the Indian government
unofficially brought out a collection of the Anderson reports for limited circulation in 1972.

      35. Nixon maintained in his foreign policy report to Congress
that through the summer of 1971 the United States and the USSR were
working on parallel lines to prevent war in the subcontinent. He
gave Moscow "credit" for "restraint, after East Pakistan went down,
to get the cease-fire that stopped what would inevitably have been the
conquest of West Pakistan as well." The Statesman (New Delhi),
December 28, 1971, and U.S. Foreign Policy for the 70s, p. 147.
The Indians, however, maintained that they held the entire decision-
making initiative during the war and that "at no stage [had] the Soviet
Union intervened themselves or on behalf of anyone else to tell us to
do one thing or another or refrain from doing one thing or another."
The Times of India, December 19, 1971.

      36. The Pakistanis had reacted bitterly to the conclusion of
the Indo-Soviet treaty. Bhutto, who was then outside the government,
had remarked that if the Soviets had been "neutral" between India and

Pakistan, Gromyko should have been in Rawalpindi to offer a similar
treaty to the Pakistani government. However, in the UN Security
Council in December the Pakistani delegate did not attack the Soviet
Union. Bhutto received a warm congratulatory message from Podgorny
when he took over as president of Pakistan, and soon after his visit to
Peking, he went to Moscow to seek Soviet friendship.

      The Security Council sessions dramatized the Sino-Soviet
rivalry with regard to the subcontinent and illustrated how it had
gotten mixed up with the strategic antagonism between the two Communist powers. As Henry Tanner reported in the New York Times
on December 6, 1971, "The two powers came to the Council with
diametrically opposed tactics. The Soviet Union was committed to
support for India and China for Pakistan. But almost immediately
the exchanges turned to the basic aspects of the ideological and national conflict between the two communist regimes."

      37. Bhutto started his presidency with enormous and unprece-
dented problems. He had to deal with a nation caught in the trauma
of defeat in a war with India. A British journalist reported, "It is as
if the entire nation had pulled a blanket over its head to avoid seeing
or being seen." Bhutto had to usher this nation to a parliamentary
democratic system of government after 13 years of military rule.
His own party, the Pakistan People's Party (PPP), had little following in Baluchistan and the Northwest Frontier province; of the 86
members of the ruling party in the national assembly, all but 20 had
been returned from Punjab. He had to devise a political system that
would allay the fears of Punjabi domination of the Sindhis, Baluchis,
and Pathans and yet assure the 45 million Punjabis that they would
not be threatened by the dictates of a possible coalition of the three
minority provinces. Anti-Urdu, that is, anti-Punjabi riots broke out
in Sind and Baluchistan in the spring and summer of 1972; the PPP
faced a vigorous political challenge from the National Awami League
of the NWFP. Peter Hazelhurst, "Pakistani Provinces on Collision
Course," The Statesman, September 4, 1972; Hazelhurst, "Fresh
Regional Tensions in Pakistan," The Statesman, August 23, 1972.
See also Dilip Mukherji's reports on Pakistan in The Times of India,
March 11, 29, and 30, 1972, and News Review for South Asia (Institute of Defense Studies and Analyses, New Delhi), February-September
1972. Also the New York Times, February 27, 1972.

      38. Bhutto claimed that he had released Mujibur Rahman from
prison in the hope that the two would be able to arrive at some kind
of an understanding so that he could tell his countrymen that Pakistan
had not lost everything in the war. When he found that his hope could
not be realized, Bhutto took refuge in a cluster of contradictory postures. In quick succession he would describe the Bangladesh defeat
as a "passing phase," express the hope that "Muslim Bengal" would

one day return to Pakistan, plead with his countrymen to recognize
the "new realities," and assert that he would recognize Bangladesh
only if Rahman agreed first to meet with him. Bhutto apparently
shared, or pretended to share, what a British reporter described as
"the average Punjabi's sentiments on Bangladesh and the unrealistic
belief that Bangladesh is merely occupied by India and would return
to the Pakistan fold if given the chance." See Hazelhurst, The Statesman, August 27, 1972. For two very different versions of the Bhutto-
Rahman "understanding" at the time of the Awami League leader's release from Pakistani prison, see Nayar, Distant Neighbors, op. cit.,
pp. 196-97.

    39. The initiative for India-Pakistan talks came from Moscow.
In February 1972 the Soviet Union sounded India out on how far it was
prepared to go to accommodate Bhutto on the prisoner of war question. The Soviet deputy foreign minister, Nikolai Firyubin, reportedly told the Indian ambassador in Moscow that Bhutto was under great
pressure from the "rightist forces" in Pakistan to get the war prisoners released. Firyubin advised the Indian envoy that it was not in the
interest of India that Pakistan be weakened. Moscow had some leverage with Pakistan and would like to retain it. A long stalemate in the
subcontinent would embolden China, which might egg Pakistan on to
another confrontation. Ibid., p. 212.

    The Simla agreements were signed on July 2, 1972. They
pledged the two countries to "put an end to the conflict and confrontation that have hitherto marred their relations and work for the promo-
tion of a friendly and harmonious relationship and the establishment
of a durable peace in the subcontinent." It took the two governments
four months of hard bargaining to agree on a new control line in
Kashmir. The Indians contended that the bilaterally agreed-upon
new line of control made the presence of the UN cease-fire supervi-
sion team superfluous. Pakistan did not agree. For a critical appraisal of the Simla accord, see G. S. Bhargava, Success or Surrender? (New Delhi: Sterling, 1972). See also News Review on
South Asia, August, September, and October 1972. The new control
line in Kashmir meant an Indian gain of nearly 500 square miles of
territory from Pakistan. In Punjab and Rajasthan, however, India
returned over 5,000 square miles of Pakistani territory.

    40. For details, see The Times of India, April 18, 1973.

    41. For a brief but perceptive analysis of these agreements,
see Mahammed Ayoob, India, Pakistan and Bangladesh (New Delhi:
Indian Council of World Affairs, 1975), Chapter 3.

    The diplomatic "norm" for the conclusion of these agree-
ments was bilateral negotiations between India and Bangladesh and
between India and Pakistan. Throughout these negotiations, the Soviet
Union advised India and Bangladesh to accommodate Pakistan to the
maximum extent possible.

42. Bhutto took 798 days to recognize Bangladesh. For the Indian reaction to the Lahore pan-Islamic conference, see The Statesman Weekly, February 23 and March 2, 1974. The Indian government, keeping up a benign face, welcomed the establishment of diplomatic relations between Islamabad and Dacca. However, for India it was evident that the right thing had happened in the wrong way. Rahman, after the Lahore conference, was generous in his praise for Pakistan. He even offered to mediate the differences between India and Pakistan. See Kuldip Nayar's interview with Rahman in The Statesman, February 28, 1974. Rahman's declared objective was now to make Bangladesh the "Switzerland of the East."

The Soviet media took a more positive view of the Islamic summit than the media in India. This was reflective of the new pro-Soviet stance of the oil-rich Islamic countries since their "oil war" with the industrialized capitalist nations. The Soviet media not only did not criticize Rahman's participation at the Lahore conference, but they highlighted his plea for closer cooperation between the Muslim nations and the "progressive" forces in the world.

The Shah of Iran was represented at the Lahore conference by a relatively unimportant member of his cabinet.

43. Bhutto received an unexpectedly warm popular welcome on his arrival in Bangladesh, but his talks with Rahman failed to resolve such bilateral issues as sharing of foreign debts incurred by the united government of Pakistan and compensation for damages done by the Pakistani army to Bangladesh property. However, Bhutto's phrase "Muslim Bengal" appealed to the orthodox elements of the Muslims in Bangladesh and soon became a popular slogan for those who opposed the secularism of Mujibur Rahman.

44. India has always aspired to an integrative role in the subcontinent; this aspiration seemed achievable after the creation of Bangladesh. In Indian elite perception, the claim of New Delhi to regional primacy rested as much on the Indian democratic model as on its military power. For a representative expression of this widely shared belief, see R. Narayanan, "Toward a New Equilibrium in Asia," Economic and Political Weekly, special number (February 1972). See also K. P. Mishra, "Trilateralism in South Asia," Asian Survey 14, no. 7 (July 1974), for an optimistic account of the integrative promise of the accords reached in 1972-74.

45. New York Times, December 7, 1975. For the events leading to the declaration of national emergency, see S. P. Seth, "Political Crisis in India," Pacific Community 7, no. 2 (January 1976), and Bhabani Sen Gupta, "India as a Regional Power," International Affairs (New York) 29, no. 2 (Fall 1975).

46. For a first-hand account of the August 15 coup, see "Gory Morning," Hindustan Times, August 23, 1975; for subsequent developments, see the New York Times, November 6, 1975.

47. After some improvement in the spring and summer of 1972, the rift between Bhutto's government and the opposition groups in Baluchistan and the Northwest Frontier province widened in 1973. In January the Baluchi tribesmen rose in an armed rebellion. In 1974, 100,000 Pakistan troops were fighting an insurgent force unofficially estimated at 6,000 to 8,000 men who were split into groups of 30 to 50 and operating in the entire area between the Afghan border and the Hab dam, 15 miles west of Karachi. Called the Popular Front of Armed Resistance, this insurgent force was allegedly receiving help from Afghanistan and Iraq. The Pakistani air force inflicted heavy casualties on the rebels, killing 800 of them in April 1974 alone. On October 15, Bhutto announced that organized insurgency had been wiped out.

In a white paper issued on October 19, the Pakistani government blamed the feudal vested interests in backward Baluchistan for inciting the tribesmen against the authorities. The tribal chieftains in Baluchistan, the white paper added, had been resisting the introduction of civil administration and modernization of the provinces.

Baluchistan province of Pakistan has a population of 2.4 million (1972) belonging to three principal tribes, the Baluchis, the Brohis, and the Pathans. In the Northwest Frontier province, the interior minister was assassinated on February 8, 1975. This led to the banning of the National Awami Party and the indefinite extension of the state of emergency in Pakistan by the national assembly. Bomb explosions were frequent in the frontier province in the summer of 1974. In October the explosions spread to Punjab. Assassinations and attempted assassinations of government and opposition leaders frequently occurred in 1973-74. An attempt on the life of Bhutto himself occurred in Quetta on August 2, 1974.

Four air force officers were court martialled and sentenced to four to five years' imprisonment on February 1, 1974, and 15 army officers were given sentences varying from two years to life on March 2, 1974 on charges of conspiring to overthrow the government. The Guardian (London), January 24, 1975, and February 10, 1975. Dawn (Karachi), February 9, 1975; August 3, 1974; and October 20, 1974. Pakistan Times (Lahore), February 2, 1974, and March 3, 1974.

Like the ruling Congress party in India, the Pakistan People's Party enjoys a two-thirds majority in parliament. With this required number voting, both governments made major amendments to the constitution that severely abridged civil liberties.

48. The Soviet media gave strong, consistent support to Indira Gandhi's political and constitutional measures against her opponents, to her efforts to impose "discipline" on her country, and to her program of economic reforms. During 1974 and the first half of 1975, the Soviet media had perceived a major right-wing "offensive" against

the Indira Gandhi government; the right-wing forces, the media alleged, were getting help from the CIA. In India the only political party that stood by Indira Gandhi was the pro-Soviet CPI. In some of the states the CPI was included in the political committees formed at different levels to oversee the implementation of the economic program, particularly the agrarian reform legislation. However, the CPI-led All-India Trade Union Federation organized a one-day labor strike on January 9, 1976, to protest a government measure reducing the amount of bonus payable to certain categories of industrial workers. This was the first organized action in India since the emergency, which had put a ban on strikes as well as on lockouts. For the Soviet media support for Indira Gandhi, see V. Shurygin, "Approved by Parliament," Pravda, July 20, 1975; V. Kondrashov, "Important Decisions," Izvestia, August 12, 1975; and Moscow Radio Tass International Service in English, July 28, 1975.

49. M. Rostarchuk, "After the Coup," Izvestia, September 2, 1975; G. Krasin, "Bangladesh: Political Guidelines," Pravda, September 6, 1975; P. Mezentsev, "After the Coup," Sovetskaya Rossiya, September 7, 1975.

50. India has a fairly diversified base of dependencies for its arms imports, but its dependence on the USSR has been expanding during the 1970s. This is more noticeable in the air force and the navy than in the army. The most sophisticated Soviet aircraft engine to be built in India so far is the MIG-21M engine. The manufacture of MIG-23 engines in India has been under discussion for some time. All of the four submarines in the Indian navy have been acquired from the USSR, which is now helping in several aspects of the naval power expansion program. In small arms India is not only self-sufficient but has also an exportable surplus.

51. Patriot (New Delhi), December 14, 1974.

52. For Brezhnev's and Indira Gandhi's speeches during the Secretary's visit, see Pravda, November 27, 1973, and Indian and Foreign Review (New Delhi) 11, no. 4 (December 1, 1973). For texts of the agreements for economic and scientific-technological cooperation, see Pravda, November 27, 1973.

No visit by any world statesman in the recent past generated such preparation in the economic ministries of the Indian government as did the Brezhnev visit. The Statesman, November 23, 1973. The timing of the visit was significant. It came soon after the October 1973 Arab-Israeli war, which had raised the Soviet image in Asia. It also came after India was seriously hit by the sudden jump in the world oil price. The price of petrol was raised by 65 percent in India on November 2, 1973; the fifth draft five-year plan, which was ready for public release, had to be drastically revised in light of the economic burden of petroleum imports.

53. The Indian foreign minister, Y. B. Chavan, applauded the Communist victories in Indochina as "dramatic changes" and as the culmination of a "heroic struggle waged by the people of Indochina to assert their independence and sovereignty and their determination to shape their destiny without external interference." The New York Times India correspondent described the minister's views as "one more Indian slap at the United States," and added, "Those slaps have been getting sharper in the past few weeks." Bernard Weintraub, "India Hails 'Dramatic Changes,'" New York Times, April 24, 1975.

54. In 1970-71 India sought an improvement in its relations with China. The issue was discussed between the two countries at several capitals, including Rangoon, Katmandu, Cairo, and Moscow. Some promise of improvement was seen by New Delhi in the earlier months of 1971, but the Soviet-backed Indian intervention in the Bangladesh struggle froze the attitude of Peking. India was now seen by the Chinese as a Soviet satellite, an instrument for the Soviet "encirclement" of China. For contacts between the two countries, see The Times of India, September 4, 1971; The Statesman, September 1, 1971; and The Hindustan Times (editorial), September 1, 1971.

The Indo-Soviet treaty did not block a certain amount of improvement in Sino-Indian relations; indeed, a thaw between India and China might help Soviet openings to Pakistan. The Indian and Chinese envoys in Moscow met three times in the spring of 1971 to discuss improvement in Sino-Indian relations, presumably with the tacit approval of the Soviet government.

The long quiet on the Sino-Indian border was broken toward the end of October 1975 when, according to India, Chinese troops crossed the eastern section of the border and killed four Indian soldiers from ambush. New York Times, November 2, 1975.

The Nixon administration wanted India to have a "balanced" relationship with the two superpowers; India, in return, sought a "mature" relationship with the United States. In Foreign Affairs 41, no. 1 (October 1972), Indira Gandhi stated that no U.S. administration during the postwar period had been willing to concede to India the right to make its independent decisions when these were at variance with U.S. perspectives. Throughout the Nixon period, Indian reporters in Washington, D.C., noted an "ugly, anti-Indian mood" in the White House. Nevertheless, relations improved with the agreement in 1973 on the disposal of the huge accumulation of $3.2 billion in Indian currency of U.S. credits resulting from the sale of PL-480 grains. The Indo-U.S. intergovernmental commission that had been set up in 1974 held its first meeting in Washington in the fall of 1975, and relatively limited areas of economic and cultural cooperation were worked out.

55. This is my own interpretation of the Indian position. See
Sen Gupta, "The Persian Gulf and the Indian Ocean," paper read at
the conference on the Persian Gulf and the Indian Ocean in International Politics, Tehran, March 25-27, 1975, under the auspices of
the Institute of International Political and Economic Studies, Tehran.
For various expositions of the Indian position with regard to the Indian Ocean, see T. T. Poulose, ed., Indian Ocean Power Rivalry:
An Analytical Study of the Littoral States' Perspective (New Delhi:
Young Asia Publications, 1974).

As regards the convergence of Indian and Soviet strategic
perceptions, it is interesting to note that K. Subrahmaniyan, Director
of the Institute of Defense Studies and Analyses, New Delhi, who attended the 14th annual conference of the International Institute of
Strategic Studies at Ste. Adele, Quebec, in October 1972, found a
"vast communication gap" between U.S., and Western, strategic
thinkers and their Indian colleagues. In a report on the conference
he wrote,

> For most of the establishments of the Western
> countries and Japan, the Cold War is not yet over.
> Only its methodology has changed. The Soviet
> Union still continues to be the major adversary.
> They still discuss Soviet penetration and policies
> in Asia and security threats to Japan and South-
> east Asia without specifying from whom, though
> making it explicit that the threat is no longer
> from China. . . . The framework, perceptions,
> and value systems of Western strategic establish-
> ments are as different from ours now as they were
> during the days of Nehru. However, till recently,
> the Westerners found an overwhelming majority
> of our elite echoing their views. Now some In-
> dians have started articulating their own world views
> and these do not always get across in view of the
> vast communication gap that exists between this
> country and the Western world.   (Hindustan Times,
> October 19, 1972.)

56. Since the late 1960s Indians have been pretty confident that
in view of the Sino-Soviet conflict the Soviet Union would not really
object to an Indian acquisition of nuclear weapons. Since the explosion of the nuclear device in India in May 1974, the Soviet media
have echoed the official Indian view that the device had been exploded
solely for the purpose of peaceful uses of nuclear energy. An Indian
who was in Moscow when the news of the Indian explosion was reported

in the Soviet media claimed that he saw a crowd of Russians "dance
with joy" in the Red Square on hearing the news. The Indian, H. N.
Trivedi, general secretary of the Indian National Trade Union Congress (the labor front organization of the ruling Congress party),
said that the explosion had "enhanced the respect for India among
the socialist countries." National Herald (New Delhi), May 25, 1974.

57. In the advertisement run by the Soviet embassy in New
Delhi in the Indian Express of September 4, 1971, it was conceded
that the Indo-Soviet treaty did not preclude "a certain amount of improvement" in Sino-Indian relations.

In May 1976 India decided to send an ambassador to Peking.
Peking agreed to send its own ambassador to India "soon after" the
Indian action. This marked the beginning of a thaw in Sino-Indian re-
lations, which had been frozen after the 1961 frontier war.

58. Indians are impressed by the consistency of the Chinese
friendship for Pakistan and hostility toward India. During the great
proletarian cultural revolution, Pakistan was about the only country
with which Chinese friendship remained completely unbruised. The
"normalization offensive" of Chinese diplomacy during the 1970s left
relations with India completely untouched. The Chinese took a dim
view of the Indian action in Sikkim, calling the annexation an act of
"imperialism" and "colonialism." Hsinhua, September 11, 1974.
The Chinese disapproval was equally aimed in the direction of the
USSR. Hsinhua, September 6, 1974. See also People's Daily, editorial, September 8, 1974.

59. As soon as Pakistan recognized Bangladesh, the Indians
were afraid that Chinese recognition would follow. However, this
recognition came only after the assassination of Mujibur Rahman
and the establishment of a military regime. "The presence of the
Pakistani and Chinese embassies in Dacca will certainly provide
enough encouragement to the unfriendly elements in Bangladesh to
stir up anti-Indian sentiment," wrote G. K. Reddy, political correspondent of The Hindu (Madras). Quoted in the New York Times,
February 28, 1974.

After the August coup the Indian government was "seriously concerned" about the developments in Bangladesh, which might
"affect the security of India." Hindustan Times, August 18, 1975.
In November the defense minister, Swaran Singh, once again expressed "grave concern" about political developments in Bangladesh
and declared that India must "keep vigil" over events across the
border. He also said that it was "very significant" that the officers
who had killed Mujibur Rahman had fled to Thailand and were "seeking asylum in the United States." The Statesman, November 29,
1975. The coup leaders left Bangkok for Lybia. The Statesman,
November 25, 1975.

In Pakistan the assassination of Rahman and the successive coups were seen as consequences of efforts by India to keep the new republic under its control. The change of regime was welcomed in the conviction that the foreign relations of Bangladesh would now be diversified and that its dependence on India and the USSR would diminish. See news reports and special articles in Dawn and Pakistan Times, November 12-28, 1975.

60. Ayoob, op. cit., pp. 25-26; Dawn, August 4, 1973. The Times of India reported in January 1975 that the increase in the defense budget of Pakistan by 4,198 million rupees (about $525 million) during the 1965-75 decade and in its armed forces by 184,000 (excluding paramilitary troops) was "disproportionately" higher than its present needs because with the "slicing away of the eastern wing, Pakistan's defense commitments have been considerably reduced." The expenditure, the report added, did not cover the arms and equipment Pakistan had been receiving "free from China and other friends." The report said, "Pakistan's armed forces are manned by a much younger generation of officers who are extremely hostile to India." All of the officers of the Pakistani armed forces had to take the oath that they would "under any circumstances take revenge" against the humiliating defeat of 1971. Quoted in Asian Recorder, 1975, p. 12597.

61. Washington Post, March 10, 1975.

62. Dilip Mukherji, "New Delhi and Moscow: Many Accords, Some Problems," The Times of India, November 30, 1974. For the Soviet response to this article, see the Moscow-dateline special article "Moscow and New Delhi: Study in Trends," in Patriot, December 14, 1974.

63. Two points are worth noting here in connection with Grechko's visit. In the formal speeches Grechko made enthusiastic references to the Indo-Soviet treaty, while his Indian counterpart did not mention the treaty at all. In the final communique, however, both sides acknowledged the importance of the treaty in Indo-Soviet relations. The second point is that leaders of the CPI were invited to an official reception given by Grechko in New Delhi. The Times of India, February 25-29, 1975; Pravda, February 28, 1975.

64. Indira Gandhi affirmed that the main thing about the Indian-Soviet treaty was that "in all these years Soviet leaders have never put pressure on us, never dictated conditions to us, never imposed their will on us." Pravda, November 28, 1973. See also Indian and Foreign Review, December 1 and 15, 1973.

65. Socialist India (New Delhi), May 10, 1975.

66. As it did with regard to Soviet arms aid to the Popular Movement for the Liberation of Angola in 1975-76.

67. The CPI-M, however, also wants an improvement in Sino-Indian relations. The only Indian Communists who oppose a Soviet presence in India are the Maoists. The CPI (Marxist-Leninist) and several other Maoist groups were banned by the Indian government after the proclamation of national emergency.

68. This assessment is based on an analysis of Indian writings on the Soviet Union during the 1970s as well as on personal interviews with arbitrarily selected representatives of different elite groups in New Delhi.

69. Since the mid-1960s the Soviet Union has been listed as the most popular country in public opinion polls conducted by the Indian Institute of Public Opinion. Only once did it falter, by flirting with the policy of equal friendship for India and Pakistan. Soviet popularity peaked in August 1972. In a poll taken in August 1973, 56 percent of the samples wanted Indo-Soviet relations to become still closer, while only 6 percent preferred a less close relationship. In contrast, only about 50 percent wanted relations with the United States to be closer than they were, while 18 percent said that they wanted a "less close" relationship. The Soviet image was better among the poor and the most highly educated. It was best in Delhi and poorest in Bombay. The U.S. image, in contrast, was found to be best in Madras and poorest in Delhi and Calcutta.

To the question "How much confidence do you have in the ability of the United States and the Soviet Union to deal wisely with world problems?" the answers were recorded as follows: for the USSR, great confidence, 30 percent; considerable confidence, 29 percent; very little confidence, 5 percent; for the United States, great confidence, 15 percent; considerable confidence, 23 percent, very little confidence, 15 percent. Among university graduates there was three times as much confidence in the Soviet Union as in the United States. Monthly Public Opinion Survey 18, no. 5 (February 1973) and 18, no. 12 (September 1973).

The Soviet connection polarizes the committed Indians. The Communist and pro-Communist press sees nothing bad and everything good in it, while the right-wing press sees India "going red" under Soviet influence. The noncommitted elite are defenders of the pervasive connection more than they are its enthusiastic advocates. Criticism of the USSR can be heard more often in government offices and in the living rooms and clubs where members of the elite gather than they can be read in print. The criticisms that have made the most impact are Dilip Mukherji's low-key complaint in The Times of India of November 30, 1974, that the Soviet Union was stalling on Indian requests for more sophisticated, high-speed, and deep-penetration aircraft and that Soviet credits could not compete with the credits being given by the soft-loan windows of the World Bank; and Kuldip

Nayar's comment in The Statesman of August 28, 1974, that the Soviet
leaders had refused to reiterate their support for the Indian position
on Kashmir and were apparently trying to adopt their 1968 policy of
cultivating both Indian and Pakistani friendship.

　　　　For the perception by the Indian elite of Soviet scholarship
as well as of Soviet analyses of world affairs, see Stephen Clarkson,
"The Low Impact of Soviet Writings and Aid on Indian Thinking and
Policy," Survey 20, no. 1 (Winter 1974). Clarkson writes,

> The low impact of Soviet writings and policy on
> Indian thinkers and policy-makers may also work
> to the advantage of the Soviet government which
> is more concerned about stability and influence in
> the subcontinent than ideological converts and
> policy disciples. While not flattering to Soviet
> ideologists, India's cool reaction to Marxist-
> Leninist ideas may be the best condition for a
> continuingly healthy long-term relationship of
> that country with the Soviet Union.

　　　　70. In a statement on September 12, 1973, Ashok Mehta,
president of the rival Congress party, asked whether several recent
attempts by Indira Gandhi to underplay the security aspects of the
Indo-Soviet treaty and its overall importance for the external relations of India indicated that India had "unilaterally dissociated itself"
from Articles 9 and 10 of the treaty. In one of her explications the
prime minister had said, "We do not have an alliance. The treaty
of friendship is not an alliance. It has no military overtones and
undertones or anything of the sort. . . . It was a morale booster at
a time when we were very much in need of it." Hindustan Times,
September 13, 1973.

　　　　71. New York Times, January 1, 1976.

　　　　72. Pravda, February 6, 1972.

　　　　73. The last of the Soviet ships left the Bangladesh waters four
months ahead of schedule. Nevertheless, according to a report in
The Statesman Weekly of March 23, 1974, the Bangladesh government
seemed more relieved at their departure than grateful for their services. Some Bangladesh officials had begun to feel "rather uncom-
fortable" about the "prolonged presence" of the Soviet force, surmis-
ing that it might be one reason for China's continued refusal to recognize the new republic. As for the Soviet view, the report added,

> The Russians . . . seem to feel unhappy that their
> good work in making Chittagong and Cox's Bazar
> ports safe and operational has not been much ap-
> preciated by the Bengalis. Soviet diplomats have

> informally regretted that some Bangladesh offi-
> cials and politicians have been rather "un-
> kindly." . . . Their disillusion, they say, is
> because they have done the salvage and mine-
> sweeping work . . . free of (considerable) cost,
> for which all they have earned is a bad name.

The Bangladesh foreign minister, Kamal Hossein, however, told me in December 1974 that his government "highly appreciated the work done by the Soviet salvage and minesweeping team."

74. The India-Bangladesh peace and friendship treaty is modeled largely on the Indo-Soviet treaty. For the text, see The Times
of India, March 20, 1972. India saw the treaty as conferring a strategic harmony on most of the subcontinent. See Girilal Jain, "The
Indo-Bangladesh Treaty," The Times of India, March 21, 1972.

75. The text of the joint communique is in Pravda, March 5,
1972.

76. For a measure of the economic, social, and political problems faced by Bangladesh, see Marcus Franda's testimony in U.S.,
House of Representatives, Committee on Foreign Affairs, hearings
before the Subcommittee on the Near East and South Asia, 93rd Cong.,
1st sess., October 31, 1973.

To quote from the annual plan of the Bangladesh government
for 1972,

> Conventionally measured income per head stood
> at about Taka 450 (US $37.50) per year . . . at
> current prices in 1969-70, the most recent nor-
> mal year. . . . The average income of the
> poorest 20 per cent of the population during the
> same period was Taka 158 ($20.00). . . . Nearly
> half of the population have serious deficiency in
> caloric intake. . . . Annual per capita consump-
> tion of clothing is less than 7.5 yards equivalent of
> coarse cloth, which means for the vast number of
> the poor little more than . . . a loin cloth or
> two. . . . Nowhere in the world is there anything
> like so much poverty shared by so many squeezed
> into so little a land area. (Quoted in Far Eastern
> Economic Review, Hong Kong, December 16, 1972.)

77. Interviews with officials of the Bangladesh Ministry of
Commerce in December 1974.

78. For a Soviet analysis of the social and economic structure
of Bangladesh, see Yuri V. Gankovsky, "The Social Structure of
Society in the People's Republic of Bangladesh," Asian Survey 14,

no. 3 (March 1974). The main point of this study is that Bangladesh
lacks the kind of urban-rural elite that can promise a successful experiment in parliamentary democracy.
       79. As I have written elsewhere,

> The main problem was that the Awami League was
> not really a political party but a poorly organized
> political movement, a loose and flabby coalition of
> a deeply-entrenched landed gentry and a relatively
> small urban middle class. Some 70 percent of the
> legislators who had been elected to the Pakistan
> national assembly and the East Pakistan provincial
> legislature on the Awami League ticket in December
> 1970 were erstwhile "basic democrats" of the Ayub
> Khan period (1958-69). Mujibur Rahman himself
> was a moderate nationalist who had been driven to
> an extreme nationalist position by the avalanche of
> events. Given a free choice, he would probably
> have been satisfied with a largely autonomous
> Bangladesh within Pakistan; however, the deter-
> mination of the Bhutto-Yahya Khan combination to
> deny the Awami League the fruits of its massive
> electoral victory, plus the volatile pressure of
> the students and youths of Dacca, had forced him
> to demand independence in the fateful days of
> March 1971.

Bhabani Sen Gupta, "Moscow and Bangladesh," Problems of Communism, March-April 1975.
       In the Soviet Union the Awami League was seen as a "cen-
trist" party in March 1970. V. Nakaryakov, commentary on Pakistan
in Izvestia, March 12, 1970. It was elevated in August to the status
of a "left" force because of its demand for a "broad political and economic improvement" in East Pakistan and its desire for "friendship
and cooperation with the Soviet Union." A. Filippov, article in
Pravda, August 14, 1970.
       80. For CPI and CPSU efforts to promote the image of the
BCP as a leading participant in the Bangladesh freedom struggle, see
New Age (New Delhi), April 11, 1971, and Pravda, January 24, 1972.
       81. Moscow Radio described the NAP-M as the "runners-up"
in the election. Moscow Radio in English, March 8, 1971.
       82. Izvestia, August 19, 1973.
       83. Welcoming the formation of the "united front," Pravda
wrote on October 23, 1973, that

the long and difficult struggle for freedom and
independence convinced the people of Bangladesh
that only the united actions of all national-
patriotic forces made it possible to achieve national independence. The two-year period of independent developments (since) has shown that
this unity is also necessary now, at the important stage of building a peace-loving, democratic, independent state. That is why the broad,
progressive public in Bangladesh considers the
creation of a united front of the three parties to
be an important step on the road to strengthening
the independence and social gains of the young
republic.

84. In December 1974 I interviewed 55 arbitrarily selected
members of the elite in Dacca. Rahman's image was the poorest
among the intellectuals, students, and small- and medium-level
traders and businessmen. None, however, saw any alternative to
his leadership, and many still hoped that he would realize his mistakes and retrieve the situation.

85. Kirit Bhaumik, "All Power to the President: Change in
Bangladesh," The Times of India, January 31, 1975.

86. Moscow Radio in Bengali 1300 GMT, August 27, 1975;
Izvestia, September 2, 1975; Pravda, September 6, 1975.

87. The Indian government sent Kewal Singh, the topmost
civil servant in the external affairs ministry, to Moscow for urgent
consultations. Kewal Singh had talks with Gromyko and delivered a
personal message from Indira Gandhi to Brezhnev. The "nonparty"
and "nonpolitical" government that has ruled Bangladesh since November 1975 assured both India and the USSR of its continued friendship.
A high-level delegation came to New Delhi in November for talks
with the Indian government. Also in November the Chinese government announced its recognition of Bangladesh, and ambassadors were
exchanged between Bangladesh and Pakistan.

88. It was no longer possible to influence Bangladesh through
India alone. The elimination of the Awami League leaders increased
the influence of Pakistan in the new republic.

89. G. W. Choudhury, Pakistan's Relations with India 1947-
1966 (New York: Praeger, 1968), p. 234.

90. Satish Kumar, "Pak Attitude Change," Overseas Hindustan
Times, January 31, 1974.

91. S. M. Burke, Pakistan's Foreign Policy: An Historical
Analysis (London: Oxford University Press, 1973), p. 367.

92. Ibid., p. 366. Sangat Singh wrote,

> If the Pakistani theme impinges on the Soviet
> Union's interests in India, the Soviet theme of
> improving relations at people's level between
> Pakistan and India impinges on the very stabil-
> ity of the ruling hierarchy in Pakistan which
> needs an external stimulus to maintain itself
> in power.
>   As such, by keeping her choices in the inter-
> national community wide open, Pakistan is not
> likely to be amenable to Soviet influence on that
> count. Also, despite the supply of arms, Moscow
> is not likely to be able to control or dissuade
> Pakistan from future adventurism against India
> in Kashmir. Pakistan's increased strength is
> likely to add to the bellicosity of her leadership.
> Whether the Soviet Union will be able to achieve
> an over-arching influence in the India-Pakistan
> subcontinent depends principally on the likely
> changes in the pattern of leadership structure
> in Pakistan.

Sangat Singh, Pakistan's Foreign Policy: An Appraisal (New York:
Asia Publishing House, 1970), pp. 160-61.

93. Dawn, December 22, 1971.

94. Interview by Dilip Mukherji, The Times of India.

95. Mohammad Ayub Khan, Friends Not Masters: A Political
Autobiography (London: Oxford University Press, 1967), p. 118.

It may be noted that Bhutto has not made any basic change
in the foreign policy developed by Ayub Khan in the 1960s, except that
he is in a better position than Ayub Khan to exploit the Sino-Soviet
conflict to the advantage of Pakistan, in view of the detente between
China and the United States.

96. Ibid., p. 199.

97. On the seventh day of the war the Chinese forces on the
Indian border were put on the alert, and this was followed by the
"ultimatum" to India. By this time "Pakistan's top military men had
formulated the following contingency plan for a joint blitz on India:
Seeking to gain for Pakistan a superior position in post-war negotiations by grabbing territories and inflicting humiliations on India, China
would occupy a big chunk of Indian land in the Northeast Frontier
Agency, while Pakistan, with much of the pressure siphoned off from
the west, would drive from the West Pakistan frontier." The Pakistani generals did not expect the Soviet Union to intervene on behalf

of India in this kind of a war, while they believed they could count on Indonesian help and, through pressure from Iran, keep the United States neutral. With this contingency plan in mind, the generals urged Ayub Khan to opt for a prolonged and expanded war. "The Chinese ultimatum of September 6 was not a 'paper' threat. For five days the world wondered and worried whether the war would escalate . . . involving not just India and Pakistan but China as well." When Ayub Khan consulted Peking about the UN demand for a cease-fire, the Chinese "gave Pakistan full freedom to make her own decision," but were "ready to come to Pakistan's rescue provided Pakistan wanted such assistance."

During the 1971 crisis, the Chinese secretly advised Yahya Khan to find a "rational solution" of the East Pakistan problem, and at no stage approved of the atrocities committed by the Pakistani army. When Bhutto went to Peking on the eve of the December war to get from the Chinese the kind of support they had offered in 1965, he could get no such assurance. "The Chinese role in the 1965 and the 1971 wars were totally different." G. W. Choudhury, "Reflections on Sino-Pakistan Relations," Pacific Community 7, no. 2 (January 1976).

98. As a Western diplomat put it, the Indo-Soviet treaty "scared the hell out of the Chinese." New York Times, February 15, 1972.

99. International Herald Tribune, July 8, 1974. Bhutto, who was speaking at the National Press Club, Washington, D.C., also said that Pakistan wanted to build a "credible deterrent" against India, to whom the USSR had transferred $2 to $3 billion worth of arms.

100. Richard Nixon, in his foreign policy report to Congress in February 1972, ruled out competing with the Soviet Union for influence in South Asia.

101. William Borders, "Kashmir Dispute Losing Its Urgency after Three Decades of Bitterness," New York Times, October 27, 1975.

102. Cited in Ayoob, op. cit., p. 61.

103. Amir Tahiri, "The Persian Gulf: The Non-Arab Littoral," paper read at the conference on The Persian Gulf and the Indian Ocean in International Politics, Tehran, March 25-27, 1975.

104. The Statesman, October 1975. Afghanistan has been receiving aid from some of the oil-rich Arab countries, too. The Indian influence on Afghanistan in the 1970s is much less than it used to be in the 1950s and even the 1960s.

105. The generals are believed to be more pro-Chinese than Bhutto. Army chief Tikka Khan's visit to Peking in early 1973 touched off a controversy in the Pakistani press over the role of

the army in foreign policy making. <u>Link</u> (New Delhi), February 11,
1973.

In May 1974 Bhutto himself made his second trip to Peking
as head of the Pakistani government. He was received by Mao Tse-
tung in a "cordial and friendly atmosphere" and had wide-ranging
talks with Teng Hsiao-ping in a "sincere and friendly atmosphere."
The joint communique on the visit welcomed the bilateral agreements
reached between Pakistan and India since the 1971 war, reiterated
the support of China (though not necessarily that of Pakistan) for the
Kashmiri people's "right to self-determination" and stressed the
need for "vigilance against tendencies toward hegemonism and expansionism." On the day of his arrival in Peking (May 11), the
<u>People's Daily</u> carried an editorial welcoming the "outstanding
statesman" from Pakistan and bitterly attacking Moscow for its policy of "interference, infiltration, domination, and subversion" of
the countries in South Asia. The "defense needs" of Pakistan were
discussed between Bhutto and the Chinese leaders, who also pledged
commodity assistance worth $.1 billion. <u>Hsinhua</u>, May 11 and 14,
1974.

106. These "positive" and "negative" tendencies stem primarily
from changes in Pakistan's social structure. See Vladimir Moskalenko,
"Pakistan's Foreign Policy," <u>Asian Survey</u> 14, no. 3 (March 1974).

107. A. R. Siddique, "A Fresh Look at Security," <u>Defense
Journal</u> (Karachi) 1, no. 1 and 2 (February and March 1975). Siddique
perceives an Indian "grand design" for the "reconquest of the subcontinent" and sees in the policies of the new Afghan regime "a formidable
threat" to Pakistan.

In the summer of 1975 the Afghan government accused Pakistan of instigating widespread antigovernment riots in Afghanistan.
Apparently Pakistan is trying to counter the Afghan-backed Pakhtoonistan insurgency with a tribal insurgency within Afghanistan that is
directed against the regime in Kabul.

108. Amir Tahiri, op. cit.

109. New York <u>Times</u>, cited in Ayoob, op. cit., p. 61.

110. Hindustan <u>Times</u>, April 1973. One of the leading strategic thinkers of India sees a linkage of U.S., Iranian, and Pakistani
interests in South Asia that is impinging on Indian interests.

> The essential point for us to grasp is that for the
> United States, Pakistan is the eastern flank of a
> crucial area where it has vital oil interests. If
> it is necessary to do certain things to please the
> Shah of Iran and to safeguard this flank from
> various threats, including its genuine democrati-
> zation, then the United States will do it--

> irrespective of India's sensibilities and interests or
> considerations of durable peace in the subcontinent
> which, to the Americans are very minor issues
> compared to their national interests. This has
> been the game for the last 25 years and continues
> to be so now. Pakistan, for them, is a pawn in
> this game. . . . The United States cannot be
> bothered about adverse consequences to India's
> security and interests.

K. Subrahmaniyan, "American Arms for Pakistan," Link, March 25, 1973.

111.   Interview by Dilip Mukherji, The Times of India, July 4, 1973.

112.   Ayoob, op. cit.

113.   New York Times, May 6, 1974.

114.   The Indian government has taken over all of the foreign refineries operating in the country. Iran, too, has assumed control over its foreign corporations.

115.   This account of the conversations between Indira Gandhi and the Shah of Iran is based on interviews with knowledgeable officials in New Delhi and Tehran, checked with journalists who covered the meetings in the two capitals.

116.   Amir Tahiri, op. cit.

117.   Tehran Journal, March 29, 1975.

118.   During the Shah's visit to Pakistan in March 1975, it was agreed that Pakistan would get 50 F-5H aircraft from Iran in the next few months to replace the outdated F-86 Sabre jets. The Statesman, March 8, 1975.

119.   Bhutto expressed serious concern to a visiting team of Iranian journalists about economic collaboration by Iran with India. Dawn, March 10, 1975.

120.   Girilal Jain, "Balanced Foreign Policy: Coping with New Realities," The Times of India, August 13, 1975.

121.   Amir Tahiri, "The Moscow Connection," Kayhan International (Tehran), October 21, 1972.

122.   Ibid.

123.   For an account of the Gilan "republic" and Soviet policy during this period, see E. H. Carr, The Bolshevik Revolution, vol. 3 (London: Macmillan, 1952).

124.   The United States did not sign the CENTO treaty, of which Britain, Turkey, Iran, and Pakistan are full members. By an executive declaration in 1958, the United States agreed to "cooperate" with CENTO. The declaration said, in part: "In case of aggression against [Iran, Pakistan, or Turkey] the Government of the United States of America, in accordance with the Constitution of the United

States of America, will take such appropriate action, including the
use of armed forces, as may be mutually agreed upon." At the
CENTO headquarters in Ankara in 1973 there were 22 Americans,
including two generals, one of whom is the chief of staff of the combined military planning staff of the treaty. In terms of phraseology,
the U.S. commitment under CENTO is not basically different from
its commitments under the Pacific treaties. However, the CENTO
documents are not treaties, since they have never been placed before
Congress for ratification. "This distinction gives the United States
slightly more flexibility to avoid engagement in Iran than in situations
involving its Pacific treaty partners." Roland A. Paul, American
Military Commitments Abroad (New Brunswick, N.J.: Rutgers University Press, 1973), pp. 25-29.

      However, the Shah of Iran took note of the fact that Paki-
stan got no help from the United States in its two wars with India and,
according to Amir Tahiri, who covered the two visits of the Shah to
Moscow as well as the two visits of the Iranian prime minister between 1972 and 1974, the Iranian leaders have tried to impress the
Soviet leaders with the fact that Iran has no military pact with the
United States nor has ever granted military bases to the United States.

      125. Moscow Radio in Arabic 1700 hrs GMT March 7, 1975;
"Friends and Good Neighbors," New Times, no. 43 (October 1972);
"Advances and Problems," New Times, no. 10 (March 1973); "Iran's
Golden Dream," Pravda, January 1, 1972; Moscow Radio in Persian
0900 GMT August 11, 1973; Moscow Radio in English, 0942 hrs June
8, 1973.

      126. Moscow Radio in Arabic 1700 hrs March 7, 1975; Moscow
Radio in Persian 0930 hrs GMT March 8, 1975; Moscow Radio in
Persian 1630 GMT January 23, 1975.

      127. New York Times, December 1, 1975.

      128. Kahyan International (Tehran), August 13, 1973.

      129. This account of exchanges between the Iranian and Soviet
leaders is based on interviews with reliable sources in Tehran and
on Iranian press coverage of the Shah's and Premier Hoveida's visits
to Moscow.

      130. Interview with an Iranian official.

6

SOUTHEAST ASIA:
STRANGERS
AS THEY MEET

Soviet perceptions of Southeast Asia in the mid-1970s betray almost an equal mixture of hope and anxiety. The hope stems from the collapse of the U.S. security system and the unlamented demise of SEATO, from the Communist victories in Indochina, and from the rise of Hanoi as the major Indochinese power.[1] The Soviet Union sees welcome opportunities that, properly exploited, should obtain it an access to the rich natural resources of Southeast Asia[2] and to its strategic seaways on equal terms with the United States.

If the Soviet Union can establish a strong political and economic presence in Communist Vietnam as the main donor of development assistance and as the chief source of strength in the affirmation by Hanoi of independence from China, the impact of this presence on the rest of Southeast Asia should not be negligible. The Soviets therefore combined complete support for the socialist construction of Vietnam with a benign attitude of friendliness toward the national-bourgeois regimes that constitute the Association of Southeast Asian States (ASEAN), which are the Philippines, Thailand, Malaysia, Singapore, and Indonesia. To be sure, Moscow is not equally warm to all of these regimes: it smiles less on Indonesia than on the Philippines, Thailand, and Malaysia. However, Soviet policy proceeds broadly from the assumption that, pressed between their fear of China and suspicions of Hanoi, in an ambience in which the protective wings of the United States are no more and with deepening internal social and economic problems, the ASEAN group of countries will be increasingly drawn to the benign blandishments of the industrialized Soviet bloc.

The USSR, to its credit, has had no involvement in the internal insurgencies in Southeast Asia. It has a more or less untarnished record of cooperation, albeit at a low level, with the bourgeois regimes of the region. Unlike the United States, it stood by its allies in Indochina until the last days of the war, saw them through their military victory, and is now rendering them substantial development assistance.[3]

The principal source of Soviet anxiety is China. Southeast Asia is the historical backyard of the Chinese empire, Peking's natural sphere of influence. The end of the Indochina war has snapped the last threads of the interests shared by the Soviet Union and Maoist China. The two Communist giants who contributed massively to the outcome of the war are now locked in an increasingly abrasive competition for influence and status in Indochina. In the first round, according to the evidence available, the Soviets have bested the Chinese. They have built a strong rapport with the leadership in Hanoi and, through that channel, with the leadership in Laos, while the Chinese influence seems to be confined only to Cambodia.[4] The Sino-Soviet rivalry in Indochina may engulf the whole of Southeast Asia in the next few years, exposing the "soft" states of the region to competing and overlapping Communist pressures. It would be frustrating for the Soviet Union if the United States were offered a Chinese crutch that would enable it to reconstruct a military presence in Southeast Asia.

Moreover, the heavy Soviet commitment of development aid to Hanoi must in itself remain a gamble with uncertain rewards. The Soviet Union cannot control Hanoi in the way it controls the countries of Eastern Europe; indeed, it must accept and even perforce encourage the independence of Hanoi. It is illustrative of the vast changes that have occurred in the universe of Communism in a quarter century that although in 1950 Mao had rejected the "third road" and firmly aligned Communist China with the USSR, in 1975 the newly established Communist regimes in Indochina proclaimed themselves as neutral and nonaligned, and this enormously ambivalent billboard was equally acceptable to Moscow and Peking.

It is in Southeast Asia, then, much more than in Northeast and South Asia, that Moscow must play the game of containing China without military entanglements with the local regimes, with limited expendable resources, and always avoiding a military confrontation with the People's Republic. Moscow therefore watches with unconcealed anxiety the responses by Peking to its strategy of containment. These responses include coolness toward Hanoi; a suddenly unfolding of competitive friendliness toward the bourgeois-nationalist regimes in Southeast Asia; active support for a residual U.S. security role in the region; pressure on the United States to reverse the process of detente with the Soviet Union; and efforts to build a concert of interests with the United States and Japan to contain the Soviet Union in Asia.[5]

The Soviet Union has no autonomous foreign policy strategy
for Southeast Asia, where its involvement has so far been marginal
except in the Vietnam war. This involvement has been limited, to a
large extent, by the Soviet conflict with China.[6] The raw materials
of Southeast Asia are attractive, but not essential for Soviet industry.
Trade with Southeast Asia adds up to less than 1 percent of Soviet
foreign trade. In the 1960s the first major setback to the Third
World policies of the Soviet Union occurred in Indonesia.

Here the local actors are weak and divided among themselves.
Of the six non-Communist countries, the five ASEAN countries and
Burma, not one is internally stable and secure. The region seethes
with peasant and youth unrest, and its economies, which are oriented
to raw material exports, are buffeted by the ups and downs of the
world capitalist economy.

Despite all this, over the years Southeast Asia has acquired
a political and strategic importance that, as a global power, the
Soviet Union cannot ignore. Its sea lanes, Soviet analysts point out,
are now an inseparable part of the domestic maritime trade of the
Soviet Union. It is in Southeast Asia that "imperialism" has suffered
a clear and unmistakable defeat in a direct military conflict with the
forces of national liberation, aided by those of world socialism.

If the retreat of the United States results in a power vacuum,
the vacuum will be immediately filled by China. A strong Soviet
presence in Southeast Asia, supplementing the stronger Soviet presence in South Asia, would go a long way toward trimming the hegemonic
ambitions of China and it would strengthen the Soviet negotiating position with the United States and Japan. An ongoing detente with the
United States and steadily expanding relations with Japan would also
reinforce the Soviet image in Southeast Asia and contribute to the
containment of China.[7]

This dialectical content of Soviet strategic thinking on Southeast
Asia generates a foreign policy of caution, persuasion, and cooperation rather than adventure, pressure, and hostility. The Soviet
Union has stepped into the slippery Southeast Asian landscape wear-
ing the mantle of a respectable and responsible global power, willing
to do whatever it can to help a cluster of "soft" states acquire stability, orderly social change, and security from external aggression.
The Soviet Union has neither the capability nor therefore the intention
of playing the role of security guarantor in Southeast Asia; what it
wants to prevent is the return of U.S. power, directly or through informal arrangements with local actors.

The Soviet leaders look with interest at trends toward an insti-
tutionally neutralized Southeast Asia, and they are perturbed because
the concept has lost in 1975-76 whatever momentum it had gained in
earlier years. Meanwhile, they continue to project their Asian

collective security model to the region without hoping to recruit any
support in the next few years.

ASEAN PERCEPTIONS OF THE SOVIET UNION

It is easier to sketch a broad framework of Soviet perceptions
of the ASEAN group of countries than to attempt the same with
ASEAN perceptions of the Soviet Union. For ASEAN, the USSR is a
largely unknown quantity. Only one of its members, Indonesia, had
extensive political and economic relations with the Soviet Union for
eight years in the 1950s and 1960s.[8] The great political discontinuity
in Indonesia as a result of the events of September and October 1965
has left the present ruling elite in Jakarta with only unpleasant
memories of that period.
The four other members of ASEAN began to build relations
with the USSR, mostly during the 1970s, and the limited sweep of
the present relationship as well as the international ambience in
which it is being constructed make the ASEAN elites look askance
at Moscow. For most of the period of the cold war, the ASEAN
elites saw the Soviet Union as a hostile power; the image was reinforced during the post-1965 escalated period of the Vietnam war.
The elite images of the outside world were controlled and shaped
by the authoritarian regimes that ruled all of these countries. The
mild breeze of detente did not reach Southeast Asia in the 1960s,
and no major realignment of external powers like that in South Asia
cast its shadow on this region. The United States did not need the
Soviet Union to contain China in Southeast Asia. The United States
enjoyed the moral, though not the material, loyalty of each of the
ASEAN countries. The Soviet role in containment of China made no
impression on the Southeast Asian ruling elites.
The cold-war image of the USSR began to lift with the announcement of the Nixon Doctrine, which proclaimed an imminent lowering
of the U.S. profile in Southeast Asia. Then came the trauma of the
Sino-American diplomatic breakthrough and with it a brutal reorder-
ing of global power equations. The puzzled and bewildered ruling
elites in Southeast Asia saw the apocalyptic enmity suddenly change
to a fledgling friendship. As the United States baptized China as a
world power and dipped its own profile in Southeast Asia, the elites
of the ASEAN capitals were almost automatically made a little aware
of the rising profile of the Soviet Union, the "other" global power.
This awareness was somewhat reinforced as the ASEAN governments turned to the USSR and the Soviet bloc as alternative sources
of aid and markets for raw materials, in their efforts to rescue
their economies from the grip of worldwide recession and inflation.

In 1970 the road to Moscow beckoned a number of ASEAN leaders. Adam Malik of Indonesia made two journeys to the Soviet capital, which was also visited by Lee Kuan Yew of Singapore, while
Tenku Abdul Rahman of Malaysia, during a stopover at the Moscow
airport, was visited there by a deputy Soviet prime minister. Exchanges of trade and of parliamentary delegations began to gather
momentum, and trade channels began to open even where diplomatic
relations were nonexistent. The ASEAN elites suddenly discovered
that Moscow was no longer hurling verbal invectives at their countries and leaders; on the contrary, Moscow was willing to offer
trade and aid without asking for an explicit political price. The
ASEAN leaders were no longer dismissed by Moscow as puppets of
imperialism but were being identified as freedom-loving people
struggling to strengthen their national independence. Within ASEAN
itself the rhetoric of cold-war anti-Communism yielded to the idioms
of neutralism and nonalignment. For most of the elites it was a
nerve-racking experience. They stopped seeing the Soviet Union as
an enemy, but they could not bring themselves to see it as a friend.

In November and December 1974, I found enormous ambivalence in the five ASEAN capitals with regard to the Soviet Union.
Presidents and prime ministers were exerting themselves to establish or improve relations with Moscow. In the Philippines, Malaysia,
and Indonesia, animated debates had been taking place within relatively small groups of powerful men about what kind of relationship
each of these countries should seek with the Soviet Union and what the
impact of those relationships would be on Peking. However, among
the elites outside these groups, there was no clear vision of the
USSR. It was neither an enemy nor a friend, an object of neither
high praise nor bitter blame. The ideological image of the Soviet
Union had vanished; most people in the universities, in the press,
in business houses, and in government did not see the USSR as interested in extending the frontiers of world Communism. The Soviet
Union was not even perceived as overly interested in a Communist
victory in South Vietnam; indeed, as we shall see in a moment, at
the end of 1974 no one in the five ASEAN capitals expected South
Vietnam to fall to the Communists. The elite groups did not see the
Soviet Union as a credible candidate for power and influence in
Southeast Asia. Whatever resources it could muster in the region
would be consumed in not very productive labor to contain the influence of China. Few seemed to expect Moscow to play a major
diplomatic or security role in post-Vietnam Southeast Asia. At a
well-attended conference on "The Great Powers and Southeast Asia,"
held in July 1972 by the Institute of Southeast Asian Studies in
Singapore, no particular attention was given to the USSR, while
China and the United States each claimed four papers. Such references as were made rather casually to the Soviet Union saw Moscow's

influence-building efforts as remaining more or less confined to
Northeast Asia, the subcontinent, and North Vietnam; Moscow was
expected to adopt a standoff posture in the rest of Southeast Asia.[9]
Even more curiously, at an equally well attended conference on the
security of Southeast Asia held in Singapore in 1974, no particular
attention was paid to the Soviet Union. Moscow was seen neither as
a provider of Southeast Asian security nor as a threat to it.[10]

The only perception of the Soviet Union that was widely shared
by the elites in all of the ASEAN capitals was that Moscow would be
locked in a struggle with China for influence in Southeast Asia during
the 1970s. This was a reassuring perception, because these elites
wish to see China contained by either the United States or the USSR,
or preferably by both. However, even in that rubric, few foresaw a
big Soviet role; Southeast Asia was, by consensus, outside the pale
of active, large-scale Soviet involvement.

This perception was generated by a cluster of assumptions.
The first was that the United States would maintain a strong residual
military and political presence in Southeast Asia for a long time and
that it would not abandon its commitment to its allies. The second
was that the war in Indochina would not end in Communist victory and
that South Vietnam would survive for many years as a non-Communist
state, while Cambodia would settle down as a neutral sovereign nation. Since the United States had virtually recognized Southeast Asia
as a zone of Chinese special interests,[11] there would be no conflict
between U.S. and Chinese power. The United States would protect
the vital interests of its Southeast Asian allies from Chinese power
ambitions, while the two together would keep off the Soviet Union as
a credible candidate for influence.

All these assumptions were shattered in the spring of 1975
when the Communist forces swept across South Vietnam and Phnom
Penh fell to the Communist-led insurgents. Thailand immediately
asked for complete withdrawal of U.S. troops and bases from its
territory within 18 months, while the Philippines moved to bring the
U.S. bases under its own control. Within five months of the end of
the Indochina war, Thailand and the Philippines jointly called for the
phasing out of SEATO. Among the unnoticed results of the Indochina
war was the change in the collective ASEAN perception of realities
within and outside Southeast Asia. The Communist victories in Indochina suddenly sharpened the diversities of Southeast Asia, and each
nation of ASEAN was now called upon to readjust its perceptions.

THE INSECURITY OF SOUTHEAST ASIA

Asian diversities are most pronounced in Southeast Asia, which
was born as a geopolitical region during World War II because of the

need to set up a separate command under the British to defend, and
later to regain, the British, French, and Dutch colonies in Asia
from Japan. Southeast Asia is a curiously ill-balanced assemblage
of territories "draped in one great elongated and branching peninsula
and a series of elaborately contorted archipelagoes stretching from
Sumatra to Luzon--a dozen or so large islands and an immense profusion of smaller ones."[12] It has the world's most complex maritime crossroads, formed by interconnecting seas and oceans, giving
it a high degree of accessibility. Over a long historical period,
therefore, it has been a meeting place of peoples, cutlures, civilizations, and ideas, and its societies have acquired a strong assimilative
character. Politically Southeast Asia has been as turbulent as heter-
ogenous. Rival imperialisms have clashed with each other for the
mastery of its lands and peoples for thousands of years. In the period since World War II, two mutually contradictory and still inter-
weaving forces have interacted in the political evolution of Southeast
Asia. These forces are the nationalism of peoples emerging from
the colonial domination of European powers and the competitive
influence-building endeavors of the United States, the Soviet Union,
China, and, since the early 1960s, Japan.

The fragmented character of international relations within the
region and the feeble quality of the internal political orders have
acted as strong incentives for intervention by external powers, especially the United States. The U.S. intervention was prompted by the
image of the region as the highly vulnerable rear guard of the world
capitalist system; this was not an unrealistic image. With the aim
of protecting the rear guard from falling to the rival, or Communist,
system, the United States tragically pitted itself against the aroused
nationalism of the Vietnamese people, who were mobilized by a
dynamic Communist leadership. The intervention finally led to the
Communist victories in Indochina. Southeast Asian regimes sought
the protection of the United States partly because each one of them
was plagued by armed insurgencies led by Peking-supported Communist groups (Soviet support ceased in the late 1950s or early
1960s) and partly because they regarded themselves as an integral
part of the world capitalist system.

As U.S. protection came to an end with the turn of the 1970s,
these regimes did not see themselves as individually much stronger
and sounder than before.[13] Insurgencies continued to threaten
Thailand and the Philippines and on a lesser scale continued to tax
the resources of Malaysia and Indonesia also. Each of these nations
had unresolved problems of large ethnic minorities that were of
doubtful loyalty to the prevailing political orders. Despite considerable economic growth since the mid-1960s, which has promoted
the ASEAN countries to the category of a middle-income group of

nations, the disparities between the rich few and the multitudes of
poor have increased, and affluence remains limited to urban islands,
insecure and ostentatious, in seas of mass poverty. In nearly all of
the ASEAN countries, a state of increasing polarization exists between small, conservative, change-resisting oligarchies with authoritarian tendencies and the increasingly radicalized student and youth
cohorts, the urban middle classes, and the deprived peasantry of the
countryside.[14]

The security gaps in Southeast Asia are, then, both internal
and external, and they have widened as a result of the folding up of
the U.S. security system. However, no security system ever devised for the region has succeeded in establishing a congruence of
the internal and external interests of the states nor between regional
interests and the interests of the security-providing external powers.
The great weaknesses of the U.S. security system were that it rested
on straw pillars, on local regimes and leaderships that were not
rooted in popular affection and support; and that it throttled the orderly
political evolution of the region.[15]

Although Southeast Asia is the geographical and historical
backyard of China, Peking has so far not offered this region a credible concept or system of security. It can be argued that the U.S.
policy of containment of China made it impossible for the Chinese
government to play a stabilizing role in Southeast Asia. However,
Peking has almost consistently been torn between a policy of cultivating relations of peaceful coexistence with the Southeast Asian
regimes and rendering moral and material help to revolutionary
elements in these countries. Even during the period since the Vietnam war, when China has set out to establish normal relations with
its neighbors and has demonstrated its readiness to extend economic
aid, three clandestine radio stations, allegedly located on Chinese
territory, have been calling for the violent overthrow of the governments in Malaysia, Singapore, Thailand, and Burma. Moreover,
China has not reversed its policy of hostility toward the military regime in Indonesia nor its policy of nonrecognition of the republic of
Singapore.

The Southeast Asian nations are anxious to normalize their
relations with China, whose preeminent position in the region they
now reluctantly acknowledge; but they can hardly look toward Peking
as a protector of the internal stability and external security of their
states, and they are far from certain that the current policy of
cooperation and good-neighborliness will survive political succession
in Peking after the passing of the present palsied leadership.[16]

During the imperial period, Britain had imposed a strategic
symmetry on Southeast and South Asia; the security shield was
Britain's unchallenged sea power. That strategic symmetry broke

down during World War II and could not be restored even after the Allies recovered Southeast Asia from Japan. Decolonization finally snapped all strategic links between the two Asian regions.

Britain, however, continued to maintain security linkages with Malaysia and Singapore until the early 1970s. The Anglo-Malayan Defense Agreement (AMDA) of 1957 provided Malaysia and later Singapore with an explicit security guarantee. The guarantor was Britain in association with Australia and New Zealand. Britain's membership in SEATO linked AMDA with the U.S. security system. Malaysia found AMDA useful during the Indonesian confrontation, but AMDA could not survive the economic and political changes in its partner nations during the 1960s. The British decision to withdraw military commitments in areas "east of Suez" eroded the defense commitments to Malaysia by Australia and New Zealand. At the turn of the 1970s Southeast Asia "failed to become a cohesive region for alliance purposes" for these two antipodean powers. [17]

AMDA lapsed in November 1971, yielding to the looser five-power defense arrangement, ANZUK, linking Britain, Australia, New Zealand, Malaysia, and Singapore to a consultative framework of defense support for the two Southeast Asian countries if either, or both, came under an external attack or threat of attack. ANZUK was no defense pact; it merely linked together two clusters of agreements in the form of letters of exchange between Malaysia and the three external powers on the one hand and between Singapore and these external powers on the other. ANZUK, then, failed to resolve the strategic divergence between Malaysia and Singapore. ANZUK virtually ceased to exist when the Labour government in Australia began to withdraw its ground forces from Singapore in 1973 and when Malaysia announced a year later that the 1971 defense arrangements were no longer operative. [18]

The only security concept, as distinct from a system, that prevails in Southeast Asia in the 1970s is the ASEAN proposal of neutralization. ASEAN was set up in 1966, with U.S. and British encouragement, to promote economic and cultural cooperation among the five members. At a special foreign ministers' meeting in Kuala Lumpur in November 1971, ASEAN issued a declaration proposing that Southeast Asia be recognized by the great powers as a neutralized region free from the power rivalries and competitive intervention of the principal actors of the international system. The fact that the declaration was issued not from one of the regular meetings of the ASEAN foreign ministers but from a special meeting suggested that neutralization was an extracurricular objective of the group, something not quite within the normal framework of the terms of reference of ASEAN. Moreover, this attempt to impose a strategic symmetry on the five Southeast Asian nations merely ignored

the territorial disputes existing among them; the diverse and sometimes contradictory strategic perceptions of the leaders of the different governments; and the very limited success achieved by ASEAN
so far, even in the realm of economic regionalism.[19] Indeed,
regionalism had made so little progress that one year after the
Kuala Lumpur Declaration a noted scholar on Southeast Asia was
constrained to remark, "If there were a verb 'to regionalize' then
a dispassionate student of regionalism in Southeast Asia might con-
jugate it thus: past, imperfect; present, indicative; future, indefinite."[20]

In November 1974 I found in the ASEAN capitals neither universal approval of the strategic concept of neutralism nor a uniform
framework of conceptual thinking. The elites in the different capitals had their own attitudes toward neutralization. The high enthusiasm in Kuala Lumpur contrasted sharply with the high cynicism
in Jakarta and Singapore. The Thai and Philippine attitude was a
mixture of interest and doubt.

The Indonesian foreign minister, Adam Malik, came out solidly
in favor of neutralization during an interview, emphasizing at the
same time that progress toward neutralization could only be by step
by step and that the first step, which was normalization of relations
between each of the ASEAN countries and China and North Vietnam,
was still some way off. Scholars at the prestigious Center for
Strategic and International Studies, the "think tank" of the Indonesian
military regime, saw neutralization as "more desirable than attain-
able." There were obviously major differences between the strategic
perspectives of the Indonesian foreign minister and those of the military leaders of the regime.[21]

On the question of neutralization the leaders in Singapore were
closer to the Indonesians than to their brethren across the Causeway
in Malaysia. In Bangkok and Manila there was even less conceptual
clarity about neutralization, though there was no lack of support for
neutralization as a desirable but distant goal.

It is in Kuala Lumpur that most of the conceptual and spatial
exercises appeared to have been done. Conceptually, the Malaysians
visualize agreements on a set of "rules" that must govern international relations in Southeast Asia at two interlocking levels, the
regional level and the major power level. At the regional level the
Southeast Asian countries must agree to respect one another's sovereignty and territorial integrity, bind themselves to the principles
of nonaggression and noninterference in one another's internal affairs, settle all interstate disputes by peaceful means, promote
regional cooperation, and develop a collective view before the major
powers on vital issues of security. They must also get rid of foreign
military bases and troops and must not allow the region to be used as

a theater of conflict in the international struggle of power. Once
the regional states have agreed on these rules, they must approach
the major powers collectively for an interlocking agreement. This
agreement must bind the major powers to recognition of the neutrality of Southeast Asia, which they must exclude from their power
struggle. They must also devise the supervisory means of guaran-
teeing the neutrality of the region.[22]

The four other ASEAN members have many reservations about
the Malaysian model, which in November 1974 looked to many of the
elites in these countries as utopian. How could one expect the USSR
and China to work together in a "supervisory council" to oversee
Southeast Asian neutrality? Did Southeast Asia have a stable balance
of power on which alone a strategic system of neutralization could
be built? How could the region be neutralized when some of the
states had security relations with the United States? Would neutralization buy as much security for Singapore as it would for
Malaysia and Indonesia? Would it not freeze the existing borders
and forever deny Sabah to the Philippines? Could neutralized regimes effectively deal with Communist insurgencies? Would neutralization not weaken the will of the states to defend themselves,
making them easy prey to intervention or aggression by a major
power? Above all, was it not utopian to talk about a neutralized
Southeast Asia when great power relations were marked by keen
competition; when a cold war went on between Moscow and Peking;
and when the Indian Ocean was becoming a zone of acute rivalry between the United States and the Soviet Union?

If ASEAN, then, is far from a firm commitment to neutralization, it seems to be equally distant from any transition from an organization for regional cooperation into a defense alliance. Indonesia has been the most strongly opposed to investing ASEAN with
security functions, partly because of the traditional distaste of
Indonesia for military pacts, but mostly because its leaders are not
willing to place their military potential at the disposal of a collectivity. Malaysia has rejected the idea of making ASEAN an instrument of collective defense because of its adherence to nonalignment.
Moreover, as long as Thailand and the Philippines were members of
SEATO, the transformation of ASEAN into a defense pact would have
made it look like an offshoot of the U.S. security system. The 1973
proposal by the Philippines for an ASEAN collective nonaggression
treaty has not passed so far, although it has been discussed at length
by the foreign ministers. This resistance to collective defense responsibility without the cement of U.S. leadership stems primarily
from the strategic discord among the five and the disdain of some
for the military capability of others. The Indonesians, for instance,
appear to entertain no great opinion about the fighting ability of

Thailand and the Philippines; both armies are thought to be in poor shape. On the other hand, the preoccupation of the Indonesian armed forces with internal security makes Indonesia incapable of undertaking regional security burdens and perhaps affects its role as defender of its national frontiers. Besides, there is also some fear in Jakarta, Singapore, and Kuala Lumpur that collective defense may involve ASEAN in guerrilla wars in Southeast Asia and thereby with such external powers as may support the insurgent elements.

The spatial framework of neutralization is also controversial. ASEAN does not represent all of Southeast Asia. Five states are outside it, the four Indochinese states and Burma. In a way, ASEAN still carries upon it the imprint of the polarization that the U.S. doctrine of containment had imposed upon Southeast Asia. The spatial inadequacy of ASEAN is acknowledged in all five ASEAN capitals, and there is a visible desire to expand the frontiers of regionalism to include the Indochinese states and Burma. It is also acknowledged, in principle, that a neutralized Southeast Asia must cover all ten nations.

However, Thailand participated in the Vietnam war in a big way on behalf of the United States, contributing 12,000 troops and permitting full-scale use of the U.S. bases on its territory for air and naval operations in support of the pro-Western regime in Saigon. So also did the Philippines, though on a much smaller scale. North Vietnam made it clear that it would have nothing to do with ASEAN as long as two of its members belonged to SEATO and permitted U.S. bases and troops on their territory. After the Paris peace accords of January 1973, all of the ASEAN governments realized the importance of repairing their relations with Hanoi, but none was ready to pay the price demanded by the North Vietnamese, namely the immediate withdrawal of U.S. troops, the dismantling of the U.S. bases, and the liquidation of SEATO.

Neutralization as a strategic concept was anchored on the assumption that the Indochina war would end with the survival of non-Communist, neutral regimes in South Vietnam, Cambodia, and Laos and that the overall balance of forces in Southeast Asia would remain decisively in favor of the non-Communist states. A Thai scholar, writing in 1971, echoed a widely shared ASEAN sentiment when he affirmed that "as far as the security and stability of Southeast Asia are concerned, it is of crucial importance that the war does not end with the immediate takeover of South Vietnam by North Vietnam."[23] At the Singapore conference of Southeast Asian security in May–June 1974, the consensus was that there was little possibility that the Communists would win in South Vietnam in the near future, and even less possibility that they would win in Cambodia and Laos.

A paper reflecting widely shared perceptions of the future of Vietnam and of its impact on Southeast Asia came to the following conclusion:

> A military or political victory of the North Vietnam- ese Communists is highly unlikely. It follows that there is not much point to speculation about the pol- icy of a Vietnam reunified by the Communists.
>
> For a fiarly long time to come, Vietnam will remain divided, not only between a Socialist North and a "non-Communist South," but also between two administrative zones in the South with indeterminate borders, the one large in area but thinly peopled and relatively isolated from the outside world, probably crystalizing in a mini-Yenan with a non-capitalist regime, the other controlling the great majority of the population and the large towns, wide open to the outside world and likely ultimately to seek sta- bility and new opportunities through a change of government, possibly by a military coup on the Portuguese model. [24]

This perception of the durability of the political status quo in Indochina survived through 1974. Of those whom I interviewed in the five ASEAN capitals in November and December 1974, less than one-third saw the possibility of the whole of Indochina going Com- munist "in the next five or six years." The rest believed that South Vietnam would survive as a non-Communist entity and that of course Cambodia and Laos would also. [25]

The perception of Hanoi's role in Southeast Asia by the ASEAN elite also showed a remarkable degree of polarization. A minority expected Hanoi to be preoccupied for the next ten years with prob- lems of internal reconstruction, neither desiring, nor capable of playing, a larger Southeast Asian role; its stance would remain largely internal, and it would adopt a foreign policy of nonalignment rather than seek an alliance with China or the Soviet Union. This perception was the strongest in Malaysia, but it was also shared by a minority in the other ASEAN countries. The majority perception, on the other hand, was that of an expansionist and aggressive North Vietnam that would combine the strategy of revolutionary takeover in the three Indochina states with active assistance to the insurgents in Thailand, the Philippines, and Malaysia. The Malaysians, with a mellower view of North Vietnamese intransigence, were appar- ently arguing with their ASEAN partners that even in a Communist Indochina, Hanoi would for many years be preoccupied with prob- lems of cohesion, reunification, and economic reconstruction and

unable to play a larger role in Southeast Asia. To ensure its inde-
pendence of China, Hanoi would seek its identity in the community of
Southeast Asian nations. Neutralization would strengthen Hanoi's
nonalignment and its candidacy for U.S. aid. Proceeding from these
assumptions, the Malaysians argued that the best way to secure
Chinese and Soviet commitment to the neutralization of Southeast
Asia would be to recruit Hanoi as a member of an expanded ASEAN.
The Malaysian thesis was unacceptable to Indonesia, Singapore, and
Thailand because they rejected the assumptions on which it was
based. It also gave Hanoi, in their view, a leading role in a neutralized Southeast Asia.

The progress of ASEAN toward neutralization halted after the
Communist victories in Indochina. The foreign ministers did not
meet in April to approve the "operational blueprint." Even verbal
enthusiasm for neutralization waned. In the perception of the ruling
elites in Bangkok, Singapore, and Jakarta, and to a lesser degree in
Manila and Kuala Lumpur, the Communist successes in Indochina
had brought about a shift in the balance of forces in the region. Each
ASEAN country now had to adjust its policies to the change in the
political map of Southeast Asia. What perturbed the ASEAN leaders
even more than the Communist victories was the decision by two
Vietnams to reunify their country by April 1976. A united Vietnam
ruled by the Communists would be an entirely new factor in Southeast
Asian politics. It might give the Soviet Union an advance outpost in
Southeast Asia. It might make the region a hotbed of the Sino-Soviet
cold war. When the heads of government of the five ASEAN countries assembled for the first time in eight years at Denpasar, in
Bali, in February 1976, they had no reason to be reassured of their
relations with Communist Vietnam, Laos, and Cambodia. Although
the meeting adopted a declaration of amity, it failed to harmonize
the strategic interests of the five nations. "Old rivalries reappeared.
Long-standing suspicions resurfaced. Sensitivities were aroused,"
reported the Far Eastern Economic Review. "Like Southeast Asia
itself, it is a complex tale."[26] In their amity declaration, the conference leaders sought to direct their efforts toward closer economic
cooperation, which the declaration said was the key to regional
stability.

THE SOVIET UNION AND VIETNAM

The strategic disarray of the non-Communist countries of
Southeast Asia is likely to help the Soviet Union build its presence
in a region in which it had practically none before 1970, at which
time Soviet perceptions of Southeast Asia began to change in a big

way. The Chinese were still hurling revolutionary invectives at the
Southeast Asian regimes.[27] The Soviets, in contrast smelled the
sweet odor of anti-imperialism in the nationalism of the elites in the
region. Victor Mayevsky, an expert on Asian security, commenting
on the "One Asia" conference organized in Manila in August 1970 by
the Asia Press Foundation, noted a change of mood: despite the
pro-Western makeup of the assembly and the Southeast Asian actors'
rejection of socialism, the deliberations lacked an anti-Communist
accent. At the present time, wrote Mayevsky, the Asian bourgeoisie
were trying to use nationalism in their own class interest. To a
large extent nationalist feelings were developing "as a reaction to
the neocolonialist policy of imperialism, great power chauvinism
and the chosen-nation concept propagated in Japan."[28] Both external
and internal factors were stimulating the growth of nationalism in
Asian countries. Trends toward regional cooperation were largely
a reaction to external intervention. Regional cooperation therefore
could not be directed against the Socialist bloc.

This was one of the first Soviet attempts to differentiate between ASEAN and SEATO. In the mid-1970s the Soviet Union sees
no major contradictions between the Communist-led regimes in
Indochina and the non-Communist states grouped together in ASEAN.
The entire Southeast Asian region will belong to the national liberation zone as soon as it is detached from the "world imperialist order."
The major contradictions in Southeast Asia are with "American and
Japanese imperialism and neocolonialism" and the "great power
chauvinism of Maoist China."

A detailed analysis of Soviet policies for Indochina during the
1970s is beyond the scope of this study.[29] However, the Soviet rule
in the Indochina war appears to have become highly complex during
the 1970-73 period. The Soviet Union has probably been nudging
Hanoi toward a negotiated peace with the United States ever since
the announcement of the Nixon Doctrine. In March 1970, when
Narodom Sihanouk paid an official visit to Moscow, the Soviets were
clearly visualizing a postwar political map of Indochina in which
Cambodia and Laos, if not South Vietnam, would continue to remain
non-Communist and neutral.[30]

When Sihanouk was overthrown by the coup of Lon Nol and
Sirik Matak, a delicate and difficult situation developed in Cambodia
for the Soviet leaders. If Sihanouk were to try to rally the neutralist
and Communist forces for partisan war, he must obviously function
from Peking, and his chief source of hardware support could only
be China and North Vietnam. This would offer the Chinese a coveted
opportunity to influence future events in Cambodia. To make the
best of a bad situation, the Soviet leaders adopted a dual policy:
continued diplomatic dealings with the Lon Nol regime, and moral

and propaganda support for the partisans mobilized by the Peking-based Cambodian government-in-exile headed by Sihanouk.

When U.S. and South Vietnamese forces invaded Cambodia on May 1, 1970, the Soviets bitterly condemned the action, and on June 12 Brezhnev gave the prophetic warning that "by widening the war in the region Washington leaders are widening the scale of their future defeats both on the military and on the political fronts."[31] Kosygin, at his press conference on May 4, went to the length of stressing that the Chinese government also had "angrily condemned the US aggression in Cambodia."[32] The Soviet media supported the "armed struggle of the Khmer people against the agressive intrigues of the US imperialists and their stooges," and Kosygin welcomed the formation of the National United Front of Cambodia but carefully avoided mentioning the formation of the government-in-exile.

The Soviets lowered their diplomatic presence in Phnom Penh by withdrawing the ambassador, and they probably gave, or offered, a certain amount of economic aid to the government-in-exile.[33] Nevertheless, Soviet nonrecognition of the Sihanouk government blocked meaningful cooperation between Moscow and the Cambodian insurgents. As Sihanouk himself correctly pointed out, "the interests of the Soviets and those of us do not coincide."[34]

The Soviet Union probably increased the volume of its military and economic aid to Hanoi in the wake of the U.S. invasion of Cambodia and looked to the North Vietnamese to counter the Chinese influence on the Cambodian insurgent leadership. What evidently disturbed Moscow most in 1970 was the Indochinese "peoples' conference" in Hanoi, which turned out to be a summit meeting of the Communist leaders of the four Indochinese states and Chou En-lai.[35] A Chinese success in contriving some kind of a socialist bloc in Asia would have been highly injurious to Soviet interests. This, however, did not happen, and despite the determination of Hanoi to remain independent of Moscow as well as Peking for the rest of the war, the Soviets focused their attention mostly on North Vietnam, publicly supporting its political stand and strategic plans but privately counseling compromise and actually helping to remove several obstacles to the successful convening of the Paris conference.[36] The Soviets publicly stood by Hanoi subsequently as well, blaming Saigon and the United States for repeated violations of the Paris accords and in private probably advising the North Vietnamese not to press for a military victory in South Vietnam, but not withholding or reducing its support when Hanoi decided to mount its final, successful military offensive.

Of greater significance was the agreement concluded in 1973 between Hanoi and Moscow providing for large-scale Soviet assistance for economic reconstruction of war-ravaged North Vietnam.

The talks between Le Duan and Phan Van Dong, the two leading
members of the North Vietnamese delegation, on one side, and
Brezhnev, Kosygin, and other Soviet leaders on the other must have
been highly satisfactory to both sides, since the Soviet leaders decided that economic and military assistance given to Hanoi so far
would be nonrefundable, a generosity that the Soviet Union had not
extended to China and North Korea during the Korean war or after
the Korean armistice.[37]

The joint committee on economic and technological cooperation
set up in 1973 has had several meetings since. According to Moscow,
the Soviet Union had completed the construction of 150 industrial and
natural resource projects in North Vietnam by 1975, including the
Thap Bu hydroelectric plant, the largest of its kind in Southeast Asia
and 70 more projects are under construction. Soviet-aided projects
cover coal and tin mines, electric power plants, cement factories,
prefab housing factories, and tool repairing plants, as well as transportation and road building projects.

The planning organizations of the two countries are working
together; 7,000 North Vietnamese technicians have been trained in
the USSR and 4,000 more are under training. An undisclosed number of Soviet specialists and technical hands are deployed in Hanoi.
A Moscow Radio broadcast told the Vietnamese in August 1975 that
"in the coming five years the Soviet Union will generously assist the
Democratic Republic of Vietnam in developing all the main branches
of its national economy."[38] Within a few weeks the two countries
concluded a five-year economic cooperation agreement integrating
their five-year development plans.[39]

Of greater import was the political declaration issued jointly
by the Soviet Union and North Vietnamese regime in Moscow in early
November, pledging the latter's support for almost all the major
directions of Soviet foreign policy except the containment of China.
The declaration, which came after four days of talks between the
Soviet leadership and a Hanoi delegation led by Le Duan, said that
the two countries "held completely identical views" on major international issues, specifically on detente, the Middle Eastern conflict,
and Portugal.[40]

On their part the Soviet leaders apparently have not too strongly
pressed Hanoi to adopt an openly anti-China position. They have
listened without protest to public tributes to China for its fraternal
assistance to North and South Vietnam by the Hanoi leaders. Soviet
dignitaries visiting North Vietnam have scrupulously avoided criti-
cizing China openly. The Kremlin sent to the 30th anniversary
celebrations in Hanoi in September 1975 one of the CPSU leaders
who is relatively unknown to the outside world, M. S. Solomentsev,
premier of the Russian republic and candidate member of the

Politburo. Evidently Moscow wanted neither to dramatize its presence in North Vietnam nor to parade its developing political understanding with Hanoi. In his speeches in Hanoi and in other places in North Vietnam, Solomentsev made no reference to China nor to the Soviet concept of collective security in Asia;[41] nor did the joint declaration issued in Moscow pledge Hanoi to support the Soviet security model for Asia.[42]

Soon after the Communist victories in Indochina, however, the Soviet media made it clear that the North Vietnamese success, which must have taken the Soviet leaders as much by surprise as it did the rest of the world, owed a great deal to the military assistance given Hanoi by the USSR. A Moscow broadcast disclosed that nearly 70 percent of all foreign military aid received by Hanoi during the entire period of the Vietnam war had been given by the Soviet Union.[43]

Confirmation of the Soviet political and diplomatic success in Hanoi after the Indochina war came more conclusively from Peking. The Chinese became suddenly cool toward Hanoi and took no particular care to hide this from the world. In view of their hostile relations with the USSR, the Chinese probably did not wish the North Vietnamese to inflict a crushing defeat on the forces of South Vietnam and thereby deal a mortal blow to the U.S. security system in Southeast Asia.

After the Indochina war, Peking and Hanoi disagreed on the U.S. role in Asia that would be desirable during the post-Vietnam period. Although Peking had been supporting a significant residual U.S. military presence in Asia as a check on the expansion of Soviet influence, Hanoi demanded total withdrawal of U.S. forces and military bases from Thailand.

When a North Vietnamese delegation arrived in Peking in August 1975 for preliminary talks on postwar reconstruction, it was not received by any top Chinese official, but only by the deputy premier in charge of economic affairs, Li Hsien-nien. The meeting lacked warmth. One report said that the Chinese were blaming the North Vietnamese for ingratitude and for their pro-Soviet policies; they were afraid that North Vietnam would grant the Soviets a naval base at Cam Ranh Bay. After a four-day stay in Peking, the Hanoi delegation, which was led by the top economic expert of North Vietnam, deputy premier Le Thanh Nghi, left for Moscow without signing an aid agreement.[44]

When Henry Kissinger was in Peking in October to arrange for Gerald Ford's visit, it was reported that the "precipitate end of the Indochina war" was among the factors that had brought about "a congruence of Chinese and United States interests in Asia" in containing Soviet influence.[45]

Only a few days before Kissinger's visit Le Duan had led an unsuccessful mission to the Chinese capital. He had left abruptly

for Moscow without signing the usual joint communique on his talks
with the Chinese leaders and without the customary return banquet
for his hosts in the Great Hall of the People. Reporting Le Duan's
visit, the New York Times said,

> The Chinese fears seemed to center on several
> developments: the suspicion that despite all
> Peking's wartime aid, Hanoi might grant a mili-
> tary base to the Soviet Union; indications that
> North Vietnam was following the Soviet line on
> issues ranging from the Portuguese situation to
> support for Prime Minister Indira Gandhi in India
> and concern that the Soviet Union was gaining the
> upper hand with the Communists in Laos, thanks
> to North Vietnam's dominant influence there. [46]

Peking, on the other hand, gave a most enthusiastic welcome
to the Cambodian leaders when they arrived in the Chinese capital in
August. The Chinese persuaded them to invite Norodom Sihanouk to
Cambodia and concluded an agreement on economic cooperation, the
details of which were kept secret except for the fact that all Chinese
aid would be given free of charge. A thousand Chinese technicians
were engaged in repairing Cambodia's war-shattered economy. [47]
Under Chinese prompting, the Cambodian leaders paid a visit to
Bangkok in October-November; the visit led to a temporary improvement in Thai-Cambodian relations, which had remained more or less
hostile for the entire period following World War II. [48] The Cambodian Communist leaders remained cool toward Moscow through
1975. [49] Some of them had a meeting with Solomentsev in Hanoi in
September, but apparently there was no political breakthrough. In
Laos, on the other hand, the Soviets were able to build a visible
presence, largely through the good offices of the North Vietnamese.

Thus the Soviet Union Union and China have gotten fully involved in the ancient frictions among the Indochinese peoples at the
end of 30 years of revolutionary war and 150 years of Western
dominance in Indochina. Having secured a much larger and stronger
foothold than the Chinese, the Soviets have determined to transfer
large-scale resources to Vietnam and Laos in the coming years, and
also to Cambodia, should the Cambodian Communists ask for aid,
provided political relations with Hanoi remain warm and mutually
beneficial.

Aid to Communist Vietnam will be an additional strain on Soviet
resources, but the political and strategic payoff may well compensate
the cost. First, an independent Vietnam could be a handy instrument
for containing China in Southeast Asia. If Hanoi can build, with

Soviet-bloc assistance, a socialist industrial infrastructure that skips capitalist development altogether, it will be a more credible example of the Soviet model of noncapitalist development than Mongolia and the Asiatic republics of the USSR, which are now cited as empirical evidence of the theory and the model. In any case, if Vietnam can modernize itself in the next 15 to 20 years, following a non-Chinese model of development and with close political and economic collaboration with the Soviet Union, the Asian image of the USSR as the pathfinder of rapid industrialization of agrarian societies will certainly be much stronger.

Second, in a region in which almost all of the states are heavily dependent on foreign aid, Vietnam will also enable the Soviet Union to demonstrate the difference between socialist and capitalist foreign aid to the developing nations.

Third, success of the Vietnamese revolution will rob Maoism of much of its charisma among the restless youth and awakening peasantry in Southeast Asia. A major role in the socialist reconstruction of Vietnam may rehabilitate the revolutionary image of the USSR in Asia, an image that now lies buried in conflict with China and detente with the United States.

At the same time, the obligation to transfer large-scale resources to Vietnam without any certainty of political return cautions the Soviet leaders against revolutionary upheavals in other Asian countries. As noted, they cannot be certain of the loyalty of Hanoi and cannot control its independence. Massive aid to Vietnam will tax the Soviet economy more than the continuing aid to Cuba because the Chinese factor will oblige Moscow to render this aid on the most generous terms. Economic cooperation will be a one-way street, at least for some time. The inevitable pluralism of Communism in Asia and the extremely high cost of building an industrial infrastructure in a precapitalist society are among the reasons why the Soviet Union cannot look with much enthusiasm on the possibility of successful Communist insurgencies in other Asian countries. This explains the Soviet anxiety to pursue a parallel policy of friendly cooperation with the bourgeois regimes in Southeast Asia and promote cooperation between these regimes and Vietnam. Hence, also, the Soviet hope that the "lessons of Vietnam" will eventually "show the peoples of Asia the great importance that a system of collective security can have, a system designed to prevent bloodshed and to promote the creation of a favorable atmosphere for cooperation in peaceful, constructive labor,"[50] that is, in peaceful evolutionary change rather than in revolutionary upheaval.

The way the Soviet leaders are trying to develop their parallel strategy for the ASEAN group of countries can be seen with some clarity in their efforts to build relations with each member of the

collectivity. Each country is unique, anywhere in the world, but in
Southeast Asia the distinctiveness of the countries is more pronounced than their similarities. The Soviet leaders must readjust
their perceptions as they turn their attention from one ASEAN country to another. Equally divergent are perceptions by the individual
ASEAN countries of the Sovier Union. The following sections of this
chapter offer an analysis of the Soviet perceptions of each of the five
ASEAN countries and of the perceptions by each of the Soviet Union.
The existing state of relations between the USSR and each of the five
is taken into account in the context of mutual perceptions, and in the
same context the areas in which these relations are likely to grow
or meet with resistance are also indicated.

THE SOVIET UNION AND THAILAND

Of the five ASEAN countries, none has a greater problem of
internal stability and external security than Thailand. At the 1972
Singapore conference on Asia and the great powers, the following
was stated:

> The great question mark in continental Southeast
> Asia is Thailand. As it is the only country never
> colonized by the European imperial powers, its con-
> servative political leadership feels unembarrassed
> in casting its ideological lot with the United States.
> The United States recently built a huge air base
> near Bangkok, from which raids into North Vietnam
> are being staged. Nevertheless, Thailand's north-
> east is heavily troubled with Communist infiltration
> and is practically lost to Bangkok. There are pockets
> of insurrections, Communist and communal, down
> south. Perhaps sensing the pressures pushing for
> eventual Chinese hegemony over continental South-
> east Asia, Thailand has shown a remarkable enthu-
> siasm as joiner in various regional groupings; it is
> a signatory to SEATO, ASA, and ASPAC, and now it
> is one of the staunchest supporters of a stronger
> ASEAN. Apparently, Thailand hopes to ward off a
> Chinese future in the illusory comfort of member-
> ship in regional security and politico-economic
> arrangements.[51]

The political changes that have occurred in Thailand and in
Southeast Asia during the last three years have widened the gaps in

its internal stability and external security. The rebellion of the university youth, supported by the urban middle class, toppled its military-bureaucratic dictatorship in 1973. An interim civilian government ruled for a little over a year, during which period a new constitution was drawn up and free parliamentary elections held for the first time in Thailand's history. The first cabinet formed after the election could not last more than a week. The second, a center-right coalition, ruled more than a year but fell toward the end of 1975 because of factional infighting.

New elections were due in April 1976, but the prospects for the emergence of a stable government were slim. Parliamentary government, a fragile plant, is threatened by urban and rural violence on the one hand and by the ever-present possibility of a military coup on the other. The Thai middle class, long under pervasive military influence, is emotionally distant from the increasingly restless youth in the cities and peasantry in the countryside. The prosperity of Bangkok stands in mocking contrast with the poverty of the villages in which 80 percent of the population of over 30 million lives. This population is growing at the rate of 3.3 percent. The increasingly politicized peasants are demanding agrarian reforms and larger development inputs in the long-neglected countryside.[52] There is a real possibility that the growing disparity between the rich and the poor will encourage the deprived rural population to turn to the "vigorous Communist party and its rural insurgent elements."[53] Strikes are becoming part of the fraying fabric of life in Bangkok itself, where nearly 8 percent of the people live in slums.[54] The buoyant economic growth of the 1960s was primarily due to the heavy U.S. military expenditure in Thailand as a result of the Vietnam war. The Thai economy essentially remains feeble. The development plans have failed to raise rural incomes as the demographic pressure on land has continued to increase; development has remained more or less confined to the urban industrial environs and is "unable and unwilling to break out into the countryside."[55] The urban industrial development, which has largely been the result of Japanese and U.S. private investment, has been hit by the worldwide recession and inflation. Anti-Japanese nationalism exploded during the 1974 visit of prime minister Tanaka, leading to a decline in the flow of Japanese capital. Meanwhile, a growing trade deficit and heavy dependence on the export of agricultural products, which are vulnerable to falling prices, threaten even the limited prosperity that urban Thailand has experienced during the 1960s and early 1970s.[56]

The Communist insurgencies in Thailand have compelled scholars to wonder whether it will turn out to be a second Vietnam.[57] The insurgency in the north engulfed six provinces in 1972, when the

government had to evacuate the entire population of three provinces.
An even more serious situation prevails in the 15 northeast provinces which constitute one-third of Thai territory. The insurgents
in this region are reinforced by infiltrations from Laos and Cambodia. The terrain of forested sandstone plateau dissected by river
valleys is ideally suited for guerrilla war. Although the number of
armed guerrillas is probably small, according to Thai official estimates not more than 5,000, certain areas on the Thai-Cambodian
border are admittedly under the administrative control of the
rebels. [58] The Thai Communist party is anti-Soviet and pro-Peking,
but its logistical support probably comes from Hanoi. Since May
1975 the insurgents have been able to count on active support from
Laos and Cambodia, support that will continue if these Communist-
ruled countries remain hostile to Thailand. [59]

It has been suggested that for the last 30 years the domestic
politics of Thailand have been strongly influenced by its foreign
policy and that Thailand can produce the political leadership necessary for the survival of its independence and sovereignty. [60] Perhaps it is more correct to suggest that domestic politics have dictated Thailand's foreign policy. Its close relations with the United
States and Japan have been conducive to the perpetuation of the political, social, and economic power of the relatively small oligarchy
of bureaucrats, military officers, merchants, and landlords. [61]
However, the close correspondence between the internal power
structure and its external patrons has finally crumbled. The compelling foreign policy task for Thailand is to normalize relations
with China and the Communist regimes in Indochina, and it is idle
to think that economic and political mating of Thailand with a host of
Communist countries can be managed without major modifications
of the Thai political and social structure.

The predicament of Thailand is enhanced by the discord between Peking and Hanoi. Bangkok moved swiftly in 1974-75 to normalize relations with Peking, and diplomatic ties were established
in the summer of 1975. The Chinese sent a quantity of petroleum,
which the Thais found to be unsuitable for their use because of a
high wax content. The clandestine insurgent radio station located on
Chinese territory, however, did not cease its propaganda. Relations
with Vietnam and Laos remained difficult and strained. The Vietnamese demanded complete withdrawal of all U.S. military personnel and dismantling of the U.S. bases. Premier Pramoj asked the
United States to pull out by March 1976, but as the deadline approached, he seemed to be under pressure to allow a residual U.S.
military presence. The pressure presumably came both from the
Thai military and China, but the Thai ambivalence angered the
Vietnamese, who also pressed Bangkok for the return of the

properties of the former Saigon regime. Another factor that con-
tinued to strain Thai-Vietnamese relations was the presence in
Thailand of a large number of political refugees from South Vietnam.
Relations with Laos worsened after the Communist takeover in
Vientiane.[62]

Even in 1974, the Thais regarded North Vietnam to be the key
to future interstate relations in Southeast Asia. They considered
it essential for regional stability for the war in Indochina not to end in
conclusive Communist victories in South Vietnam, much less in
Cambodia and Laos. When I was in Bangkok in November 1974 no
one believed it would. Thai strategic thinkers, however, were already wondering which of the Communist giants, China or the USSR,
had more leverage with Hanoi. Contacts with Hanoi had been established in Paris only to reveal that the North Vietnamese wanted
total and unconditional Thai neutrality as the price for normal relations. This was not the price that the Thai ruling elite was ready to
pay in 1974.[63] Peking was willing, even anxious, to see a U.S.
military presence in Thailand. While this was reassuring, most
Thais asked whether Peking was in a position to persuade or pressure Hanoi to accept a similar position. The Soviet Union was seen
as interested in reunification of Vietnam under the leadership of
Hanoi. This made the Soviet Union less responsive to the Thai
strategic thinking, which now centered on the theme of "not to swing
too much to any one side."[64] Nevertheless, the Thais expected
Hanoi to lean more on Moscow than on Peking, if only for historical
reasons, and they began to wonder if the road to good neighborly
relations with Hanoi did not lie through better relations with the USSR.

Elite perceptions of the emerging realities in Indochina, then,
suddenly enhanced the importance of the Soviet Union for Thailand
toward the end of 1974. During an interview, the editor of a leading
Bangkok newspaper said he regretted that Thailand had not responded
to overtures that had been coming from Moscow since the mid-
1950s. He said, "Now it seems Thailand needs the Soviet Union to
build bridges to Hanoi and also to protect itself from an overdose of
Chinese influence." That the Thai government should invite the
the Soviet foreign minister to visit Bangkok for the relatively unimportant business of the conclusion of a cultural cooperation agreement is indicative of the importance given by it to a political dialogue
with Moscow.

In November 1974 I found the Thais most reluctant to get involved in the Sino-Soviet cold war. In fact, the new strategic stance
of an equal distance from the major powers, which had been devised
in the foreign office in 1974, sought its primary justification in the
need to keep out of the Sino-Soviet conflict. Nevertheless, some
Thais realized that wittingly or otherwise they were getting involved

not only in an increasingly acute Sino-Soviet competition for influence in Southeast Asia but also in the possible differences and disputes among the Indochinese states. This became unavoidable after the Communist victories in Indochina. Thailand was now deeply entangled in the emerging differences between North Vietnam and Cambodia, between North Vietnam and China, and between Cambodia and Laos. Enmeshed with each strand of this complex web of ancient and contemporary differences was the deepening conflict between China and the Soviet Union.

Of all the Communist powers, close and distant, the Thais have the mellowest images of the USSR. They seem to have forgotten their hostile perception of the Soviet Union, which they no longer see as an aggressive or subversive threat to their security, except in the case of the traditionally anti-Communist minority in the military and the bureaucracy. This is probably the result of the passing of the Thai self-image of "an anti-Communist nationalist power in Southeast Asia." Thanat Khoman, former foreign minister and veteran diplomat, said in an interview that anti-Communism had ceased to be in Thailand's national interest; Thailand must learn to live with its Communist neighbors. However, the Thais are reluctant to concede a security management role in Southeast Asis to the USSR. In August 1974 the national security council regarded the Soviet naval presence in the Indian Ocean to be a matter of great concern to Thailand.[65] Foreign Minister Chatichai Choonivan, a former major-general, stated on August 16 that Thailand wanted SEATO to expand its military strength in view of Soviet naval expansion in the Indian Ocean, but only two days later he modified his position by saying that "the presence of the Russian naval fleet in the Indian Ocean as such does not pose a threat to Thailand."[66] When I asked foreign office officials whether Thailand would concede the Soviet Union equal access with the United States to the sea lanes of Southeast Asia, the answer was in the affirmative.

Between 1973 and 1975, after a decade of a practically marginal relationship with the USSR, the Thais have prepared the ground for the development of economic and trade relations, which will probably flourish in the next five years. The ban on Soviet films has been lifted, and cultural exchanges have received some momentum. The Soviet Union has held its first trade exhibition in Bangkok, and arrangements are being made to open a Thai exhibition in Moscow. Without asking for reciprocal rights, the Soviet Union has permitted the Bangkok Bank to open a branch in Moscow. The Singapore-based Narodny Bank has agreed to participate in a joint industrial venture. Russian ships belonging to the Singapore-Soviet shipping company have begun to carry Thai exports on the route from Bangkok to the Southwest United States. At the Thammaset University, two young daughters of a former Thai ambassador to the Soviet Union, both graduates of Moscow State University, have started the first Russian classes in Thailand. Thailand has established diplomatic relations with all of the East European countries and concluded trade agreements with some of them. [67]

The Soviet perception of Thailand changed with the collapse of its dictatorial regime in 1973. Soviet analysts saw in the student rebellion a rising tide of anti-American nationalism that had found its strength in the victory of the North Vietnamese people against U.S. aggression. [68] The formation of a provisional civilian government in Thailand was a welcome development; more so was the beginning of the withdrawal of U.S. troops. [69] Moscow was even more pleased when the parliamentary election led to the formation of the coalition government in March 1975. A report in Pravda noted "positive changes" in Thailand that were bringing into national focus the importance of "progressive social and economic reforms, the securing of broad democratic rights for the people, and the pursuance of an independent foreign policy."[70] When Thailand asked for the complete withdrawal of U.S. troops by March 1976, it was, in the Soviet perception, "gradually becoming a new link in the broad front in the struggle against imperialist military involvement in Asia from the Japanese islands to the Mediterranean coastal areas." However, the "enemies of progress" still held strategic positions in the country. "The political struggle in Thailand is proceeding under difficult conditions."[71]

The Soviet Union has firmly indicated its interest in steadily widening economic and trade relations with Thailand. The Soviet Union could do with Thai rice and maize, and Thailand may accept a Soviet role in the development of its transportation, electric power, and mineral resources. The Soviets may gain a political role in Thailand if it can help bring Bangkok and Hanoi together. The Soviet leaders seem to be somewhat worried about the future of the big U.S. naval base at Sattahip, the facilities of which the United States may continue to enjoy even after the withdrawal of U.S. forces from Thailand. [72] If Hanoi makes nonuse of these facilities by the United States one of the preconditions for normalization of relations with Thailand, it is likely to receive Soviet backing.

The political message of Moscow is addressed to the "progressive bourgeoisie" of Thailand. According to an Australian expert attached to SEATO, the Soviets, with their "good guy" image, are trying to radicalize the central bureaucracy, especially those agencies that are concerned with internal security, which are the police, communications, mass media, transport, education, and public health. [73] They evidently value the relations they have already established with the Thai business community, for the Soviets reportedly objected when the Thai government decided in 1974 to set up a state trading corporation to conduct trade and business transactions with all Communist countries.[74]

Meanwhile, the Soviet Union is bracing itself for a keen economic competition with China in Thailand. On December 2, 1974, the Bangkok Nation ran a four-page special supplement on the occasion of the opening of the Soviet trade fair. Its front page carried the following affirmation:

> The Soviet Union is not afraid of the People's Republic of China's commodities.
> The competition will mean nothing to the Soviets, because it is based on the businessmen of Thailand.
> If they approve of the quality of the Soviet commodities, they will put faith on the Soviet commodities by themselves.
> Therefore, there is no problem for the Russians.

THE SOVIET UNION AND THE PHILIPPINES

Among the ASEAN countries, the Philippines has shown the utmost alacrity in normalizing relations with the Communist world. Considering the fact that Manila had no diplomatic relations with any Communist country even in 1971, it is truly remarkable that in 1975 it had established diplomatic relations with the Soviet Union and China, with all countries of Eastern Europe, with Mongolia, and also with North Vietnam. For more than 25 years the sheet anchor of Manila's foreign and defense policy was its deep and expansive political, economic, and security relations with the United States. The U.S. alliance, U.S. bases, U.S. commerce, and U.S. culture dominated the national life of the Filipinos.

In the early 1960s, however, the Filipino ruling elite began to "turn east."[75] President Diosdado Macapagal and President Sukarno jointly fathered the concept of Maphilando, a confederative association of the Malay nations of the Philippines, Indonesia, and Malaysia. Maphilando, however, died in the confrontation between Indonesia and Malaysia. Its place was taken in 1967 by ASEAN, of which the Philippines was a founder member. Thus, although the Philippines is a kind of a detached bit of the Caribbean and an off-shore East Asian island, it has finally decided to identify itself with Southeast Asia, giving this basically Indian Ocean community of nations a geopolitical extension into the Pacific Ocean.

Within ASEAN, however, relations among the three Malay
nations have never been completely cordial. Between Manila and
Kuala Lumpur stands the disputed territory of Sabah, the former
British Borneo. This is one reason why the 1973 proposal of the
Philippine foreign minister, Carlos Romulo, for a nonaggression
pact among the ASEAN countries did not find support in Jakarta and
Kuala Lumpur.

The great paradox in the history of the Philippines in the past
30 years is that in spite of the powerful and expansive U.S. security
umbrella, the Philippines has not known internal peace and security.
The Huk insurgency of the postwar years was suppressed, though
not entirely eliminated, by the late 1950s, but guerrilla insurgencies
have plagued the Philippine cities and villages throughout the postwar
period. A determined and large insurgent force has been fighting
for autonomy in the largely Muslim provinces in Mindanao Island,
with help from such diverse sources as Saudi Arabia and the Chinese
People's Republic.[76]

The Philippines joined the U.S. alliance system in Asia and
contributed troops to the U.S. wars in Korea and Indochina because
its U.S.-oriented ruling elite shared the U.S. perception of Communism, a perception that was reinforced by the Communist insurgency within the republic itself. The social and cultural background of this elite has not changed very much during the last 75
years. As George E. Taylor has pointed out, the elite stole the
Filipino revolution from the masses at the turn of the century and
made peace with the United States for guarantees of social power.[77]
To social power was added political power when the United States
granted independence to the Philippines in 1946, preserving extensive military and economic rights for itself. Even today political
and social power in the Philippines is wielded by an oligarchy of
some 200 families.

In the mid-1970s the Philippines is for the first time left without the U.S. security system in Asia. Unlike Thailand, the Philippines has not asked for complete withdrawal of U.S. troops and
bases. The objective of President Marcos is to place the bases
under Philippine sovereignty and to turn them into "economically
productive facilities" as well as military installations. The bases
involved are the Clark air base, an enormous facility of 130 acres
with 10,000 servicemen and 15,000 U.S. dependents, and the naval
base on Subic Bay, which employs 7,000 Filipinos and poured
$77.5 million into the local economy in 1974. Of the two bases, the
Subic is considered the more critical for U.S. strategic power in
the Pacific, being an integrated repair, supply, and maintenance
base for the Seventh Fleet. There is no comparable facility between
the Philippines and Pearl Harbor. Marcos told a New York Times

correspondent in September 1975 that he would be willing to give facilities within the bases to the United States, since he "recognized
the need to maintain the balance of power in the Pacific."[78]

It is interesting that Hanoi established diplomatic relations
with the Philippines in 1975 without pressing Manila for withdrawal
of the U.S. troops and dismantling of the U.S. bases. The agreement
on the establishment of diplomatic relations pledged the two countries
to nonparticipation in actions detrimental to the independence, sovereignty, unity, and territorial integrity of either party. Neither is
to grant its territory to another state as a base for direct or indirect
aggression against any country in the region. The Philippines, then,
assured Hanoi that the U.S. bases will not be used for hostile military operations against any country in Southeast Asia and that
Manila would not object to the reunification of Vietnam.[79]

Even in the mid-1960s the Philippine government stirred
gently toward opening trade relations with the Soviet Union and the
Eastern European countries. Nothing much happened in that direction except the visit of an industrial delegation to the USSR in 1967
for trade talks. Things began to change, however, at the turn of
the decade. A combination of political and economic factors, including serious youth and middle-class unrest in Manila and other
cities and a sharp decline in exports, persuaded the government in
1970 to turn more seriously to the socialist bloc. In September
1970 Romulo hinted at a press conference that diplomatic and commercial relations with the Communist countries were in prospect.
About the same time Nicanor Yniguez, chairman of the house committee on foreign affairs, led a congressional group to the Soviet
Union and reported on his return that the Soviet leaders had offered
to set up refineries in the Philippines with an assured supply of
crude, on condition that Manila pay for the equipment out of the
operational proceeds over 15 years at 2 percent interest.[80] Carmelo
Barbero, a member of the delegation, said further that the Soviet
leaders had offered financial assistance, equipment, and technicians
for oil exploration and had indicated their willingness to offer financial military aid also.[81] In his report, Yniguez recommended establishment of diplomatic and economic relations with the USSR,
arguing that the independence and security of India had remained un-
altered despite "Red assistance."[82]

Indo-Soviet relations became a subject of much interest in
Philippine ruling circles during 1970-71. Executive secretary
Melchor visited New Delhi twice to study this relationship; he also
went to Moscow to probe for aid for oil prospecting and rural elec-
trification and became an ardent advocate of formal relations with
the Soviet bloc.[83] Similarly, Representative Antonio M. Diaz,
after a visit to the Soviet Union in June 1971, said that Moscow was

willing to help with the Philippine railway system, with rural elec-
trification, and with shipping. [84]

In 1971 the ruling elite was split into two groups, the supporters and the opponents of economic and diplomatic relations with the
Communist countries. Opposition was the strongest in the Senate,
which in December 1970 rejected a House proposal aimed at facili-
tating the opening of trade relations with the USSR. The government,
however, was determined to progress in that direction. Marcos, in
his message to Congress in early 1971, declared that the Philippines
"will abandon its old policy and open widespread trade and diplomatic
relations with Communist countries." The foreign policy council
now came out in favor, and by the end of the year the Senate had
passed a bill permitting the government to borrow from Communist
countries to finance major economic projects without establishing
diplomatic relations. [85] Romulo, in an article printed in the Manila
Bulletin of February 17, 1971, outlined the new Philippine perception of the Soviet Union as follows:

> We in Asia are beginning to feel the impact of a
> Soviet Russian offensive, something we have never
> experienced before. The Soviets have sent mis-
> sion after mission to almost all countries of the
> region except mainland China; she has put up trade
> fairs in Singapore and Malaysia and has in turn
> received missions from these countries. There is
> no denying the growth of Soviet presence. Although
> most wonder what all this portends, these countries
> are taking Soviet diplomacy in good faith, and are
> basking, in fact, in the unabating friendliness of
> the Russians. Russia has become an important
> trading partner and source of technical assistance
> and loans for some countries of the region. [86]

Romulo was evidently telling his countrymen that it was not in the
interest of the Philippines to lag behind.

The Soviet Union helped. It offered trade without diplomatic
relations and in December 1972 bought 5,000 tons of copra. When
Imelda Marcos visited the USSR in March 1972, she was received
by Kosygin, and the conversation lasted two and a half hours. A
group of Soviet visitors to the Philippines was given the red carpet
treatment in June and even invited to attend a discussion in the department of defense. [87]

Marcos, however, could not normalize relations with Moscow
without also simultaneously normalizing relations with Peking. In
fact, his overtures to Moscow were also meant to signal a message

to Peking, which the Chinese were quick to pick up. The Chinese
duplicated the Soviet benignancy. In May 1971 Chou En-lai received
a visiting Filippino trade delegation and declared that China was
"waiting with open arms" to establish diplomatic relations with
Manila. [88] China, too, offered trade prior to diplomatic relations,
making it clear at the same time that the Philippines should not
move too close to Moscow. When Imelda Marcos visited China in
1974, she was overwhelmed with hospitality and was received by
Mao Tse-tung himself. China offered to supply the Philippines with
considerable quantities of oil and immediately shipped the first con-
signment to Bataan; it also offered to buy more of the major export
items of Manila, which are copra, coconut oil, sugar, copper, and
wood. [89]

After the return from China of Imelda Marcos, resistance to
normalization of relations with the Communist powers collapsed in
the national security and foreign policy councils. These two bodies
now concluded that normal relations with China and the Soviet Union
were "in the highest interests of the Philippines."[90] Diplomatic
relations were established with both in 1975.

In written answers to my questions, former president Diosdado
Macapagal, a member of the national council, said that a combination
of internal and external factors had removed the hostile perceptions
of the Soviet Union and China and persuaded the Philippines to seek
the friendship of both. The internal factors were a decline of exports, a need for capital, and the pressing priority of "vigorous
economic and social development." Soviet aid was considered necessary for building an industrial infrastructure; there were "highly
placed advocates" of economic collaboration with Moscow within the
administration. The external factors were the termination of prefer-
ential trade relations with the United States in July 1974 and the
detente between Washington and Moscow. Detente, more than anything else, removed the Filipinos' hostile image of Communism.
Macapagal, who during his presidency had followed a strong anti-
Communist line, now believed that cooperation with the Soviet Union
and China would "strengthen the economic and social institutions of
the Philippines." He was, however, doubtful about political cooperation because of the appeal of Communism to the masses of a country
like the Philippines "where the gap between the few rich and the
multitudinous poor has hardly narrowed down in nearly three decades." Macapagal disclosed that the Soviet proposal for Asian collective security had not been discussed in the national security
council and foreign policy council. Like the rest of the elite in
Southeast Asia, Macapagal saw the Soviet proposal as mainly directed against China. In November 1974 he had no vision of Indochina going Communist "in the next decade or so, " but he seemed

to welcome the idea that each of the Southeast Asian countries might
adopt state policies of liberal socialism, which, he said, would
strengthen regional cooperation and better protect the independence
and territorial integrity of each nation. [91]

Even a man like Macapagal, then, had traveled a long way
within a short few years, from uncompromising anti-Communism to
limited cooperation with the Communist world, and from unbridled
private enterprise to liberal socialism. Others in the ruling circles
were more outspokenly bitter about the erstwhile anti-Communism
of the Philippines. Ambassador J. V. Cruz, who accompanied
Imelda Marcos to China, told the Manila Rotary Club in September
1974 that "for far too long" the Philippines had "entertained myths
and fallacies that wrapped our vision of the world and distorted our
foreign policy. . . . The important thing is that we will finally come
to grips with reality. We will be dealing with the world as it is, not
as we wish it were or as we hope it were."[92]

Toward the end of 1974 the members of the Philippine elite
were proud of the fact that the two Communist giants were competing
with one another to woo their country; it suddenly bestowed on the
Philippines an international importance it had hardly enjoyed before.
The smiles of Moscow and Peking improved the domestic image of
Marcos and made his martial law administration a little more toler-
able to his critics. The older-generation Communists of the pro-
Soviet Communist party came out in the open with an offer of cooperation to build Marcos's "new society"; with the president's blessing
they went to the insurgent regions to persuade the armed guerrillas
to abandon the path of violence. However, they met with only limited success. As it happens in almost all closed oligarchies, in the
Philippines there is a great polarization of social forces beneath the
false surface of order. The Communist probe, as George E. Taylor
correctly observes, is not among the provincial Huks but among the
campus intellectuals and mercantile interests. Only urbanized
Filipinos think in national terms; many of these are of the elite,
which controls commercial enterprises and vast tracts of farm land
as well as political power and is traditionally conservative and
change-resisting. Nevertheless, their entrenched position is undermined by the nationalism of the expanding middle class, of the radicalized youth, [93] and of the unionized workers in the factories and
farms whose political complexion is said to be changing rapidly. It
is the nationalism of these potentially and actually change-demanding
elements that is the target of the pro-Soviet Communists. He who
captures Filipino nationalism captures the Philippines. In the
Philippines, as in Thailand, the ruling elite is not in command of the
nationalism of the middle class, the youth, and the urban and rural
proletariat.

Soviet perceptions of the Philippines changed sharply in the mid-1960s, when Soviet analysts woke up to the upsurge of bourgeois nationalism in that country. In the Soviet vision, a broad-based coalition of intellectuals, radicalized youth, left-wing trade unions, and remnants of the Huks emerged as a platform of anti-U.S. nationalism. The underground leaders of the banned Philippine Communist Party (PKP) raised the slogan of an anti-imperialist united front, and anti-U.S. sentiments surfaced even in middle-class behavior toward U.S. residents in Manila.[94] The coalition called for a state of national democracy. Soviet analysts now focused on radicalizing changes within the national bourgeoisie; these alone could drive a wedge between Manila and Washington and prevent a slither toward Maoist-led peasant uprisings. The Marcos regime, which had slowly begun to respond to the demands of the radicalizing nationalists, was now a target of both praise and gentle pressure. In May 1971 Izvestia welcomed the setting up of a Philippine board of investment and said that what the country needed was an independent national economy, the "American monopolies have the Philippine economy by the throat." To the U.S. stranglehold was now added the "very strong pressure" of the Japanese monopolists; if timely measures were not taken to correct the situation, "the country could find itself economically even more dependent on Japan than it already is on the USA."[95] In January 1972 Izvestia praised certain aspects of the "new society" program of Marcos and then went on to point out how exposed the country was to Maoist violence and terrorism. "The social structure of the Philippine society is characterized by a great polarization of poverty and wealth. . . . This polarization, which has reached the limit, is one of the main reasons for the political extremism in the Philippines, where the landlords maintain heavily armed private armies for the sake of retaining their privileges."[96] A year later Pravda printed the first report from Vladimir Grigorovich, the first Soviet journalist to get permanent accreditation in Manila. The report portrayed the picture of a country in which feudal barons were resisting land reform proposals of Marcos and where a tense situation had been created by antigovernment demonstrations of "feudal, separatist and extreme leftist elements." The insurgency in Mindanao and Sulu, justified by the ruthless exploitation of the peasants by the landlords, was being exploited by "ultrarevolutionaries," thus harming the "anti-imperialist movement" of the broad strata of the Philippine people.[97] After this correspondent made an officially conducted tour of Mindanao in February, his report strongly implied that the insurgents were receiving arms from China.[98] In March 1975 a Moscow Radio broadcast saw in the results of the presidential referendum evidence of a strong popular desire for social change and better government.

In the Philippines "there is now a marked tendency to shape an independent line [of foreign policy] particularly in relations with other
Asian states."99 The support by Manila for neutralization of Southeast Asia was commended, although this did not exactly square up
with the presence of U.S. troops and bases on Filippino territory.
The broadcast continued as follows:

> [However,] the dominant tendency in the Philip-
> pines' foreign policy today is the desire to re-
> evaluate the country's role in a constantly
> changing world and first and foremost among
> other developing countries. A number of devel-
> opments show that the Philippines desires more
> resolutely than before to participate in the com-
> mon struggle the young national states are wag-
> ing against military actions of the imperialists.
> This particularly applies to the economic field.
> The Filippino public has clearly expressed it-
> self against the imperialist attempt to shift the
> burden of the present economic crisis in the
> capitalist world over on the shoulders of the
> developing countries.100

The Philippines was now broadening its cooperation with the socialist world. Diplomatic relations had been established with all of the
Eastern European countries, and similar relations with the USSR
were "on the agenda." The first joint Soviet-Filippino enterprise,
the Philsov shipping line, was inaugurated in 1974.101 This was to
be only the beginning; it was important that Marcos implement his
social and economic program with speed and vigor and expand and
intensify his cooperation with the socialist bloc. This would not
only serve the interests of the Philippines but also contribute to
stability and security in Southeast Asia.102 After the establishment
of diplomatic relations between Manila and Hanoi, Pravda observed
that the prerequisites had been created for rebuilding relations
among the Southeast Asian nations on a new basis.103
    These commentaries and observations carry an implicit stra-
tegic content. The Soviet Union wants the Philippines to move
closer to North Vietnam while developing economic relations with
the Soviet bloc. The emphasis is on the (hopefully) growing links of
Manila with the anti-imperialist nationalism of the Asian states,
which in Soviet thinking is the dividing line in Asia between the developing countries and the United States, Japan, and China.

THE SOVIET UNION AND MALAYSIA

Despite the well-known differences in their strategic interests and perspectives Malaysia and Singapore are the two countries in Southeast Asia that have explicitly or implicitly indicated their readiness to give the Soviet Union a direct or indirect role in the management of regional security. Neither has responded positively to the Soviet concept of collective security, but the Malaysian concept of a two-tier neutralization system for the region makes the Soviet Union, together with the United States and China, a guarantor of Southeast Asian security. The prime minister of Singapore, Lee Kuan Yew, has often spoken in favor of a strong Western, especially U.S., security role in Southeast Asia; his second preference is for a stable balance of external powers in the region, which he considers necessary for the security of Singapore not only from China but also from its two large, immediate neighbors, Malaysia and Indonesia. In the absence of a significant U.S. security role in Southeast Asia, Singapore will probably see the USSR more clearly as the only credible countervailing power opposed to the Chinese People's Republic.

In March 1970 Malaysia's then prime minister, Tenku Abdul Rahman, gave tacit approval to Soviet naval patrols in the Indian Ocean, provided the "peace and stability (of the Southeast Asian nations) was not disturbed."104 His successor, Tun Razak, moved closer to the Afro-Asian community and was the most enthusiastic ASEAN champion of neutralization.

The Malaysian middle class is more Third-World oriented than its counterparts in Thailand and Singapore; it has a broadly benign image of the USSR. It is a self-confident elite that is in charge of Malaysian affairs. Though the country is still plagued by insurgents, both at the border with Thailand and in Sarawak, and the insurgency along the Thai border seems to have gotten worse since 1974 and has strained relations between the two neighbors, nevertheless, the regime in Kuala Lumpur rejects the idea of great-power involvement in the country's internal security; this it argues, would only enable the Communist rebels to appeal to the nationalist sentiments of the broad masses.105 The Soviet noninvolvement with the Malaysian Communist Party (MCP) since the early 1960s and the party's pro-Chinese position help the Malaysian elite to see the USSR as a moderate global power more interested in the friendship of the bourgeoisie than in promoting the cause of revolution.106

The insecurity of Malaysia stems basically from the potentially explosive ethnic situation in the country. One-third of its population is Chinese, and the commanding position of the Chinese population in the national economy makes it the first and the easiest target of the relatively backward Malays. The Chinese population feels threatened by the declared government policy of reserving the lion's portion of the national cake for the Bumiputras, the "sons of the soil." The Malays, on their part, are nervous about the Chinese community's loyalty to China. However, the ruling elite refuses to see the Soviet Union as a countervailing power; its members affirm their ability to deal with the ethnic problem and seem to take the declaration of good-neighborliness by Peking in relaxed good faith.

According to a U.S. scholar, there is perhaps no country in Southeast Asia where "the graph of official cordiality with Moscow registers such a quiet but steady rise as in Kuala Lumpur."[107] Nevertheless, the Malaysian elite wishes to keep a respectable political distance from Moscow, as also from China and the United States. They have not entirely forgotten the days when the Soviet Union gave unstinted support to Sukarno's "Crush Malaysia" cry; the memory, however, is stronger in the minds of the older generation, which also has a strong religious and cultural resistance to Communism.

The Soviet image is better among the younger generation belonging to the 25 to 35 age group, though not among the university youth, the sympathies of which seem to lie in the direction of Peking and Hanoi.[108] Refreshingly youthful men head most of the desks in the Malaysian foreign office. They speak with a candor that is conspicuously lacking in the other ASEAN capitals. They discuss issues and problems of foreign policy with knowledge, clarity, and self-confidence, in striking contrast with their counterparts in Manila, Bangkok, and Jakarta.

My discussions in the winter of 1974 with some of these people and with other Malaysians belonging to the universities, the press, parliament, and the political parties brought out the following broad framework of Malaysian perceptions of the Soviet Union during the 1970s. As a global power, the USSR is becoming increasingly involved in the affairs of Southeast Asia, and it is up to the regional powers to see to it that Soviet involvement remains constructive and helpful and does not aggravate the social, political, and strategic disparities already existing in the region. If Soviet involvement remains correct and relatively low, it is possible to avoid major contradictions between the Soviet strategic interests in Southeast Asia and the national interests of the local states.

The principal Soviet concern is to prevent Southeast Asia from turning into a Chinese sphere of influence; a keen Sino-Soviet competition for influence in the region is therefore inevitable. Small powers cannot expect to exploit to their own advantage conflicts and quarrels among the big powers. In this respect the Sino-Soviet cold war is qualitatively different from the bipolar cold war

of the 1950s and 1960s. Any effort to use the Soviet Union as a
countervailing power is an invitation to Moscow to intervene in the
international conflicts of Southeast Asia. The regional states should
therefore try to keep an equal distance from Moscow and Peking,
while cooperating with both on mutually beneficial terms.

The industrialized socialist bloc is a source of development
assistance and trade that the Southeast Asian nations can ignore only
to their own disadvantage. Even for states that are determined to
encourage private enterprise and foreign investment there are areas
in the economy that can be developed with the help of the Soviet bloc.
Furthermore, it is in the interest of the Southeast Asian countries
to seek stable, long-term markets for some of their agricultural
products within the Soviet bloc. In any case, countries like Malaysia
that have a favorable trade balance with the USSR must sooner
rather than later buy capital goods and specialized services from
the Soviet Union, if only to balance the trade.

The Soviet anxiety for a stable security system in Asia stems
from multiple factors, including the Soviet capability to intervene in
local wars and the Soviet reluctance to get involved in local wars.
Whatever the merits of the Soviet concept of collective Asian security, there is no possibility of its realization as long as the Sino-
Soviet cold war continues. On the other hand, the Soviet Union is
taking a favorable view of the neutralization of Southeast Asia. The
concept has also been supported by China and it has not been opposed
by the United States. Hanoi, too, has indicated its interest, provided the region is rid of U.S. troops and bases. The Malaysians
are afraid that if ASEAN fails to assemble a regional security system based on neutralization, the initiative would pass on to Indonesia, acting in cooperation with the United States and Japan to make
some kind of U.S.-backed security arrangement, or to Hanoi, which
might push the Soviet model of collective Asian security.

The Malaysians have been more concerned with regional politics than with developments in the larger, global, universe. The
anti-Communism of Malaysia in the 1950s and 1960s, it is pointed
out by one of the country's best-known scholars,[109] had been shaped
more by events within Southeast Asia than by the bipolar cold war.
The Communist insurgency justified dependence on British military
protection; AMDA was needed to ward off the Indonesian confrontation. It was the Communist insurgency and the attitude of the Soviet
Union and China to Malaysia and its enemies that had compelled
Kuala Lumpur to adopt a hardened anti-Communist line.

As soon as Jakarta called off the confrontation in 1966 and
this action was welcomed by Moscow, the Malaysian foreign policy
stance began to shift from the extreme right to the middle. An official statement in mid-1966 described Malaysia as "non-aligned but
not neutral."[110]

What concerns the Malaysian elite is not so much the transformation of the international system from bipolarity to multipolarity
as the impact of this transformation on problems of Southeast Asian
stability and security. As they look at the Southeast Asian universe,
they see two slightly contradictory aspects of the changing international order, one "chaotic," the other "conspiratorial." The
"chaotic" aspect is created by the collapse of the U.S. security system; the "conspiratorial" by the fear that the logic of Sino-U.S.
detente might not relegate Southeast Asia to a sphere dominated by
China.[111] Only by taking the initiative to build a new regional order
could the Southeast Asians bend the chaos to their own advantage and
dispel the "conspiratorial" possibilities. Malaysia took the lead in
the direction of a regional order by becoming the first ASEAN country to establish diplomatic relations with China on May 31, 1974, and
even before that, on May 30, 1973, with North Vietnam.

The Malaysians would probably welcome the evolution of Vietnam as an independent Communist power in Asia. For the present
they welcome the nonalignment of the Communist regimes in Indochina and hope that, once relations between Hanoi and Bangkok are
normalized, the concept of neutralization will gather a new momentum because, as I was told by a perceptive observer of the Southeast
Asian scene, "ASEAN will realize that it is of the highest importance
to do everything possible to detach Indochinese Communism from the
Communism of China and the Soviet Union, and try to merge it in
the mainstream of Southeast Asian nationalism."[112]

In the mid-1970s the Soviet Union sees Malaysia as a country
of unfolding economic and political relations. The image of Malaysia
as an offspring of British imperialism and its outpost in Southeast
Asia, an image that was strong in the 1960s, began to melt away with
the turn of the decade. In 1969-70 Moscow still denounced the Malaysian defense links with Britain, but the focus of attack had shifted
from Kuala Lumpur to London. In 1971 Pravda was convinced that
Malaysia was "striving for peace"; it even discovered something that
wasn't really there: a high degree of interest in the Soviet proposal
for collective Asian security among the progressive elements.[113]

The "peace-loving" image became stronger as Malaysia identified itself with the Afro-Asian community; as pro-Soviet Friendship
societies sprouted in its cities; as Malaysians attended meetings of
the Afro-Asian People's Solidarity Association; as the exchange of
delegations expanded; and as Kuala Lumpur stepped up economic
cooperation with the Soviet bloc. During and after Tun Razak's
Moscow visit, the Soviet media described Malaysia as a leading
member of the national liberation zone, as a country "pursuing a policy of turning from an agrarian and raw material appendage of U.S.
monopolies into an industrially developed state."[114]

Since 1970 the Soviet Union has "flooded" Malaysia with offers
of economic assistance and joint venture proposals, only a few of
which the Malaysians have accepted so far. In 1971 the Soviet Union,
through its ambassador in Kuala Lumpur, submitted a list of 40 industrial and technological projects, including the development of tin
mining. Moscow offered to send specialists to initiate these projects
and to train Malaysians in the USSR, including personnel of the
armed forces and the state-owned airline.[115] During Tun Razak's
visit to the Soviet capital, agreements were signed for economic,
technological, scientific, and cultural cooperation. Since then economic relations have been expanding. The Soviet Union is now the
single largest buyer of Malaysian rubber. Since 1973 Malaysia has
been importing Soviet tractors, machine tools, and automobiles.
Work is in progress on a hydroelectric and flood control project with
Soviet assistance. Russian ships ply a regular freight route between
the Black Sea ports and Malaysia, delivering heavy industrial items
and collecting rubber and other Malaysian exports.[116]

THE SOVIET UNION AND SINGAPORE

In 1965, when Malaysia and Singapore separated from one another and became two sovereign nations, Lee Kuan Yew, the socialist
prime minister of Singapore, told a U.S. correspondent, "If Malaysia played host to American troops, Singapore would offer a base to
the Soviet Union."[117] This theatrical rhetoric was of course meant
to emphasize the extremely poor strategic relationship between the
neighboring nations rather than to signal a pro-Soviet foreign policy.
A strategic unity was imposed on Singapore and Malaysia by their
membership in AMDA and ANZUK; the linkages were provided by
Britain, Australia, and New Zealand.

When Lee Kuan Yew's People's Action Party (PAP), with its
avowedly socialist program, swept into power in the state's first
election in 1966, many feared that Singapore would be turned into a
Communist enclave. In a decade, however, Lee and his colleagues
have built Singapore into a "global city," an island of capitalist affluence in a sea of relative poverty: a former minister of his cabinet described Singapore to me as a "social-capitalist state." Its per
capita income is second only to that of Japan in Asia.

Midway during this decade, Lee Kuan Yew realized that the
Soviet Union, with its expanding naval power, would soon become a
major user of the huge modern port facilities of Singapore, and he
began to look at the Soviet Union through lenses of enlightened self-
interest. In 1970 Lee told another U.S. reporter that the Soviet
advance into the Indian Ocean was "natural," and this reporter wrote

after the interview: "It is believed in Singapore that once Moscow
develops its naval strength from the eastern Mediterranean into the
Indian Ocean, this island city-state becomes a natural choice as a
warm water port for the Soviet Indian Ocean fleet and the big Pacific
fleet based at Vladivostok."[118] As the Commonwealth prime ministers were conferring in Singapore in 1971, two Soviet battleships
sailed majestically past the windows of the conference hall, and
Lee's comment was that this was nothing to get excited about.

The Singapore government concedes that the sea lanes across
the Indian Ocean are now part of the merchant marine lifeline between
European Russia and the Soviet Far East.

> Karachi, Bombay, Colombo, Mauritius, and Singa-
> pore are the only Indian Ocean ports able to meet
> the full needs of the Soviet merchant marine and
> naval fleet, and Singapore has ambitions to be one
> on which civilian Russian ships will come to rely
> most--bring their rubles to spend on the goods
> and services on the sale of which Singapore's fu-
> ture livelihood depends. Apparently acting under
> strong Anglo-American pressure, the Singapore
> government has not so far allowed armed Soviet
> vessels to use the port's services, although it did
> permit in 1972 a "mother" ship (itself unarmed but
> capable of supplying armed ships at sea) to bunker
> and take on supplies.[119]

More than 500 Soviet ships put in annually at Singapore, and a
joint Soviet-Singapore shipping company has been in business since
1969. Aeroflot makes regular flights to Singapore, where there are
more Soviet business offices than in any other Asian capital. The
first Singapore-Soviet joint industry, a watchmaking plant, seems to
be somewhat symbolic of the relationship between the two countries.
Although the first Soviet ambassador to Singapore took up his office
only in 1968, the Soviet embassy, located in the exclusive neighbor-
hood of Cluny Road, adjacent to the Singapore University, is one of
the largest in Asia. Soviet scholars research at the university and
at the Institute of Southeast Asian Studies, temporarily located on
the campus.[120]

Lee Kuan Yew is known for his strong support for a major U.S.
security role in Southeast Asia and has often spoken of the "threat"
faced by the regional states from an expanding Soviet naval presence
in the Indian Ocean. In May 1973, while on a visit to Tokyo, Lee
proposed the formation of a naval task force by the United States,
Japan, Australia, and perhaps Europe to safeguard the "freedom of

the Indian Ocean, promote peaceful development of Southeast Asian neutrality and offset the threat of the growing Soviet fleet. "[121] Lee, then, would like to see Southeast Asian neutrality protected by a dominant Western security role in the region. This kind of an external security ambience would correspond with the domestic economic policy of Singapore and offer it protection from the ambitions of Malaysia and Indonesia. However, Lee seems to have kept other options open. He visited Moscow once each year between 1968 and 1971. The 1971 visit, which lasted eight days, did not exactly produce a political rapprochement, but it paved the way for further economic and technological cooperation.

The great vulnerability of Singapore comes from its population, 67 percent of which is Chinese. The vast majority of these people have a strong pull toward China. The Singaporean is an English-educated Chinese who claims to have abandoned his Chinese identity but is incapable of losing his Chinese mind and personality. The refusal of Peking to recognize the independence and sovereignty of Singapore and the deep-seated Chinese character of the bulk of the population makes the members of the elite of Singapore psychologically and culturally insecure despite the fact that they live in one of the stablest and best-governed Asian states. It was announced in May 1976 that Lee Kuan Yew would be visiting Peking in a short while, indicating a dramatic improvement in Singapore's relations with the PRC. Another reason for this insecurity is the Malay nationalism of Indonesia and Malaysia.

For ten years the elite of Singapore felt secure in the U.S. security system without being formal consumers of this security; the United States protected Singapore from China. Now that very little is left of the U.S. security system in Southeast Asia, Singapore is under strong pressure to readjust itself to the new realities. In 1974, a few weeks before a visit to the United States, Lee Kuan Yew supported the Thai demand for withdrawal of all U.S. troops within a specified period. "You might as well make a virtue out of a necessity," he told the New York Times. "Tell me, what is the value of American soldiers on the ground today? Once upon a time, two and a quarter years ago, there was no Congressional resolution that said bombs could not be used in Southeast Asia without Congressional approval. We all know that no American soldier will fight again in a guerrilla war in Asia. "[122]

In Washington Lee received the assurance he sought that the United States would stand by its allies and its commitments in Southeast Asia, where it would maintain a presence for a long time. [123] For Singapore that assurance shaped perceptions of Southeast Asia more profoundly than it did the perceptions of the other ASEAN elites. In November and December 1974 I did not come across a single citizen of Singapore who was not certain that the then existing political map of Indochina would continue for a long time. [124]

The Chinese nature of the population of Singapore should prevent Lee Kuan Yew from seeking Soviet protection against Peking even if he personally prefers such a course, which he does not at present. However, he will go on expanding nonmilitary relations with the Soviet Union, looking at neutralization of Southeast Asia with disdain and hoping, with his foreign minister, that the United States, the Soviet Union, China, and Japan will eventually come to a strategic understanding among themselves in the Pacific-Asian region and that the political fallout of that understanding will promote stability in Southeast Asia.

The Soviet leaders, on their part, seem to understand the peculiar security problems of Singapore and take a more benevolent view of Lee Kaun Yew's "pro-imperialism" than that of some of the other Southeast Asian actors. Pravda, for instance, while taking Lee to task for his 1973 proposal for a multilateral naval task force in the Indian Ocean, was unusually mild in its criticism; much more than Lee, it blamed the Chinese People's Republic for allegedly approving the proposal. At the same time, Pravda took some pains to convince the Singapore premier that the USSR had neither "any bases scattered along the Indian Ocean littoral nor a powerful naval presence."[125] The Soviet leaders are evidently pleased with the state of their relations with Singapore and expect them to improve further. The short-term objective of Moscow is to get port facilities for the armed ships of its Indian Ocean fleet; in the new balance of power in Southeast Asia after the Indochina war, it will not be surprising if Lee extends this facility to the Soviet Union.

The Soviet leaders seem to believe that the strategic posture of Singapore will now be determined by the policies of Peking. Soviet propaganda tries to remind the Singaporeans that they can only weaken the stability of their society if they move closer to China. Moscow probably believes that the elite of Singapore listen to this kind of propaganda with more interest than the elite in Malaysia because the people of Singapore are equally afraid of the hostility of China and of its friendly embrace.[126]

Meanwhile, the Soviet Union is impressed with the economic performance of Singapore, with the efficiency of its administration, and with Lee's no-nonsense attitude toward all the major powers. Singapore shows the rest of Asia that nothing succeeds like success, whether dealing with the capitalist West or the socialist USSR.[127] The Soviet Union signed a cultural and scientific cooperation agreement with Singapore on November 7, 1974. The immediate Soviet objective is to get the remarkable facilities of the former British naval base at Changi for servicing ships of the Soviet navy. The first Soviet destroyer stopped at Singapore in 1971, and I found that Soviet diplomats in Singapore were "reasonably optimistic" that Russian warships would soon be given facilities to dock, refuel, and repair that would be equal with those given to U.S., British, and other maritime vessels.

Singapore is a tiny city-state, and it can hardly play a significant political or security role in Southeast Asia. Its prosperity and progress and even its survival depend on an equilibrium of social and political forces not only in the region but also on a global scale. It made the best of the stability provided for 25 years by the overwhelming U.S. power, but now that stability is no more. The ASEAN countries still do not feel insecure, because China is deceptively benign and the Communist rulers of Vietnam are too busy putting their own battered house in order, but this comfortable ambience may change.

Meanwhile the Soviet Union can be expected to court Lee's industrial enclave with sustained fortitude. Nothing promotes the Moscow "good-guy" image in Southeast Asia more than its friendship with Singapore. In a reverse way, then, Singapore is as important for the Soviet Union in Southeast Asia as is Hanoi. As Dick Wilson has observed, "The fact that Mr. Kosygin, the Soviet prime minister, paid an official visit to Singapore earlier than did any British prime minister sheds more light on the relative Russian and British assessment of Singapore's potential <u>future</u> role in their own plans than it does on their estimate of its existing importance."[128]

THE SOVIET UNION AND INDONESIA

By virtue of its size, population, and resources, Indonesia is the leading power in Southeast Asia; however, its political leaders have been more conscious of its leadership role than capable of playing a regional integrative role. Sukarno's foreign policy, despite its ideological glitter, had a distinctly destabilizing impact on the region. The concept of Maphilindo had an integrative content, but Sukarno found more drama in confronting Malaysia than in patiently building a pan-Malay confederation with the leaders of Malaysia and the Philippines. Instead of integrating the Malay-speaking noncontinental Southeast Asia, Sukarno in fact contributed greatly to the polarization of the area, not only between the "progressives" and the "reactionaries," but also among the major powers. His "united front" foreign policy, which aligned Indonesia with China, North Vietnam, and North Korea, pushed several Southeast Asian regimes to security dependence on the United States and encouraged the United States to build a military presence in the region.[129] In the final years of his

rule Sukarno aligned himself with China against the Soviet Union,
thus exposing Southeast Asia to the uncertain blasts of the Sino-
Soviet conflict.

The Suharto military regime, which came to power in October
1965 on the bloody ruins of the once seemingly pervasive Indonesian
Communist Party (PKI), did not make a total formal break with
Sukarno's foreign policy. Indonesia continued to remain nonaligned
and did not join the U.S. security system. However, under Suharto
foreign policy became an instrument for internal development.
Stripping themselves of the old linkages with the Communist world,
and without new security ties with the Western powers, the leaders
of the military regime became excessively sensitive about geographical gaps--Indonesia is a vast island chain stretching over
3,000 miles--and the problem of integrating a nation of many cultures and ethnic diversities. The strong anti-Communism of the
regime reflects to a large extent a psychic state of insecurity, somewhat enhanced by the realization that the ownership of energy resources exposes Indonesia to the crosscurrents of a new competition
among the industrialized nations, on the one hand, and between the
developed and the developing nations, on the other.[130]

For several years the domestic and foreign policies of the
Suharto regime were deliberately directed toward close economic
and somewhat less close political cooperation with the United States
and Japan, leading to criticism both at home and abroad for an apparent shift to the Western camp. Suharto's main objective, however, was to correct the "imbalance" of Sukarno's nonalignment
and to restore some symmetry between the domestic economic development of Indonesia and its external relations. The Foreign
Investment Law of 1976 opened the country to the inflow of foreign
private capital, with which Indonesia is able to develop its extractive
industries, notably petroleum, tin mining, timber, and fisheries.

The paradoxical combination of a strong anti-Communist policy
and a refusal to formally associate itself with the U.S. security system in Asia produced an inevitable ambivalence in the foreign policy
of Indonesia in Southeast Asia and in the wider world. Though nonaligned, Suharto for several years kept away from the annual summit
meetings of nonaligned nations, on the ground that these meetings
had admitted a number of Communist countries.[131]

Indonesia joined ASEAN and became a champion of regional
cooperation, but it resisted all ideas of investing the association with
any security functions. Although rhetorically it wanted Southeast
Asia to be equidistant from all great-power rivalries, it was strongly
in favor of a continuing U.S. security role in the region. Indonesia
remained neutral in the Indochina war, but its leaders made no
secret of the importance they attached to the survival of the non-

Communist regimes in South Vietnam, Laos, and Cambodia. The
Indonesian leaders wanted relations between China and each of the
ASEAN countries to be normalized, but they were not prepared to
take any initiative to normalize their own relations with Peking.
Indonesia maintained diplomatic relations with Hanoi, but it was unwilling to bring Hanoi within the community of Southeast Asian
nations.[132]

The ambivalence in the Indonesian perspective on Southeast
Asian security became evident in March 1970 when the pro-U.S.
coup in Cambodia threatened to enlarge the Indochina war. The
cabinet split in its appraisal of the Cambodian crisis. The right
wing of the military leadership wanted Indonesia to rush to the aid
of the Lon Nol regime, even with an expeditionary force, while the
centrists, supported by Adam Malik, were against getting involved
in the Cambodian civil war. The government decided to move in two
directions at the same time. It sent a secret small military mission to Phnom Penh to make observations and to discuss with the
Lon Nol regime its immediate military needs, and Suharto invited
20 Asian governments to deliberate on a solution of the Cambodian
crisis. When Malaysia politely turned down his request to host the
conference, Suharto decided to convene it in Jakarta. The invitation was predictably declined by as many as ten, including China and
all of the countries of South Asia.

With the sole exception of Indonesia, the ten countries that
finally attended each had either a security treaty with the United
States or membership in one or another of the U.S.-sponsored or
supported military alliances. The conference, then, at once acquired an anti-Communist and pro-U.S. image, which had not been
the intention of Suharto. His first adventure in international diplomacy had been inspired by the mistaken belief that Indonesia could
mobilize the disparate and discordant nations of Asia to seek an
agreed solution to the crisis in Cambodia. The adventure failed.
The Jakarta conference had no impact on the Cambodian crisis.
When it met, U.S. and South Vietnamese forces had already invaded
Cambodia; a week after it ended, the Cambodian foreign minister
announced that the invading forces would remain until the North
Vietnamese and Vietcong forces had been defeated. In July the
Indonesian cabinet rejected a cabled request from Cambodia for
arms.[133]

The major contradiction in Indonesian thinking about regional
security involves a high degree of security-role awareness and a
low degree of willingness to assume security responsibility. The
contradiction probably stems from the already noted inherent sense
of insecurity. In spite of all its strength, the regime lives in per-
petual fear of the apparition it claims to have virtually annihiliated,

which is Indonesian Communism. In recent years the regime has
lost the esteem of large sections in its own constituency, especially
the youth and the urban intelligentsia, who had played a heavy role
in the massacre of the PKI cadres and supporters in 1965. The
government has been accused of large-scale corruption and inefficiency and criticized for its failure to arrest urban and rural unemployment and effect a more equitable distribution of the fruits of
development. The widespread student riots during Tanaka's visit
to Indonesia in 1973 were in part an expression of disenchantment
with the performance of the Suharto regime.[134] The economic
problems became worse when exports began to shrink in the early
1970s as a result of the recession in Japan and the other industrialized countries.

Nobody doubts the stability of the regime. There is no organized opposition, and only mild and controlled dissent is permitted
to surface; but in the mid-1970s the Indonesian house is not in such
order as would enable its leadership to take a relaxed view of the
domestic and international environments. Hence the extreme reluctance of the government to take the initiative of normalizing relations with China, although it did not lose much time in extending
diplomatic recognition to the Communist governments in Saigon and
Phnom Penh after the end of the war in Indochina.

Indonesian concepts of the security of Southeast Asia center
around four basic points. First, each nation must rely primarily
on its own national defense and "national resilience" to protect itself
from external aggression; dependence on an external power can only
enfeeble its own will and capability to defend itself. Second, there
should be bilateral and even regional "pooling of experience" to deal
with insurgencies, especially those occurring in border regions.
Third, Southeast Asia must not be dominated by a single power or
combination of like-minded powers. Fourth, although neutralization is a desirable strategic goal, effective neutralization would require both a balance of power within Southeast Asia that is not
weighted in favor of the Communist states and a stable external
balance of power that will simultaneously neutralize Chinese hegemonism, Soviet expansionism, and U.S. interventionism.[135]

The Indonesian elite appears to have a sharper image of a
steadily lengthening shadow of Soviet power falling over Southeast
Asia during the 1970s than do the elites in other ASEAN capitals.
At the Singapore conference on Southeast Asian security in 1972, an
Indonesian scholar-diplomat saw the Soviet Union as posing the
largest challenge to the United States and China in the 1970s; hence,
he explained, the Sino-U.S. detente. He expected the Sino-Soviet
conflict to continue unabated and even to deepen further. The Soviet
threat was forcing China to increase its nuclear striking power. The

Soviet Union, in turn, was bracing itself to meet the Chinese threat on a global front. In Asia the Soviet Union would try to build a cordon sanitaire around China by "tightening up" its relations with India and Bangladesh, by "winning over Vietnam from the Chinese," and by courting the other Southeast Asian regimes in order to keep them neutral and friendly. At the same time the USSR would continue to strengthen its naval presence in the Indian Ocean, which serves as a linkup between the Russian fleet in the Middle East and the Pacific Ocean. With a permanent sizable presence in the Indian Ocean, the Soviet navy would take an active part in the encirclement of China; keep a watch on Pakistan, China's ally in South Asia; and maintain a power vigilance on the oil routes from the Middle East to Japan, Australia, New Zealand, Western Europe, and the United States.[136]

Unwilling to bow to Peking, in recent years the Indonesians have shown an increasing willingness to improve their relations with the Soviet Union. Adam Malik told me in an interview that Indonesia was seeking Soviet assistance to build its growth industries, which have been generally neglected by U.S. and Japanese investors. Soviet help could also be useful in developing transportation and in surveying mineral resources. Besides, Indonesia was interested in finding stable markets for its rubber, tin, and forest products in the socialist bloc.

Adam Malik had visited Moscow several times since 1970 and had found the Soviet leaders generally sympathetic to Indonesian problems, though not necessarily to the Indonesian regime. They were quite willing to resume development assistance. Both parties had learned their lessons from melancholy experience in the 1960s and were anxious to avoid the mistakes of those years. Indonesia would not like to be overly dependent on outside powers and would accept Soviet aid only for projects that would contribute to genuine growth and development. Malik did not visualize political cooperation in the near future, but he said that Soviet friendship was becoming a political necessity and would help the regime improve its domestic as well as its international image.

The Soviet leaders have ambivalent perceptions of the Indonesian military regime. The duality of Soviet policy for Indonesia, which represents a combination of cautious cooperation and strong criticism of aspects of Indonesian domestic and foreign policies, corresponds to the split Soviet image of the country. The Soviet Union has resumed economic and trade relations with Indonesia, but the political and strategic distance between the two remains wide. The collapse of the PKI as a powerful domestic political force gives the Soviet Union considerable freedom of action, but the continued arrest of people, including military officers, for political reasons and the rigid military grip on the political system make it difficult

to build an effective constituency in Indonesia that could demand
closer relations with Moscow.

When Soviet-Indonesian friendship had reached its peak in the
late 1950s and early 1960s, Indonesia was strategically less important to the Soviet Union than Egypt and India because of its geographic distance from the USSR and because of the Soviet noninvolvement in Southeast Asian affairs. However, the relationship had
acquired a superficial ideological correspondence that is still miss-
ing in Soviet-Indian relations. Sukarno's "Nasakom" came very
close to the Soviet concept of national democracy.

It is possible that it was this ideological harmony that persuaded Khrushchev to commit the Soviet Union to the fantasies and
follies of Sukarno. Between 1958 and 1964 Indonesia became the
nation in the Third World that was most favored by Moscow. The
Soviet Union transferred considerable military hardware to Indonesia
during the West Irian campaign and the confrontation with Malaysia
and gave it the most powerful navy in South and Southeast Asia.[137]

The economic aid of $370 million was largely misspent by
Sukarno. Little work was done on the projects the Soviet Union had
agreed to help build, which were the first Indonesian steel plant at
Tjilegon; a nuclear reactor; a superphosphate plant at Tjilatjap; an
industrial complex in northern Sumatra; and mechanized farm
projects and road construction in Kalimantan--although, according
to Soviet sources, 90 percent of the machinery and other equipment
for these projects had been supplied.[138]

In the 1970s the strategic importance of Indonesia to the Soviet
Union has greatly increased. A friendly Indonesia is of considerable
help to Soviet naval interests in the Indian Ocean; more precisely
it is necessary for unfettered use of the strategic Malacca Straits.
A hostile Indonesia can create problems for the USSR both in the
Malacca Straits and in the Indian Ocean. Indonesian friendship can
also be helpful in improving the Soviet image in the Islamic Middle
East and in the OPEC. Without Indonesian support there is little
future in Southeast Asia for the Soviet concept of collective security.
Since the Communist victories in Indochina, Indonesia is the only
viable Southeast Asian country that is potentially capable of taking
the initiative to reconstruct a regional security system excluding
the Communist powers.

Predictably, the Soviet attitude toward Indonesia changed after
the announcement of the Nixon Doctrine and after the establishment
of a stable Soviet naval presence in the Indian Ocean. Between 1966
and 1969 the Indonesian military regime sent several plenipoten-
tiaries to Moscow, including Adam Malik, in hopes of obtaining
spare parts and a settlement of its debts, but Moscow made no response. However, Malik's 1970 visit to Moscow proved to be

unexpectedly fruitful. The Soviet Union accepted a settlement of the total Indonesian debt at $750 million and agreed to a new schedule of repayment. They also offered to resume work on some of the old projects, including the nuclear reactor, the steel plant, and the superphosphate plant. About a year later a Soviet team of experts arrived in Indonesia to study which of the projects should be taken up. It was mutually agreed that the nuclear reactor should not be built. In 1971 the Soviet Union offered spare parts for the Indonesian navy and air force, but by then two-thirds of the Soviet-built naval ships and 90 percent of the aircraft had gone out of operation and the offer was rejected by Jakarta.[139]

From 1971 on the Soviet Union mixed friendship diplomacy with sharp media criticism in dealing with the Suharto regime. At times Soviet diplomacy became suddenly bold. In 1972, for example, the USSR offered Indonesia a treaty of peace and friendship on the model of the Indo-Soviet treaty. The Indonesian leaders must have been surprised by the move, especially since during the 1971 crisis in the subcontinent their sympathies had been with Pakistan and they had taken their time to recognize the republic of Bangladesh. Adam Malik told a Singapore audience in April 1972 that Indonesia had rejected the Soviet offer. "We have no need for a treaty like that now," he explained. "Our need is not the same as India's."[140]

At the same time, the Soviet media kept on attacking the Suharto regime for its anti-Communism, for its alleged pro-Western policies, and for its refusal to broaden the base of cooperation with the socialist countries. Izvestia warned Indonesia in 1972 that its non-alignment was taking a pro-Western slant and that it was moving toward security collaboration with the United States.[141] The same newspaper also saw Indonesia as under U.S. pressure to yield service facility for ships of the 7th Fleet operating in the Indian Ocean.[142]

Soviet analysts perceived Indonesia as a country "literally besieged by imperialists" and as a "victim of collective neocolonialism." The Western powers and Japan were threatening its economic independence and political sovereignty. U.S. and Japanese foreign capital had reduced Indonesia to an "agrarian-raw material appendage of the capitalist system." The two imperialist powers were trying to outbid one another for control of Indonesian petroleum resources. Soviet analysts also saw the Indonesian military leadership as an incohesive group, split between ultrarightists and rightists. A big social divide separated the officer class from the rank and file. The regime was far from stable. There were yawning gaps in the economy. Development was uneven and lopsided, resulting in growing unemployment, greater urban-rural stratification, and increasing discontent among the urban youth and the rural poor.[143]

This dim view of the Indonesian polity on the part of the Soviet Union did not prevent a steady improvement in mutual relations. In November 1974 Adam Malik publicly declared that the Soviet Union had no involvement in the abortive coup of 1965.[144] When he visited Moscow a month later, he was seen for the first time by one of the top Soviet leaders, Nicolai Podgorny. The visit led to the conclusion of an agreement on economic and technological collaboration. The Soviet bloc resumed economic aid to Indonesia. Evidently one of the topics discussed between Malik and his Soviet hosts was Asian collective security. The joint communique declared that the two countries had agreed to build their relations on the principles of peaceful coexistence. Both saw "processes in Asia" developing favorably for "consolidation of peace and security" on the basis of "joint efforts and cooperation among the states of Asia." Inter-Asian relations should develop on the basis of the Bandung principles, which were "the nonuse of force, noninterference in internal affairs, and broad and equal cooperation among the states."[145]

Earlier, in March, Nokolai Firyubin, the Soviet deputy foreign minister, had met with Adam Malik at Jakarta and, as already noted in Chapter 4, notified him of the Soviet claim that the Indian Ocean "is a free sea which could be used by any country." Firyubin also asked for Indonesian support for the Soviet proposal for Asian collective security. Malik later told a news conference, "We do not reject the idea, but it is still not clear to us."[146]

In Southeast Asia, then, the Soviet Union has embarked in the 1970s on a large-scale mission to win friends and influence people. The Soviet and Southeast Asian leaders are still strangers to one another, except in North Vietnam, where the Soviet leaders have to deal with extraordinarily subtle and tough Communists, hardened in the world's longest internationalized civil war.

The Soviet leaders have begun their diplomatic operations in an area in which the United States still enjoys considerable prestige and even affection. Even the Vietnamese Communists have asked for U.S. aid, and Gerald Ford, in his Pacific Doctrine message, has not closed the door on Communist Vietnam. If relations between Vietnam and the United States become normal, clearing the way for U.S. aid, the Vietnamese dependence on the USSR may be reduced.

The political climate in Southeast Asia is, then, extremely uncertain in the mid-1970s. The Soviet presence in the non-Communist countries of the region can grow only slowly, and it must take substantial economic form before the USSR can assume real political and strategic importance.

NOTES

1. The Southeast Asia Treaty Organization (SEATO) began to lose its effectiveness as a collective defense organization even in the late 1960s. Pakistan formally withdrew in 1972. SEATO had no collective involvement in the Vietnam war; the contributions made by Thailand and the Philippines were made more as allies of the United States than as members of the treaty organization. In July 1975 President Ferdinand Marcos and Premier Seni Pramoj declared in a joint statement that the role of SEATO would be gradually curtailed, and the announcement was welcomed in Pravda on July 29 as a step dictated by the "logic of events in Asia and throughout the world." When Thailand and the Philippines jointly decided in September 1975 on the phasing out of SEATO, the New York Times in an editorial on September 28 observed that "From beginning to end, the United States essentially acted alone in Vietnam."

That Hanoi was emerging as the major power in Indochina became clear by the end of 1975, when North and South Vietnam were moving toward reunification at an unexpectedly accelerated pace and Hanoi established its dominant role in the political development of Laos. See the New York Times, October 28 and 29, 1975, and November 2, 4, and 9, 1975.

2. Southeast Asia produces 62.5 percent of the world output of tin concentrates, 89.9 percent of rubber, 98.4 percent of abaca, 54 percent of coconut, 19.9 percent of rice, 2.2 percent of copper ore, and 1.4 percent of petroleum. United Nations Statistical Yearbook, 1975 (New York: the UN, 1975).

3. The failure of the U.S. administration to get congressional approval for military and economic aid to South Vietnam and Cambodia in the last months of the Indochina war made a deep impression on Southeast Asian capitals. See Bangkok Post, April 26, 1975, and The Strait Times (Kuala Lumpur), May 2, 1975.

The U.S. political influence on its one-time allies in Southeast Asia diminished sharply after the Indochina war. In the UN voting on the Arab-sponsored resolution branding Zionism as a racist ideology, none of the Southeast Asian governments voted against the resolution, despite intense U.S. lobbying to get the resolution defeated in the General Assembly. New York Times, November 11, 1975.

4. New York Times, November 4, 1975.

5. Ibid., October 19, 1975.

6. Foreign policy can be said to be nonautonomous when it is primarily a response to the initiatives of rival actors. Khrushchev probably sought to put together an autonomous policy for Southeast Asia through his diplomatic initiatives in Burma and Indonesia in the

1950s and 1960s. In Vietnam, especially during the 1965–75 period, the Soviet Union mainly responded to the U.S. escalation, and the scale of the response was to a significant extent determined by its competition with China.

7. In November and December of 1974 I found unmistakable evidence in the ASEAN capitals that the U.S. search for a detente with the USSR had improved the Soviet image in the minds of the elite. During interviews, most Southeast Asians mentioned the fact that the United States had "conceded" strategic parity to the Soviet Union as "conclusive proof" of the rising military power of the USSR. Similarly, one of the commonest arguments advanced in favor of economic cooperation with the Soviet Union was, "If Japan can invest large resources in Siberia, why shouldn't we build economic relations with the Russians?"

8. The period began with Sukarno's two-week visit to the Soviet Union in 1956 and ended with his visit to Moscow in 1964. Relations began to cool in 1963, when the PKI moved close to Peking, drawing Sukarno with it.

9. The papers read at this conference have been published as New Directions in the International Relations of Southeast Asia: The Great Powers and Southeast Asia (Singapore: Institute of Southeast Asian Studies, 1973).

10. The conference was sponsored jointly by the Institute of Southeast Asian Studies and the International Institute of Strategic Studies in London. A decision was taken between them not to publish the papers read at the conference.

11. After the announcement of the Nixon Doctrine, the mainstream of Southeast Asian thinking on the U.S. role in the region was that the United States, while theoretically conceding Chinese "legitimate interests" in Southeast Asia, would still keep Chinese influence limited both by virtue of its own relations with the countries in the area and with the cooperation of Japan. See Pracha Guna-Kasem, "The Future Role of the United States in Southeast Asia," and Goh Cheng Teik, "The United States and Southeast Asia," in New Directions in the International Relations of Southeast Asia, op. cit., pp. 92–103.

12. Charles A. Fisher, "Geographical Continuity and Political Challenge in Southeast Asia," in Conflict and Stability in Southeast Asia, ed. Mark W. Zacher and R. Stephen Milne (New York: Anchor Books, Doubleday, 1974), p. 4.

13. Some Southeast Asian scholars take a dim view of the stability of the political orders existing in the different countries.

> The mass protests against social injustice are being
> ignored by the ruling elites of Southeast Asia, and

> instead all over the region we are witnessing the
> further entrenchment of dictators and their few
> conservative rich supporters. In fact, the
> masses, as a rule, are still effectively excluded
> from significant participation in politics. If this
> condition of affairs persists--and there are no
> impelling indications to the contrary--Southeast
> Asia, with its newly aware and groaning masses
> of the deprived and the hungry may prospectively
> deserve its old unflattering description as "a re-
> gion of revolt." I will only insert an adjective,
> "a region of communist revolt."

Alejandro M. Fernandez, "On the Future of Southeast Asia," in New
Directions in the International Relations of Southeast Asia, op. cit.,
p. 31.

14. While in the 1960s the major destabilizing factors were
ethnic, racial, and tribal, in the 1970s the political orders are under
increasing pressure from secular forces, that is, from politically
mobilized students, the unionized working class, and organized
peasants. In December 1974 university students demonstrated in
Malaysia and Singapore in support of the marching peasants or pro-
testing the large-scale layoffs of industrial workers.

> Indeed the most important and far-reaching feature
> of the trouble in Malaysia is that for the first time
> the Malay Government is being confronted not by the
> Chinese but by the Malay students, the privileged
> sons of the soil, many of whom have strong com-
> mitments to the traditional and Islamic ways of
> life. The hungry peasants in whose support the
> students demonstrated are also Malays.

Denzil Peiris, "Revolt of the Young: New Phase in Malaysia and
Singapore," The Times of India, January 7, 1975.

In November 1974 a massive demonstration by peasants
and students near the gates of Government House in Bangkok took the
Thai elite completely by surprise. Signals of rural unrest had been
reaching the capital for several weeks, but no one in Bangkok appeared to take them seriously. When on November 26 some 2,000
peasants marched the streets of Bangkok, several newspaper editors
told the author that it did not portend any serious problem because
the peasants were not capable of organized action. Peasants had by
that time threatened to burn rice fields if the government did not
intervene in their dispute with landlords over farm-renting fees.

The government did not stir. On November 29 a demonstration of
several thousand farmers was joined by students and others and
swelled to a crowd of 20,000, forcing the government to accept most
of the peasant demands. What shocked the Thai establishment even
more than the combined demonstration of peasants and students was
that a number of Buddhist monks took part in the protest, in violation
of the vow each monk has to take that he will have nothing to do with
politics. See Bangkok Post, November 11, 12, and 30, 1974.

15. The cardinal U.S. error in Southeast Asia was the
perception of a homogeneity that never existed. If
all the Southeast Asian countries were not basically
alike, there was no reason for them to stand, or
"fall," like dominoes. In retrospect, however, it
is striking how close America came to make the
domino theory a self-fulfilling prophesy. For nearly
a generation, US power in Southeast Asia was so
pervasive--and so polarized events--that the region
for a time acquired some of the characteristics the
Americans attributed to it. "Communism" and
"anti-Communism" were accepted as adequate
terms for unrelated problems--like ethnic insurgency in Thailand or civil war in Laos; or fear of
the Chinese in Indonesia; or fear of Vietnam in
Cambodia. . . . In Singapore--which prospered
as a supply center for US forces--it made sense a
year ago for Lee Kuan Yew to express his island's
vulnerability in terms of a "Communist threat"
rather than the nationalist resentment of his neighbors of Singapore's disproportionate affluence.
Such approaches made sense because America
made them make sense. The key to Southeast Asia's
temporary polarization was not what the United
States military interests produced in Vietnam, but
the regionwide massiveness of the intervention itself. . . . Events in Southeast Asia for a decade
hung not on the outcome of the Indochina war, but
on the outcome of America's impulse to intervene.

T. D. Allman, "The Bastion That Never Was," Guardian (London),
February 16, 1974.
16. Interviews with arbitrarily selected members of the political elite in the ASEAN capitals in November and December 1974
yielded contradictory and splintered images of China. Most Southeast Asians saw China as one of the major world powers mostly

because of the detente between Peking and Washington. The majority, 63 percent of 250 persons interviewed, had serious doubts about the stability of China's present diplomacy of peaceful coexistence with its Southeast Asian neighbors. They expected a return to the revolutionary foreign policy of the 1960s sooner or later. Only 37 percent believed that the present policy would continue. Almost everyone visualized a strong Sino-Soviet competition in Southeast Asia. To the question, "In which parts of Southeast Asia are the Chinese likely to acquire strong influence?" 57 answered, "continental Southeast Asia." The others avoided a precise answer.

17. K. Jackson, "New Zealand and Southeast Asia," Journal of Commonwealth Political Studies, March 1971. For a brief but perceptive study of British, Australian, and New Zealand defense commitments to Malaysia and Singapore, see Chin Kin Wah, The Five Power Defense Arrangements and AMDA (Singapore: Institute of Southeast Asian Studies, 1974). See also Peter Lyon, "Reorientations in Southeast Asia: ANZUK and After," Round Table, April 1972. For fuller studies, see Michael Leifer, et al., Constraints and Adjustments in British Foreign Policy (London: Allen & Unwin, 1972); and T. B. Millar, Australia's Defense (Melbourne: Melbourne University Press, 1965).

18. Neither of the host powers (or the former consumers of alliance security) has misplaced expectations about the Five Power Defense Arrangements as instruments for its national security. Singapore, while showing a greater public support for the Arrangements than Malaysia, has nevertheless come a long way from her sense of heavy dependence both economically and militarily on the British presence and is unlikely to be too perturbed by a "second withdrawal" under another British Labor Government. For Malaysia, whose espousal of neutralization has meant an increasing public de-emphasis on Five Power Defense, an ideal situation could be one in which the pace of disentanglement from the Commonwealth defense connection corresponds to the pace of gradual evolution toward a new regional order. This is unlikely to be realized as the Australian "withdrawal" has shown and any new British withdrawal is likely to show, that change within the five power partnership is more an immediate function of domestic factors among the guest powers. (Wah, op. cit., p. 15.)

19. The different perspectives of the five ASEAN countries on regional security came into sharp focus at a conference on regionalism held in Jakarta in October 1974 under the auspices of the Center for Strategic and International Studies. Adam Malik, in a paper, regretted the slow and limited progress made in regional cooperation and emphasized the "negative possibilities" of great power detente. Detente, he said, might split the world into spheres of influence and might proceed without any regard for the interests of the weaker powers. The lack of an external power equilibrium in Southeast Asia, he suggested, contributed to the security gap in the region. In a multipolar world, he said, it was illusory to look for "a single structure of peace." Shri M. Ghazali bin Shafie of Malaysia rejected the idea of a collective security role for ASEAN. It had no "collective, common response to security," he added. Southeast Asia faced three kinds of security issues, internal, regional, and external. There was an "unfortunate conjunction of conflict situations within the same territorial and time frame resulting in their fusion and transformation into one vast conflict environment that is rather more complex than the sum total of its parts." It was necessary, he said, to break the "vicious cause and effect circle" and deal with each level of security issues separately from the others. Indonesian Times, October 29, 1974.

About the actual performance of ASEAN in the field of regional cooperation, Lee Kuan Yew gave the following account at the opening session of the fifth ministerial conference in Singapore on April 13, 1972:

> In the first year, August 1967 to August 1968, there were 102 recommendations. None was implemented. In the second, August 1968 to December 1969, of 161 recommendations, 10 were implemented, that is, 6.2%. In the third year, December 1969 to March 1971, of 207 recommendations, 22 were implemented--10.6%. In the fourth year, March 1971 to April 1972, of 215 recommendations, 48 were implemented--22.3%.

The Mirror (Singapore), April 24, 1972.

20. Peter Lyon, "ASEAN and the Future of Regionalism," in New Directions in the International Relations of Southeast Asia, op. cit., p. 157.

21. Adam Malik is sometimes jokingly described as the foreign minister of Malaysia.

22. For a closely argued presentation of the Malaysian view of neutralization, see Shri M. Ghazali bin Shafie, "The Neutralization

of Southeast Asia, " Pacific Community (Tokyo), October, December 1971.

23. Somsakdi Xuto, "Prospects for Security and Stability in
Southeast Asia," Pacific Community, October–December 1971.

24. The author of this paper cannot be identified unless the
sponsors of the conference change their decision not to publish the
papers read at the conference.

25. The question asked was, "Do you visualize the four Indochina states being ruled by the Communists in the next five or six
years ?"

26. Far Eastern Economic Review, March 5, 1976.

27. At the beginning of 1970 China still saw the Asian people's
revolutionary storm rising with great vigor. The New China News
Agency (NCNA), in a report dated February 13, 1970, said, "In the
sixties Marxism-Leninism-Mao Tse-tung thought won great victories
in its polemics and great struggle against modern revisionism. In
this great battle the 'peaceful transition,' 'parliamentary road' and
other counter-revolutionary nonsense peddled by modern revisionism went bankrupt." The true Marxist-Leninist parties became
stronger. "The gunshots of the people's revolutionary armed struggle resounded in the vast areas from the western coast of the Pacific
to the eastern coast of the Mediterranean Sea." The "heroic Vietnamese people" had persevered in people's war; the "courageous
Laotian patriotic people" and their armed forces had persisted in
armed struggle; the Communist party of Burma had carried on its
armed struggle for over 20 years, relying on its own efforts, and
since 1964 "under the guidance of the party's revolutionary line of
'winning the war and seizing political power'" the Burmese people
have brought about a new situation in their revolutionary armed
struggle characterized by its vigorous development; in recent years
the Communist party of Malaya has united still more closely with
the people of various nationalities of the country and expanded the
revolutionary armed forces; the people's armed forces of Thailand
were fighting in the North-eastern, Northern, Central and Southern
parts of the country; after the Naxalbari rising in 1967 "a vigorous
revolutionary situation has appeared in the whole of India"; under
the leadership of the PKI the revolutionary Indonesian people "have
revolted against the white terror of the Suharto fascist military regime"; and the "heroic North Kalimantan people" had established
guerrilla bases in some areas. Mixan, Supplement B, no. 1
(January–February 1970), p. 20.

28. Pravda, August 21, 1970.

29. The 1970–75 period of Soviet involvement in the Vietnam
war remains an unexplored field of study at this time. For the
origins of the Soviet involvement, see Allen M. Cameron, "The

Soviet Union and Vietnam: The Origins of Involvement, " in Soviet
Policy for Developing Countries, ed. W. Raymond Duncan (Waltham,
Mass.: Blaisdell, 1970). For a perceptive analysis of Soviet and
Chinese competitive involvement in Vietnam, see Donald S. Zagoria,
The Vietnam Triangle (New York: Pegasus, 1967).

30. This was quite clear in the conversations that took place
between the Soviet leaders and Sihanouk. See reports in Pravda,
March 17 and 18, 1970

31. Izvestia, June 13, 1970.

32. Pravda, May 5, 1970. This was one of the rare occasions
when Moscow stressed a common stand taken by Peking on a major
world issue.

33. Tass, August 7, 1970. In the days before the fall of
Phnom Penh, Moscow withdrew its diplomatic staff from the embassy, leaving three nondiplomatic personnel in charge; the Cambodian embassy in Moscow, however, continued to remain side-by-
side with the mission of the government-in-exile, with which the
Kremlin had no official relation.

34. NCNA, July 13, 1970.

35. The conference was held in Hanoi on April 24-26, 1970.
On the 25th Chou En-lai gave a banquet in honor of the four delegations; on the following night the four delegations gave a banquet in
honor of the Chinese premier. The Chinese government issued a
statement on the occasion of the Indochina summit. Soviet newspapers reporting the conference took no notice of the Chinese presence; similarly, Chinese reporting ignored the Soviet Union as a
strong supporter of the Indochinese Communists. Kosygin sent a
message to the summit. Pravda, April 30, 1970; Izvestia, April 28,
1970; NCNA, April 28, 1970, and May 3, 1970.

36. New York Times, May 14, 1974.

37. Moscow Radio in Vietnamese, 1500 hrs GMT, August 28,
1975.

38. Moscow Radio in Vietnamese 1300 hrs. GMT August 25,
1975.

39. New York Times, November 4, 1975.

40. Ibid.

41. Moscow Radio in English 1403 GMT September 2, 1975;
also, Moscow Radio Peace and Progress 1030 hrs GMT September 3,
1975. Pravda devoted its entire fourth page on September 2 to articles prepared by Nhan Dan, the Vietnamese official newspaper.

42. New York Times, November 4, 1975. However, the joint
declaration did extol the principles on the basis of which the Soviet
security model is to be built in Asia.

43. Moscow Radio in Vietnamese 1500 hrs GMT August 25,
1975. The commentary said that Soviet ships carried two-thirds of

the military supplies to North Vietnamese ports, defying U.S. aircraft.

According to Washington estimates, Communist aid to Hanoi totaled $1.2 billion in 1972; $1 billion in 1973; and $1.7 billion in 1974, when for the first time it surpassed U.S. aid to South Vietnam ($1.2 billion). Communist military aid to Hanoi in 1974 amounted to $.4 billion, as against $.7 billion worth of military aid given by the United States to Saigon. New York Times, March 20, 1975.

Soviet military and economic aid to Hanoi totaled $705 million in 1967 and $415 million in both 1970 and 1971. Chinese military aid was $145 million in 1967, $85 million in 1970, and $75 million in 1971. New York Times, April 13, 1972.

The retreating South Vietnamese forces left $5 billion worth of military equipment and ammunition in South Vietnam, much of which the Communists were not expected to put to use because of lack of spare parts and expertise. New York Times, May 2, 1975.

44. New York Times, August 19, 1975.

45. Fox Butterfield, "Peking is Disappointed but Still Patient on U.S. Ties," New York Times, October 19, 1975.

46. Fox Butterfield, "Hanoi-Soviet Tie Worries Peking," New York Times, November 4, 1975.

47. New York Times, August 19, 1975. One of the reasons for the coolness between Peking and Moscow could be the Chinese occupation of the Parcels islands about 500 miles to the north of the Spratly islands on the China sea. The Parcels, which are some 200 miles east of the area where the anti-Communist South Vietnamese regime had been exploring for oil, were occupied by a Chinese military force consisting of MIGs, missile ships, and ground troops. They encountered no opposition. The occupation drew Soviet criticism, but no public objection from Hanoi. New York Times, February 1, 1974. The Parcels islands, which are claimed simultaneously by Vietnam, the Philippines, and China, are shown as Chinese territory on Soviet maps. New York Times, February 10, 1974.

48. New York Times, October 28 and 29, 1975.

49. Immediately after their takeover of Phnom Penh, the Cambodian Communists denied that there were North Vietnamese troops in their armed forces and rejected suggestions that they were under the influence of Hanoi. "The Cambodians have looked to Peking for protection against domination by the historically expansionist North Vietnamese. Hanoi's relations with Moscow contain a similar desire to balance the influence of China, Vietnam's traditional enemy." Flora Lewis, "A Possible Resurgence of Ancient Asian Frictions," New York Times, May 2, 1975.

50. Vladimir Kudryavtsev, "Favorable Opportunities,"
Izvestia, February 6, 1973.

51. New Directions in the International Relations of Southeast
Asia: The Great Powers and Southeast Asia, op. cit., p. 30.

52. M. Rajaretnam and Lim So Jean, ed., Trends in Thailand
(Singapore: Singapore University Press, 1973), pp. 22-25.
A survey conducted in 16 provinces in the Central Plains
in 1967 showed that 48.8 percent of the rural families were tenants
and that about 95 percent of the tenant farmers were in debt. Tenant
farming is most common around Bangkok, where more than 80 percent of the farmers are tenants, and in the adjoining provinces of
Pathumthani, Thonburi, and Samutprakan. It is in these provinces
that an organized peasant movement seems to be emerging. Ibid.,
pp. 42-45.

53. David Morell, "Thailand: Military Checkmate," Asian
Survey 12, no. 2 (February 1972).

54. New York Times, September 24, 1975.

55. Rajaretnam and Jean, op. cit., p. 24.

56. Bangkok Bank Monthly Review 12, no. 5 (May 1972).

57. L. S. Girling, "Northeast Thailand: Tomorrow's Vietnam?" Pacific Affairs 46, no. 2 (January 1968); Daniel Wit, Thailand:
Another Vietnam? (New York: Charles Scribner's Sons, 1968),
pp. 191-95.

58. Rajaretnam and Jean, op. cit., pp. 16-22. The 15 north-
eastern provinces have an area of 64,500 square miles. Unofficial
estimates put the guerrilla force at about 10,000.

59. In November 1975 relations between Thailand and Cambodia suddenly warmed up, probably at Chinese bidding. Several
Cambodian Communist leaders visited Thailand, and the visit was
returned by the Thai foreign minister. The two countries agreed
to establish diplomatic relations and promote mutual cooperation.
However, the warmth seemed to have disappeared in a matter of
months; in the spring of 1976 the old animosities returned. In any
case the Thai insurgents would turn to Hanoi and Laos if the Cambodian Communists ceased their support, a probability that the
Cambodians would like to control. New York Times, November 2
and 18, 1975.

60. Donald E. Neuchterlein, Thailand and the Struggle for
Southeast Asia (Ithaca: Cornell University Press, 1965), preface.

61. The main reason why there has been no land reform in
Thailand, despite the fact that a land reform committee was set up
by the government in 1972, is that most of the land to be purchased
for distribution to the poor peasants belongs to members of the royal
family and high-ranking government officials. Prachthipatai,
August 24, 1972, Survey of Thai and Chinese Press, U.S. Embassy,
Bangkok.

"The military predominance in the Thai power structure has long been the nature of things and its influence has been so pervasive in terms of values, beliefs, and, most important of all, interests." Rajaretnam and Jean, op. cit., p. 90.

62. David A. Andelman, "Thai-Laotian Friendship Unravels on the Mekong," New York Times, October 30, 1975.

63. In 1973 Thanat Khoman, the former foreign minister, made secret contacts with the North Vietnamese in Paris on behalf of the military regime in Thailand. He found the terms offered by the North Vietnamese unacceptable. Interview with Thanat Khoman.

64. The new strategic thinking, as explained by a spokesman of the Foreign Affairs ministry in June 1974, was to get rid of "excessive" relationships with any major power including the United States and maintain "healthy relations" with each one of them. The Bangkok Nation, June 7, 1974; the Bangkok Star, June 4, 1974.

65. The Bangkok Post, August 30, 1974.

66. Ibid., August 16, 1974.

67. Ibid., September 3, 1974; October 26, 1974; and November 28, 1974.

68. Pravda, October 19, 1973. For a typical example of the earlier, negative image, see V. Shurygin, "Events in Thailand," Pravda, November 20, 1972.

69. Pravda, May 6, 1974.

70. V. Shurygin, "Thailand's New Coalition," Pravda, March 15, 1975.

71. Moscow Radio Peace and Progress in Mandarin to Southeast Asia, 0830 hrs GMT March 6, 1975; I. B. Bulay, "Thailand: American Outpost in Asia," USA: Economics, Politics, Ideology, no. 8 (August 1973); also, Moscow Radio Peace and Progress, in English to Asia, 1030 GMT March 13, 1975.

72. For Soviet concern about the future of the Sattahip naval base, see Moscow Radio Peace and Progress, in English to Asia, 1030 GMT March 13, 1975.

73. Francis P. Serong, in a paper drawn up in August 1974, also said that while Chinese influence was to be seen mostly in the insurgent regions in north and northeast Thailand, Soviet influence was visible in the urban areas as well as in Southern Thailand. The Bangkok Nation, August 28, 1974.

74. The Bangkok Nation, September 21, 1974.

75. Significantly, Diosdado Macapagal, the Philippine president between 1961 and 1965, a stern anti-Communist and a strong ally of the United States, entitled a collection of his speeches, The Philippines Turns East (rev. ed., Manila: Mac Publishing House, 1970). For the country's Southeast Asian identity, see ibid., pp. 37-40.

76. For a first-hand report of the insurgency, see Fox Butter-field, "Philippine Rebels Vow to Keep Up Fight for Self-Rule," New York Times, September 5, 1975.

77. George E. Taylor, The Philippines and the United States: Problems of Partnership (New York: Praeger, 1964), preface.

78. Fox Butterfield, "Marcos Outlines Campaign for More Control over Bases," New York Times, September 7, 1975.

79. Pravda, August 14, 1975. At the same time, the foreign minister of South Vietnam, Nguyen Thi Binh, objected to Manila's participation in the 1975 nonaligned summit at Lima on the ground that there were U.S. bases on its territory. When the two Vietnams are reunited, their government will probably press Manila for either abolition or total control of the U.S. bases.

80. Soviet Activities in Southeast Asia, 1970 (Bangkok: SEATO, 1971), p. 14.

81. Ibid.

82. Bulletin (Manila), September 17, 1970.

83. Lim Yoon Lin, ed., Trends in the Philippines (Singapore: Singapore University Press, 1972), p. 29.

84. Philippine Herald (Manila), June 23, 1971. "The Philip-pines . . . is now in the same situation as India was before 1956 and it is time this country explored the possibility of securing aid out-side of the United States for the development of untapped oil re-sources." Bulletin, March 15, 1970.

85. The Chronicle (Manila), October 15, 1971.

86. He also tried to convey the message that once trade and diplomatic relations were established with Moscow, it would be easier to work out similar relations with Peking.

87. Chronicle, June 11, 1972. For Imelda Marcos's visit to Moscow, see Chronicle, March 30, 1972.

88. Rajaretnam and Jean, op. cit., p. 31.

89. Philippine Daily Express, October 28, 1974.

90. Ibid.

91. Macapagal also made these additional points. (1) The Philippines should have balanced relations with Moscow and Peking. (2) The Philippines could not antagonize China in view of the "uncon-trolled Maoist-oriented rebellion amongst some Filipinos." And (3) the ASEAN countries were keeping each other informed about the progress toward normalization of their relations with the Communist powers.

92. Philippine Daily Express, October 28, 1974.,

93. The Philippines has one of the world's highest birth rates. Its population of 35 million is multiplying at the rate of 3.5 percent a year.

94. Justus M. van der Kroef, "The Soviet Union and Southeast Asia, " in The Soviet Union and the Developing Nations, ed. Roger E. Kanet (Baltimore: Johns Hopkins Press, 1974), p. 92. See also New York Times, October 4, 1971.
    Van der Kroef writes,

> In the present Philippine climate of widening public
> discontent with, and dissent from, the present con-
> stitutional establishment, the two-party system and
> its corrupt political ancillaries, the severe social
> and economic inequalities and excessive dependence
> upon the US in economic and foreign policies, the
> Soviets are exceptionally well suited to enlarge
> their influence slowly, steadily, and in a disciplined
> way, utilizing especially a new and more radical
> Philippine nationalism that finds adherents ranging
> from the bourgeoisie and professional groups to the
> industrial and rural proletariat. (Pp. 95-96.)

95. Vladimir Kudryavtsev, "The Philippines: Yesterday and Today," Izvestia, May 26, 1971.
96. Yu. Popov, "The Philippines' New Constitution, " Izvestia, January 19, 1972.
97. Vladimir Grigorovich, "Encounter with Manila," Pravda, January 9, 1973.
98. Vladimir Grigorovich, "The Island of Mindanao and Further South," Pravda, February 11, 1973.
99. Moscow Radio, March 1975.
100. Ibid.
101. Soviet ships of the company carried Philippine cargo at prices 10 to 15 percent lower than the charter rates charged by Western shipping companies. For the popularity of this measure, see Philippine Daily Express, editorial, October 28, 1974.
102. Moscow Radio in English to Southeast Asia 1100 GMT March 16, 1975.
103. Pravda, August 14, 1975.
104. Bangkok Post, March 22, 1970.
105. For the nature of the insurgency that still persists in Malaysia, see 1975 Yearbook on International Communist Affairs (Stanford: Hoover Institute Press, 1975), pp. 375-78. Unlike those in Thailand, the Malay insurgents do not seem to have large rural areas under their administrative control. The Malaysian government claimed in 1974 that 75 percent of the "entire Communist fighting forces in Sarawak" had laid down their arms since the launching of the "peace campaign" in October 1973.

106. A Malaysian Communist Party delegation attended the CPSU 21st Congress in January 1959. Since then there has been little organizational link between the MCP and the CPSU.

107. Van der Kroef, op. cit., p. 79.

108. The population of Malaysia is overwhelmingly young, 65 percent being below the age of 25. In 1966 approximately 35 percent of the young people were in educational institutions. Yong Mun Cheong, ed., Trends in Malaysia (Singapore: Singapore University Press, 1974), pp. 76-77.

109. Stephen Chee, "Malaysia's Changing Foreign Policy," in Trends in Malaysia, op. cit., pp. 76-77.

110. Cited in Peter Boyce, Malaysia and Singapore in International Diplomacy (Sydney: Sydney University Press, 1968), Document 5, p. 44.

111. Stephen Chee, op. cit., p. 48.

112. Pran Chopra, noted author, editor, and analyst, interviewed in Kuala Lumpur.

113. Pravda, December 29, 1971.

114. Moscow Radio in English to Southeast Asia 1949 GMT August 30, 1973.

115. Soviet Activities in Southeast Asia June 1970-July 1971 (Bangkok: SEATO, 1971), pp. 8-9.

116. Moscow Radio in English to Southeast Asia 1949 GMT August 30, 1973; also, in English to Southeast Asia 1100 GMT August 30, 1973.

117. New York Times, September 17, 1965.

118. Los Angeles Times, March 13, 1970.

119. Dick Wilson, The Future of Singapore (London: Oxford Paperbacks, 1972), p. 28.

120. The Soviet embassy in Singapore keeps a close watch on developments in Southeast Asia, and its officials speak about Singapore with unconcealed respect. Forty business houses or firms of Singapore, representing a cross section of the business community, ran advertisements in the Strait Times alone congratulating the USSR on its 57th anniversary. The Times published a four-page supplement laden with articles by Soviet publicists.

121. Strait Times, May 12, 1973.

122. New York Times, April 24, 1975.

123. New York Times, May 12, 1975.

124. The intellectual community in Singapore tends to be conformist; there is very little serious dissent from the thought processes of the political leaders. Although more than one cabinet minister has regretted this "intellectual sterility" (Far Eastern Economic Review, August 5, 1972), the academic community seems to be still awed by the intellectual acumen of Lee Kuan Yew and the

foreign minister, S. Rajaratnam. For a highly critical view of the regime, see T. K. S. George, Lee Kuan Yew's Singapore (London: Andre Deutsch, 1974).

125. Pravda, May 15, 1973.

126. For a typical sample of Soviet anti-China propaganda to Singapore, see Radio Peace and Progress in Mandarin to Southeast Asia 0830 GMT August 9, 1973.

127. The Soviet journal New Times, no. 37 (1973), wrote about Singapore,

> True enough, in its eight years of independence the republic has made marked economic progress. No longer does it merely process and reexport raw materials from, and deliver West European goods to, neighboring Indonesia and Malaysia. Today it is a leading manufacturing center, where one or two industrial enterprises start nearly every week. Its port, fourth in the world in the amount of cargoes handled, operates at capacity, taking ships virtually from all the world over. Singapore boasts the biggest refineries in Southeast Asia; it is also fast becoming the main dry-dock in this part of the world for tankers carrying Middle East oil. This has all served to boost employment, especially in comparison with the other Asian countries.

128. Wilson, op. cit., p. 29.

129. Robert A. Scalapino, Asia and the Great Powers: Implications for an International Order (Washington, D.C.: American Enterprise Institute for Public Policy Research, 1974), pp. 42-43.

130. Indonesia is the only Southeast Asian country to be a member of the OPEC. Indonesian petroleum reserves are relatively small, between 2 to 3 percent of world reserves stocks. The petroleum, however, is of a high quality, with a very low sulphur content. In 1974 Indonesian oil was selling for $10.8 a barrel. Oil is now the most important branch of the economy, accounting for 55 percent of all export earnings. Some 30 foreign petroleum companies operate in Indonesia, of which 19 are based in the U.S. Since 1968 foreign investment in the Indonesian oil industry has exceeded $1 billion. The petroleum industry is controlled by Pertamina, the state-owned corporation, but about 90 percent of the extraction is done by foreign companies. The 1974 oil output was 70 million tons. Production is expected to rise to 3 million barrels a day by 1980, the present level of extraction in Kuwait. Far Eastern Economic Review, October 1, 1973; November 12, 1973; December 24, 1973; February 11, 1974; and March 4, 1974; Newsweek, February 18, 1974.

131. O. Sumoto Roesnadi, "Indonesia's Foreign Policy," in
Trends in Indonesia, ed. Yong Mun Cheong (Singapore: Singapore
University Press, 1972), pp. 60-73. Indonesia resumed its atten-
dance at nonaligned summits in 1970.

132. In November 1974 I found the North Vietnamese mission
in Jakarta manned by a few junior diplomats; the gate was locked 24
hours, and there was very little sign of activity. The North Vietnamese official who received me said that relations between Jakarta
and Hanoi were "correct."

133. Asian Almanac 8, no. 52 (December 26, 1970), p. 4339.
The right-wing military leaders wanted to send an expeditionary
force to Cambodia, hoping that this would enable Indonesia to get
U.S. military aid to "replenish their rundown arms and equipment."
Michael Leifer, "Indonesia's Future Role," The World Today 26
(December 1970). See also Lau Teik Soon, Indonesia and Regional
Security: The Djakarta Conference on Cambodia (Singapore: Insti-
tute of Southeast Asian Studies, 1972).

134. There seemed little doubt that one of the chief
failures of the Suharto regime so far had been its
inability to harness or integrate the so-called
Generation of 1966 and give its members a sense
of useful participation in the new scheme of things.
This group's restlessness was aggravated by the
fact that, being both socially mobilized and highly
literate, it felt its new alienation all the more
keenly for having lent its early support so strongly
to the Suharto regime.

Robert Shaplen, Time Out of Hand: Revolution and Reaction in Southeast Asia (New York: Harper & Row, 1969), p. 191.
I found students in the campuses in Jakarta disappointed
with the economic policies of the government, which they said had
created a new class of rich people, made the gap between the rich
and the poor wider, and brought about widespread corruption. They
also resented what one of them called "too much influence" of the
United States and Japan on the country's economic life. I got the
impression that the campus youth, while still decidedly turned
against the Sukarno period, nevertheless missed the radical ethos
of the regime they had helped so much to destroy.

135. Based on interviews and discussions in December 1974
with officials, scholars, journalists, and members of parliament in
Jakarta.

136. Nugroho, "Southeast Asian Perceptions of the Future of
the Region," in New Directions in the International Relations of Southeast Asia: The Great Powers and Southeast Asia, op. cit., pp. 7-19.

137. A U.S. scholar has given three reasons why Indonesia
became Moscow's "most favored nation" in the Third World between
1958 and 1963: (1) the size of the country and its growing stature
in the Afro-Asian community; (2) an "obvious rapport" between
Khrushchev and Sukarno; and (3) a "temporary absence of serious
competition on both sides," that is, from the United States and
China. Charles B. McLane, Soviet-Asian Relations, Vol. 2 of
Soviet-Third World Relations (New York: Columbia University
Press, 1973), p. 78.

138. Moscow Radio in Indonesian 0930 GMT February 12, 1970.

139. The amount of military aid given to Indonesia by the
Soviet Union is controversial; some put the figure at $1.2 billion.
Indonesia received from the Soviet Union a heavy cruiser; 7 destroyers; 6 submarines; dozens of torpedo and coastal craft; over 150
fighters and bombers, including some 2 dozen MIG-21s; and miscel-
laneous artillery and antiaircraft weapons, including SA-2 missiles
at three known sites.

Between 1966 and 1969 several Indonesian dignitaries
went to Moscow in search of spare parts, but the Soviet Union did
not help. For Soviet aid to Indonesia, see Stephen P. Gilbert and
Wynfred Joshua, Guns and Rubles: Soviet Aid Diplomacy in Neutral
Asia (New York: American-Asian Education Exchange, 1970), pp.
32-39; The Military Balance 1970-1971 (London: International Institute for Strategic Studies, 1971), pp. 63-64; Wynfred Joshua and
Stephen P. Gilbert, Arms for the Third World: Soviet Military Aid
Diplomacy (Baltimore: Johns Hopkins Press, 1969), p. 73; and
Marshall I. Goldman, Soviet Foreign Aid (New York: Praeger,
1967), pp. 125-34. The accord reached during Malik's 1970 visit
was carried by Antara, the Indonesian news agency, on August 31,
1970.

140. Asian Recorder, 1972, p. 10794.

141. Izvestia, December 9, 1972.

142. Izvestia, February 10, 1972.

143. Moscow Radio in Indonesian 1130 GMT August 4, 1973;
Moscow Radio in Indonesian 1130 GMT March 14, 1975; V. Ivanov,
"Indonesia: Foreign Monopolies' Offensive," International Affairs,
January 1968; Ye. A. Kutovaya, "The United States and Indonesian
Petroleum," USA: Economics, Politics, Ideology, no. 10 (October
1974).

144. Strait Times (Singapore), November 6, 1974. An Indonesian parliamentary delegation visited the USSR in 1973, and Indonesia received a Soviet parliamentary delegation in 1974. A labor
delegation from Indonesia attended the May Day celebrations in the
Soviet Union in 1973. In 1975 East Germany and Czechoslovakia
became large buyers of Indonesian natural rubber. After an absence

of ten years, Jakarta attended the Leipzig Fair in 1975. In that
year Soviet-Indonesian trade doubled the figure of 1965.

　　　　Adam Malik said in 1973 that if Moscow invited Suharto
for a state visit, "the Government will think over it." However, by
the end of 1975 no invitation had come; nor has a major Soviet leader
visited Jakarta since deputy premier Mazurov's presence at the
August 1965 anniversary of Indonesian independence. Far Eastern
Economic Review, June 8, 1973; Moscow Radio in Indonesian 1130
GMT March 14, 1975.

　　　　145. Pravda, December 28, 1974.

　　　　146. Indonesian Times, March 11, 1974. One result of the
Firyubin-Malik meeting was a widening of Soviet development aid.
Malik had declared in March 1970 that "all Asian countries, including Indonesia, have rejected the Soviet Union's proposal for a regional
security arrangement [sic]." Sunday Times (Singapore), March 8,
1970.

SOVIET PERCEPTIONS OF JAPAN

Historic Enemies

In the middle of the nineteenth century, by a narrow margin of seven months, Russia lost to the United States the race for the "opening up" of Japan.[1] Since then until the present time, Moscow has encountered two rivals on the eastern shores of Asia: Japan and its patron, the United States. The eastward expansion of Csarist Russia brought it into conflicts with the territorial and maritime interests of Japan.

The Sakhalin and Kurile islands on the Sea of Okhotsk have oscillated between Russian and Japanese possession. Russia lost the southern half of Sakhalin to Japan as a result of the Russo-Japanese War of 1904-1905, while Japan lost the southern half of Sakhalin, as well as the Kuriles, to the Soviet Union as a result of World War II.[2]

Four islands, two of them belonging to the Kurile archipelago, which the Soviet Union took at the end of World War II, are claimed back by Japan. These islands, Habomai, Shikotan, Kunashiri, and Etorofu,[3] constitute what the Japanese call the Northern Territory; they still block a peace treaty between the USSR and Japan. "Throughout history Russia has been untrustworthy," declared the Rengokai, a united front of eight Japanese nationalist groups formed to protest the terms of the Treaty of Portsmouth, which was concluded between the two in 1905 through the good offices of the United States.[4] Seventy years later one can still hear similar exclamations from many in Japan.

In this century, within a span of 40 years the two Pacific neighbors have fought three wars and numerous skirmishes over fishing

rights in the waters of the ocean and the seas. Two of the wars were
not even declared. In 1904 Japan invaded Russia without declaring
war, something that Stalin never forgot, although Lenin had welcomed
the war as a catalyst for the Russian revolution.[5] In 1905 most Japanese felt that the United States had deprived Japan of the fruits of victory in the war with Russia.[6] In 1936-38 the Soviet and Japanese
armies fought an undeclared war along the Soviet-Manchurian-
Mongolian border.

On August 8, 1945, two days after the dropping of the atomic
bomb on Hiroshima, the Japanese ambassador in Moscow called on
Foreign Minister V. M. Molotov with the request that the Soviet
Union transmit the eve-of-surrender peace proposals of Japan to the
United States and Britain. Molotov told his visitor that as of August
9 the Soviet Union would be in a state of war with the Japanese empire. Five months earlier the Soviet government had notified Japan
of the termination of the neutrality pact the two countries had concluded in April 1941.[7] Japan regarded the Soviet invasion as an act
of treachery.

In 1945 the United States denied the Soviet Union a foothold in
Japan. However, Soviet troops had overrun Manchuria and North
Korea as well as Southern Sakhalin; the United States also permitted
them to occupy the Kuriles. Like Theodore Roosevelt in the first
decade of the century, successive U.S. presidents since World War II
have wanted to see Russia and Japan locked in a relationship of "balanced antagonism."[8]

Despite the "historic antagonism," or more correctly because
of it, Japan owes much of its historical development to its massive
northern neighbor. Confrontation with Russia enabled the Japanese
to sharpen their insular talent for exploiting the rivalries among the
great powers to their own advantage.[9] It was the victory over Russia
in 1905, rather than the victory over China some 20 years earlier,
that aroused the imperial hunger of Japan. Although it could not
secure any territorial gains from Russia except Southern Sakhalin,
the Treaty of Portsmouth virtually formalized a Japanese imperial
sphere in Korea and Manchuria.[10]

In 1918 Japan made another attempt to detach substantial portions of Siberia from the control of the young Soviet state. Violating
its understanding with the United States, which stood for only limited
intervention against the Bolshevik regime, Japan deployed four to
five divisions in 1920 in the Siberian region between Vladivostok and
Khabarovsk in the east and Manchouli and Chita in the west and expanded its field of operation to include Northern Sakhalin. The U.S.
and allied forces evacuated Siberia in 1920, but the Japanese forces
elected to remain until 1922 in the Amur basin and until 1925 on
Sakhalin. "Throughout this period the army sought energetically to

advance the interests of its White Russian proteges, to secure control of the Siberian railways for itself, and, especially through the
Siberian economic assistance committee, to integrate the economy
of the region with that of Japan."[11]

The Siberian adventure failed, but it settled for the next 20
years the struggle that had been going on within the ruling circles in
Japan, between those who wanted to use relations with the West as
the major instrument for development and those who stood for securing a Japanese empire in Asia. Both elements wanted Japan to become independent, wealthy, and powerful. However, providence had
endowed Japan with little arable land and few industrial minerals
with which this ambition could be realized. Japan was hopelessly dependent on foreign sources for the raw materials and markets necessary for modernization. "Broadly speaking, the Japanese had two
alternatives: a strong alliance with the West, from which would follow goods, services, ideas and military support, or a sphere of
their own on the Asian continent by means of which they might become independent of the West."[12] Those who favored the first, the
"continental activists" (tairiku-nonshu), also stood for "cast off
Asia" (datsu-A).

No Japanese government, of course, pursued one policy to the
exclusion of the other; but the Asian empire-builders won. Within
six years of the termination of the Siberian intervention, Japan began a systematic penetration of Manchuria and then of China. Until
1941 the Soviet Union pursued what in effect was a policy of neutrality and noninvolvement, as long as there was no threat to its own
territory or to Mongolia. If that was appeasement, it was "an appeasement without illusions and offered from a position of strength."[13]
Nevertheless, Soviet neutrality was of considerable help to the Japanese empire-building.

The Soviet-Japan neutrality pact that was concluded on April
13, 1941, was also helpful. It enabled Japan to conduct the Pacific
war against the United States, Britain, and China without undue worry
about its frontiers with the USSR or about the security of its Man-
churian domain. It also enabled the Soviet Union to concentrate on
the war with Germany without having to fight simultaneously in the
Far East. That the wartime rulers of Japan had little understanding
of the considerations that prompted Joseph Stalin's decision to sign
the neutrality pact became evident when in 1944, with the Pacific war
turning definitely in favor of the allies, Japan offered sweeping territorial concessions to the Soviet Union--predominance in the Pacific
Far East and an equal sphere of influence in southeast Asia--if Moscow were to walk out of its alliance with the United States and join
forces with Japan. Stalin had decided to go along with the U.S. decision to demand total defeat and unconditional surrender. Even after

Stalin rejected the feelers, the Japanese government tried in vain to persuade him to mediate between Japan and the United States. [14]

Stalin had apparently decided that the elimination of Japan as a power would be of great benefit to Soviet postwar interests in the Pacific-Asian region. If the atomic bombs had not hastened the Japanese surrender, and if the Pacific war had continued for more months, Soviet forces would have entered Japan proper, and the postwar history of Japan would have been entirely different.[15] Stalin, however, had accepted the U.S. supremacy in postwar Japan; his primary preoccupation was with Eastern Europe. When the United States denied the USSR all opportunities to influence events in postwar Japan, Stalin's protests were mild. Later he was gravely displeased with the U.S. occupation policy, which included retention of the imperial system, nonliquidation of the Japanese general staff and armed forces, and rehabilitation of the big-business oligarchy, but he could only warn the United States that it was repeating in Japan the mistakes the allies had committed with regard to Germany in 1918. [16]

It was not only that the Soviet Union had no direct means after 1945 to influence developments in Japan. The Soviet Union itself destroyed what could have been a powerful indirect instrumentality for influencing Japanese affairs. The occupation allowed the Moscow-oriented Japanese Communist Party (JCP) to function openly for the first time as a political organization, and within four years it had become a major force in Japanese politics. In the Diet elections in 1949 the JCP polled 9.3 percent of the votes and captured 35 seats in the lower house. However, Stalin killed the efforts of the JCP leadership to build a "lovable party." At the bidding of the Cominform, the JCP was obliged to swing to a "revolutionary" line of industrial and urban violence and was quickly suppressed by the Occupation. It lost all of its Diet seats in the 1952 election and for 20 years ceased to be a major political force in Japan. [17]

Relations Normalized

At the San Francisco Peace Conference in 1951, the Soviet Union spelled out its strategic concept for Japan, that of an unarmed, neutral nonpower. This was to remain more or less unchanged through the 1950s and 1960s. In 1951, of course, the Soviet Union was in a position of strength derived from its anti-Japan security and friendship treaty with the People's Republic of China. At the San Francisco conference the Soviet delegate, Andrei Gromyko, spoke for the USSR and also for the People's Republic of China, which had not been invited to attend. Japan, insisted Gromyko, must not maintain substantial armed forces nor conclude a military alliance with any country. The Straits of Soya, Nemuro, Tsugaru, and Tushima, the sea lanes of Japan to the Pacific Ocean, must be demilitarized and opened to the peaceful maritime commerce of all nations, but passage of warships should be restricted only to nations that are adjacent to Japan. The rights of China to Manchuria, Taiwan, and various other islands off the Chinese coast must be restored. The Soviet right to Sakhalin and the Kuriles must be formally recognized, but the Ryuku and Bonin islands, occupied by the United States, should be restored to Japan.[18]

Article 2 of the San Francisco Peace Treaty contains the renunciation by Japan of that portion of Sakhalin and the islands adjacent to it over which Japan had acquired sovereignty as a result of the Treaty of Portsmouth. The USSR was not named as the power to whom these islands had to be renounced. If the Soviet Union had signed the treaty, which it did not because the People's Republic of China was no party to it, its claim to the Northern Territory would have been formalized. Since it did not sign, the Japanese government, with tacit U.S. consent, took the stand that Article 2 was not binding on its relations with the USSR and that the ultimate fate of the Kurile archipelago should be settled in a future peace treaty to be signed between the two countries. At the same time the Japanese refused to negotiate a peace treaty with the Soviet Union until the Northern Territory was returned to them.

Between 1952 and 1956 the Soviet Union took a number of initiatives to normalize relations with Japan, trying at the same time to strengthen the already substantial opposition within Japan to the Japanese security relations with the United States.[19] Normal relations with Japan became politically important in 1954 when the Soviet Union returned control of Port Arthur to China and agreed to withdraw its troops from Manchuria by May 1955. Also, within Japan public opinion was generating pressure on the government to normalize relations with the USSR and China. This, many Japanese thought, would minimize Japanese dependence on the United States.[20]

In December 1954 Ichiro Hatoyama became prime minister, pledging a foreign policy shift from total dependence on the United States to "an amended policy of dependence." There were, however, strong differences within the cabinet and in the government factions in the Diet about opening negotiations with the Soviet Union and about the modalities of negotiations, since Moscow had no officially recognized mission in Tokyo.[21] Informal contacts over several months, however, led to the opening of formal talks in London in June 1955. The Soviet Union submitted a 12-article draft peace treaty that more or less reaffirmed its 1951 strategic concept for Japan, seeking to formalize its possession of the Kurile islands but dropping its demand for the annulment of the security treaty between Japan and the United

States. This last-named concession came after protracted negotiations, together with a territorial gesture: the Soviets agreed to return to Japan the islands of Habomai and Shikotan, which are adjacent
to Hokkaido, after the conclusion of a peace treaty. Japan was on the
verge of accepting the Soviet offer when U.S. Secretary of State John
Foster Dulles intervened, warning Japan that if it agreed to the Soviet
proposal, the United States would be constrained to annex Okinawa. [22]

In the meantime the Soviet veto had blocked the admission of
Japan to the United Nations. Japan now moved to normalize relations
with the USSR, putting aside the territorial issue as well as the question of a peace treaty. Talks were resumed in September 1956 on
five subjects: an end to the state of war; establishment of diplomatic
relations; repatriation of Japanese war prisoners still held in the
Soviet Union; implementation of a fisheries agreement worked out
through bilateral contacts; and Soviet support for Japanese admission
to the United Nations.

Hatoyama visited Moscow in October, and a joint declaration
was issued on October 19, 1956, under the signatures of the Soviet
and Japanese prime ministers. At the same time the two countries
signed a fisheries agreement, an agreement for cooperation in the
development of trade and commerce, and an accord for the rescue of
persons in distress at sea. Diplomatic relations were to be established at once. On the question of territory the joint declaration
said, "The Union of Soviet Socialist Republics, in response to the desire of Japan and in consideration of her interests, agrees to transfer the Habomai island and the island of Shikotan to Japan, provided,
however, that the actual transfer of these islands shall be affected
after the peace treaty between Japan and the USSR is concluded."
The joint declaration was ratified by the Diet on November 27, 1956.
On December 12 the instruments of ratification were exchanged, and
on the same day the UN Security Council was convened to recommend
the admission of Japan to the General Assembly. Two days later
Hatoyama tendered his resignation as prime minister. [23]

For 15 years thereafter Japan had a succession of prime ministers, none of whom showed any particular interest in improving relations with the Soviet Union. On the other hand, its security relations with the United States deepened and involved Japan in the U.S.
security system for Asia.

No Japanese prime minister was prepared to move toward a
peace treaty with the USSR on the basis of the terms negotiated in
1956. After the extension of the revised security treaty between the
United States and Japan in 1960, the Soviet attitude on the Northern
Territory hardened. In a memorandum to the Japanese government,
the Soviet leaders declared that none of the northern islands would be
returned as long as Okinawa remained under U.S. control. Later

they took the rigidly legalistic stand that the territorial question had
been settled and could not be reopened. [24]

Changes in the 1970s

In the 1960s the Soviet Union watched the rising economic
power of Japan with a mixture of admiration and apprehension. What
alarmed the Soviet leaders was that this economic power would soon
be translated into political and military power as an integral force
within the U.S. security system for Asia. They closely followed the
growing contradictions between U.S. and Japanese economic and
commercial interests in Asia and elsewhere, as well as the resentment and opposition within Japan to the government's unenthusiastic
cooperation with the U.S. military operations in Indochina. It was
at this time that Japanese studies began to receive special attention
in the Soviet Academy of Sciences.

The U.S. predicament in Vietnam in the late 1960s sharpened
the Soviet observation of Japan. In the Guam, or Nixon, Doctrine in
1969 the Soviet leaders saw the collapse of the U.S. security system
in Asia. At this juncture of Asian-U.S. relations, which was bound
to make qualitative changes in U.S. relations with Japan, the Soviet
leaders seriously revised their earlier strategic concept of the future
role of Japan in Asian affairs. The changing realities and expectations began to create new images of Japan in the Soviet mind. My
inquiry into Soviet perceptions of Japan begins with the advent of the
1970s.

To some extent the changing Soviet perceptions of Japan correspond to its growing importance for the Soviet strategic portfolio for
Asia during and beyond the 1970s. The Soviet Union needs Japan's
advanced technology and its capital to develop the untapped resources
of Siberia. Even in the 1950s the Soviet Union had tried, without success, to attract Japanese help for Siberian development. The situation now was very different, and Moscow took another initiative to
improve relations with Japan. This initiative was well timed: the
traumas of the 1970s made the Japanese responsive.

What the Soviet Union has been able to get from Japan and what
Japan has refused to yield come out in the following pages. In evaluating the gains and the gaps, it is important to remember that the
Soviet leaders themselves do not expect a dramatic breakthrough in
their relations with Japan. They seem to realize that the relationship will take time to rise to their expectations and that much patient
effort will be needed. The task of Soviet foreign policy in the 1970s
is to lay the "foundation for good neighborly relations . . . over a
really historically long period of time," as Brezhnev defined it during Tanaka's visit to Moscow in October 1973. [25]

Two years later the Soviet media played up a Tass interview with Tanaka's successor, Takeo Miki, in which the Japanese premier took a long-distance view of relations between Moscow and Tokyo. "I am confident," Miki declared, "Japan-Soviet cooperation will be of historic significance in the 21st century!"[26] Meanwhile, both nations have been trying to gain advantages, and neither seems to have done badly in these difficult and complex transactions.

Economic Breakthrough

During the 1950s and 1960s the Soviet leaders realized that they had no political blandishments with which they could bridge the divide with Japan. They therefore adopted the twin policy of continued political attack, with piercing invective and propaganda aimed at the Japanese antiwar psyche, and step-by-step improvement of "nonpolitical" relations. Thus in the 1960s relatives of Japanese who were buried in the Russian earth were permitted to visit their graves. An agreement was signed for the collection of sea tangle in the waters near Habomai and Shikotan islands. The Japanese airline was the first foreign line to be granted a Siberian route to Europe. Japanese resistance to the Soviet proposal for a cultural exchange program at the "people's level" held up a comprehensive cultural accord, but unofficial cultural exchanges continued.[27]

In the field of fisheries, many problems arose because of what the Soviet leaders called "reckless fishing" by the Japanese. Since fish is part of the Japanese staple and provides a livelihood to many millions, the Soviet Union did try to use the fisheries problem to generate internal pressure on Tokyo to normalize relations. After the conclusion of the fisheries agreement in 1956, a Northwest Pacific fisheries convention was set up, with three Soviet and three Japanese representatives. It met annually to determine the yearly catch of salmon, herring, and crabs and to make recommendations for conservation and for expansion of fisheries resources. The Soviet Union has frequently accused Japan of violating the conservation rules and held Japanese vessels and fishermen for alleged violations of the agreed-upon boundaries, but nevertheless, the fisheries issue appears to have been brought within mutual control, although the detention of Japanese fishermen by the Soviet Union continued to abrade the relationship.[28]

The trade between the Soviet Union and Japan was insignificant until 1956. The normalization of relations raised hopes in the USSR that Japan might be persuaded to take part in the development of Siberian resources. The sixth five-year plan, adopted in February 1956, held out to Japan the prospect of long-term supplies of fuel,

coal, and forest resources as well as a large market for Japanese
machinery and consumer goods. The first trade pact was concluded
in 1957 with mutually conferred most-favored-nation treatment. The
first substantial increase in the volume of trade, $147 million, was
registered in 1960 as a result of deferred payment facilities granted
by Japanese companies.

Thereafter, trade continued to increase impressively, awakening the interest of the big corporations in the Soviet Union as a trading partner.[29] In 1966 the pattern of trade agreements covering
three-year periods was changed to one of five-year periods to correspond to the Soviet five-year plans. When the volume of trade passed
the annual figure of $400 million, the Soviet Union found Japanese
business houses responsive to the idea of setting up an "unofficial"
Japanese-Soviet economic cooperation committee.[30] This committee held its first session in March 1966. The Soviet Union shifted
the emphasis from trade to economic collaboration and gradually unfolded what to the Japanese was an enticing as well as frightening
portfolio for the development of forest and energy resources in
Siberia and Sakhalin.

The Joint Economic Cooperation Committee (JECC) devoted its
first two years, as a Japanese newspaper put it, to little more than
"getting acquainted with one another."[31] However, the ice broke in
1968 when an agreement was signed for the development of Siberian
forest resources with Japanese technology and with Japanese credits
worth $.1 billion. In 1969 the committee decided on the construction
of a modern port at Nakhodka on the Wrangal Bay, and an agreement
was formalized in the following year.

It took the Japanese a little time to realize what the Soviets
knew from the beginning: economic cooperation between nations can
hardly remain nonpolitical. In 1970-71 it became quite clear to the
Japanese that they could not contribute to the development of
Siberian fuel resources without significantly adding to Soviet military power and helping the Soviet Union gain its strategic objectives
in Asia. The shrewd businessmen who constituted the Japanese delegations to the annual sessions of the JECC discovered that, although
it had not been the case when dealing with China, economics could
not be separated from politics while dealing with the Soviet Union.[32]
There was just not that much public opinion in Japan in favor of collaboration with the USSR. There was no Soviet lobby in Japan that
was remotely comparable to the Peking lobby.

The Soviet Union, which had been spending about 16 percent of
its annual budget for Siberian development, saw in the pressing need
of Japan for fuel an opportunity to secure much-needed technology
and capital for Siberian projects.[33] The Japanese had shown genuine
interest in exploiting the natural gas deposits on Northern Sakhalin to

feed the burgeoning industrial complex on the island of Hokkaido; however, they found in 1970 that the Soviet Union was not interested in exclusive development of these natural gas deposits but wanted to link the North Sakhalin project with a second natural gas project in Yukutsk and an oilfield development project at Tyumen. The Soviet explanation was that the deposits on North Sakhalin were too small for economical exploitation without simultaneous development of the much larger deposits in Yukutsk; in any case, development of the North Sakhalin natural gas would make no contribution to the development of Siberia.[34] The Japanese had visualized limited commercial collaboration between an export-oriented natural gas project on Sakhalin and the industrial complex at Hokkaido. They were now offered 10 billion cubic meters of natural gas a year from Sakhalin and Yukutsk or none at all! To consume this vast quantity, the pipeline would have to be expanded to Japan proper and the gas supplied to the Pacific belt zone. The larger dimensions of the new Soviet proposals inevitably raised questions of political and strategic import. Would it be safe to make an extensive industrial complex in Japan dependent on Soviet natural gas? Would the much-larger capital be forthcoming in the existing climate of Japanese-Soviet relations? How would China and the United States react?[35]

When it came to the question of oil, the differences between Soviet and Japanese approaches became ever larger. The Japanese were interested in the Tyumen oilfields as well as in the joint exploration of natural gas and oil on the continental shelf around Sakhalin. The development and transportation of oil would call for a pipeline 2,400 kilometers long to Irkutsk and, from there, another pipeline of 4,300 kilometers to Nakhodka. The project had unmistakable military implications, and it involved territory over which the Soviet Union and China were engaged in a cold war.[36] Nevertheless, it was a priority item for the JECC through 1973 as the world energy crisis obliged Japan to seek diversified sources of fuel supplies.

In September 1973, however, the Soviet Union drastically modified the quantity of crude it would export to Japan from the Tyumen oilfields. The original understanding was that the export to Japan, over a 20-year period, would range from 25 million tons of crude to 40 million tons a year when the project was completed. The Soviets now told the chairman of the oil subcommittee of the JECC, Hiroki Imasato, that the peak delivery would not exceed 25 million tons a year.[37] The Soviet Union, however, claimed that it was not deviating from the original commitment, since it would be exporting 15 million tons of oil products a year, including gasoline refined at the refinery to be built at Nakhodka, to a group of Japanese industries centering around Idemetsu Kosan, a corporation that had been doing business with the USSR since the mid-1950s.[38]

The Soviet strategy, as the Japanese understood it, was two-fold: (1) to utilize Japanese technology and credits as far as possible for Siberian development rather than for the purpose of meeting the energy demands of industries in Japan and (2) to broaden its clientele among the medium and small industrial units in Japan. This strategy met with immediate resistance in the Gaimusho (the Japanese Foreign Office). A Gaimusho "source" announced that the government had to take an "extremely cautious view" of the Tyumen oilfields project because the reduced annual crude quota had dampened the spirit of "political and business circles." Also, it would now be even more difficult to get the United States interested in joint investment in the project. Above all, China was showing "strong repulsion" to Japanese participation in the development of Siberian oil, which looked to Peking like "participation in the Soviet Union's operation for the encirclement of China."[39]

Undaunted by the Gaimushu recalcitrance and encouraged by the perception of the critical need of Japan for a stable long-term supply of energy, the Soviet leaders presented at the March 1974 session of the JECC an integrated portfolio of six Siberian projects for which they sought Japanese collaboration. These were (1) a paper mill with an annual output of 1.5 million tons in the Yeniseisk area north of Lake Baikal; (2) the Tyumen oilfields; (3) oil and natural gas prospecting on the Sakhalin continental shelf; (4) the natural gas project at Yukutsk; (5) the coking coal project at South Yukutsk; and (6) the forestry development project with the new port on Wrangel Bay. Some of these projects were open to third-party, especially U.S., participation. For all of the six projects, the Soviet Union asked for total credits worth $5 billion, half of which should be in U.S. currency. [40]

In late March the first basic contract for Japanese collaboration in some of these projects was signed, with provision for a Japanese bank loan of $450 million, and concrete agreements were reached on plans for prospecting for natural gas at Yukutsk and on the Sakhalin continental shelf. [41] The Tyumen oilfields project, however, presented Japan with further problems. The Soviet Union revised the project for the second time in two years. The original construction plan, as I have noted, included two pipelines; the second revision provided for the construction of 4,000 km of pipelines and 3,000 km of railroads. The Amur-Baikal Railway (to the Japanese, the Second Siberian Railroad) would be a double-track line beginning at Lena city and terminating at Komsomolsk Na Amur. The Soviets asked Japan for bank loans of $2.4 billion to cover the new project. [42]

The second revised project "stunned" the Japanese. The Soviet Union was asking them to finance the construction of a project that would alter the strategic face of the Siberian Far East! Moreover, the Soviet leaders made it clear that they regarded the six Siberian projects as a package and that they intended to divert from each project some funds to build the new railway, for which they neither needed nor were asking for Japanese participation. All they wanted was to use part of the Japanese loan for the Tyumen oilfields project to buy material and equipment for the railway. It was nothing more than a trade transaction. [43]

The Soviet project was tantalizing to the recession-caught Japanese transportation and steel industries, but opposition came from the Gaimusho as well as from the Japan Defense Authority (JDA). Both looked at it from the strategic-political angle and from the angle of Japanese relations with China. If the project were built, a Gaimusho source warned, it would sharply bolster the military strength of the Soviet Union in the Far East and strengthen the transportation base of the Soviet Pacific fleet. The JDA observed that the railway would increase the "Soviet military threat to China" and "directly affect" Sino-Japanese relations. [44]

The Soviet leaders had predicated their strong bargaining posture on the serious economic and resource crisis in Japan, and events proved that they were not entirely wrong in their appreciation of the Japanese predicament. Immediately after Prime Minister Tanaka's return from Moscow (see below), representatives of the leading corporations impressed upon him the urgency of economic collaboration with the Soviet Union, and from what Tanaka told them it appeared that he had already committed his government to the Tyumen oilfields plan. [45] He announced at a meeting with officials of the Ministry of International Trade and Industry that 80 percent of the funds for the project would be provided by the Export-Import Bank and that the details would be worked out in negotiations between the Keidanren (Federation of Japanese Economic Organizations) and a person of ministerial rank to be appointed by the Soviet government. [46]

Japan, however, was not prepared to go into the Tyumen oilfields project without U.S. participation, which was needed to dispel both Chinese and Japanese fears. Japanese and U.S. firms concluded an agreement with the Soviet Union in April 1974 for joint exploration of natural gas in Yukutsk with $1 billion in credit. [47] In June Japan agreed to contribute capital and equipment for the development of coking coal at Yukutsk. This was followed by an accord on prospecting for gas and oil on the Sakhalin continental shelf, for which Japan agreed to give credits worth $100 million. By April 1975 the Japanese committed well over $1.5 billion in credits for the development of three major and two relatively minor Siberian projects, and negotiations were going on for another $1 billion credit for the construction of two large pulp-and-paper plants. Each of

these projects contributed directly or indirectly to the construction
of the Baikal-Amur Railway. [48]

In 1974 the Soviet Union sought Japanese cooperation in building a 4 million kilowatt nuclear power plant in Sakhalin. They asked
for credits to buy "facilities" in Japan and offered repayment in nuclear energy transmitted through a submarine cable to be built between Sakhalin and Hokkaido. The Soviet offer was discussed in Moscow with a visiting Keidanren mission led by its chairman, Kogoro
Uemura. Earlier, the Soviet Union had offered cooperation in the
entire nuclear fuel cycle from mining of natural uranium to refining,
molding and processing, and reprocessing.

In March it had offered the sale of enriched uranium at lower
than U.S. prices: an obviously attractive offer since the United
States, the sole supplier of enriched uranium to Japan, had notified
Tokyo that it would not renew the existing uranium supply agreement
when it expired in 1982. The immediate Japanese reaction to the
Soviet offer had been mixed. The government predictably reacted
with "extreme caution." Some of the questions raised in official and
business circles were as follows: What kind of safeguards would the
Soviet Union ask to prevent weapons-purpose use of enriched uranium?
Would the Soviet Union get unwarranted insight into Japan's nuclear
aspirations? Could Japan depend on the USSR for a stable supply of
enriched uranium and nuclear-generated electricity? A section of
the press, however, took a milder view of the Soviet offer and pleaded
for an objective response to it. Japan needed to diversify its sources
of enriched uranium imports, it was argued. It had already contracted to buy enriched uranium from France. The Soviet Union,
which had constructed the world's first nuclear power plant, was engaged with the United States, France, and Britain in cooperation for
the development of nuclear technology for peaceful purposes. Japan
could benefit from nuclear collaboration with the USSR, and the government therefore should look in this direction "in a forward-looking
manner." [49]

To be sure, until the middle of 1975 the Soviet Union could not
get from Japan as much participation in Siberian development as it
had asked for; but what it got probably surpassed its own expectations. The first government-to-government trade agreement, covering the period 1971-75, was concluded in September 1971. It projected an increase in the total volume of trade from $791 million in
1971 to $1,277 million in 1975.

Actually, the trade turnover proved to be much larger. According to a West German newspaper, Japanese exports to the Soviet
bloc rose from $2.1 billion in 1973 to $4.2 billion in 1974, and imports from $2.8 billion to $3.6 billion. The share of the socialist
bloc in the total exports of Japan grew from 5.7 percent to 7.6

percent, while its share in the total imports of Japan declined from
7.3 percent to 5.9 percent. [50] Each of the major Siberian projects
locked the two nations in long-term collaboration. A Soviet reporter
wrote the following in April 1975:

> Now we have the Sakhalin project covering a ten-
> year period, the Yukut project for 20 years, the
> purchase of equipment in credits extended over
> 8 to 16 years. . . . The year 2000 . . . is
> featuring more and more in business transactions
> between [the two nations]. . . . In other words,
> there is mutual trust . . . and there is belief in
> a peaceful future. [51]

Political Thaw

The postwar political deadlock between the Soviet Union and
Japan loosened up under the impact of the Sino-U.S. diplomatic breakthrough in the summer of 1971. The July 15 announcement that
President Nixon would visit Peking in early 1972 on his own initiative
shocked Moscow as much as it unnerved Tokyo. As the United States
and China turned to one another over the divide of 22 years, the
Soviet Union and Japan also turned toward one another, as if in a
spontaneous reaction.

At the United Nations the chief Japanese delegate, Aichi, sought
a meeting with Gromyko in September to find out if Moscow were willing to back, directly or indirectly, the Japanese effort to keep Taiwan
a member of the world body while conceding the China seat to Peking.
Gromyko reaffirmed the Soviet stand on the question of Chinese representation but was quite impressed with the insight he obtained into
the Japanese nervousness about a Sino-U.S. rapprochement. Aichi
invited Gromyko to visit Japan. In less than three weeks the Kremlin
notified the Japanese government that the Soviet foreign minister
would be in Tokyo in January to attend the second bilateral ministerial
conference. [52] The first one had been held in 1957.

Between the announcement of the visit and Gromyko's arrival in
Tokyo, Soviet-Japanese mutual perceptions became largely parallel.
Both had genuine apprehensions about a Sino-U.S. rapprochement;
but each saw the other in a predicament that was worse than its own.
The Soviet leaders saw Japan as brutally jolted by the humiliating way
it had been treated by its mentor, the United States. They concluded
that Japanese-U.S. relations had reached a turning point and that the
shaken Japanese trust in the United States would not be easily restored. The Soviet leaders also saw Japan as deeply disturbed and

hurt by the exaltation of China, by one stroke of U.S. diplomacy, to
the level of a world power at par with the United States and the USSR.
They had a vision of a Japan genuinely afraid that the United States
would use its friendship with China to limit its economic and political
influence in Asia. At a slight remove from these images lurked the
Soviet leaders' own fear of the emergence of a compact by the United
States, Japan, and China to contain the Soviet Union.[53]

The Japanese saw a Soviet Union the primary foreign policy
concern of which was how to contain China. If China and the United
States came close to one another, Moscow would be in dire need of a
friendly Japan, and it would therefore do everything in its power to
prevent a Sino-Japanese detente. The Japanese also saw the focus
of Soviet diplomacy shifting to Asia, where it had already shored up
substantial gains by intervening in the war in the subcontinent. A
leading Japanese newspaper wrote as follows:

> What is most important is to grasp the strategic
> moves of Soviet diplomacy, which can be called
> very positive and bold, in the midst of the grow-
> ing tendency of international politics toward a
> multi-polarization. The Soviets have secured
> recognition of the status quo in Europe and con-
> solidated the "Brezhnev structure" at home;
> under this strategic set-up, they have a sys-
> tematic plan to advance into Asia, diplomatical-
> ly, politically and militarily. As a result of
> Pakistan's defeat in the December war, the
> southern advance of the Soviet Union has sur-
> passed the achievements of Czarist Russia. In
> June 1969 Brezhnev put forward a concept of
> collective Asian security. If there is a Nixon
> grand strategy, there is also a rivaling
> Brezhnev grand design to counter the ap-
> proaching Sino-U.S. rapprochement, the ef-
> fects of Peking's presence at the United Na-
> tions. . . . It is said that the aspect of the
> Soviet Union's southward advance is symbol-
> ically manifested in the moves of the Soviet
> navy. The treaties concluded with Egypt and
> India have secured the Soviet navy a safe outlet
> to the Mediterranean and the Indian Ocean. Is
> it certain that the Soviet approach to Japan does
> not contain the same kind of strategic consider-
> ation?[54]

The Soviet initiative of 1971-72 proved to be more productive economically than politically. Neither among the LDP factional leaders nor in the Sato cabinet was there a consensus on political cooperation with the Soviet Union. The whole concept was so traumatic for the Japanese political elite that it was not even seriously considered in the concealed and quite mystical decision-making apparatus in Tokyo. [55]

Besides, Sato himself was fast losing his grip on political power. He had succeeded in getting the revised U.S.-Japanese security treaty accepted by the Diet and the Japanese people, but his negative China policy, which looked foolish in the face of the coming Nixon visit to Peking, had humiliated him in the eyes of his own people. It was quite clear in January 1972 that Sato's days as prime minister were numbered; he was definitely not in a position to initiate a policy of political cooperation with the USSR even if he wanted to, which he did not. [56]

Nevertheless, Gromyko's two days in Tokyo in January 1972 were not politically barren. They marked a thaw in Soviet-Japanese political relations. In effect Gromyko had offered Japan a compromise on the Northern Territory; a stable, assured resource base in Siberia; the growing Siberian market for Japanese machinery and consumer goods; Soviet support with which to counter hegemonic thrusts by China; and a military role for Japan in the Pacific region, preferably as an independent power but, if Japan so desired, even in conjunction with the United States.

All Gromyke specifically asked for was an assurance that Japan would not develop relations with China to the detriment of Soviet interests. What he was able to get from Japan was, in effect, an assurance that no rapid normalization of relations with China was foreseen and that Japan had no intention of hurting Soviet interests in the Pacific-Asian region. [57] He also received encouraging Japanese responses to the possibility of cooperation in Siberian development.

The communique issued on his talks with the Japanese leaders was deceptive. It did not mention the Northern Territory, although the Japanese had made it one of the major topics of discussion; nor did it reveal the political and strategic issues that dominated the talks. It merely said that the two governments would start negotiations for a peace treaty before the end of 1972; that they would hold bilateral annual consultations at the ministerial level on major issues concerning the two nations; and that they would make efforts "for realizing reciprocal visits of the heads of the two Governments." [58] In the economic field the Japanese government not only agreed to adopt a positive attitude toward cooperation but also to associate itself with the "unofficial" negotiations. It also agreed to extend cooperation to the scientific, technological, and cultural spheres.

That Moscow was not fully satisfied with the results of
Gromyko's visit is a conclusion that seems to be justified by the
brief notices the visit received in the Soviet press.[59] However,
Soviet diplomacy in Japan was now to seek new directions. The improvement of relations called for patience and persistence, qualities
in which Soviet diplomacy is seldom wanting. Much depended on what
the other major international actors did and did not do in respect to
Japan and the rest of Asia. In Soviet commentaries on Japan, the
references to militarism largely disappeared and the criticism of
its security treaty with the United States was muted. The focus was
on the rising Japanese economic status; on the way this status came
into conflict with the U.S. domination of Asia; on Japanese trade and
fiscal problems with the United States; on the conflict of interests
between the monopoly capital of Japan and southeast Asian nationalism, and on the interimperialist rivalries between Japan, the United
States, and the European Economic Community (EEC).

In Japan, on the other hand, the results of the Gromyko visit
were received with greater enthusiasm. Sankei described it as "an
epoch-making event," while Mainichi said that it had produced "great
results." Foreign Minister Fukuda noted a change of nuance in the
Soviet attitude to the Northern Territory. What pleased the Japanese
most was the Soviet recognition of the importance of Japan. Moscow
now appeared to be eager to appease Japan, if only because of its
fear that China would draw closer to the United States. The Japanese
government found in the Soviet Union some strength in dealing with
Peking, and its foreign ministry drew the lesson that Japan was now
inextricably caught in an intensifying Sino-Soviet conflict and that
while dealing with one it must closely watch the reaction of the other.[60]

There was no official Chinese comment on Gromyko's talks
with the Japanese leaders. However, on the eve of Gromyko's arrival in Tokyo, Peking made it known through the leader of a visiting
Japanese businessmen's delegation that "it is better for Japanese
businessmen to tie up with China, which abounds in resources, without putting [Japanese] energy into the development of Siberia."[61]
A Japanese correspondent reported from Peking that in the Chinese
perception, the Soviet Union was now appeasing the Japanese militarists, who were opposed to normalization of Sino-Japanese relations. The Soviet Union was offering Japan "a recognized zone of
expansion in Northeast Asia" and keeping security relations with the
United States intact.[62]

The Soviet leaders were evidently more nervous about Nixon's
visit to Peking before it took place than after its concrete results became known. The Tass summary of the Shanghai communique carried in Izvestia of March 1, 1972, noted the wide divergence of views
of the United States and China on most of the major issues discussed

and the limited area of detente reached between the U.S. President and the Chinese leaders. The most important gain, it noted, was that "political contacts" had been established between Washington and Peking. [63] In any case, Soviet analysts found little evidence that Nixon and Chou En-lai had put together the scaffolding of an alliance of the United States, Japan, and China against the USSR. On the contrary, the Sino-U.S. detente appeared more to have bruised U.S.-Japanese relations. Japan, the foremost U.S. ally in Asia since the war, found itself left out in the cold as the United States proceeded to repair its relations with China, the historical rival of Japan in Asia. A report in Pravda indicated that the Japanese government believed that Washington and Peking were joining together to create a new balance of power in the world and that the foreign affairs ministry was worried that in moving close to China the United States was sacrificing the interests of Japan. [64]

The trauma of the approaching U.S.-Chinese rapprochement was indeed far greater for Japan than for the Soviet Union. The Japanese government noted with dismay that in the fall of 1971, while it had been toiling at the United Nations, with full U.S. backing, to marshal votes for its "dual representation" theory for China and Taiwan, Henry Kissinger had been making secret trips to Peking to beat a path for the presidential pilgrimage. [65] The Japanese press comments were full of anguish, hesitating to speak the unspeakable and reluctant to think the unthinkable. The Japanese saw their own and U.S. China policy as moving on parallel lines betraying a "basic strategic difference." It was not unlikely, warned Mainichi, that the United States would work with China to curb the economic position of Japan in southeast Asia and prevent a revival of Japanese militarism. [66] Other newspapers noted that the United States was now pursuing an independent China policy without consultation with its principal ally in Asia and that Nixon's visit to Peking was part of a new U.S. global strategy, in the framing of which Japan had been assigned no part at all. These perceptions reinforced the demand that Japan work out its own independent China policy and make an independent contribution to the lowering of international tensions. [67]

In February the Japanese looked with anguished interest at Nixon's foreign policy report to Congress and came to the widely shared conclusion that the U.S. president was not willing to concede to Japan an autonomous role in Asia. Nixon was seeking to build a new five-power international order and a four-power balance in the Pacific-Asian region. Japan was ostensibly given a crucial role in ensuring peace and stability in Asia, but in reality it must play this role "leaning entirely on the U.S." and sharing the burden of the U.S. security system. The theoretical concept of equality and reciprocity was mutilated by the operational expectation that the allies of the

United States, Japan particularly, would gradually take over the heavy U.S. military and security burden without trying to interfere with the U.S. monopoly of political initiatives. During the transition from the politics of confrontation to the politics of negotiation, the allies of the United States were expected to strengthen its negotiating position and not to make their own independent contribution to a global relaxation of tensions. This was nothing short of "thrusting Japan away," of asking Japan to be happy with "an American peace in Asia." It was nothing short of giving Japan notice that when it came to the question of advancing or protecting U.S. interests, the United States was "not prepared to make any allowances" for the economic power of Japan. [68]

The Shanghai communique appeared to reassure Japan as much as it did the Soviet Union that the concrete results of the Nixon visit were less traumatic than the visit itself. Mainichi observed that the talks had not produced anything "earthshaking," and that there had been no "drastic" change in U.S. policy toward Taiwan. Government sources "welcomed" the removal of the basic cause of tension in Asia, namely the confrontation between the United States and China. Most Japanese now saw "fear of the Soviet Union" as the principal motivation that had led China to invite Nixon to Peking; the Sino-U.S. rapprochement would therefore be primarily directed against the USSR. Most commentators agreed that the Nixon visit to China had changed the "framework of international relations in Asia" and that it was now essential that Japan seek a "new U.S.-Japanese cooperation structure," revise its stand on Taiwan, normalize relations with China, and steadily improve relations with the Soviet Union. [69]

The almost parallel Soviet and Japanese perceptions of the "concrete results" of Nixon's visit to Peking provided no great stimulus for closer relations between Moscow and Tokyo. For Japan, the compelling task was now to normalize relations with China, independently of the United States, and thus retrieve its self-image and affirm its importance to the United States; for Moscow, the most important task was to make U.S.-Soviet detente the mainstream of the world's immutable transition to peaceful coexistence. Soviet analysts expected several other streams to gather strength during the transition period. These were the relations of China with the United States, of Japan with the USSR, of China with Japan, and of Western Europe with the Soviet bloc. All of these streams were to be subdued by the mainstream of U.S.-Soviet detente, which alone could keep the Sino-Soviet cold war under control. [70] For different reasons, the Nixon administration also appeared to share this perspective.

Even before Nixon's visit to Peking, the fate of the Sato cabinet had been doomed. The LDP had split into two nearly equal

factions over Sato's China policy, and maneuvers had begun to re-
place him with another prime minister.[71] After the Nixon visit,
Sato tried to retrieve some of the lost ground by conceding before a
Diet committee that "Taiwan is part of the People's Republic of
China."[72] He also established diplomatic relations with Mongolia,
as he had agreed to do during Gromyko's visit to Tokyo, and sent an
unofficial mission to Hanoi to initiate economic relations with North
Vietnam.

All of this, however, was too little and too late. The serious
balance of payments crisis with the United States, of which the "textile war" was only one of the manifestations, could not be settled
without seriously reducing the global trade surplus of Japan within a
very short time, without reducing exports to the United States and
increasing U.S. imports into Japan, without opening the Japanese
economy to a larger inflow of U.S. investment, and without revaluing
the yen. These highly unpalatable, self-inflicted injuries had to be
compensated elsewhere. The business houses and LDP factional
leaders saw China as the only country from which substantial compensation could come, and they were mortified that the Nixon visit
had given U.S. businessmen a head start over Japan in the race for
the China market. They eased Sato out in July 1972, since with him
at the helm in Japan, there could be no dramatic improvement in relations with China.[73]

The inauguration of Kakei Tanaka as prime minister was a
"somewhat unusual phenomenon" in Japanese politics. He was the
first leader of the "career politicians' group" in LDP to become
prime minister; his predecessors had all been bureaucratic politicians.[74] He was chosen for his vitality and executive ability; his
choice meant "an infusion of new blood in the hardened arteries of a
deeply conservative political structure dominated by thoroughbreds
and bureaucrats."[75]

Tanaka promised the development of a welfare society, an environmental facelift for the entire Japanese archipelago, and independent action in the realm of foreign policy. Although normalization of relations with China was his first priority, Tanaka's installation as prime minister was not unwelcome to the Soviet Union. As
minister in charge of MITI in the Sato cabinet, he had shown some
enthusiasm for cooperation in Siberian development and had often indicated that this could reduce the "thick American shadow" over
Japan.[76] He was not a man of the Zaibatsu (big business), with which
he lacked inseki, by which the Japanese mean "usual inside relationship." Nor was he an intellectual, a member of the prestigious
Todai Club. Last but not least, he was relatively young and stood
for a generous infusion of young blood in the palsied Diet galleries
of LDP.[77]

When Tanaka went to Washington to meet with Nixon, Soviet
analysts believed that the theme of the talks "was not so much bilateral trade and economic relations as the very nature of relations"
between Japan and the United States. A reexamination of the "foundations of Japanese-American relations" had become necessary because "Japan's growing economic potential is altering its position
within this alliance."[78] In spite of the sweeping concessions made
by Tanaka to balance trade between Japan and the United States, or
probably because of them, the Soviet Union expected the "contradictions between the world's two largest imperialist powers" to continue and even widen, compelling Japan to take independent decisions
to protect and enhance its vital interests. Tanaka's pilgrimage to
Peking in September 1972 was seen more charitably in Moscow than
in the capitals of southeast Asia. It was a mistake, Soviet analysts
asserted, to hasten to normalize relations with China merely because
the United States had slapped Japan in the face while moving earlier
in that direction. This undue haste had enabled China to get a much
better deal than it would have gotten if Tanaka had gone to Peking
from a position of strength and not one of weakness. It also activated
Chinese hegemonists and Japanese militarists to strive for cooperation against the Soviet Union. On the other hand, the fact that Tanaka
had acted independently of Washington and was anxious to deliver a
Tanaka shokku to the United States demonstrated the qualitative
change that had occurred in the hitherto closed relationship between
Japan and the United States.[79]

In the Soviet perception, international relations were developing in a favorable way on a number of fronts as 1972 yielded to the
new year. The agreements concluded in Paris in January 1973 paved
the way for complete withdrawal of U.S. troops from Indochina. The
crisis of the capitalist system was seen to be worsening. Each of
the major industrialized nations was plunged into inflation and business recession, and the fiscal war continued to reduce the value of
the dollar. The world energy crisis began to cast its warning shadows.
The Soviet Union had shown no particular anxiety to open peace treaty
negotiations with Japan since Gromyko's visit to Tokyo.[80] Economic
relations were nevertheless growing steadily, though far below Soviet
needs and expectations.

Since the fall of 1972, diplomatic soundings had been going on
for a meeting between Brezhnev and Tanaka. The Japanese premier
had to come to Moscow after his journey to Peking. There was some
problem with the timing. Tanaka apparently wanted a summit in the
summer: this was the main content of his letter to Brezhnev in
March 1973. The letter was delivered personally by the Japanese
ambassador, his first meeting with the general secretary, a gesture,
on Brezhnev's part, that he was serious about improving relations

with Japan. The theme was quickly picked up by such leading specialists on Japanese affairs as Leonid Zamyatin and Vladimir Kudryavtsev.
The political contacts that had been going on between the Soviet Union
and Japan, they said, should now lead to negotiations for a peace
treaty. If no progress in that direction had been made so far, it was
because Japan had tried to play diplomatic games with the USSR. However, "it is apparent that a realistic outlook is beginning to prevail in
Japan with respect to development of relations with the Soviet Union
in the present international situation."[81]

The Brezhnev-Tanaka summit was fixed for August but was
shifted, at Soviet request, to October. Although the Soviet leaders
were preoccupied all of these months with such important issues as
Brezhnev's meeting with Nixon and the gathering storm in the Middle
East, they apparently devoted considerable time and attention to a
close look at Japan and its maverick prime minister. According to
Japanese and Soviet sources, they came to the conclusion that, first,
the Sino-Japanese rapprochement did not offer Japan much relief in
its economic crisis, nor did it appear to have given Japan a new
identity in Asia and the world.

Second, Japanese relations with the United States continued to
remain in disarray, with little possibility of equilibrium being restored in the near future. Third, the economic and resource crisis
had considerably eroded Tanaka's popularity with his own people.
Furthermore, Japanese economic primacy in Southeast Asia was
meeting with an increasing nationalist challenge, a phenomenon not
particularly distasteful, both to the United States and China.[82]

The Japanese perception of 1973 did not exactly bubble with
self-confidence. The Gaimusho, in an "unofficial" appraisal, saw
the triangular relationship of the United States, the USSR, and China
as dominating international relations; Japan was caught in the swirls
of this volatile relationship both as a pawn and a potential catalyst.
The appraisal expected both the United States and China to be more
inward looking in 1973 than in the year before. The United States,
however, would fasten its diplomacy mainly on its detente with the
Soviet Union and maintain its "power position." China's main effort
would be to improve its relations with the United States and to normalize relations with its neighbors so that it could take on the Soviet
Union with greater self-confidence.

As for the Soviet Union, its principal foreign policy task was
to contain China; with that in view it would strive to strengthen the
detente with the United States and further improve relations with
Japan. The Sino-Soviet conflict would have a spillover effect on international relations in most of Asia.[83] Outside the Gaimusho, some
Japanese saw the triangular U.S.-Soviet-Chinese relationship as
highly unstable, mainly because of the huge power gap between China

and either superpower. If the United States sought Chinese friendship to check the Soviet Union, then Moscow would be obliged to look
for new allies to balance its two adversaries. [84]

As preparations for the Brezhnev-Tanaka meeting went on, the
Soviets saw the Japanese prime minister in a weak bargaining position both domestically and internationally. The Japanese had almost
mirror perceptions of the USSR: it needed large-scale participation
by Japan in Siberian development, not only to balance the new Tokyo-
Peking relationship, but also to counter the friendship between the
United States and China.

These mirror perceptions led to some hard maneuvering to
prepare the agenda for the summit. Moscow informed Tokyo through
an eminent Japanese nonofficial, Shigeyoshi Matsumae, the president
of Tokyo University (the Todai), that it would like to put Asian collective security at the top of the agenda. Within the framework of a new
security system for Asia, the questions of the Soviet-Japanese peace
treaty and of the Northern Territory, as well as of Siberian development, could be discussed. The same suggestion was also conveyed
to the Gaimusho through an unnamed member of the CPSU central
committee who was in charge of Japanese affairs. According to this
official, "Asian security should come first. The territorial question
is a minor question that can be settled if a peaceful coexistence
structure in Asia is established firmly."[85] What Brezhnev was trying to tell the Japanese leaders in the fall of 1973, far more clearly
than Gromyko could have done in January 1972, was that the Soviet
Union would be flexible and even magnanimous on the territorial
question if Japan were to take a constructive official position on a
collective security system for Asia.[86]

The "current of history" took Tanaka to Moscow in October,
as he himself put it to the Japanese reporters traveling with him in
a special JAL plane. He was strongly impressed by the vastness of
Russia and the richness of the Russian earth, which, he mused, must
have resources "probably for one to two thousand years." He was
in a fighting mood, slightly nervous, and therefore eager to show his
self-confidence. "My journey is meaningful in itself," Tanaka reflected, "it does not have to be made meaningful." He was the first
Japanese premier to visit the Soviet Union in 17 years; none before
him had ever journeyed to Washington, Peking, Moscow, Paris,
Bonn, and London, and this had all been done in less than one and a
half years. "All figures are borne in my mind," he assured the reporters. "No one will be able to argue me down."[87]

Tanaka had reason to be nervous and tough. His visit to the
Soviet Union had aroused a uniform nationalist demand in Japan that
he return, if not with the four northern islands, then at least with a
Soviet promise to link the return of the islands with the conclusion of

the peace treaty. His confabulations with the LDP factional leaders and with his cabinet colleagues had led to a rigid brief for him and Foreign Minister Ohira: they must push to the fore the settlement of the territorial question and make this the premise for the peace treaty, and economic cooperation in Siberia should be made contingent on a settlement of the territorial issue. They could listen to all the Russians had to say about the Soviet design for collective Asian security, but they must not give any impression that Japan would take part in a Soviet-sponsored security system.[88] Tanaka had been criticized at home for giving in too much to the Chinese; he must salvage his image by showing his toughness in Moscow. The popularity of his government had slumped sharply. A diplomatic success in Moscow might balance his failure to check inflation and rising prices at home. Tanaka had made a dramatic departure from the traditionally impersonal style of Japanese diplomacy, and now he saw himself a prisoner of the popular expectations he had aroused.[89]

At the summit Brezhnev appeared to be more accommodating than Tanaka. He did not raise the Asian collective security question directly at all; nor did he object to having Tanaka raise the territorial issue. The summit, nevertheless, was rough going because Tanaka doggedly pursued the territorial question, returning to it every time he spoke and arguing his points at length. Reportedly Brezhnev was so "disgusted" with Tanaka's style that he was reluctant to join the second day's session. When at that session too Tanaka stuck to the territorial issue, Brezhnev, according to a Soviet source quoted by a Japanese newspaper, "finally exploded in anger. . . . He was so angry that he told the prime minister to stop discussing the matter." The Soviet source told this newspaper, "If Tanaka's approach had been more moderate, Brezhnev might have permitted the employment [in the joint communique] of expressions more advantageous to the Japanese side."[90]

In fact, the Soviet position on the Northern Territory was no longer rigid. Brezhnev had told the CPSU central committee in December 1972 that the Soviet-Japanese summit meeting would try to settle "questions remaining from the time of the second world war and to provide a treaty basis for relations between our countries. We seek a mutually acceptable accord on the entire range of questions under discussion."[91] On another occasion the CPSU had agreed with a delegation of the Japanese Communist Party that the peace treaty should be linked with the return of the smaller islands of Habomai and Shikotan to Japan, leaving the status of the two larger ones, Kunashiri and Etorofu, for future negotiation.[92] On October 11, 1973, Pravda and Izvestia, in reporting Tanaka's luncheon for the Soviet leaders, printed the prime minister's statement that he had discussed with the Soviet side the question of "the conclusion of a peace treaty based on a resolution of the territorial question which is the most important unsolved problem in our relations."[93] This was indicative of Soviet agreement or acknowledgment that without a settlement of the territorial issue there would be no political breakthrough between the USSR and Japan.

In the joint communique there was no direct reference to the Northern Territory; all that the Japanese delegation could obtain, after hard bargaining, was the following oblique reference:

> Realizing that the settlement of unresolved questions remaining from the time of World War II and the conclusion of a peace treaty would contribute to the establishment of genuine good neighbor and friendly relations between the two countries, the two sides held talks on questions involving the content of a peace treaty. The two sides agreed to continue talks on the conclusion of a peace treaty between the two countries at an appropriate time in 1974.[94]

It seems reasonable to infer that Brezhnev wanted a peace treaty that would provide the framework for political and strategic cooperation between the Soviet Union and Japan for peace and security in Asia without any formal assault on the Japanese security relationship with the United States. If Japan agreed to this kind of a peace treaty, the Soviet Union would go a long way to satisfy the Japanese demand for return of the Northern Territory.

In the field of economic cooperation, Tanaka evidently went much beyond the brief he had been given in Tokyo prior to his departure for Moscow. He agreed to involve the Japanese government in the negotiating process within the framework of the JECC and also to have direct periodic intergovernmental discussions. The Soviet leaders preferred exclusive Japanese participation in Siberian projects but conceded that third-party participation was not "ruled out."[95] Another plus point for Siberian development was the conclusion of an agreement for scientific and technological cooperation, as well as an accord for cooperation in the field of peaceful uses of nuclear energy. [96]

In assessing the results of the Moscow summit, the Japanese newspapers referred to the "sternness of international politics" and the "hard realities of the outside world," which made it extremely difficult for a country like Japan to pursue an autonomous foreign policy. They noted the poor returns from Tanaka's meetings with the French president, the West German chancellor, and the British prime minister: there was little hospitality in Western Europe for Japanese capital and goods. Similarly, the USSR was determined not

to return the Northern Territory: "The wall of Moscow is thick."
The Moscow talks failed to be politically productive because the "mo-
tives" of the two sides were different. The Soviet leaders sought to
improve relations with Japan as part of their world strategy. Japan
was for Moscow "a steppingstone toward Asia." Japan, on the other
hand, had no comprehensive foreign policy strategy. Its eyes were
riveted on the narrow issue of the Northern Territory. Tanaka had
tried to use Japanese relations with China and the United States as
levers, only to realize that these were not strong enough to bend the
tough denizens of the Kremlin. [97]

In fact it was Japan rather than the Soviet Union that had to
yield on the Northern Territory. Tanaka, as noted, agreed in Moscow that Japan would participate in Siberian development despite non-
resolution of the territorial question. He even committed the Export-
Import Bank to provide 80 percent of the credits Japan might be required to put in for the development of the Tyumen oilfields. After
his return from Moscow Ohira said that the territorial issue could
be settled only in the course of development of Japanese-Soviet relations (thus conceding the basic Soviet position): "it would not be
proper for Japan to follow parallel lines forever," meaning that Japan
could not go on making a resolution of the territorial question a precondition for its involvement in Siberian projects. [98] A section of the
Japanese press pleaded for greater understanding of the Soviet stand
on the Northern Territory. Soviet "caution" was dictated by the politics of postwar Europe and the Soviet territorial problem with China.
Besides, one of the islands, Kunashiri, had been developed as a fisheries base, and there might be considerable domestic opposition to
its return to Japan. Japan should also take into account Soviet fears
that, once restored to Japanese sovereignty, these islands might be
developed as military bases. [99]

The debate within and outside the Japanese government on the
results of the Moscow meeting led to a broad consensus on three issues. First, the diplomatic explorations by Japan in three continents
had only confirmed the Japanese national policy not to dismantle the
existing structure of its international relations, that is, its security
relations with the United States, but only to try to "add some plus
points to it." Second, Japan could not, especially in the circumstances created by the world energy crisis and the global recession,
refuse to participate in Siberian development, and that participation
should be determined by the viability of each project and the capital
resources available. Also, Japan should not go in for the oilfields
project without simultaneous U.S. participation. Third, in improving its relations with the USSR, Japan must take care not to alienate
China. [100]

In 1974 the Japanese government tried without success to persuade any one of the three top Soviet leaders to visit Tokyo. Tanaka
wrote to Brezhnev and Kosygin and received their replies. Moscow
did not show any eagerness to resume negotiations for the peace
treaty. The Japanese government had no alternative to making "pro-
motion of economic cooperation for Siberian development and other
purposes" the first task of its diplomacy with the USSR in 1974. Conclusion of the peace treaty with a settlement of the territorial issue
now came second. Powerful elements in the LDP wanted to use
China to gain concessions from the Soviet Union. "These people hold
the view," reported Asahi in September 1974, "that Japan must rely
on the power of China, which is in confrontation with the Soviet Union,
if it wants to bring the Soviet Union, which has been reluctant to take
up the territorial problem with Japan, to the conference table."[101]
Japan initiated peace treaty negotiations with China, only to find that
concluding a treaty on the terms insisted on by Peking would jeopar-
dize its relations with the Soviet Union.

For the Soviet Union the Brezhnev-Tanaka meeting was a positive gain, but not positive enough to warrant too much optimism. The
meeting put a governmental stamp on the economic breakthrough. It
improved the political weather in Japan, but there was no sunshine
yet. A leading Soviet analyst now perceived Japan as a country of
"great potentialities" that had "still not found itself." Its ruling bourgeoisie, as in the United States, was divided among those who wanted
relations with the Soviet Union to improve markedly and those who
either wanted no improvement at all or would permit only slow and
cautious steps toward improvement.[102] The hard core of opponents
of improved relations belonged to the military, to the big corporations,
and to the older generation of bureaucratic politicians, whose memory
of the past prevented them from taking a bold step to the future.

Opposition also came from the powerful China lobby. Peking
was able to influence the domestic politics of Japan to a degree that
was still beyond the grasp of the Soviet Union. Among the intellectuals in the universities and the mass media, the ideological-cultural
pull toward China was matched by a cynical power-political perception
of the Soviet Union. In short, in comparison with that of the United
States and China, the partisanship of the Soviet Union in Japan was
still weak, amorphous, and ineffectual.[103]

The Soviet Union was directing great efforts in Japan toward
filling this vacuum. The gains shored up between 1972 and 1975 were
not quantitatively insignificant, although their political value was
still not kinetic. Nearly 65,000 Japanese visited the USSR during
these three years as tourists or members of official and unofficial
delegations. Some of the big business houses, especially those in
the fields of steel, shipbuilding, construction, machine tools,

refrigeration, electric power, and oil exploration, became supporters of Siberian development.

The Japanese-Soviet Trade Association set up in 1973 became
a lobby of some importance. By early 1975, 22 Japanese firms
opened offices in Moscow. Several hundred medium-sized and small
Japanese enterprises formed associations of their own to press for
major shares of Siberian business. The USSR-Japan Association
had 15 chapters in 1975 in the Soviet Union, from Sochi on the Black
Sea to Nakhodka in the Far East. Its counterpart in Japan is said to
have as many chapters. The Dietmen's League to Promote Friendship between Japan and the Soviet Union, which was set up in 1973,
is said to have 500 members. The agreements for scientific, technological, and cultural exchanges have enabled thousands of Japanese,
including scientists, technicians, university professors, architects,
composers, writers, actors, and artists, to visit the USSR. There
is even a Japanese-Soviet expert committee for peace in Asia, which
held its second session in Moscow in 1974.

A consular agreement has led to the opening of Soviet consulates
in Osaka and Sapporo and of Japanese consulates in Nakhodka and
Leningrad. Soviet and Japanese planes fly through Siberia, and there
is also an air route between Niigata and Khabarovsk. The leading
Japanese trade unions have linkages with the Soviet Trade Union Congress, with which they hold joint sessions. In a major cultural relations drive, the Soviets translated 439 Japanese books into Russian
in 1973 alone, among which were works by leading writers such as
Yusanari Kawabata, Kenzaburo Oe, Takeshi Kaiko, Shusaku Endo,
and Seicho Matsumoto. Hundreds of Russian books translated into
Japanese are sold in Japan at nominal prices. Front organizations
have been formed among elected local officials, and delegations of
prefectural governors, mayors, and local assemblymen have visited
the Soviet Union.[104] Major Japanese newspapers and news agencies
station their reports in Moscow. A small corps of Soviet correspondents reports systematically on Japanese affairs. The major opposition political parties, including the Japanese Socialist party, the
Communist party, and the Komeito, maintain contacts with the Soviet
leaders through visits by top party officials.

Soviet experts on Japan expect big changes to occur in the
Japanese domestic politics in the late 1970s and early 1980s. They
are certain that the economic crisis will continue. Japan will have
to face up to the resource nationalism of the developing nations in
Asia, including the oil-rich countries of the Middle East. The coming years will witness social and political polarization. Analysts
have noted the political weakness of successive prime ministers and
the inability of their governments to solve social and environmental
problems.[105]

In the 1950s and 1960s, Soviet propaganda to Japan used to be in the form of outbursts of anger and bitterness, but in the 1970s it is persuasive, as if the propaganda chiefs have decided that the Japanese, so long brainwashed by the Americans, have to be told why they find their nation in one predicament after another in spite of its great economic power. Thus, after the widespread hostile demonstrations in the southeast Asian capitals during Tanaka's visit in 1974, Moscow Radio broadcast a commentary by a leading Soviet expert on Japanese affairs, explaining why Japan had become the target of Asian hatred and anger. This was because Japan's role in southeast Asia was being determined by the monopolists' ever-growing appetite for markets and profits and because the rulers of Japan had not basically changed their "too powerful orientation toward the United States." Too dependent on the United States, Japan becomes, willy-nilly, a partner of U.S. imperialism, which prevents it from playing a truly constructive role in the development of the southeast Asian countries. A Japan controlled by the monopolists and by the United States cannot expect to win the hearts and minds of the freedom-aspiring people of Asia. China cannot deliver Japan from its predicament. Peking is trying to draw Japan into its hegemonic design and an anti-Soviet alliance. "If this path is taken, nothing will come out of it except submission to interests which are alien to Japan."

Japan, however, has a third alternative that would mean a "genuine national policy" and would rid it of the "excessively great influence of extraneous forces." This is the policy of peaceful coexistence with each of the three major powers, the United States, the USSR, and China, and a "balanced relationship" with the two superpowers. With the USSR, Japan could then develop many-sided long-term relations based on "full equality, mutual benefit, and noninterference in each other's internal affairs." There would be no question of subordinating the interests of one to those of the other.[106]

The coveted Soviet foreign policy objective, then, is a Japan independent of the United States and China, with a balanced relationship with the United States and the USSR. Japan can be expected to move toward a balanced relationship only if it significantly loosens its political and security ties with the United States. The Soviet leaders therefore note with approval every autonomous action in the diplomacy of Japan, such as its support for the Arab demand that Israel withdraw from all territory occupied in the war of June 1967, its recognition of the revolutionary regimes in South Vietnam and Cambodia, and its economic and commercial relations with North Vietnam and North Korea.

However, the Soviet Union is not in a position to accelerate the pace of the Japanese exit from the U.S. security orbit. The power that can do that is the United States itself, by pressing Japan for actions Tokyo may consider to be against its best interests.

Indeed, for all practical purposes Japan in the mid-1970s is politically and diplomatically independent of the United States. The four-power relationship has become so dynamic that Japan can use it as effectively as any of the other three. As long as the LDP is in power, Japan will maintain its close strategic links with the United States, all the more so because the United States has ceased pressing Japan to assume a security role in Asia since the communist victories in Indochina and because China has become a supporter of the security treaty between the United States and Japan.

A new Japanese style of dealing with the two conflicting communist giants has emerged in 1975-76. Japan is now inclined to use its relationship with the one to wrest concessions from the other. Furthermore, Japan seems to be quite prepared to incline toward one to curb the influence and stature of the other. When Takeo Miki became prime minister after Tanaka's resignation, he sent Foreign Minister Miyawaza to Moscow to resume the peace treaty negotiations. Miyawaza found the Soviet leaders unwilling to meet the Japanese demand for the return of the four northern islands.

Japan had already initiated peace treaty negotiations with China, which had been deadlocked over Japanese refusal to accept the so-called antihegemony clause, which the Chinese had quite stubbornly declared was aimed against the Soviet Union. The Soviets themselves had warned Japan not to accept the antihegemony clause.

Toward the end of 1975 Miki reversed the Japanese position and indicated his willingness to accept a mutually agreeable draft of the antihegemony clause in the Sino-Japanese peace treaty under negotiation. This made Gromyko hurry to Tokyo in January 1976. In contrast to 1972, Gromyko now offered to return two of the four islands, and all that he asked for was a firm Japanese commitment that it not be a party to the anti-Soviet moves of China.

Miki announced after Gromyko's departure that his government would still sign the peace treaty with China with its antihegemony clause. What was more significant was Miki's declaration that Tanaka's policy of equidistance from China and the USSR no longer suited Japanese interests. In other words, Japan must play poker with all the major powers and cannot afford to bind itself to any rigid foreign policy posture.[107]

Strategic Stalemate

The main roadblock to political cooperation between the Soviet Union and Japan is the high degree of strategic disharmony that still exists between the two powers in the middle of the 1970s. Throughout the postwar period, Japan has been a main pillar of the U.S.-

sponsored global security system, and in Asia Japan has been the fulcrum of that system. The Soviet Union has become used to regarding the U.S. military presence in Japan as a direct threat to the security of the USSR and its actual and potential friends in Asia. Japanese military strategists have become equally used to perceiving the Soviet Union as the power that poses the greatest threat to the security of Japan and its allies in Asia. However, the hard and ultra-hard Soviet images of the Japanese security relations with the United States have mellowed enormously since 1971-72. The Soviet leaders realize that there can be no strategic harmony with Japan as long as it remains in the U.S. military embrace. However, what alarms the Soviet Union is that Japan may lend its great economic resources to refurbish the U.S. security system in Asia and may become its deputy manager. The collapse of the U.S. security system in Southeast Asia and its uncertain credibility even for Northeast Asia provide the Soviet leaders with an ambience in which they must try to persuade Japan, with the hope of greater success than in the past, that its "true security and lasting leadership role" lies in loosening its military ties with the United States.

The long-term Soviet objective is to harness Japan as one of the principal pillars of an Asian collective security system. "We believe that Japan, one of the leading nations of Asia, should play an important part in establishing a collective security system in this part of the world," said a Moscow Radio commentator on December 12, 1969, within six months of the launching of the Asian collective security concept by Brezhnev.[108] In fact, Japan was one of the first countries with the governmental leaders of which the Soviet leaders engaged in a diplomatic monologue on prospects of an Asian collective security system replacing that of the United States. Moscow was even encouraged by the fact that Sato, then the prime minister of Japan, did not react entirely negatively, at least in his first public reaction, to the Soviet concept. However, the Japanese government took a dim view of the Soviet initiative from the beginning, if only because Japan did not have the least desire to opt out of the U.S. security system.

The essential precondition for the Soviet security model for Asia was explained by Mikhail Suslov, a member of the CPSU Politburo, to Tomoni Narita, chairman of the Japanese Socialist Party, in July 1970. Suslov told Narita that an Asian collective security system required "the withdrawal of U.S. troops from Indochina; the dissolution of SEATO; and the abrogation of the Anzas Pact, the U.S.-Japanese security treaty, and the defense treaties with South Korea and Taiwan."[109] The JSP had been the first and only group in Japan to show a positive interest in the Soviet concept. In December 1969 Moscow Radio pleaded with Japan to "propose a conference of all nations in the Asian and Pacific region to deliberate the measures

that would be necessary for the creation of a realistic basis for a
collective security system in this part of the world. "[110]

It is interesting to note how and why Soviet strategic perceptions of Japan have changed so remarkably with the progress of the
1970s. For 27 years after the end of World War II, the Soviet Union
saw Japan as a major factor for insecurity in Asia, both as a military ally of the United States and as an autonomous imperialist power
of growing economic weight. Protected by the U.S. nuclear shield,
Japan, in the Soviet perception, allowed the United States to build
hundreds of military bases on its territory and even to station nuclear
warheads at some of these bases. It aligned itself completely with
the U.S. policy of containing the USSR and China during the 1950s
and 1960s. During the Korean War and the Vietnam War it functioned
as a forward base for the U.S. line of containment. It willingly undertook special responsibilities for the defense of South Korea and
Taiwan.

The Japanese "ruling clique" systematically projected to its
own people the image of the Soviet Union as its principal enemy. As
the economic power of Japan grew, the monopolists who controlled
the economy embarked upon an imperialist policy of economic expansion in the Far East and in Southeast Asia. At first they operated
as junior partners of U.S. monopolists; but in the 1960s they began to
elbow out the Americans from several Asian markets.

Meanwhile, under U.S. patronage and instigation, the Japanese
"ruling clique," a coalition of reactionaries, militarists, and monopoly business houses, adopted an ambitious military buildup program
in violation of the Japanese constitution. This military program
generated and fed upon a growing demand that Japan play a military
and political role in Asia that corresponded to its economic power.
Ostensibly this militarism was meant to protect the economic lifeline of Japan, but the real purpose was, at first, to join hands with
the United States in policing the lines of containment; and later, to
fashion a Japanese empire in the Pacific and Southeast Asia. The
militarists' guideline was the concept of a greater Asian co-prosperity
sphere, the dream of the 1930s that had doomed Japan. [111]

This hard image of Japan acquired an additional edge when
Nixon announced the Guam Doctrine following his meeting with Sato.
The meeting led to an indefinite continuation of the security treaty between Japan and the United States, albeit with major revisions, with
the return of Okinawa to Japanese control. The Soviet Union realized
that the reversion of Okinawa would reinforce the Japanese demand
for the restoration of the Northern Territory. As noted, Moscow
immediately adopted a hard line on the territorial issue because "the
whole of Japan has been Okinawa-ized. "[112] A commentary in Pravda
concluded that the revised treaty gave Japan a "more positive role"

in the U.S. post-Vietnam Asian strategies. The U.S. intention was
to "widen the scope of the alliance" in order to link it with the U.S.
system of alliances spanning the entire Pacific-Asian region. The
renewal of the treaty was seen as a strong stimulus for remilitariza-
tion in Japan, as follows:

> The automatic renewal of the treaty is related to
> the desire of the USA to turn Japan into a center
> for carrying out the "Guam Doctrine," into the
> policeman of Asia, to whom Washington would
> like to transfer the dirtiest part of suppressing
> the national liberation movement. . . . Thus,
> the renewed "security treaty" and the "Guam Doc-
> trine" complement one another, as it were, and
> become what is actually the military-political
> program of the alliance of U.S. and Japanese im-
> perialist circles. This is not a defensive alliance,
> but an aggressive one.[113]

The ultra-hard image continued through 1970 and part of 1971.
Pravda, in a strongly worded editorial in December 1970, warned
Japan that aligning with U.S. imperialism might involve it in future
Vietnam-like conflicts. The Soviet leaders, however, also continued
to convey the image of Japanese militarist imperialism to its dim-
visioned victims. "Up to now," elaborated the Pravda editorial,
"the postwar expansion of Japanese imperialism has been largely
economic in nature. The talks between Sato and Nixon indicate that
Japan's ruling circles are ready to reinforce economic penetration
by political means and if necessary by military means as well."[114]
The Singapore correspondent of Izvestia reported that a new "military bloc" was being created in Asia, under U.S. initiative and in-
spiration. "The central place in it is reserved for Japan."[115] The
official organ of the Soviet government expanded the theme with
greater forcefulness in May 1971, as follows:

> The more powerful Japan becomes in economic
> respects the more clearly do expansionist yearn-
> ings show up in its foreign policy. These yearn-
> ings are for the regions in Asia that one might
> call traditional for Japanese imperialism: the
> southeast. . . .
>   Two-thirds of Japan's so-called economic
> and financial assistance is given to countries of
> southeast Asia. . . . Step by step Japan is
> crowding its protector and competitor--the USA--

out of the markets of southeast Asia; and in such
countries as Thailand, Cambodia, Indonesia,
Malaysia and Singapore, it has already overtaken
the USA in trade. . . .

Japanese loans, made at very high interest
rates, are accompanied by a strict policy of binding the countries to Japanese goods. In short, the
whole policy is aimed at establishing Japanese
hegemony in the countries of southeast Asia. . . .

The interests of the Japanese monopolies that
are resurrecting their prewar imperialistic appe-
tites are incompatible with the interest of the developing countries of southeast Asia. These countries know from past experience that economic
hegemony will be followed shortly by political
hegemony and then by military hegemony as
well.[116]

Since 1972 the Soviet Union has been trying to develop a new
strategic perception of Japan, but without much clarity of vision.
The increasing political and diplomatic independence of Japan goes
hand in hand with its willing security dependence on the United States.
The Soviet leaders do not seem to be clear about whether the independence or the dependence is more important. Both Moscow and Peking
want Japan to play a military role, but the Soviets want Japan to develop its own independent military strategic posture, while the Chinese
apparently prefer to see Japan continue to maintain its strategic linkages with the United States.

The Chinese want Japan to rearm within limits as an anti-
Soviet power in Asia. During Tanaka's visit to Peking, Chou En-lai
told him, "China welcomes the reinforcement of Japanese military
strength as a potential counterweight to Soviet aggression."[117] The
Chinese foreign minister, Chi Peng-fei, told a visiting socialist Diet
member in December 1973 that while it was "desirable" that Japan
extricate itself from the U.S. security system and build its independent military strength, this would not be a "realistic" step at the
present time because without U.S. "protection" Japan could not defend itself from the Soviet Union.[118]

This strategic agreement among the United States, China, and
Japan puts the Soviet Union in a particularly difficult situation. In
fact, it deprives Moscow of any credible strategic concept with which
to entice the Japanese ruling elite. The Soviet Union can only cater
to the growing Japanese self-pride and the strengthening Japanese desire to play an independent role in Asian and global affairs, and this
is what the Soviet propagandists and diplomats have been trying to do.

However, they are stonewalled by the deep-seated Japanese opposition to large-scale militarization. Not many Japanese are willing to pay the costs of an independent national defense system.[119] This is not to suggest that the Soviet arguments fall only on deaf ears. The fact remains that even those Japanese who want their country to build its own independent military force do not subscribe to the Soviet strategic design for Asia.

JAPANESE PERCEPTIONS OF THE USSR

Japanese perceptions of the Soviet Union are shaped partly by historical memories but largely by Japanese perceptions of the three major powers and of the relationship existing among them and by its self-image. As the Japanese look at the tripartite relationship, they are more impressed by rivalries and conflicts of interest than by detente. They see detente as too fragile and narrow to generate confidence that the three major international actors have shifted from confrontation to a plateau of peaceful coexistence. In any case, only one of the three has a certain amount of detente with the two others, while the Soviet Union remains engaged in a cold war with China. The detente, says Shinsaku Hogen, adviser to the external affairs ministry, is highly unstable because the superpowers are still engaged in an arms race and are still "competing furiously" for influence "in the gray zones of the world."[120] "Peaceful coexistence," writes a Japanese scholar, "is the will of the Soviet Union and the United States to avoid a nuclear war, and perhaps nothing else."[121] The weakest link in the tripartite framework is China, much of the foreign policy resources of which are consumed by an intensifying cold war with the USSR. The withering of the U.S. security system in Asia, writes a Japanese specialist in Chinese affairs, places the Soviet Union in a position of vantage because China lacks the power to match its adversary. The principal Soviet objective in Asia is "out-and-out" containment of China, an objective that cannot be achieved merely by an alliance with "powerless India." The Soviet Union will therefore vigorously compete for the friendship of Japan and the countries of Southeast Asia. China, too, will woo Japan, because of its fear of the Soviet Union. Since it lacks matching influence-building resources, China is likely to mount a two-pronged strategy to weaken Japan by increasing its intervention in domestic politics and by economic competition in Southeast Asia.[122]

A weak, unstable, and limited detente is evidently more agreeable to Japan's interests than a strong, wide, and stable one. The rivalry among the three principal powers enhances the importance of Japan to each and enables Japan to navigate for larger diplomatic

options. In Japanese perceptions, the U.S.-Soviet detente in the
wake of the U.S. decision to pull out of Vietnam reduced the importance of Japan to Washington; a stable and firm superpower detente
would probably freeze the status of Japan as that of a reluctant junior
partner of the residual U.S. security system in Asia.[123] The Japanese are equally afraid of a stable Sino-U.S. detente, which, they
believe, can operate only to the detriment of Japan's interests.[124]
What they mortally fear is a detente between the USSR and China.
They seem to be certain that this will not happen in the next ten years,
and their own policy is designed to ensure that Japan makes no contribution to that undesirable eventuality.

The uncertainties of the tripartite relationship and Japan's in-
extricable involvement in the triangular competition for influence
and power have produced in the Japanese mind split images of each
of the three major powers. Is the United States the motherly mentor
in whose lap Japan can continue to find succor and satisfaction; or is
it an unfriendly Victorian father castigating a prematurely successful
son and ejecting a challenge from within the nest? Is China a cultural mother from whose central strength Japan cannot separate its
future; or is it the oversized sibling with whom rivalry and competition for Asian leadership is unavoidable? Is the Soviet Union a welcome alternative source of investment returns and oil and natural
gas, and even a potential ally that Japan may need in order to maintain its independence and identity from an expansionist or hegemonic
China; or is it a darkly threatening superpower dangerously tempting
Japan to break away from its U.S. moorings?[125]

The emotional and intellectual involvement of Japan with the
United States and China is far greater than its tie with the Soviet
Union, a situation that is not always to the disadvantage of Moscow.
The debate on relations with the United States goes on endlessly in
all departments of Japanese society; except among the teen-age youth,
the United States is still among the countries the Japanese like most.
China is a different story. It lures, fascinates, repels, and frightens
the Japanese people. In the opinion polls not many Japanese say that
they like China, although those who like China far outnumber those
who say they like the USSR. Although hundreds of Japanese delegations have visited China and many politicians--more non-Communists
than Communists--have had access to top Chinese leaders, and although there is a corps of highly perceptive and knowledgeable China
experts in the universities and the press, China is less open to the
Japanese tourist than the USSR. Chinese affairs are penetratingly
and extensively reported in the Japanese newspapers, the Peking-
based correspondents of which seem to be systematically taken into
confidence by the Chinese leaders on matters relating to Soviet "aggression." In contrast, there is little systematic reporting on the

USSR in the Japanese press, and Soviet studies are yet to be set up in the universities as a serious discipline.[126]

"China, like America, divides the Japanese people," a Japanese newspaperman who had been a correspondent in Peking for several years told me in Tokyo.

> The lure for China is of two kinds. Cultural-- and here the pull is strong and widely shared, particularly by men belonging to the older generations. Political-ideological--this is the impact People's China has on the young. Many Japanese turn to China out of disgust with Japan's blind pursuit of growth and with the many ills of rapid industrialization.
>
> However, China has been Japan's most frustrating experience since the normalization of relations in 1972. The Japanese people do not know what kind of relations they want with China. Some think of China as a rival and an adversary. Others see no basic conflict between an industrialized Japan, whose major interests lie in the Pacific, and an essentially agrarian China, with its population concentrations in the north and the south. The Chinese appear to think that they have Japan on the leash by virtue of their friendship with the United States. China wants Japan's cooperation to keep the USSR off Asia, and as long as China remains militarily weak and the United States uncertain about its commitments in Asia, the Japanese will be well advised to keep their distance from Russia. That doesn't mean Japan moves too close to China, but you must realize that the Japanese consider today's China to be much less of a threat than the USSR.[127]

To be sure, many in Japan resent the upsurge in the international stature of China, especially since they believe that China has not earned its position but has been elevated to it by the United States. They also resent the Chinese behavior toward Japan. Yoshikazu Sakamoto, for instance, points out that the publicly recognized principle underlying Japanese diplomacy has always been that Japan must stand in a superior position with regard to China, whether by itself or as an ally of the United States or the countries of Europe. The Japanese resented Nixon's opening to China, he says, because "this is the first occasion in the history of modern Japanese diplomacy in which another Asian nation has achieved a position of political and military superiority over Japan."[128]

There are powerful factions in LDP, JDA, and Gaimusho that are opposed to any deference to Chinese preeminence in Asian and world affairs. One of the officials I interviewed remarked with some bitterness that the Chinese leaders had developed the habit of "publicly advising Japan as to how we should run our foreign policy." To the question, "Do you find the advice useful?" his prompt reply was, "Of course! It helps us understand how the Chinese mind is working."

The majority in the Japanese establishment, however, find it easier to live with Chinese prestige than with Soviet power. First, the Japanese see the United States and China working together to limit the power and influence of the USSR. They do not permit themselves to turn against China because this might mean turning against the United States. Second, they seem to believe that the United States would not allow Peking to hurt Japanese interests.

There is also a subtle strain in current Japanese thinking about the Soviet Union. Because many Japanese now regard it as inevitable that Japan will steadily be drawn into the long-term process of Siberian development, Japan must at the same time do everything it can to limit the Soviet political and strategic role in the Pacific-Asian region. From conversations with several persons close to JDA as well as to the Japanese foreign office, I received the impression that a consensus exists among the factional leaders of LDP that relations with the Soviet Union should be managed on two simultaneous levels: economic cooperation and strategic resistance. This policy seems to be acceptable to the Broad Japanese public, and it is reinforced by the current Japanese perception of Soviet power. Newspapers often refer to the "strategic lead" taken by the USSR over the United States, although what the Soviet Union has gained is no more than strategic parity. A specialist in Soviet affairs, who heads the only institution in Japan that is engaged in a systematic study of the Communist societies, told me that the most significant Soviet advance in recent years was its demonstrated capability to intervene in local conflicts. Gone were the days, he added, when the United States could get away with unilateral intervention.

Each display of Soviet naval power in Asian Pacific waters is "news" for the Japanese press and a subject of "informed comment." In May 1973 a Soviet fleet of four ships passed through the Taiwan Strait, the first Soviet naval presence in those waters since 1949. The Japanese press linked this display to the visit of a high-power Chinese delegation to Tokyo to discuss operational agreements in the light of the joint Tanaka-Chou communique of September 1972.[129] A JDA spokesman saw the Soviet naval presence in the Taiwan Strait as part of the Soviet determination to secure free access to all the high seas in the world.[130]

In July-August 1973 a fleet of ten Soviet ships held a month-
long maneuver in the Pacific Ocean "in the direction of Guam," advancing, as one Tokyo newspaper put it, into "Nixon's bathtub." JDA
saw this maneuver in the central Pacific Ocean as "the final stage in
the USSR's global maritime strategy."[131] Much in the same vein,
the Soviet naval presence in the Indian Ocean reinforces the Japanese
perception of the USSR as a power capable of operating, and determined to operate, a global diplomacy. The Japanese see three principal objectives of the Soviet naval expansion in the Indian Ocean:
"to endorse the Soviet Union's expansion of political power as far as
the subcontinent and Southeast Asia";[132] to "deter the advance in the
Indian Ocean by US missile-SSN's";[133] and to keep a sharp watch on
the developments in the Middle East.

The Japanese seem to believe that the Soviet Union has brought
much of South Asia under its influence, if not control; that India is
"socializing" itself under Soviet influence if not under its direction;
that the Soviet Union has already secured naval base facilities in
India and perhaps in Ceylon and Burma; and that Moscow has already
secured an edge over China in the competition for influence in Southeast Asia. [134]

The traditional Japanese respect for power is clearly evident
in the current Japanese perceptions of the Soviet Union. It is the
rise in Soviet power that has persuaded the United States to seek a
detente with Moscow, and once the United States has begun the process the Japanese, with their habitual flair for imitation, cannot lag
far behind, as a retired diplomat told me during an interview. Although Japanese scholars have a rather dim view of Soviet economic
prospects and think poorly of the bureaucratic efficiency of the USSR,
they do not as a rule expect political instability to develop within the
USSR in the foreseeable future. On the contrary, they tend to view
the Soviet system as quite stable and resistant to change. [135] The
perception of Soviet stability strengthens the desire to invest in
Siberian development.

No one in Japan visualizes a dramatic upswing in relations
with the Soviet Union. "Step by step, things are happening between
Japan and the USSR," said a senior official, "and perhaps a lot more
will happen in the years to come." The Soviet Union has markedly
expanded its contacts with various layers of Japanese society, but
unlike China it has had little influence on Japanese domestic politics.
"China divides our people," the official continued, but "the Soviets
unite."

There was a broad national consensus, shared even by the
JCP, that political relations with the USSR could not improve significantly until Moscow had settled the issue of the Northern Territory
to the satisfaction of Japan. Japan would not settle for anything less

than all of the four islands, the senior official affirmed, but others
told me that the Japanese stand was not that rigid. Did the USSR
ask for a political price for restoration of the islands? The answer
was no, it did not, although the Soviet leaders argued that a mutually
satisfactory settlement of the territorial issue could come only after
friendly, good neighborly relations between the two nations had been
established. Didn't that mean that the islands were being held as a
bait for better political relations? One could interpret it that way if
one wished, came the reply, but the unchangeable position of Japan
was that the islands must be returned because they had always been
under Japanese sovereignty and had been seized as fruits of victory
in World War II.

Economic cooperation in Siberia was going ahead independently
of the territorial issue, the official went on; but the age-old distrust,
the limited amount of capital for investment, and sheer national interest placed unavoidable limitations on the volume of the possible
Japanese contribution to Siberian projects. Would he care to compare the relations of Japan with the USSR to its relations with China?
"China is an emotional phenomenon in Japan and therefore very controversial," came the reply. There were two China lobbies; the
Peking lobby was now much more powerful than the Taiwan lobby.
"There are no emotions while we deal with Russia. We can proceed
more objectively, guided only by our national interests. On the
Soviet side too there is a lot of objectivity and much wish to demonstrate friendliness." The relations with the two Communist neighbors were nearly equal, with the important exception that over a
billion dollars of Japanese investment had been committed to Soviet
projects in Siberia, while no major Japanese investment had yet been
made to develop resources in China. Did that mean that over the long
run Japan was going to develop a greater stake in Soviet than in Chinese friendship? The answer was no. The Soviets would have built
the Siberian projects anyway. They had a far greater capability to
assemble the industrial infrastructure. Hard-headed Japanese businessmen were guided by cold realities, and they were investing in
projects that they believed will yield sure, stable results.

"Relations with the Soviet Union would have been much better
if the Russians had been more generous on the territorial issue, if
they smiled all the time, instead of smiling only now and then," observed the editor of a daily newspaper, a self-confessed student of
Soviet affairs. He did not believe that Japan would ever get all the
four islands back; in fact one of them, Kunashari, had been developed
as a fisheries base and the Soviet Union was not likely to return it to
Japan.

"However absurd it may sound, the Japanese capitalists are
the strongest advocates of better relations with the USSR." Soviet

support in industry and business was quite large and affected hundreds of medium and small units. It was nonsense to suggest that economic cooperation had no political implications; in fact, the political distance between Moscow and Tokyo slowed the pace of economic collaboration.

Even if Japan had the resources to develop Siberian oil, natural gas, coal, and nuclear power, which it clearly didn't have, it would be too dangerous to make Japan heavily dependent on the USSR for the supply of strategic raw material and fuel. In any case, Japan could not be expected, in the existing state of the relationship, to make a significant contribution to Soviet military power. [136]

The postwar generation of the Japanese ruling elite has been used to seeing the Soviet Union as a hostile power, if not an enemy. This Soviet image, however, has not been shared by the majority of the Japanese people, at any rate not during the 1970s. In a national public opinion survey in early February by Chuo Chosasha, the Central Research Service in Tokyo, only 22 percent expressed fear that "some foreign country might attack Japan in the future"; 47 percent felt there was no threat to Japan from any foreign country. Only 13 percent named the Soviet Union as the possible source of attack, while 11 percent named China. The 87 percent who did not name the USSR were later specifically asked if they feared any attack from that direction. Only 8 percent said that they did, while 45 percent said they did not and the rest had no answer. Fear of an attack by the USSR was highest, 26 percent, among those who supported rearmament and lowest, 8 percent, among those who stood for a reduced self-defense force; 44 percent of those who feared an attack from "some foreign country" were also listed as "pro-rearmament." [137]

Far more of the Japanese thought that their national security was endangered by the presence of U.S. bases on Japanese territory. In April 1970 a _Kyodo_ survey, conducted with a national sample of 3,000, of which 85 percent were successfully interviewed, asked: "Are you afraid that if American planes took off from their bases here to fly into combat, some ally of the attacked nation might retaliate against Japan or don't you have any such fear?" Over 77 percent said they did fear such a possibility, while 8 percent said they did not. [138]

In the mid-1970s the hostile image of the USSR seems to have been blurred even in the minds of the ruling elite, except for the minority that stands firmly in support of rapid rearmament. None of the 65 Japanese interviewed by me in Tokyo in October 1974 described the USSR as a power hostile to Japan. [139] However, their image of the Soviet Union as a power friendly to Japan was not so unambiguous. Only 10 among the 65 saw the USSR as a friendly power, while the rest listed that country as a power that seemed to be interested in Japanese friendship.

Similarly, the Soviet Union is no longer seen to be an expansionist, aggressive power; in fact, among those who take a special interest in international affairs, the image of the USSR is that of a "generally cautious, status-quo defending power." Furthermore, few Japanese have an ideological perception of the Soviet Union; most of the persons interviewed saw it as a superpower motivated by the global interests of the Soviet state rather than by the interests of international Communism. The ideological image is somewhat stronger among the university youth; out of 50 students sampled in one of the universities in Tokyo, 14 said that they saw the Soviet Union first as a Communist power.[140] The fact that the CPSU does not have the best of relations with the majority of the Communist parties in Asia is not unknown to the Japanese public. China, despite its rapprochement with the United States, commands a much stronger ideological image in the Japanese mind than does the Soviet Union.

The Soviet Union continues to be among the least liked countries in Japan. In a Sankei opinion poll in March 1975, only 2 percent said they liked the USSR, which, however, had the dubious distinction of being more liked than the two Koreas and Taiwan. The number of those who disliked the Soviet Union was the highest among people in their 60s and the lowest among those in their 30s.

These statistics do not necessarily indicate that the Japanese public is not interested in better relations with the USSR. An opinion poll during Tanaka's visit to Moscow showed that 74 percent of the sample was following the prime minister's talks with the Soviet leaders with strong to moderate interest, and 53 percent wanted deeper relations, 34 percent thought that the existing state of relations was sufficient, 11 percent were against any deep involvement with the USSR, and only 1 percent did not want friendly relations with Moscow at all.[141] In October 1974 the widely shared stance was that Japan should try to "gradually" improve relations with the Soviet Union. Among the 50 university students sampled, as many as 45 were in favor of "gradual and cautious" development of Japanese-Soviet relations.[142]

The Japanese mind is used to interpreting the present in terms of the past, and historical memories are therefore generally strong. Thus people born during the Taicheo period, that is, between 1915 and 1925, who still have strong memories of World War II and of the Soviet "treachery" in invading Japan in 1945, offer various degrees of resistance to improvement of relations with Moscow. The younger generation, born either immediately before or during the war or after the surrender, has a more open mind. Since 60 percent of the people involved in the decision-making process still belong to the Taicheo generation, there is much emotional and psychological resistance to a rapid improvement of relations with the Soviet Union.[143] At the same time, this generation also recalls the ability of Japan during the first three decades of the century to advance its interests by playing poker with the powers, and it should not be imagined that they are entirely blind to the possibilities of manipulating the differences among the major world powers in order to advance the interests of Japan.[144]

The Soviet Union is not popular with the left-wing opposition in Japan, but its standing is better with the Socialist and Communist parties. The JSP has established a relationship with the CPSU. Its leaders confer at regular intervals with the CPSU leaders, and it is the only major political group in Japan that has given some support to the Soviet concept of a collective Asian security system. However, the JSP chairman's support for the Chinese-sponsored antihegemony clause in a Sino-Japanese peace treaty incurred Soviet displeasure in the spring of 1975, although the chairman's move was criticized by the "pro-Soviet faction" of the JSP.[145]

The JCP independence of the Soviet and Chinese Communist parties has, paradoxically, helped Soviet image-building in Japan. Independence has enabled the JCP to return to its policy of the late 1940s of building a "lovable" Communist party relevant to the felt urges and needs of the broad strata of the Japanese people. Its successive electoral successes since 1972 have once again made the JCP one of the major political forces in the country. Its image is more positive among the younger generations than among the older, but even those who are opposed to JCP emergence as a ruling party concede that it is doing constructive work and that it is no longer a stooge of Moscow or Peking. Unlike the Chinese Communist Party, the CPSU has maintained its contacts with the JCP despite its independence, apparently ignoring the fact that in public opinion polls some 30 percent of the people listed as JCP supporters declared their dislike for the USSR.[146] Leaders of the Keomoto Party have also visited Moscow more than once and conferred with Soviet leaders. All of these three opposition parties advocate substantially diminishing, if not completely terminating, Japanese security ties with the United States. Each of them supports the idea of nonaggression and friendship treaties between Japan and each of the three major powers and a reduced self-defense force, ideas that also enjoy the backing of a number of leading Japanese intellectuals.[147]

Although the Soviet Union is disliked by the vast majority of the Japanese electorate, paradoxically, the Soviet hope of a radical improvement in its relations with Japan is pinned on the Japanese voter. A change of government in Tokyo can only be to the Soviets' advantage if the Kremlin does not mishandle its Japanese diplomacy.

In the unlikely event of a JSP-JCP coalition ruling in Japan in the next five to ten years, the Soviet Union will probably launch a

massive friendship drive, offering a benign settlement of the territorial issue in return for a peace treaty formalizing the relationship
of peaceful coexistence, which as a Japanese scholar correctly points
out, already exists for all practical purposes between the two countries.[148] However, even for a leftist government in Tokyo it would
not be easy, nor good politics, to dismantle the present framework
of Japanese international relations.

This is understood at the Yoyogi, the headquarters of the JCP,
no less than in the JSP. A JCP source told me in October 1974 that
if the party came to power in coalition with other progressive forces,
it would not "destroy" the existing structure of Japanese foreign
policy but would try to remove only those "gross inequalities" that
seriously circumscribed Japanese sovereignty. A center-left coalition would probably try to lower the U.S. security burden in Japan
and balance the still-continuing security relationship with treaties of
friendship and nonaggression with the USSR and China. A certain
balancing of Japanese relations with the United States is inherent
even in the present policy of equal relationship with Moscow and
Peking. It does not allow a tilt toward the USSR except as a tentative
short-term maneuver to deal with specific unacceptable thrusts from
China; but in deft Japanese hands, it does permit playing poker with
the cards concealed.

NOTES

1. The Russian and American races for Japan began almost
simultaneously. The Czarist government sent Vice-Admiral Putiatin
to Japan in 1852. He arrived at Nagasaki in August 1853, and was
promised that Russia would be given first priority in a trade agreement. However, Commodore Matthew C. Perry had sailed into Edo
Bay in July 1853, and he succeeded in concluding the first treaty with
Japan at Kanagawa on March 31, 1854. See G. A. Lensen, The
Russian Push Toward Japan (Princeton: Princeton University Press,
1959), for detailed accounts of the Russian bid to open up Japan; see
also G. A. Lensen, Russia's Japan Expedition of 1852 to 1855
(Gainesville, 1955), pp. 60-68.

2. At the Crimea Conference in February 1945, an agreement
was reached by Roosevelt, Churchill, and Stalin that the Soviet Union
would enter the war against Japan "on the side of the Allies" two or
three months after the surrender of Germany and the termination of
the European war, on condition, among others, that "the former
rights of Russia violated by the treacherous attack of Japan in 1904
shall be restored." Apart from restoration of Soviet interests in
Manchuria, the agreement provided that "the southern part of

Sakhalin as well as the islands adjacent to it shall be returned to the
Soviet Union," and "the Kurile islands shall be handed to the Soviet
Union." "Yalta Conference Documents," International Affairs (Mos-
cow), September 1965.

      For Russo-Japanese competition for these island groups
even in the eighteenth century, see James Murdoch, A History of
Japan: The Tokugawa Epoch, 1656-1828 (London, 1926), pp. 512-15.

      3. In area, Habomai is 102 square kilometers; Shikotan, 255
square kilometers; Kunashari, 1,500 square kilometers; and Etorofu,
3,139 square kilometers. For maps prepared by the Japanese Ministry of Foreign Affairs, see Savitri Vishwanathan, Normalization of
Japanese-Soviet Relations, 1945-70 (Tallahassee, Fla.: Diplomatic
Press, 1973), pp. 52-54.

      The Japanese claim that Habomai and Shikotan do not belong
to the Kurile islands. Their main argument is that the four islands
have always been Japanese, that they were never occupied by Russia,
and that the wartime deal was purely a territorial acquisition by the
Soviet Union as a result of the Japanese defeat.

      4. Shumpei Okamoto, The Japanese Oligarchy and the Russo-
Japanese War (New York: Columbia University Press, 1970), pp.
196-200.

      5. It is suggested that Lenin was among the Russian revolu-
tionaries who received money from Japan during the Russo-Japanese
war. Vadim Medish, "Lenin and Japanese Money," The Russian Review 24, no. 2 (April 1965): 165-76; Bertran D. Wolfe, Three Who
Made a Revolution (New York: The Dial Press, 1948), p. 280.

      6. Okamoto, op. cit., Chapters 7-8. Okamato documents the
feeling of the Japanese people that they were deprived of their legitimate fruits of victory.

      7. Adam B. Ulam, Expansion and Co-existence: Soviet For-
eign Policy, 1917-1973 (2nd ed., New York: Praeger, 1974), p. 394.

      8. G. A. Lensen draws some parallel between the Japanese
attack on Russia in 1904 and Pearl Harbor. See his review of John
A. White, The Diplomacy of the Russo-Japanese War (Princeton:
Princeton University Press, 1964), in The Russian Review 24, no. 2
(April 1965): 186-87.

      9. In the nineteenth century Russia, with the help of France and
Germany, prevented Japan from gaining a foothold in China in spite
of Japan's victory in the Sino-Japanese War. Russia also frustrated
Japanese plans in Korea. At the dawn of the twentieth century Japan
sided with Britain and thus isolated Russia from France and Germany
and successfully challenged its old rival. Andrew Malozemoff,
Russian Far Eastern Policy, 1881-1904 (Berkeley: University of
California Press, 1958), pp. 25-45.

      10. Okamoto, op. cit., Chapters 3 and 5.

11. James W. Morley, The Japanese Thrust into Siberia 1918 (Freeport, N.Y.: Books for Libraries Press, 1972), p. 309.

12. Okamoto, op. cit., pp. 46-47.

13. Ulam, op. cit., p. 201. The neutrality treaty pledged the two powers to respect the inviolability of their satellites, Manchuko for Japan and Outer Mongolia for the USSR.

14. The terms offered by Japan for Soviet help during the last year of World War II can be seen in Shusen shiroku (Historical Record of the Ending of the War) (Tokyo: Ministry of Foreign Affairs, 1952), pp. 155-68.

For a decade after 1906, relations between Russia and Japan were cordial even though Japan had its alliance with Britain. If the Secret Convention signed in 1916 had been implemented, the Far East might have become an exclusive Russo-Japanese domain, but the Bolshevik Revolution frustrated Russian efforts to cooperate with Japan in the Far East. For the terms of the Secret Convention see Victor Yakhontoff, Russia and the Soviet Union in the Far East (London, 1932), p. 379.

15. The Soviet Union, however, claims to have made a substantial contribution to the Allied victory over Japan. It had made a thorough preparation for the war, assembling 1.6 million soldiers for the lightning strike into Manchuria and northern China. In 15 days the Soviet army defeated the Kwantung army of almost one million. History of the Great Patriotic War of the Soviet Union, Vol. 5 (Moscow, 1963), pp. 551-55. For the territorial and strategic gains of the USSR from the war, see Ulam, op. cit., p. 395.

16. Stalin cabled to Harry S. Truman, "Russian public opinion would be seriously insulted if the Russian armies were not to receive an occupation zone in some part of Japan proper." The specific Soviet proposal was for occupation of half of the island of Hokkaido. The United States denied the Soviets an occupation zone, but Moscow doggedly fought for its claim to a share in shaping Japan's postwar reconstruction. The United States had the full support of the Japanese to keep the Soviet Union out. In the extensive literature on the U.S.- Soviet contest over Japan after World War II, see Rodger Swearingen and Paul Langer, Red Flag in Japan (Cambridge, Mass.: Harvard University Press, 1952); Shigeru Yoshida, The Yoshida Memoirs: The Story of Japan in Crisis (London, 1961); Supreme Commander for the Allied Powers, Political Reorientation of Japan, September 1945 to September 1948, vol. 2 (Washington, D.C.: U.S. Government Printing Office, 1949); Documents Concerning the Allied Occupation and Control of Japan, vol. 2 (Tokyo: Ministry of Foreign Affairs, 1951); Correspondence between the Chairman of the Council of Ministers of the USSR and the President of the USA and the Prime Minister of Great Britain during the Great Patriotic War of 1941-1945, vol. 2 (Moscow: USSR Ministry of Foreign Affairs, 1957).

17. Hans H. Baerwald, "The Japanese Communist Party: Yoyogi and Its Rivals," in The Communist Revolution in Asia: Tactics, Goals, and Achievements, ed. Robert A. Scalapino (2nd ed., Englewood Cliffs, N.J.: Prentice-Hall, 1969), pp. 212-33.

18. For the various Soviet proposals and major Soviet statements, see Collection of Official Foreign Statements on the Japanese Peace Treaty, vol. 2 (Tokyo: Ministry of Foreign Affairs, 1951). Also Vishwanathan, op. cit., pp. 43-51.

19. In December 1951 Moscow awarded the Stalin peace prize to Oyama Ikuo in recognition of the important role played by the "progressive elements" in Japan. Stalin's 1952 New Year message to the Japanese people was very warm in its expression of hope for Soviet-Japan good-neighborliness. In July 1952 Moscow Radio suggested the solution to the "Japan problem" by the withdrawal of U.S. troops and the granting of equal rights to other countries. In August 1953 Premier Malenkov declared that with the achievement of a truce in Korea, the time had come to normalize relations between the USSR and Japan. In 1954 the Soviet Union did not oppose the admission of Japan to the UN Economic Commission for Asia and the Far East (ECAFE), and it invited Japan to send members to an ECAFE delegation to study Soviet agriculture and fisheries. In May 1955 Moscow declared that in seeking normal relations with Japan, neither the USSR nor China demanded that Japan discontinue its friendly relations with other nations.

Shigemitsu, foreign minister in the Ichiro Hatoyama cabinet, announced on December 11, 1954, that Japan was willing to normalize relations with its Communist neighbors without disturbing its cooperation with the "free world." Foreign Minister Molotov replied in a Moscow broadcast that the Soviet Union was ready. Moscow instructed its representative, A. I. Dominitsky, who was not recognized by the Japanese government, to deliver a note to the foreign affairs ministry of Japan. Despite this ministry's opposition, Hatoyama saw the Soviet representative at his residence. See Sovieto nenpo (Annual Report of Soviet Affairs) (Tokyo: Cabinet Research Office, 1952-56). Also, Vishwanathan, op. cit., pp. 61-69.

20. It is significant that after the October 12, 1954, accord between the USSR and China, Moscow for the first time offered to normalize relations with Japan within the existing framework of Japanese relations with the United States. Sovieto nenpo, op. cit., 1955, pp. 670-72.

21. Vishwanathan, op. cit., pp. 67-72.

22. Ibid., pp. 79-80. Vishwanathan's sources are Japanese, including Shunichi Matsumoto, Moscow ni kakeru niji (Tokyo, 1966), which is probably the most authentic account of the London negotiations, since he was the chief Japanese negotiator. Dulles, however,

denied that he had specifically threatened the annexation of Okinawa. Department of State Bulletin, September 10, 1956, p. 406.

 23. Vishwanathan, op. cit., pp. 81-89.

 24. The commander of the Far Eastern Military District of the USSR warned in January 1960 that if Japan became involved in military plans against the USSR the Soviet people would find it difficult to understand why Habomai and Shikotan should be returned to Japan, since the two islands could easily be used by foreign military forces. Pravda, January 20, 1960. In September 1964 Khrushchev told a visiting Japanese parliamentary delegation that he would be reluctant to return the two islands to Japan until the United States pulled out of that country. Pravda, September 20, 1964. The Soviet leaders, then, were never rigidly against returning these islands but were waiting for the best moment for their restoration.

 In 1966-67 Japan hinted more than once to the Soviet Union that if the four islands were restored Japan would be interested in large-scale participation in Siberian development. Asian Almanac, pp. 1442-43, 2252, 2609.

 It is quite probable that the Japanese moves to normalize relations with the Soviet Union mellowed the Chinese stand on normalization of Sino-Japanese relations. On August 17, 1955, Chou En-lai told a visiting Japanese delegation that normalization could proceed without the abrogation of the security treaty between Japan and Taiwan and that nongovernmental agreements could precede the establishment of diplomatic relations. This led to the Japanese policy of "separating political affairs from economic affairs," and a mosaic of nongovernmental relations evolved between China and Japan prior to the establishment of diplomatic relations in 1972.

 25. Pravda, October 9, 1973. The Brezhnev speech, at a luncheon in honor of Tanaka, yields an insight into Soviet foreign policy objectives in Japan. Brezhnev declared that the Soviet Union proceeded "from the premise that [Japan] can and should play an important part in the joint efforts of states and peoples to strengthen world peace and develop peaceful cooperation among all countries." Soviet-Japanese relations had improved a great deal, but "this is still not enough." Efforts should now be directed toward "more thoroughgoing improvements." The peace treaty should put these relations on a "sounder footing."

 26. Moscow Radio in English 1222 GMT February 21, 1975.

 27. Cultural exchanges gathered momentum after the Soviet rift with China in the early 1960s.

 28. Vishwanathan, op. cit., Chapter 4.

 29. This sharp improvement was partially made possible by a relaxation of the COCOM embargo on trade with the USSR. Japanese exports included large freighters. Oriental Economist (Tokyo), January 1959 and April 1960.

30.   The Japanese "unofficial" delegations to Communist countries are almost always manned by people very close to the ruling
establishment, sometimes by former cabinet ministers and on occasion even by officials of the Foreign Affairs Ministry and the Ministry
of International Trade and Industry.   Officials are "detached" from
these ministries to join particular missions.

31.   Asahi, February 12, 1970.

32.   Nihon Keizai, February 19, 1970.

33.   Kosygin told the newspaper Mainichi in 1969, "In view of
Japan's interest in expanding economic relations with our country,
we could undertake a certain acceleration in the development of this
area with an eye to satisfying our domestic requirements as well as
to supplying exports to Japan."   Cited in Yu. Bandura, "USSR and
Japan: Dictated by Life," Izvestia, January 14, 1972.

34.   The Japanese were "shocked and surprised" that the Soviet
Union should engage in serious negotiations on the basis of "slipshod
data" and wondered if they could accept the revised data as reliable.
Nihon Keizai, February 19, 1970.

35.   Nihon Keizai, September 29, 1971.

36.   Mainichi, February 20, 1972, said:

> However, in the light of the environment in which
> Japan is now placed in East Asia and the fluid in-
> ternational situation, it is not appropriate to take
> up the problem only from an economic angle.   We
> hope for prudence with which to work for expan-
> sion of Japanese-Soviet economic relations after
> giving full thought to what is politically to the
> benefit of our country, in the situation where the
> national interests and expectations of China, the
> Soviet Union, and the United States are complexly
> entangled with one another.
>
> Of course, the biggest problem in this joint de-
> velopment plan lies in the point that it entails
> permanent transactions between nations with dif-
> ferent political structures.   On the Japanese
> side, there is the fear that the Soviet Union may
> possibly stop supply.   (Sankei, February 9, 1972.)
>
> In this respect, we can say it is pertinent that
> Japanese business circles are taking a cautious
> attitude toward their cooperation in the con-
> struction of pipelines in the area which may be
> directly linked to the intensification of tension

at the present stage, at which China-Soviet relations are threatened with a possibility of an
armed conflict. (Nihon Keizai, September 29,
1971.)

37. Asahi, September 6, 1973; Yomiuri, September 7, 1973.
The original export figure had aroused much interest among Japanese
businessmen. The Soviet Union had presented the Tyumen oilfields
project at the JECC meeting in February 1972 and had surprised the
Japanese delegation by its readiness to "receive a survey mission to
the actual scene even tomorrow." Japan was getting ready to send a
survey mission in May. Business circles were expecting that the retirement of Sato as prime minister would bring in a government that
would be able to find $1 billion for investment in the project.

The Keidanren (Federation of Japanese Economic Organizations) chairman, Kogoro Uemura, remarked, "China, the United
States, and various Middle East countries took interest in the development of Japanese-Soviet economic cooperation over a political
article called oil. With such a point included, it can be said that
Japanese-Soviet economic relations have entered the second stage."
Asahi, February 25, 1972.

38. Asahi reported on September 6, 1973, that some of the
leading Japanese oil-refining companies, including Idemetsu Kosan,
had agreed under a deferred payment formula to import products of
the Nakhodka refinery and were "furiously competing with one another to receive orders" for the construction of the refinery.

39. Tokyo shimbun, September 11, 1973. "Our country's receiving structure has been cut into two groups--the Japanese-Soviet
Economic Committee and the oil products import group. This means
that Japan's position is extremely weakened in negotiating with the
Soviet Union." Yomiuri, September 7, 1973.

Asahi, on September 6, 1973, emphasized the military
spinoff of the oilfields project: the Soviet Union would be able to expand its Pacific navy and its armed forces in the Far East and reinforce its troops along the border with China without having to depend
on its traditional oil resources.

40. Nikkon Kogyo, March 27, 1974.

41. Mainichi, April 28 and 30, 1974. The Soviet vice-minister
for foreign trade, Alhinov, who signed the documents for Moscow,
told reporters that Japan would become the Soviets' "biggest trade
partner" in the near future. The agreement, he said, had been
greatly influenced by the recent hike in the interest rates of the U.S.
Export-Import Bank and the refusal of West Germany to give loans
to the USSR at low interest.

42. Yomiuri, March 28, 1974.

43. Yomiuri, March 29, 1974; Asahi, March 29, 1974.
Alhimov told the Japanese members of the JECC, "If Japan desires
to purchase 25 million tons of Tyumeni oil every year on a long-
range basis, it will have to participate in the railway construction in
the form of granting credit for the purchase of materials and equipment." The railway itself was not connected with the six projects
open to Japanese participation, but the projects were being offered
as a package, not as six separate units. Mainichi, evening edition,
April 4, 1974. This was confirmed by Kosygin himself when he had
a surprise one-hour meeting with Tanaka at the Sheremechevo airport in Moscow on April 5. Tanaka pleaded that the "resource problem" be settled "one by one, giving priority to those which are easy
to settle." To which Kosygin's "blunt" reply was, "No. Our projects
for development of Siberia are not separated from one another at all."
Asahi, April 9, 1974.
        44. Kanagawa shimbun, April 1, 1974. At a conference of
LDP factional leaders on April 4, Tanaka, faced with the somewhat
exaggerated argument that the railway would enable the USSR to establish a powerful naval presence in the Pacific and Indian Oceans,
made the rather laconic statement that his government would certainly "cope with" the Soviet plan "from the point of view of security
of our country." Yomiuri, April 5, 1974.
        The business houses were divided, but even those who had
persistently promoted the cause of Siberian development could not
overlook the political-strategic implications of the railway, all the
more because bank loans to the tune of $3.5 billion would need the
direct involvement of the government. Yomiuri, April 5, 1974.
        The only way to pacify the critics was to have U.S. par-
ticipation. Foreign Minister Ohira took up this question when he
met with Nixon in the White House on May 21 but could get nothing
more reassuring than a promise that the United States would study
the matter "positively." Yomiuri, May 22, 1974.
        45. Mainichi, evening edition, October 17, 1973.
        46. Mainichi, October 18, 1973.
        47. Theodore Shabad, "With Capitalist Aid, Siberia Is Open-
ing Up," New York Times, April 24, 1974.
        48. V. Syrokomsky, "Soviet-Japanese Trade Thrives,"
Literturnaya gazeta, no. 14 (April 2, 1975), p. 14; see also his
"Bridge Across the Sea," Literaturnaya gazeta, no. 15 (April 9,
1975), p. 14.
        49. Mainichi, April 3, 1974; Asahi, April 6, 1974; Sankei,
July 24, 1974; Yomiuri, March 24, 1974.
        50. Die Wirtschaft Des Ostblocks (Bonn), August 24, 1975.
        51. Syrokomsky, op. cit.
        52. Mainichi, September 28, 1971.

53. Discussion with a Soviet journalist in Tokyo.

54. <u>Nihon Keizai</u>, January 21, 1972.

The Japanese Foreign Affairs Ministry saw the visit as "harbinger of a new diplomatic offensive to be launched against Japan in opposition to the U.S.-Chinese rapprochement." <u>Tokyo shimbun</u>, November 28, 1971.

"It is now undeniable that the Soviet Asian policy is being developed toward China, with which it must be aware of a long confrontation in the future." <u>Mainichi</u>, January 12, 1972.

Gromyko was seeking a "balance in the Far East" to the approaching improvement in Sino-U.S. relations; his visit was also aimed at preventing an improvement in Sino-Japanese relations before an improvement in Soviet relations with Japan. <u>Sankei</u>, January 14, 1972.

Gromyko's party included his wife and Kapitsa, chief of the Far Eastern Affairs section in the Soviet Foreign Ministry and an authority on China. <u>Yomiuri</u>, evening edition, January 18, 1972.

55. A Japanese newspaperman says that Japanese decision-making follows a "piling-up" formula in which decisions go through a protracted bureaucratic process and are announced after they have been "predicted" in the newspapers. <u>Nihon Keizei</u>, March 18, 1975.

For insights into the Japanese decision-making style, see Philip W. Quigg, "Japan in Neutral," <u>Foreign Affairs</u> 44, no. 2 (January 1966); Derek Davies, "Which Way to Turn?" <u>Far Eastern Economic Review</u>, February 19, 1973.

56. Nevertheless, Gromyko invited Sato to visit Moscow for talks with Brezhnev. This was immediately resisted by the factions in LDP that were working for Sato's exit. Sato's resistance to normalization of relations with China apparently made him important to the Soviet leaders. <u>Nihon Keisai</u>, January 16, 1972. See also Fukuda's remarks in <u>Yomiuri</u>, January 25, 1972.

57. Japanese press reports of Gromyko's talks in Tokyo throw revealing light on the Soviet negotiating style. Gromyko suggested an agenda of only economic cooperation topics. Fukuda took up the position that the "instability" of Japanese-Soviet relations stood in the way of economic cooperation; political relations should therefore be stabilized with the return of the Northern Territory to Japan. The first day's discussion actually centered on the triangular relations of Japan, China, and the USSR, with U.S.-Japanese and Sino-U.S. relations in the background. <u>Tokyo shimbun</u>, January 25, 1972; <u>Asahi</u>, January 24 and 25, 1972.

The Japanese were apparently quite surprised that Gromyko did not denounce the Japanese security relations with the United States and did not demand withdrawal of U.S. troops from Japan as a condition for the return of the northern islands. <u>Tokyo shimbun</u>, January 26, 1972.

Gromyko confessed that it was not within his power to suggest a solution to the territorial issue. When the two sides agreed that negotiations for a peace treaty should be started in 1972, it was presumed that the territorial question was linked with the peace treaty: a major gain for Japan. Tokyo shimbun, January 25, 1972.

In return, the Japanese side agreed to consider positively the Tyumen oilfields project and to associate government representatives with the JECC negotiations; this was apparently done despite some opposition from the Foreign Office. Asahi, January 25, 1972; Mainichi, January 25, 1972.

On relations between Japan and China, Gromyko stated at a press conference, "I agree to normalization of Japan-China relations, but Soviet interests should not be sacrificed for that purpose." Tokyo shimbun, January 29, 1972.

The reconstruction of the comprehensive design put forward by Gromyko for the improvement of Soviet-Japanese relations is based on interviews I conducted in Tokyo with officials of the Japanese government who cannot be identified.

58. For text of the communique, see Pravda, January 28, 1972.

59. All that appeared in the Soviet press about Gromyko's talks in Tokyo, apart from the text of the joint communique, was a 300-word report in Pravda on January 24, 1972. It is quite possible that the Soviet leaders did not wish to play up the talks, in view of their delicate situation, before a full assessment of the results could be made.

60. Yomiuri, January 29, 1972; Mainichi, January 28, 1972; Tokyo shimbun, January 28, 1972; Sankei, January 28 and 29, 1972.

Nihon Keizai (January 29, 1972) reported that according to "foreign ministry leaders," the USSR had "tactfully checked" an alliance between the United States, China, and Japan.

Sankei (January 29, 1972) said, "It will be a good idea to conclude a peace treaty on condition of the return of Habomai and Shikotan and to study an intermediary plan to continue negotiations with regard to the return of Kunashari and Etorofu."

61. Mainichi, January 22, 1972.

62. Asahi, January 29, 1972.

63. Tass appeared to give more importance to the secret conversations between Nixon and the Chinese leaders than to the contents of the communique. Pravda (March 1, 1972) suggested that the agreement reached in Peking should be judged by the "practical steps" the two nations took in the future, while the trade union paper Trud (February 29, 1972) found that the "concrete results" achieved by Nixon were "minimal."

64. Pravda, February 27, 1972.

65. Yomiuri, October 6, 1971. Sato, again with full U.S. support, was resisting the three principles put forward by China for normalizing Sino-Japanese relations; by doing so, Sato was in reality struggling to maintain the individuality of Taiwan. Nixon, on the other hand, was probably moving toward abandoning Taiwan to the Peking regime. Yomiuri, April 25, 1972; Tokyo shimbun, April 27, 1972.

66. Mainichi, October 7, 1972.

67. Asahi, December 1, 1972; Tokyo shimbun, December 2, 1972.

68. Tokyo shimbun, February 10, 1972; Mainichi, February 10, 1972; Yomiuri, February 11, 1972; Nihon Keizai, February 10, 1972; Asahi, February 13, 1972; Sankei, February 11 and 19, 1972; Mainichi, February 13, 1972; Nihon Keizai, February 13, 1972; Sankei, February 19, 1972.

The image of a "tough" United States was somewhat reinforced by the concessions Japan was obliged to make in February 1972 to obtain a year's "truce" in the U.S.-Japanese "trade war." Japan agreed to increase its imports of U.S. farm products and peripheral electronic computer equipment. Mainichi (February 10, 1972) reported the news under the headline "Japan-US Trade War Ends in Japan's Complete Defeat."

69. Mainichi, February 28, 1972; Yomiuri, February 29, 1972; Nihon Keizai, February 29, 1972.

70. Interview with a leading Soviet scholar on Asian affairs.

71. Sankei, September 23, 1971.

72. Sankei, February 29, 1972.

73. Far Eastern Economic Review, September 30, 1972.

74. For the internal composition of LDP, see Robert A. Scalapino and Junnosuke Masumi, Parties and Politics in Contemporary Japan (Berkeley: University of California Press, 1971), Chapter 3.

75. Kei Wakaizumi, "Japan's Role in International Society: Implications for Southeast Asia," in Japan as an Economic Power and Its Implications for Southeast Asia, ed. K. S. Sandhu (Singapore: Institute of Southeast Asian Studies, 1974), pp. 75-87.

76. Sankei, July 27, 1972; Far Eastern Economic Review, September 23 and 30, 1972.

77. The Todai is the Tokyo Imperial University. Of the 12 postwar Japanese prime ministers, 8 have been members of the Todai. For the hold of the Todai on government and business, see Herman Kahn, The Emerging Japanese Superstate (London: Penguin, 1973), pp. 73-76.

The internationally insecure Japanese are beginning to identify the "self-made man" image of the

prime minister with their own international repu-
tation. Some of them disgustedly refer to themselves as nari-kin, as the upstart nouveau-riche
of global society, who have forfeited their proper
claim to culture and family background. One
senior official remarked contemptuously that the
Japanese had become "the NCOs of the world,
taking orders from the generals of the developed
countries and passing them to the poor bloody infantry of the developing nations. Everyone knows
that warrant officers are disliked both by the officers and the troops," he added. Many Japanese
feel that if ever they were a member of the Rich
Man's Club, they are now being blackballed, while
China is swiftly taking over any claim Japan may
have had to speak for Asia.

Derek Davis, "A Crisis in Identity," Far Eastern Economic Review,
February 26, 1973.
        Tanaka was 57 when he became prime minister. The
Tanaka faction in LDP has the largest number of younger LDP Diet-
men.
        78. Pravda, August 4, 1972.
        79. Vladimir Kudryavtsev, "Wandering in Search of New Path,"
Izvestia, November 2, 1972; Victor Mayevsky, "Searching for a New
Course," Pravda, December 17, 1972; M. Yurchenko, "Instigators
from Peking," Izvestia, December 14, 1972; Leonid Zamyatin, "Put
Relations with Japan on a Treaty Basis," Sovetskaya Rossia, March
13, 1973. For a typical Southeast Asian reaction to Tanaka's visit
to Peking, see Bangkok Post, editorial, September 30, 1972.
        80. This was in spite of several Japanese attempts to nudge
Moscow in that direction.
        81. Zamyatin, op. cit.; V. Kudryavtsev, "For Genuine Good-
neighborly Relations," Izvestia, March 13, 1973.
        82. Discussion with Soviet scholar, see note 73; Tokyo shimbun,
October 12, 1973.
        83. Asahi, January 5, 1973.
        84. Asahi, January 11, 1973.
        85. Mainichi, July 4, 1973; Nihon Keizai, July 6, 1973.
        86. The Soviet attempt to pressure Japan to bow to the Asian
collective security concept generated the first serious discussion in
the Japanese press about the Soviet security plan. Japanese analysts
found the Soviet plan wanting in several vital aspects, and all agreed
that it was primarily designed to isolate China in Asia. For representative comments, see Mainichi, July 4, 1973; Yomiuri, August
20, 1973.

87. Yomiuri, September 27, 1973; Asahi, October 6, 1973.

88. Sankei, August 17, 1973; Mainichi, August 30, 1973.

89. After the intrafactional discussions, one of the government leaders affirmed that "if there is no step forward as to the
territory, we will refuse to lend any economic cooperation." Tanaka
and his supporters came to the conclusion that if Japan pledged economic cooperation without obtaining results on the Northern Territory, it would "lower" the "internal and external evaluation" of his
visit. After two meetings with Ohira, Tanaka finally decided to link
economic cooperation with the Northern Territory. Mainichi, September 20, 1973.

90. Tokyo shimbun, October 12, 1973.

91. Cited in Kudryavtsev, op. cit.

92. The chairman of the Japan Communist Party, Miyamoto,
who was leading the JCP delegation, proposed that "reversion of
Kunashari, Etorofu and the Northern Kuriles can be discussed, after
the US-Japan security treaty is abrogated. But for the time being,
it is requested that a Japan-Soviet peace treaty be concluded and that
Habomai and Shikotan be returned." To this the CPSU side replied,
"We will seriously think of the matter as a diplomatic question." The
JCP supports the Japanese demand for reversion of all of the four
islands, and claims that if it is returned to power, it will succeed in
getting them back. Sankei, September 29, 1971.

93. A high government official interviewed in Tokyo said that
coverage of the Tanaka statement in the major Soviet newspapers
meant that Moscow conceded that the territorial issue was the most
important unsolved problem between Japan and the USSR. He also
said that the wording of the joint communique required "very hard
bargaining."

94. For the text of the joint communique, see Pravda, October
11, 1973. The official mentioned in the previous note said that the
Soviet leaders had tried very hard to incorporate in the opening para-
graph of the joint communique phrases implying that Soviet-Japanese
cooperation was contributing to peace and security in the Far East
and Asia. Finally the Soviet leaders accepted the Japanese phraseology, "to the cause of peace and stabilization in the Far East and the
world over."

95. However, Japan wanted to become the major foreign partner in Siberian development, as indicated by Tanaka and Ohira after
their return from Moscow. Mainichi, October 23, 1973.

96. Concrete results of the technological cooperation between
the Soviet Union and Japan can be seen in the report by Sergy Losev
broadcast over Moscow Radio in English 2300 hrs GMT, March 16,
1975.

97. Nihon Keizai, October 12, 1973; Sankei, October 12,
1973; Tokyo shimbun, October 11, 1973; Asahi, October 12, 1973.
98. Mainichi, October 27, 1973.
99. Tokyo shimbun, October 11, 1973
100. Mainichi, October 23, 1973.

The Peking correspondent of Asahi reported that the
Chinese leaders were paying "uncommonly great attention" to the
Tanaka-Brezhnev talks. They regarded each of the major topics
under discussion, the territorial question, Siberian development,
and Asian collective security, to be "directly or indirectly connected
with the security of China." Asahi, October 11, 1973.

Another Japanese correspondent in Peking reported that
since the announcement of the Moscow summit, the Chinese media
had mounted strong support for the territorial claim of Japan on the
Soviet Union. The Chinese leaders had become extremely sensitive
to the slightest Japanese nod to the Asian collective security concept,
partly because they felt uneasy and uncertain about future Japanese
foreign policy. "There is a sense of distrust about Japan." The
Chinese leaders believed that the honeymoon was over between Japan
and the United States and that Kissinger's "power diplomacy" might
"push Japan out of the U.S. nuclear umbrella" and then "there will
be no knowing where Japan will head for." Yamato shimbun, September 26, 1973.

Chou En-lai congratulated Tanaka and Ohira on their
"hard struggle" in Moscow. Nihon Kezai, October 11, 1973. Chang
Hsiang-shan, vice-president of the China-Japan Friendship Association, said the Chinese were pleased that the Moscow communique
made no reference to Asian collective security. Mainichi, October
10, 1973.

In January Teng Hsiao-ping, the Chinese deputy premier,
advised Japan not to go in for the Tyumen oilfields project without
U.S. participation. Nihon Kezai, January 12, 1974. In June China
offered to consider Japanese participation in developing mineral resources as well as petroleum. Yomuiri, June 6, 1974. A little
later it offered to export 1 million tons of crude to Japan in the
second half of 1975 and up to 100 million tons a year by 1979-80 if
Japan were to participate in a big way in developing Chinese petroleum
resources. Sankei, August 16, 1974.
101. Asahi, September 10, 1974.
102. Kudryavtsev, op. cit. Kudryavtsev, who is a member of
the CPSU central committee and Izvestia's political correspondent,
wrote in that paper on February 7, 1974:

It is well known that Japan's policy is determined basically by the state-monopoly structure

of its economy; but among businessmen there
are also farsighted politicians who, instead of
chasing after temporary advantages, realize
that under present international conditions there
cannot be stable and genuinely national foreign
policy without mutual understanding between
Japan and its neighbor, the Soviet Union.

103. See commentary by Victor Mayevsky in Pravda, August
18, 1974.

104. I. Latyshev, "The Way to Goodneighborliness," Pravda,
February 27, 1975; Moscow Radio in Japanese, 1400 GMT, February
27, 1975; Moscow Radio in English, 2300 GMT, March 16, 1975.

105. The Pravda correspondent in Tokyo attributed the resignation of Tanaka in November 1974 to

the deep crisis that has gripped Japan's bourgeois society in the past few months. Underlying this crisis are an exacerbation of class contradictions in the country and a general increase
in dissatisfaction with the policies of the ruling
circles. . . . Tanaka is leaving, but the problems that generated the crisis--inflation, rising
prices, economic decline--remain. Also remaining are the irreconcilable contradiction between
labor and capital and the growing resistance of
the progressive parties, labor unions, and mass
democratic organizations to the attempt to shift
the entire burden of economic difficulties onto
the shoulders of the working people. All of this
is causing a further deepening of the crisis situation in the country.

Pravda, November 29, 1974. See also Izvestia, November 14, 1974.

106. Kudryavtsev, "Wandering in Search of a New Path," op.
cit.; Kudryavtsev, in Izvestia, February 7, 1974, op. cit.; Mayevsky,
op. cit.

107. For Miyazawa's talks in Moscow, see Moscow Radio in
English 1211 GMT January 18, 1975. For reports of Gromyko's
talks in Tokyo and Miki's announcement, see the New York Times,
January 1976. On May 1, 1975, in the wake of the Communist victory in South Vietnam, Miyazawa had announced that Japan would
recognize the new regime in Saigon, move closer to the ASEAN countries, and "maintain equal distance from the Soviet Union and China."
Sankei, May 1, 1975.

108. This commentary is interesting because it announced that in the forthcoming general election in Japan "The Soviet people's sympathy is with those who are aware that to start a new military bloc under the protection of the USA and Japan is dangerous, and support those who are opposed to such a policy."

109. Mainichi, July 20, 1970.

110. Moscow Radio in Japanese 0915 GMT December 26, 1969.

111. These and similar images of Japan stud each and every commentary written on that country in Soviet journals as well as in the Soviet press during the 1950s and 1960s. These images were projected in the only serious monograph written on Japanese foreign policy up until the mid-1960s, D. V. Petrov's Japan's Foreign Policy since World War II (Vneshniaia politika yaponii posle vtoroi mirovoi voiny) (Moscow: Izdatel'stvo "Mezhdurnarodnye otnoshenaii," 1965).

However, around the mid-1960s, Soviet analysts began to take note of the soaring economic power of Japan, which lent an entirely new dynamism to the Japanese international status. The harnessing of Japanese economic power to U.S. military power in Asia became the most alarming possibility, and between 1965 and 1971 this was the focus of Soviet invective. At the same time, Soviet analysts expected the great economic power of Japan to sharpen and widen the interimperialist contradictions between Japan and the United States. I. Latyshev, "Diplomatiia Tokyo: Novye Orientiry," in MEMO, no. 5 (1970), a work of considerable scholarship and sophistication, is a blend of the two perceptions, although the perception that Japan would soon translate its economic power into political and military power as an active partner of the United States still predominates. The image of Japan competing with the United States and the EEC as an equal power center within the capitalist system becomes much clearer in D. V. Petrov, Japan in World Politics (Yaponiya v mirovoy politike) (Moscow: Mezhdunarodnye otnoshenaii, 1973).

112. "Okinawization," Pravda, June 23, 1970. For a more complete projection of the ultra-hard image, see also Victor Mayevsky, "Dangerous Security," Pravda, June 23, 1970; V. Kudryavtsev, "Shortsighted Step," Izvestia, June 24, 1970; A. Biryukov, "Operation Treaty Revision," Pravda, January 7, 1970; Yu. Bandura's review of the Japanese White Book in Izvestia, October 22, 1970; his commentary on the draft fourth defense plan in Izvestia, April 30, 1971; and B. Chekhonnin, "Remember the Lessons of History," Izvestia, October 8, 1970. Some of these articles stressed the capability of Japan to go nuclear at very short notice.

113. Mayevsky, op. cit.

114. "Dangerous Deal," Pravda, December 16, 1970. This editorial saw the Japanese military role as primarily directed against the USSR and the "countries of the socialist commonwealth."

115. "Dangerous Plans," Izvestia, December 16, 1970.
Later in July the Tokyo correspondent of Izvestia reported the formation of an "unofficial military bloc" in the Far East for the security
of the Philippines, South Korea, and Taiwan. "The creators of this
new aggressive alliance are assigning Japan an ever greater role in
it." Izvestia, July 6, 1971.

116. V. Kudryavtsev, "Zaibatsu on the Attack," Izvestia,
May 13, 1971.

117. Asahi, December 16, 1972. After his return from
Peking, Tanaka approved the fourth defense plan, doubling Japan's
defense budget, and said, "China, too, expressed understanding of
Japan's defense power."

118. Mainichi, December 17, 1973.

119. The Soviet strategic stance outlined here can be seen in
Yevgeny Rusakov, "Tangle of Contradictions," Pravda, October 2,
1974; V. Vinogradov, "According to the Pentagon's Recipes,"
Krasnaya Zvezda, March 6, 1975; and G. A. Orinova's review of
Zbigniew K. Brzezinski, The Fragile Blossom: Crisis and Change
in Japan (New York: Harper & Row, 1972) in U.S.A.: Economics,
Politics, Ideology, no. 5 (May 1973).

120. Sankei, June 28, 1974. Hogen is a former cabinet minister.

121. Hisahiko Okazaki, A Japanese View of Detente (Lexing-
ton, Mass.: D. C. Heath Co., 1974), p. 48.

122. Tooru Yano, "New Stage in Sino-Japanese Relations and
International Relations in Asia," Review (Tokyo), March 1974.

123. Asahi, September 23, 1973.

124. Nihon Keizai, January 14, 1972.

125. Derek Davies, "A Crisis in Identity," Far Eastern Economic Review, February 26, 1973.

126. There are three centers of Soviet studies in Japan. The
Oa Kyokai, or Institute for the Study of Communism and Communist
Countries, is the oldest and the best known. With 180 members
drawn from the universities, the press, business houses, and the
government, it holds 12 to 15 discussions each year and publishes
Review, a quarterly journal in Japanese and English, as well as
short monographs. It is funded by the ministry of external affairs
and private companies and receives no external money. Run by its
suave and learned executive director, Hirota, it has linkages with
sister organizations in the United States, Europe, and Britain and
has been paying some attention lately to Communist nations in Asia
and Eastern Europe also.

At the Keio University in Tokyo, the Society for Soviet and
East European Studies, recently set up with Kenzo Kiga as chairman,
has 50 to 60 members, drawn from the academic community. The

members meet once a year to review their individual studies, and the society issues an annual report. It does not conduct research nor have any students, and it gets its funds from the universities, with some government money for the annual session. There is also the Society for Russian Studies, which is concerned mostly with Russian language and literature. (I am thankful to Mr. Hirota and Professor Kiga for this survey.)

In contrast to the field of China, no serious Japanese study on the Soviet Union has so far been published in Japan. The majority of the scholars working in the Soviet field are economists. At the National Defense College, a woman professor of international relations, Kuniko Miyauchi, is in charge of Soviet affairs.

Marxism, however, occupies a "predominant" position in the university curriculum, especially in the economics departments. See Hiroaki Aono, "Marxism in Post-war Japan," Review, no. 33 (June 1972). According to a 1962 survey, 78.7 percent of the student activists said they were very much interested in Marxism.

> But a significant change seems to be occurring
> in their view of Marxism, for easily one-half
> of those respondents sympathetic to Marxism
> also supported another ideology or other ideolo-
> gies--most frequently, for example, Humanism,
> Existentialism, or Nihilism. Such an eclectic
> attitude toward Marxism very sharply contrasts
> with that monolithic and absolutistic approach
> that prevailed among pre-war Japanese Com-
> munists.

Kazoko Tsurumi, Student Movement in 1960 and 1969: Continuity and Change, Research Papers No. 5, Series A (Tokyo, Institute of International Relations, Sophia University), p. 15. For a fuller study of the attitude of Japanese people toward Marxism, see Tsurumi, Social Change and the Individual: Japan before and after Defeat in World War II (Princeton: Princeton University Press, 1970).

Southeast Asian studies were initiated in Japan only in the mid-1960s as a result of U.S. prodding and initially with U.S. funds. Philip W. Quigg, "Japan in Neutral," Foreign Affairs 44, no. 2 (January 1966).

127. In 1973 Ikamu Dan, a composer who went to China with a cultural delegation, exclaimed after his return to Japan, "Europe is exhausted. America is sick. In Japan we don't have people anywhere, just materials. Japan is being dehumanized and people are being reduced to the levels of tools and machines. China is clean and healthy

in every respect. It has a limitless future." Quoted in Derek Davies, "A Crisis in Identity," op. cit. Socialist party leaders visiting China often speak in idyllic terms of what they see in Chinese towns and villages.

128. Yoshikazu Sakamoto, "Changing Japanese Attitude Toward World Affairs," in Peace Research in Japan (Tokyo: University of Tokyo, 1971).

129. Mainichi, May 17, 1973.

130. Yomiuri, May 19, 1973.

131. Yomiuri, August 15, 1973.

132. Mainichi, March 24, 1971.

133. Tokyo shimbun, April 2, 1974.

134. I was often asked by people I met in Tokyo why India was "socializing" itself under Soviet influence. At a seminar there were a number of questions suggesting that India was under tremendous Soviet influence. The questioners were incredulous when I pointed out that in the Soviet Union, India was regarded as a country that had chosen the capitalist path of development, and all that the Soviets urged the Indians to do was to make their capitalism independent of "international monopoly-capitalism." For typically expansive views of the Soviet influence on India, see reports on Brezhnev's visit to Delhi in Tokyo shimbun, December 4, 1973; Mainichi, December 3, 1973; and Asahi, December 2, 1973.

135. Okazaki, op. cit., p. 85, said:

> In spite of the obvious necessity for economic
> reforms we find no evidence that a majority of
> Russia's people are pressing for fundamental
> reform which might even touch the basis of its
> system. . . . In any case, the evolution of the
> Russian political, economic, and social condi-
> tion is extremely slow, and we have good reason
> to believe that the situation in the Soviet Union
> will be very like the present one even at the end
> of the 1970s. . . . We can define Russia as a
> status quo power with a certain achieved stability
> as a result of its fifty-year history since the
> revolution.

For Japanese perceptions of the Soviet economy, see Kenzo Kiga, "Possibilities of Change in the Economic System of the Soviet Union," Review, no. 34 (November 1972).

136. This editor, whose newspaper is believed to reflect the thinking of the government, also made these additional points. It would not be easy for Japan to build a balanced relationship with the

United States, the Soviet Union, and China, although that was quite
a desirable objective. More realistically, Japan would continue to
improve its relations with the two Communist giants within the steadily loosening framework of its special relations with the United States.
For Japan it was of considerable advantage for a conflict situation to
exist between Moscow and Peking, though a war between the two would
place Japan into a perilous position. Japan was in a most paradoxical
situation, in that the demand for an independent role was strong and
growing stronger every year but that there was no clear idea of the
role Japan could play outside the framework of the U.S. role in Asia.
Japan couldn't be the Asian France. Although it was true that Japan
could not make effective diplomatic use of its economic power without
military power, the editor was certain that the Japanese people would
not permit large-scale rearmament and therefore that Japan would
remain a nonmilitary power for at least another ten years.

    137. Douglas H. Mendel Jr., "Japanese Defense in the 1970s:
The Public View," Asian Survey 10, no. 12 (December 1970).

    138. Yoron Chosa, July 1970.

    139. The question was put somewhat differently to various
persons: Is the Soviet Union still hostile to Japan? Do you look at
the USSR as a hostile neighbor? Does the Soviet Union still appear
to be hostile or aggressive toward Japan? Do the Japanese people
still see the USSR as hostile, belligerent and aggressive? The purpose of these questions was the same: to draw out one facet of current Japanese perceptions of the USSR.

    140. The question put to the students was, When you think of
the Soviet Union, which of these images comes up in your mind first:
(1) The Soviet Union is a Communist power interested in advancing
the cause of Communism all over the world; (2) the Soviet Union is a
global superpower primarily interested in protecting and advancing
the interests of the Soviet State; (3) the Soviet Union is a Communist
superpower whose global interests include the advancement of Communism all over the world. Fourteen listed the first image, 20 the
second, and 16 the third.

       On March 25, 1975, in a Sankei opinion poll, 8 percent
of the samples listed China as the country they liked, while those
who liked the Soviet Union were only 2 percent. In the opinion polls
since 1970, the number of those who liked the USSR never reached
beyond 3 percent and the likers of China beyond 15 percent. Once,
however, China was disliked by more of the Japanese than Russia
was. In a Jiji sampling in May 1970, 33 percent said they disliked
China and 32 percent said they disliked the USSR. Yoron Chosa,
July 1970.

       In December 1973 in a Sankei opinion poll, 16 percent of
the teenagers said they disliked the Soviet Union, while 37 percent

listed the United States as the country they disliked. Sankei, January 5, 1974.

141. A deeper relationship was advocated by 63 percent of the men and 58 percent of the teenagers, a sentiment also shared by more than 50 percent of all samples below the age of 50; 39 percent would support a peace treaty with the USSR on the basis of return of the two small islands, Habomai and Shikotan, leaving the future of the two large ones, Kunashiri and Etorofu, to be negotiated later, while 35 percent believed Japan should wait until all of the four were restored. Those who favored a package or phased reversion of the islands were almost equally divided: 41 percent and 39 percent, phased reversion being more acceptable to younger people. Sankei, October 13, 1973.

142. Out of the 50 students, 20 said they did not trust the Soviet Union; 16 said they did; and 12 said they did not distrust Moscow now as they used to before.

143. I am grateful to Masaru Ogawa, editor of the Japan Times, for this insight.

144. I asked a high-ranking Japanese official whether Japan was not already playing poker with the powers. His reply, with a twinkle of a smile in his eyes, was, "Does it look as if we were?" "You have a lot of experience," I suggested. "Oh, yes!" he said, "but that was a very different world."

145. Mainichi, April 26, 1975.

146. In a public opinion poll in June 1973, the positive and negative images of the JCP were equally divided at a 40 percent level. A year later, in July 1974, 46 percent had a negative image of the party and 36 a positive image. The most negative images were held by those who were 60 and older, while the most positive images were held by people younger than 40. Only 4 percent of the people in their 60s said the JCP still stood for a violent revolution, and this image was recorded by only 1 percent of the teenagers. Sankei, July 11, 1974.

In the 1972 lower-house election, the JCP increased its seats to 38 from 14 (it had 35 seats in the 1949 house, its highest for more than 20 years), polling 10.5 percent of the 52 million votes cast by an electorate of 70 million. This made the party the third largest, after LDP and JSP. After the 1974 election to the upper house, the JCP pushed itself to the third place in both Diet houses. Its seats increased from 11 to 20, and the gains came much more from local than from national constituencies. The JCP polled 12.8 percent of the votes in the local constituencies and 9.4 percent in the national constituencies; in the former, its gain over the 1971 upper-house election was 10.7 percent. Yearbook on International Communist Affairs, 1975 (Stanford: Hoover Institute Press, 1975), pp. 356-57.

147. Among those who broadly agree that Japan should broaden
its security relationships with treaties of friendship with the USSR
and China are Yoshikazu Sakamoto; Takeshi Ishida; and Shinkichi
Eto, the noted specialist on China. See Eto's "Japan and America
in Asia during the Seventies," The Japan Interpreter 7, nos. 3-4
(Summer-Autumn 1972), in which he writes: "Finally, a peace treaty
with the Soviet Union would provide new opportunities to strengthen
economic relations, and on that foundation a nonmilitary treaty of
friendship could follow. Should Japan succeed in building such a combination of treaties as a subsystem within the framework of Sino-
American peaceful coexistence, the same pattern could probably be
applied elsewhere in Asia."

Japanese scholars are not blind to the possibility that
Japan may develop close political relations with either of its two
massive Communist neighbors. "As the international situation
changes, we cannot preclude a situation in which common political
interests develop between Japan and a Communist country." Okazaki,
op. cit., p. 90.

"An alliance between Japan and China may not be a realistic proposition in the short run, but in the long run, especially if the
United States should assume the attitude of an onlooker adhering to a
new noninterventionist principle, a Peking-Tokyo axis might well
enter the realm of possibility." Rinjiro Harako, "Prospects for Relations with the USSR," Survey, Autumn 1972.

148. Okazaki, op. cit., p. 98.

In tracing the extended presence-building of the Soviet Union in Asia during the 1970s, I have adopted as my guidelines or organizing concepts, on the one hand, Soviet perceptions of the international environment, of the major actors and forces in the world, of the balance of forces in Asia, and of individual Asian countries; and on the other hand, Asian perceptions of the Soviet Union, of the other two major world powers, and of the international situation in general, and also Asian self-images.

It is my hypothesis that relations between and among nations reflect their perceptions of one another. Relations are friendly if the mutual perceptions are compatible and reinforce one another, while relations are hostile if the mutual perceptions are grossly incompatible and antagonistic. This hypothesis leads to a number of related hypotheses. Relations between nations are the friendliest when their mutual perceptions of the international realities mirror one another and their perceived national interests converge. Relations are the poorest when the nations look at the world and at each other through distorted mirrors, when they have antagonistic images of the world, of themselves, and of their national interests. In the same vein it is possible to measure the scale of friendliness and hostility between and among nations by measuring the degree of compatibility and incompatibility of their perceptions of the international realities, their respective national interests, and their self-images. Furthermore, if the perceptions of nations tend to change from divergence to congruence, it is possible to predict that their mutual relations will improve, the pace and substance of improvement depending on the degree of convergence their perceptions acquire. On the other hand, if the perceptions of nations tend to change from congruence to divergence, their relations are changing from warm to cold. If the divergence becomes wide and self-reinforcing, their relations are becoming hostile.

THE IMAGE SYSTEM

It is now generally recognized that foreign policy decision makers react, not to international realities, but to their images of these realities. "It is what we think the world is like, not what it is really like, that determines our behavior."[1] Decisions involve choices among preferences from an order of available alternatives. Both the ordering of preferences and the choices are determined by the images the decision makers have of their own nations (national self-images) and those they have of the world outside. The self-image, a product of historical experience colored by folklore, involves the egos, dreams, ambitions, and aspirations of the ruling elite. To a large extent it influences the decision makers' perceptions of the world outside.[2]

A national image system is a combination of its self-image and its image of the external world. It is the total cognitive, affective, and evaluative structure of the nation as an actor.[3] The image system tends to be stable. When not too rudely shaken, it tends to restore itself. In any case, it has strains of continuity, especially when a nation has had a long history and its people have had a wealth of shared experience. The image system, though stable, is not static; in fact, it is highly dynamic, since it is constantly fed by "messages" received from the internal as well as external universe. Within the image system, the self-image is most change resisting. It survives even revolutionary political transformation within a nation. The self-image of the Soviet Union has a strong Russian content, while the self-image of the People's Republic of China is rich with the reconstructed image of the glory and greatness of the Middle Kingdom.

The image system is most stable during the continuum of the political system, both at the national and international levels. At times of discontinuities, however, the image system is shaken. It can be grossly distorted by dramatic changes in the internal political system or in the external world, when messages hit some vital part of the structure. Pearl Harbor distorted the U.S. image of Japan. The atomic bombs dropped on Nagasaki and Hiroshima made the world look very different to most international actors. Nations had to readjust their lenses when Sputnik I pierced the barrier of space and orbited the earth. In the 1970s the world changed when Nixon announced his journey to Peking. It changed once again when the oil power of the Middle Eastern countries hit the industrial nations of the West in a dramatic demonstration of the power of the weak over

the strong. It changed still once again when the United States acknowledged defeat in Vietnam and the whole of Indochina was taken
over by the Communists.

ASIAN IMAGES

Some general remarks seem to be necessary to underline certain characteristics of Asian image systems. The Asian nations
have passed through many discontinuities in the course of history.
They are "new" nations with ancient civilizations; their "newness"
and "oldness" often mingle but do not mix. The Japanese have
undergone an identity crisis that the Germans have not known, although both were vanquished in World War II and had to start their
lives anew. The identity crisis of Singapore stems from the contradiction between its ethnic composition, which is Chinese, and its
nationalism, which its leaders want to be non-Chinese and Singaporean.
In its own way, each Asian nation seeks to reconstruct its ancient
history and derive from it messages with which to build its self-
image.

However, on the whole this self-image, shaped in the clay of
history and folklore, is far from internalized and remains the
property of relatively small elite groups. The elite groups, especially those of the first generation after independence, are intellec-
tually more firmly linked with the former imperialist powers than
with their own historical traditions. As agents of modernization,
they often see themselves and their nations in the images of the advanced countries of the West.[4] Asian self-images therefore generally lack the timber of continuity and stability that characterizes the
self-images of nations that have enjoyed long cultural and national
continuity.

The relative fragility of Asian self-images stems also from
the lack of shared conscious experience. Where this experience
exists, as in China, Vietnam, Japan, and to a lesser degree in
India, the national self-images have elements of considerable
strength. These elements are lacking in Sri Lanka, Malaysia, the
Philippines, and Thailand, which became independent without going
through long periods of anti-imperialist struggle.

When it comes to foreign-policy decision making, the operational role of the Asian self-image becomes conspicuously restricted.
The operative image then is that of a very small group of people,
sometimes a single leader, as in Iran, or a single leader aided by a
select number of not easily identifiable advisers, as in India. The
authoritative character of most Asian political systems forecloses
popular participation in foreign-policy decision making. The low

level of the information flow, domestic as well as international;
authoritarian control of the mass media; and censorship of news and
views prevent the formation of "counterimages" among elite groups
who do not share the images of those who are in power.

The decision makers must, of course, make their foreign
policy "popular," but they often manipulate, control, and distort information in order to plant on the public mind the images of the external world that they either hold themselves or manufacture for
political ends. From time to time Asian leaders have planted on the
minds of their people simulated images of the outside world. These
images can be hostile as well as benign. The new nations often need
hostile images of external powers to be able to mobilize their own
resources for cohesion and unity. These images are fragile when
they do not even approximately reflect reality; they can be stable
when they do reflect, if not reality, at least the mass perception of
reality. The leaders of Pakistan once planted on their people the
simulated hostile images of the USSR and China. These images were
easy to erase; but the hostile image of India corresponds with the
historical and emotional experience of the Pakistani and therefore
remains firm and unshaken.

The new nations of Asia inaugurated their careers during the
cold-war period, and it was only natural that their images of the
world would be shaped by the "reality" of the cold war. The majority
of these nations started the first years of independence with strong
linkages with the West; only at the beginning of the 1950s did some
of them develop the self-image called nonalignment. The nonaligned
wished to have a foreign policy, while the aligned had only foreign
relations.

However, whether it was foreign policy or foreign relations,
each of the new nations sought, almost as a rule, two linkage
processes with the rich and the strong of the world outside: the
process of security and the process of development. The direction
each nation could turn for security and development was determined
by the hostility-friendship dimensions of international politics.
Those who felt that their regimes were threatened by stronger
neighbors or by internal challenge, or both, generally turned to the
United States and other Western powers for security as well as development. Only those who did not feel so threatened, such as India,
Indonesia, and Ceylon, could opt for nonalignment, a diplomatic
instrument aimed at obtaining development assistance from both
power blocs without becoming a partisan of the interbloc cold war.[5]

In North and Southeast Asia, the hostility-friendship images
of the cold war meshed rather easily with the prevailing image system of the ruling elites. In Japan the enemy image of the Soviet
Union found hospitable ground in the Japanese view of the USSR,

which was quickly internalized. The Southeast Asian ruling elites responded readily to the cold-war images of China and the Soviet Union because they meshed with their own world view.

Asian memories are long. The Japanese know this more than anyone else; even today the Southeast Asians have not forgotten the Japanese imperial role of the 1940s. They want Japanese capital and technology, but are not willing to give Japan a political or strategic role in Asia. The Japanese often contrast their own political and military "untouchability" in Asia with the smooth integration of West Germany in the Western European political system and the Atlantic defense system.

In Japan and Southeast Asia, the cold war images of the Communist powers have had surprising longevity because of the prolonged hostility between the United States and China and also because of the Vietnam War. The cold-war image of China collapsed only after Nixon's visit to Peking. We have noted the way in which Japan raced to normalize its relations with China and the way its relations with the Soviet Union improved as a result of the Nixon "shock." In Southeast Asia the cold-war images of the Communist world broke down more completely after the Communist victories in Indochina and the retreat of U.S. power from that region.

In the mid-1970s there has been a widespread diffusion of the hostility images of the Communist world all over Asia, but it cannot be said that friendly images of the Communist powers have set in firmly. From Japan to Iran, hardly any Asian nation views the USSR as an enemy or a hostile power or even as an aggressive and expansionist power. Numerous channels of economic and commercial cooperation with the Soviet Union have been established within a remarkably short period of time. The image systems of the Asian ruling elites have been receiving friendly messages from Moscow and Peking;[6] but these messages also proclaim the ongoing cold war between the two Communist giants. The erstwhile Asian allies of the Western powers have tentatively and somewhat tremulously clapsed the extended hands of Chinese and Soviet friendship. Their mood is cautious and hesitant; they want to look carefully before taking steps toward unfamiliar and hitherto forbidden pastures.

The Asian mood is not uniform or monolithic: nothing in Asia is. The mood varies from capital to capital and even among political actors in the same government. In Tokyo, Kakei Tanaka was regarded as "pro-Soviet," and his successor, Takeo Miki, is thought to be "pro-Chinese." In Jakarta, Adam Malik would probably like to develop cooperative relations with Moscow faster than the military leaders of the regime are willing to stomach. There are, in fact, serious constraints to the growth in relations of most Asian countries with the USSR. Japan, for instance, is not in a

mood to consider political and strategic relations with the Soviet
Union as long as it does not get back the four northern islands. The
ASEAN countries have no major economic portfolios on the basis of
which in-depth economic and commercial relations with the Soviet
Union could develop in the immediate future. Pakistan would like to
get everything the Soviet Union might be willing to part with but is
not ready to bow to Soviet strategic demands. Iran, on the other
hand, has begun to build cautious strategic linkages with the USSR
within the overall framework of its friendly ties with the United
States.

SOVIET IMAGES

If Asian images of the Soviet Union are tentatively mellow in
the mid-1970s, how do they compare with Soviet images of Asia?
In Chapter 1 we said that the Soviet world view, as well as its
self-image, is shaped largely by the Marxist-Leninist theory of
historical progression. We also saw how the Marxist-Leninist theory
is applied by the policy maker to chart the broad course of Soviet
foreign policy. Soviet foreign policy in the last quarter of the
twentieth century will have to deal with the complexities of the entire world.
Soviet foreign policy is a formidable industry, involving, as
Gromyko told the 24th congress of the CPSU, "thousands of people"
belonging to the party, the government, the universities and research institutes, the media, and what in the non-Soviet world
has come to be called the interest groups.[7] This would suggest
that the foreign policy decision-making process draws together con-
verging and contending viewpoints of competing and cooperating
groups.
Even though Marxism-Leninism frames the cognitive map of
the decision makers, the Soviet image system has become greatly
sophisticated during the 1960s and early 1970s; to some extent the
Soviet mind can see the world as others see it.[8] Within the socialist bloc, the Soviet Union shows an increasing awareness of the dis-
tinctive character and special needs of each of the Eastern European
countries. Even the Brezhnev doctrine does not deny the rights of
individual Eastern European countries to follow their own chosen
paths of development, as long as the paths remain essentially socialist. In foreign policy, too, the Romanians have been following an
independent line on such sensitive issues as relations with China and
the Arab-Israeli conflict. The Soviet Union also maintains fraternal
relations with a number of "independent" Communist parties. The
Soviet leaders, then, are better equipped in the 1970s than in the

1960s to comprehend the changes that are taking place in international politics. Marxist-Leninist theory enables them to comprehend the basic processes of change in the Third World.

Alex Inkeles looks upon the Soviet Union as a "development model."[9] The Soviet state is still the most developed of the developing states. The Marxist-Leninist doctrine is essentially a doctrine of development. It is more applicable to the countries jogging along the rough uphill and often precipitous road from agrarian backwardness to industrialized modernity than it is to industrially advanced societies.

The Soviet Union projects its development image to the Asian countries and to the Third World. This image is likely to have a greater appeal in Asia as the development of the Soviet Union itself assumes more and more maturity, enhancing its capability to play a more significant developmental role in the countries of the Third World. This role is already quite significant, but it will probably become more and more so as time passes.

The Marxist-Leninist development model, however, is not economic but political. In it, politics takes command. Development comes through class struggle and, in the current epoch, through increasing working-class control of the means of production and distribution. The Soviet developmental role in Asia and the Third World is, then, basically a political role, even if we choose not to call it an ideological role. Whether the Soviet Union has political and strategic relations with one Asian country or economic and commercial relations with another, the Soviet leaders will continue to preach struggle and conflict to their allies, friends, and non-friends in Asia, not because they have a pathological fascination for tension and war, but because they believe that progressive development and change comes out of the barrel of struggle and conflict, both at the domestic and international levels.

Ever since the birth of the Soviet state, the Kremlin has been using the theory of struggle between two world systems as an analytical tool to interpret international relations. "Struggle" is a message that is a recurrent input of the Soviet image system and it is reinforced by the historical experience of the USSR. The Soviet leaders, then, will continue to see each interaction between the principal forces at the national and international levels as a struggle. There can be no detente nor peaceful coexistence without struggle; nor can there be peace or development. The Soviet Union cannot therefore accept the bourgeois theory of convergence. What the Chinese see as the efforts of the two superpowers to establish a joint global hegemony is seen in the Soviet Union as gaining, as a result of 60 years of struggle, a coequal status in what used to be a world dominated by capitalism. The struggle will go on. The conviction that the world will eventually be dominated by socialism will remain unsullied.

The question that disturbs the West and also a good deal of Asia in the 1970s is whether the Soviet Union will be inclined to use its newly acquired interventionist capability to transform struggles and conflicts into instruments of rapid expansion of Soviet influence. In short, will there be more Angolas, and if there are, what kind of uncertainties and traumas will visit the international relations of the 1970s and beyond? In the three decades since World War II the world has lived with more than a dozen U.S. military interventions in Asia, Africa, and Latin America. Will it be able to live with half a dozen Soviet interventions without being blown out in a nuclear war?

Although it would be foolhardy to predict future Soviet behavior, it is possible to hazard a number of guesses on the basis of current trends and processes in the Soviet Union and in the rest of the world. The Soviet operational code of struggle and conflict counsels caution, not adventurism. Struggle and conflict occur within a large time-frame; when time is an ally, there is no room for precipitate action. What the analytical concept of struggle and conflict prescribes as policy input is action rather than adventure. It is only through action that the strength and weakness of the adversary can be tested relative to one's own. Only through struggle and action can one know what can be achieved and what can not.

Conflict offers opportunity only when it can be controlled and made use of, not when it disappears. The Soviet leaders have been extremely sensitive about controlling conflict.

One means of conflict control that they have systematically adopted is the deliberate maintenance of a large gap between a proclaimed foreign policy objective and the means employed to achieve that objective.[10] During the Cuban missile crisis, for instance, the Soviet Union was clearly not deploying resources that could suggest that it was ready to risk a nuclear war with the United States. Both in Vietnam and in the Middle East, Moscow carefully avoided a confrontation with the United States. If the Soviet Union intervenes in a local conflict, it will choose the most favorable time and place and the given correlation of forces. The intervention in Angola was well timed and well chosen. It paid off. The Soviets may decide to intervene in a civil war in Rhodesia if they are invited to do so by the Africans.

The main Soviet use of its interventionist capability will probably be in the neutralization of the interventionist capability of the United States. If neither side intervenes, local wars will be won or lost on the scale of the correlation of local forces. Even by extending indirect interventionist assistance, the Soviet Union could tilt the

scale in favor of the forces it would support and thus gain considerable influence in southern Africa.

In the Soviet cognitive map of the world, nothing is nearly so
important as the safety, security, strength, and continued development of the Soviet state and the socialist bloc.[11] The base of
strength of the Soviet world of tomorrow lies in the Soviet state of
today. The Soviet leaders will therefore take no action that can endanger the socialist bloc or seriously threaten the gains already
achieved in the different world regions. It is unlikely, then, that
they will provoke another war in Korea or the Middle East. If war
breaks out, they will probably concentrate on neutralizing Western
intervention. At the same time, the campaign to spread Soviet influence, to weaken capitalism, and to win friends and allies in the
Third World will continue unabated and even with greater vigor.
The capitalist crises of the 1970s, which have turned out to be parts
of a general crisis of the industrial democracies of the West, seem
to have revived Soviet faith in the Marxist-Leninist dogma that
capitalism is digging its own grave.

What strikes one most about the Soviet system in the mid-
1970s is its stability and continuity. The 25th congress of the CPSU
in February-March 1976 was for all practical purposes a continuation of the 24th congress, held five years before. Both the leadership and the basic domestic and foreign policies have remained unchanged. This does not mean that the forces of change in Soviet
society are not growing, but it does mean that the forces of change
are under control and will probably remain so for the next decade.[12]
Meanwhile, the leadership may well succeed in increasing the capacity of the economy to satisfy the steadily rising demand for consumer goods to a point at which the fear of consumer rebellion
would become diffused. A Harvard University study in the late
1960s came to the conclusion that "Soviet citizens seem much less
concerned with winning political rights and constitutional guarantees
than with gaining more personal security and an improved standard
of living."[13] The situation has not changed in the mid-1970s.

Despite the structural stability of the Soviet image system,
Soviet perceptions of the world have changed in recent years. Images
of the United States began to change in the post-Stalin period and are
now very different from what they used to be even in the 1960s.
Soviet leaders, diplomats, officials, and analysts travel all over the
world, engage in varied, complex negotiations, enter into numerous
multifaceted transactions, consume a vast quantity of information
and interpretative material from the world outside, and speak with
and listen to people belonging to different political systems and national cultures. In short, they have the opportunity to see the world
as others see it.

The Soviet image of Asia has changed significantly during the 1970s, as we have tried to show in this volume. The U.S.-satellite, imperialist puppet image of the countries once closely tied with the United States has disappeared. Their sins have been forgiven even if they have not trooped to the confessional. Japan is seen as an emerging independent international actor; its bourgeoisie are perceived to be split between "reactionary" and "realistic" elements with a sprinkling of the "peace loving" in their ranks. The ASEAN leaders are seen as national patriots, not completely liberated from the hangover of the emasculating imperialist connection, but steadily regaining their national liberation aplomb. The Shah of Iran is perceived as an enlightened despot, a modernizer, somewhat intoxicated by his oil power. The image of India remains high, fed with stuff coming from the sacrosanct mouths of the highest leadership. India stands on a tall pedestal in the gallery of Asian images in the Kremlin mind.

COMPARATIVE IMAGES

A comparison of Soviet perceptions of Asia and Asian perceptions of the Soviet Union leads to the following matrix of relative images:

1.   The Asian ruling elites do not see the USSR as an enemy or hostile power. They are not prepared at this time to see the Soviet Union as a reliable friendly power.

2.   The Soviet leaders do not see the Asian countries as puppets of imperialism; instead, they see them as progressing toward the behavior of independent local and international actors.

3.   The widest degree of divergence exists in the Soviet and Japanese strategic perceptions.

4.   The widest degree of convergence exists in the Soviet and Indian strategic perceptions.

5.   There is a certain degree of consonance of the Soviet image of Japan and of the Japanese self-image. However, the Japanese do not share the self-image of the USSR.

6.   The Japanese images of the United States and China are completely at variance with the Soviet images of these two powers. The Japanese world view and the Soviet world view differ fundamentally.

7.   The ASEAN ruling elites do not share the Soviet perceptions of the United States. They are not entirely unresponsive to the Soviet messages on China, but they have a higher and clearer perception of the Sino-Soviet conflict, which creates a credibility gap for the Soviet messages.

8. The Soviet strategic perception of Southeast Asia and the ASEAN strategic perception of that region diverge.

9. The Soviet and Indian perceptions of the international configuration and alignment of forces have a strong element of similarity. Their images of China largely mirror one another. The Soviet image of India and the Indian self-image show a great deal of congruence. The Indian image of the Soviet Union and the Soviet self-image are not so congruent but are still compatible.

10. The strategic perception of the subcontinent by Pakistan differs fundamentally from the Soviet strategic perception of that area. Pakistan does not share the Soviet perception of China and the United States and is not responsive to the Soviet self-image. The Soviets do not see Pakistan in the way the Pakistani ruling elite see their own nation.

11. The Soviet perception of Iran agrees to some extent, but not entirely, with the Iranian self-image. The same can be said of the Iranian perception of the Soviet Union.

12. Iranian and Soviet strategic perceptions of the Persian Gulf still diverge, but the divergence is tending to narrow and points of convergence are tending to emerge.

13. The Iranian ruling elite do not share the Soviet perceptions of the United States and China.

14. Both the Iranian and Soviet ruling elites see their countries as neighbors, between whom peaceful cooperative relations should prevail.

AN OVERVIEW: SOME PREDICTIONS

From Japan to Iran, spanning three geopolitical regions of Asia, the Soviet Union has embarked upon a multifaceted diplomatic enterprise in the 1970s. With the collapse of the walls of containment, the Soviet Union has for the first time in history cast its shadow across the entire Asian land mass as well as across the Asian waters. There is hardly any Asian country with which Moscow does not have some kind of mutual intercourse, although with the majority of the Asian nations the level of relationship is still slender. Through effective intervention in conflicts, the Soviet Union has registered its claim to a major role in Asian conflict management and therefore in the management of the emerging pattern of Asian security. The Soviet Union has various levels of security relationship with Iran, Afghanistan, India, Bangladesh, Vietnam, and Laos; this relationship is strong only with Afghanistan, India, and Vietnam.

In strategic terms, the Soviet Union is seeking in Asia what we have termed a series of interlocking "inner balances," to match

its strategic balance with the United States. The Soviets probably
attach considerable priority to the "inner balance" in North Asia (the
Western Pacific) and the intermeshing regions of the Persian Gulf
and South Asia; both areas are geographically close to the USSR.
The search for "inner balances" compels the Soviet Union to operate
diverse foreign policy strategies at four intersecting levels.

1. At the level of global politics it has to contend with the
United States, the power that has held sway in Asia for 25 years
since the last war, has extensive strategic and economic interests
in the continent, and still enjoys considerable good will and friendship, as manifested in its relationships with Japan, China, Indonesia, Pakistan, and Iran.
2. At the adversary level, the Soviet Union has to contend with
China and seek its containment and isolation. In view of its detente
with the United States and conflict with China, it must also contend
with the limited friendship between China and the United States.
3. The Soviet Union also has to deal with a group of countries
that, because of its past experience and affiliations, still regards
Moscow with varying degrees of distrust, suspicion, and fear and is
willing to cooperate only to the extent it must.
4. There are also countries that have developed close linkages
over the years with the USSR and can be regarded as its friends and
allies in Asia. Even these countries, which include India and Vietnam, regard their Soviet connection as an instrument with which to
gain their own strategic objectives rather than as sign posts of
Soviet presence in Asia.

Resources permitting, it is now relatively easy for the USSR
to extend its spatial presence in Asian affairs. Over the years the
Soviet Union has sought to build an in-depth presence in a carefully
selected Asian geographic and demographic zone. The zone of intensive Soviet involvement has so far run from the Arab East
through the Persian Gulf and through the subcontinent to Southeast
Asia. This zone is supremely important in strategic raw materials,
human resources, and commercial and communication lifelines.
Part of this zone is also close to the USSR. Within it, many of the
"local wars" of the postwar period have been fought, and in it are
located the "leading contingents" of the anti-imperialist struggle.
It is within this zone that Communism has obtained its first victories
since Cuba.
For the rest of the 1970s, the main thrusts of Soviet diplomacy
in Asia will probably be focused on four countries: Japan, Vietnam,
India, and Iran. Japan has become unusually important, not only
because it can do a great deal to help the Soviet Union develop the

fuel and other resources of Siberia, but also because of the increasing ability of Tokyo to manipulate the Sino–Soviet conflict to its own advantage. In a North Asian balance of power, the Soviet Union can equal the United States only if it can neutralize the impact of the security relationship between Japan and the United States or can get the support of China. The Soviet–Japanese economic relationship has gathered some strength, but it is still far short of Soviet requirements and expectations. The Soviet economic leverage is weak because all Moscow can offer Japan are projects that will yield lucrative results only after a number of years.

The strategic divide inhibits economic collaboration on a larger scale. In fact, it blocks any dramatic improvement in Soviet–Japanese relations. The Soviets believe that they have taken a big step to placate Japan by offering to return two of the four northern islands. Japan, however, is not likely to be pleased with less than three, and in any case Japan is not prepared to pay the price the Soviet Union has asked for, which is strategic cooperation to contain Chinese influence in Asia and the world. The Soviets would make a great mistake if they forced Japan to choose between Moscow and Peking: Japan would choose Peking. The Soviets therefore are likely to trod cautiously, with careful attention to the domestic political changes in Japan in the next five years. The situation in Japan may change somewhat in favor of the Soviet Union if a left–liberal coalition replaces the LDP as the ruling party after the next election. In that event, Moscow may dangle more carrots. On the whole, however, the conflict with China seems to have become the greatest roadblock to further Soviet penetration of Japan.

Reunified Vietnam, ruled by Communist leaders friendly toward Moscow, presents the Soviet Union with a number of foreign policy opportunities in Southeast Asia. In the first place, Communist Vietnam may lessen the Chinese influence in the region. Hanoi is already trying to steal the leadership of the revolutionary elements in Southeast Asia away from Peking.[14] It is Hanoi, not Peking, that is cast in the main anti–U.S. role in Southeast Asia since the U.S. retreat from that region. A conflict between Peking and Hanoi should be most pleasing for the USSR; there could be no greater evidence of Chinese hegemonic ambitions in Southeast Asia. In an extreme situation, such a conflict might even tempt the Soviet Union to intervene on behalf of Hanoi.

Through Vietnam, the Soviet Union may hope to maintain certain kinds of pressure on the ASEAN group of countries. For instance, Moscow could find itself in a position to bargain with a government in Bangkok for strategic advantages in return for mediation between Thailand and Vietnam. The Soviet strategic presence in Southeast Asia and the Indian Ocean would be more effective if Moscow

were granted base facilities by Vietnam. Of some particular significance is the close political rapport between Hanoi and New Delhi.
This rapport has grown since 1971, that is, since the diplomatic
breakthrough between Washington and Peking. Whether the rapport
leads to strategic or logistical cooperation between India and Vietnam will be one of the developments worth watching during the next
few years.

The Soviet prospects in Indochina are not all rosy, however.
For many years both Vietnam and Hanoi will be a heavy drag on
Soviet economic resources. In view of the China alternative of Vietnam, Moscow will have to extend aid on the most generous terms.
It must tread its path in Vietnam most warily, carefully avoiding the
mistakes made in China in the 1950s and never being completely sure
that it could count on Hanoi in a contingency. If the United States and
Japan decide to aid Hanoi substantially, the options of Vietnam will
increase and its dependence on the Soviet Union will diminish. In the
process of building friendly relations with the ASEAN countries, the
Soviet Union will be annoyed if its close ally, Vietnam, promotes and
supports revolution in these countries. A conflict between Vietnam
and China may suck in the USSR against its better judgment.

The stablest Soviet relationship in the Third World has been
with India. In several ways this has been different from the other
bilateral relationships that exist between either the Soviet Union or
the United States and any Third-World nation. It did not begin with
superpower involvement in a local conflict. The Soviet leaders came
to India in the mid-1950s with offers of development aid to enable the
Indian leaders to build a series of industrial projects that they, especially Nehru, wanted to build but for which India had neither resources of its own nor assistance from the Western countries. The
Soviet Union also gave India political support on Kashmir, an input
India badly needed in order to establish its ownership of the vale of
Kashmir. Once the Soviet developmental presence was established
in India, it was relatively easy for the two countries to weave a shared
global strategic outlook. Indian nonalignment harmonized with the
post-Stalin Soviet tapestry of international relations. The fact that
the Indo-Soviet friendship had an anti-China orientation from the beginning came to be known only in the late 1950s.[15] By supporting
their Indian friends against their Chinese brothers during the Sino-
Indian border conflict, the Soviets imparted to their Indian relationship a long-term strategic importance that is not likely to be eroded
even when (and if) there is a rapprochement between Moscow and
Peking. Since the mid-1950s the Soviets have helped the Indian ruling elite with what the latter have wanted to achieve on their own but
could not without substantial external aid. The Soviet Union has
helped India build a network of strategic industries, a state sector in

the economy, and an infrastructure of defense industries, each a widely shared desideratum. It has helped India retain its hold on Kashmir, intervene in the Bangladesh struggle, usher in the republic of Bangladesh, and thereby dismember Pakistan. Whether it was the explosion of the Indian nuclear device or the annexation of Sikkim or the declaration of the national emergency, each major action of the Indian government has received either enthusiastic Soviet approval or significant noncriticism. The Soviet Union has repeatedly tried to elevate India to the status of a world power. Indians therefore claim, with more than enough evidence, that the relationship has been entirely in India's favor and that India has gotten a great deal from it without yielding anything against its will or its interests.

The stability of the relationship is assured by the current global alignment of forces and the pattern of major-power involvement in the politics of the subcontinent. Even if Indira Gandhi wanted to loosen the pervasive ties of India with Moscow and reach out to Washington and Peking, her signals would not be likely to be picked up by the two principal adversaries of the Soviet Union unless she could demonstrate in a credible way that India could act independently of the Soviet Union on major world issues. In other words, the subcontinent has gotten so entangled with the triangular U.S.-Soviet-Chinese relationship, and especially with the Sino-Soviet conflict, that no marked change in the Chinese, and therefore U.S., stance on India can be expected until such time as the triangular relationship should change.[16]

However, it is difficult to see how the Soviet Union can obtain additional payoffs from its Indian connection in the next few years. The authoritarian lurch in Indian politics since June 1975 has enabled the prime minister to bring the internal environment completely under her control, and the Soviet influence on Indian internal politics, which was never strong, is now marginal. The Soviet influence would grow if India were to become involved in another military conflict with Pakistan or China, but the chances of another conflict are slim.

The Indian bargaining position, then, has become stronger. Indira Gandhi should be able to reject pressures to move in any direction not of her own choosing. The very magnitude of the relationship has generated expectations and demands on both sides that neither may find it easy to fulfill. India has been asking the Soviet Union for goods of better quality at competitive world prices, while the Soviet Union has been asking for further coordination of the two economies, for better Indian performance, and for quicker absorption of the material received.

Indira Gandhi has been trying since 1973 to break India's isolation from much of the world, which India had earned by its intervention in East Pakistan in December 1971. Although she has not succeeded with the United States and China, she has had considerable success with Iran, Kuwait, Egypt, and Indonesia, countries that are not among the best friends of the USSR in Asia and the Middle East. India's relations with West Germany, France, and Britain are also highly positive. At the same time, India has close ties with Iraq and Vietnam, and the Eastern European countries are playing an increasing role in its development. India's international alignments, then, remain quite well balanced. If Indira Gandhi decides to move closer to the Soviet bloc, it will be an act of her own choice and decision. However, she does not seem to have any such intention. [17]

If the Soviet Union earnestly tries to revive its efforts to bring about an economic cooperation grouping in the Persian Gulf and South Asian region, it will have to enlarge its influence in Iran, a country that has in recent years assumed a great importance in the Soviet strategic thinking for these two interlocking regions. The relations of India with Pakistan are not likely to improve qualitatively in the near future unless the Shah of Iran exerts himself more strongly in this direction than he has so far. The Soviet Union will also have to depend on the Shah for the legitimacy of its interests in the Persian Gulf region, and it will also have to depend on its relationship with the Shah for its position in a regional security system if such a system emerges from the current trends in that region.

The Soviets, as noted, have been catering to the newly found national pride of the Iranian ruling elite. The Soviet image of the Shah and of Iran does not differ radically from the self-image of the Iranian ruling elite. The Shah also accepts the USSR as a global power with a "legitimate" interest in the security of the Middle East.

For the Shah, the Soviet Union has three strategic values. First, he wants to cement Iranian-Soviet economic relations with long-term, mutually profitable deals and to get from his northern neighbor as much development assistance as he may be able to absorb without distorting his political and economic system.

Second, he wants friendly relations with the Soviet Union to keep Moscow from polarizing the political forces in the Gulf region and pushing the region to the brink of interstate or intrastate conflicts.

Third, he wants to use his friendship with the USSR as a leverage with the United States, as he candidly made it clear in his interview with C. L. Sulzberger on October 5, 1975. This interview is quoted in Chapter 2. The Shah does not want the Soviet Union to penetrate the Gulf region in a big way. He wants the balance of forces in that region to remain in favor of the conservative, nonradical elements. At the same time, he needs Soviet cooperation for regional stability as well as to further Iranian economic development.

The direction in which future developments in the Persian Gulf region will move depends to a large extent on the way events develop in the Middle East. Iranians make no secret of their fear that another Middle Eastern war will lead to further Soviet penetration of the Middle East and Persian Gulf region, further polarize the political and social forces, and radicalize even the conservative Arab ruling elites. Iranian foreign ministry sources told me in March 1975 that Iran could hope to gain control of the regional environment, in cooperation with Iraq and Saudi Arabia, only if the superpowers succeeded in establishing a stable mechanism of peace in the Middle East. The Shah and his aides took a dim view of the scenario sketched by Robert C. Tucker in 1974 of U.S. military intervention to protect the Middle Eastern oil supplies of the Western world in the event of another cutoff of petroleum by the producing nations in the wake of a new Arab-Israeli war. In the Iranian view, a U.S. military intervention would at once invite Soviet counterintervention and plunge the entire area into "emotional turmoil and political chaos."[18]

Most Iranians do not see the USSR as a friendly country. The memory of the first decade of the postwar period is still strong, especially among the midele-aged and elderly groups of the population. The Iranian armed forces, which continue to be trained by several thousand U.S. advisers, mirror the Western world view and constitute the strongest anti-Soviet group in Iran.

However, the Soviet Union has some appeal for the university youth and among the more moderate of the clandestine leftist elements. It is probably of some significance that in the foreign ministry there are people who look back to the period when Iranian relations with the Soviet Union used to be quite friendly. One such official reminded me that the two countries had a neutrality and nonaggression pact from 1927 to 1939. "We may be moving back to that kind of a relationship," he mused.

The most widely shared sentiment among the Asian ruling elites in the mid-1970s is in favor of having friendly relations with the Soviet Union, if Soviet friendship can be obtained without a high political or strategic price. The most widely shared belief is that conflicts involving Asian nationalism and Western imperialism have enabled the Soviet Union to build its presence in Asia and that more conflicts of this nature would lead to further Soviet penetration of Asia, especially since Moscow now has its own interventionist capability. What limited but could not contain the Soviet Union in Asia for a quarter century was the might and power of the imperialist United States; what has helped the expansion of the Soviet presence in Asia in the 1970s is the disarrayed and clumsy retreat of that imperial power from much of Asia. The Soviet Union's actual ally in Asia, then, is not Asian nationalism but Western imperialism, particularly an imperialism that has exhausted itself by overextending its global role and overspending its material and spiritual resources. The imperialist "protection" has polarized Asian conflicts, intrastate as well as interstate and has enabled Moscow to project itself as the patron-angel of the anti-imperialist forces. In Soviet perception, as we have noted, the anti-imperialist struggle in Asia is likely to intensify in the coming years, assuming an increasingly domestic dimension and polarizing the domestic political forces in already highly stratified societies. If the pattern of Asian conflicts changes, the Soviets may well be wary of intervention because intervention will involve the Soviet Union in domestic conflicts, with consequences that are, to say the least, extremely unpredictable.

Once the nationalist regimes in Asia face the Soviet Union without the protective crutch of imperialism, Soviet interactions with Asian countries enter a highly complex phase of the mutual acceptance-rejection syndrome that imperialism has screened off all these years. The Soviets have to contend with various manifestations of Asian nationalism. In Japan they have to heal the wounds they inflicted on the Japanese nationalist psyche by seizing territory as war booty. Elsewhere in Asia they have to choose between friendly cooperation with the national bourgeois regimes and cultivation of the forces of revolutionary change. The former course will increase the demand on Soviet economic resources without assured promise of political and strategic rewards; the latter course will be even more expensive, with results that are even more uncertain.

In the 1970s the Soviet Union is a superpower, a global power, and a Communist power. The United States has been, and continues to be, a superpower, a global power, and an anti-Communist power. It is the Communist image of the Soviet Union and the anti-Communist image of the United States that have clashed for 25 years across the Asian land mass. The ideological competition between the world's two mightiest powers has distorted international relations in Asia. By the mid-1970s the United States is tending to be less anti-Communist. Its imperial role in Asia has markedly diminished. If the Soviet Union finds that the enchanted days of the anti-imperialist struggle are over in Asia, it may well weary of its enthusiasm about Asian nationalism.

NOTES

1. Kenneth E. Boulding, "National Images and the International System," The Journal of Conflict Resolution 3 (1959). See Figures 1 and 2 for measurements of compatible and incompatible images as reflective of the hostility-friendship scale of relations among nations.

2. For the image as an organizing concept in the study of international relations, see Kenneth E. Boulding, The Image (Ann Arbor: University of Michigan Press, 1956); Ole Holsti, "The Belief System and National Images: John Foster Dulles and the Soviet Union," Ph.D. dissertation, Stanford University, 1962; Holsti, "The Belief System and National Images: A Case Study," Journal of Conflict Resolution 6 (1962); Raymond A. Bauer, "Problems of Perception and the Relations between the United States and the Soviet Union," Journal of Conflict Resolution 5 (1961); Eric Bronfenbrenner, "The Mirror Image in Soviet-American Relations," The Journal of Social Issues 17 (1961); J. C. Ray, "The Indirect Relationship between Belief System and Action in Soviet-American Interaction," master's thesis, Stanford University, 1961; M. Rokeach, The Open and Closed Mind (New York: Basic Books, 1960); Alexander L. George, "The 'Operational Code': A Neglected Approach to the Study of Political Leaders and Decision-Making," International Studies Quarterly, June 1969; Michael Brecher, "Elite Images and Foreign Policy Choices: Krishna Menon's View of the World," Pacific Affairs 40 (Spring-Summer 1967); Nathan Leites, Kremlin Moods (Santa Monica, Calif.: Rand Corp., 1964); John Stoessinger, Why Nations Go to War (New York: St. Martin's Press, 1974); William Buchman and Hadley Cantrill, How Nations See Each Other (Chicago: University of Illinois Press, 1953); Otto Klineberg, The Human Dimensions in International Relations (New York: Holt, Rinehart and Winston, 1955); and William Welch, American Images of Soviet Foreign Policy (New Haven: Yale University Press, 1970).

3. Boulding, "National Images and the International System," op. cit.

4. Edward Shils, The Intellectual between Tradition and Modernity: The Indian Situation (the Hague: Mouton, 1961); John Usneen and Ruth Hill Usneen, The Western Educated Man in India (New York: Dryden, 1955); Harold Isaacs, Images of Asia (New York: Capricon, 1962); Hugh Tinker, Ballot Box and Bayonets: People and Government in Emergent Asian Countries (New York: Oxford University Press, 1964).

5. Jawaharlal Nehru defended his nonalignment policy frequently on the ground that India had no enemies. When, in the wake of the border war with China, he asked for U.S. and Soviet military aid, he conceded that this made a qualitative change in nonalignment. See his "Changing India," Foreign Affairs 41, no. 3 (April 1963).

6. Lewis Richardson's hostility rate model tells us that the rate of hostility of nation A toward nation B depends on the level of B's hostility toward A. If A's hostility toward B perceptibly lessens, B's hostility toward A is also likely to lessen, though not necessarily at a matching rate. Anatol Rapoport, "Lewis F. Richardson's Mathematical Theory of War," Journal of Conflict Resolution 1 (September 1957).

7. Pravda, April 4, 1971. Western sovietologists differ on
the role played by the interest groups in making of foreign policy de-
cisions and allocating foreign policy resources. Scholars like Robert
Conquest and Michel Tatu claim that Soviet foreign and domestic policy decisions stem primarily from intricate and unending "palace intrigues" and personal infighting among the CPSU leaders. Conquest,
Power and Policy in the USSR (New York: St. Martin's Press, 1962);
Tatu, Power in the Kremlin: From Khrushchev to Kosygin (New York:
Viking Press, 1969). Marshall D. Shulman in his Stalin's Foreign
Policy Reappraised (Cambridge, Mass.: Harvard University Press,
1963) and his "Some Implications of Change in Soviet Policy toward
the West," Slavic Review, December 1961, takes the view that Soviet
foreign policy and decisions are taken largely in response to changes
in world power relationships. For a middle position, see Sidney I.
Ploss, "Studying the Domestic Determinants of Soviet Foreign Policy,"
Canadian Slavic Studies 1, no. 1 (Spring 1967).

8. Jan Triska and Finley concluded in their 1968 study of
Soviet foreign policy that decision making was confined to a relatively
small group belonging to the CPSU politburo and the top echelons of
the government. However, "party and government roles are frequently fused in the persons who dominate the formulation of broad goals
and the selection of specific courses of action for important international engagements." Also, it is misleading to suggest that foreign
affairs officials are trained in a single uniform mold: "more and
more role differentiation and more and more differentiation in experience and training is evident." Over two-thirds of the men who
run the Soviet foreign affairs agency were found to have spent most
of their careers in non-party roles. Soviet Foreign Policy (New
York: Macmillan, 1969), pp. 108-109.

9. Alex Inkeles, Social Change in Soviet Russia (New York:
Simon and Schuster, 1971), p. 422.

10. George, op. cit.; Roger Hilsman, To Move a Nation (New
York: Doubleday, 1967), pp. 161-65; Theodore Sorensen, Kennedy
(New York: Harper & Row, 1965), pp. 676-78.

11. Triska and Finley, op. cit., pp. 113-14, wrote:

> Indeed, virtually all Communist leaders after
> 1917 have acknowledged the power of the Soviet
> Union as a necessary condition for the success-
> ful spread of Communism. Since then no be-
> havior demonstrably aimed at preserving or ad-
> vancing the welfare of the USSR has been subject
> to unambiguous condemnation as antithetical to
> the interest of world communism, a situation
> Stalin recognized and fully exploited. Now with
> a record of fifty years of Soviet policy before us,

one can objectively say only that preservation of
the Soviet Union as a nation has remained the
most basic canon of Soviet foreign policy. The
rest is relative.

12. For possible avenues from which pressures for change
may come in the next decade or so, see Zbigniew K. Brzezinski,
Soviet Politics: From the Future to the Past? (New York: Research
Institute on International Change, Columbia University, 1975).

13. Alex Inkeles and Raymond A. Bauer, The Soviet Citizen:
Daily Life in a Totalitarian Society (New York: Athenaeum, 1968),
p. 7.

14. "Hanoi Bids Rebels Step Up Efforts in Southeast Asia,"
New York Times, March 1, 1976.

15. See Bhabani Sen Gupta, Fulcrum of Asia: Relations Among
China, Pakistan, India and the USSR (New York: Pegasus, 1970),
Chapter 3.

16. Bharat Wariavwalla, a research fellow at the Institute of
Defense Studies and Analyses, Delhi, believes that Indo-Soviet relations have gotten into an impasse and that "the Soviets have also decided to reduce their involvement and de-escalate their relations
(with India)." See his comment in a paper in The Persian Gulf and
Indian Ocean in International Politics, ed. Abbas Amirie (Tehran:
Institute for International Political and Economic Studies, 1975), pp.
214-15. There is, however, no evidence in support of Wariavwalla's
opinion.

17. In February 1976 the United States government "firmly
turned its back" on quiet feelers by India for better relations "until
Prime Minister Indira Gandhi becomes openly friendlier toward the
United States." "U.S. Freezing Out India in Reaction to Mrs.
Gandhi," New York Times, February 29, 1976.

18. Interview with an Iranian official in Tehran. Tucker's
scenario can be seen in Robert C. Tucker, Commentary, 1974.

BHABANI SEN GUPTA is currently working as a Research Associate at the Institute of Defense Study and Analyses, New Delhi. He has been professor and head of the Division of Disarmament Studies, School of International Studies, Jawaharlal Nehru University.

Dr. Sen Gupta has specialized in Indian and Asian Communism and in Soviet and Chinese policies toward Asian nations. He has also written extensively on Indian and Asian strategic issues. He obtained his doctoral degree in political science from the City University of New York and in 1967-70 was a senior fellow of the Research Institute on Communist Affairs, of the East Asia Institute, and of the Southern Asia Institute at Columbia University. He was a senior fellow at the Research Institute on International Change, Columbia University, from 1974 to 1976, and he undertook this study with a Rockefeller Foundation Fellowship for the Study of International Conflict.

Dr. Sen Gupta's publications include The Malacca Straits and the Indian Ocean (1974), Communism in Indian Politics (1972), and Fulcrum of Asia: Relations Among China, India, Pakistan, and the Soviet Union (1970). He has contributed chapters to several volumes on international politics published in the United States since 1970, and his articles have appeared in numerous scholarly journals, including China Quarterly, Orbis, Asian Survey, International Affairs, Pacific Community, and Problems of Communism.

* SOVIET POLICY TOWARD THE MIDDLE EAST
SINCE 1970

> Robert O. Freedman

* CHINA AND SOUTHEAST ASIA: Peking's Relations
with Revolutionary Movements (expanded and updated
edition)

> Jay Taylor

* INTERNATIONAL POLITICS IN EAST ASIA
SINCE WORLD WAR II

> Donald F. Lach and
> Edmund S. Wehrle

SOVIET NAVAL DEVELOPMENTS: Capability and
Context

> edited by Michael MccGwire

SOVIET NAVAL POLICY: Objectives and Constraints

> edited by Michael MccGwire
> Ken Booth, and John McDonnell

SOVIET NAVAL INFLUENCE: Domestic and Foreign
Dimensions

> edited by Michael MccGwire,
> and John McDonnell

* CHINA AND JAPAN--EMERGING GLOBAL POWERS

> Peter G. Mueller and
> Douglas A. Ross

THE NEUTRALIZATION OF SOUTHEAST ASIA

> Dick Wilson

*Available in paperback as a PSS Student Edition.